ISBN 978-1-330-10962-5
PIBN 10028093

1 MONTH OF
FREE
READING

at

www.ForgottenBooks.com

By purchasing this book you are eligible for one month membership to ForgottenBooks.com, giving you unlimited access to our entire collection of over 1,000,000 titles via our web site and mobile apps.

To claim your free month visit:

www.forgottenbooks.com/free28093

English
Français
Deutsche
Italiano
Español
Português

www.forgottenbooks.com

Mythology Photography **Fiction**
Fishing Christianity **Art** Cooking
Essays Buddhism Freemasonry
Medicine **Biology** Music **Ancient**
Egypt Evolution Carpentry Physics
Dance Geology **Mathematics** Fitness
Shakespeare **Folklore** Yoga Marketing
Confidence Immortality Biographies
Poetry **Psychology** Witchcraft
Electronics Chemistry History **Law**
Accounting **Philosophy** Anthropology
Alchemy Drama Quantum Mechanics
Atheism Sexual Health **Ancient History**
Entrepreneurship Languages Sport
Paleontology Needlework Islam
Metaphysics Investment Archaeology
Parenting Statistics Criminology
Motivational

NEW EDITION

OF THE

BABYLONIAN TALMUD

Original Text, Edited, Corrected, Formulated, and
Translated into English

BY

MICHAEL L. RODKINSON

SECTION JURISPRUDENCE (DAMAGES)

TRACT SANHEDRIN

Volumes VII. and VIII. (XV. and XVI.)

NEW YORK
NEW TALMUD PUBLISHING COMPANY
1117 SIMPSON STREET

EXPLANATORY REMARKS.

In our translation we adopted these principles:

1. *Tenan* of the original—We have learned in a Mishna; *Tania*—We have learned in a Boraitha; *Itemar*—It was taught.

2. Questions are indicated by the interrogation point, and are immediately followed by the answers, without being so marked.

3. When in the original there occur two statements separated by the phrase, *Lishna achrena* or *Waïbayith Aema* or *Ikha d'amri* (literally, "otherwise interpreted"), we translate only the second.

4. As the pages of the original are indicated in our new Hebrew edition, it is not deemed necessary to mark them in the English edition, this being only a translation from the latter.

5. Words or passages enclosed in round parentheses ( ) denote the explanation rendered by Rashi to the foregoing sentence or word. Square parentheses [ ] contain commentaries by authorities of the last period of construction of the Gemara.

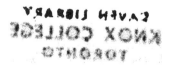

TO HIM

WHO RANKS AMONG THE FIRST PHILANTHROPISTS OF
OUR CO-RELIGIONISTS

ABRAHAM ABRAHAM, Esq.

IN RECOGNITION OF HIS GENEROUS DEEDS TOWARD PROMOTING
LITERATURE IN GENERAL AND JUDAISM IN PARTICULAR,
THIS BOOK IS MOST RESPECTFULLY DEDICATED BY
THE TRANSLATOR

MICHAEL L. RODKINSON

NEW YORK
IN THE MONTH OF ELUL, 5662
(SEPTEMBER 18TH, 1902)

A WORD TO THE READER.

MANY books have been written by the scientists of the last century, and many lengthy articles have appeared in the various periodicals, concerning the Jewish *high court*, and this tract, which, if extracts were given, would make an entire bulky volume in itself. However, we deem it best to give the reader the information where these are to be found. The time during which the Sanhedrin were established is the main topic of their discussions. Zunz, for instance, gives the time from King Simeon of the Maccabees. Jost states that it was from the period of Hyrcan. And an anonymous writer in " Israelitische Annalen," Vol. I., pp. 108-134, maintains that they were established at an exceedingly earlier date, and that the Greek name " Sanhedrin " was changed during the time of the second Temple. At all events, Schürer, in his " Jüdische Geschichte," wrote a lengthy article on this subject, in Vol II., from p. 188 to 240 (where there is to be found a bibliography of the subject), concluding with his opinion that the *high court* began at an earlier time. Z. Frankel, too, in his article, "Der gerichtliche Beweis," Berlin, 1848, claims that the establishment of the jury in the entire civilized world was taken from the Sanhedrin. All this was written in Germany. An English book by Rabbi Mendelsohn also treats upon this topic. We, too, will have something to say concerning this in our forthcoming " History of the Talmud." We are inclined, in many respects, however, to accept the opinion of Reifmann, given in his Hebrew book, " Sanhedrin," Warsaw, 1888. He says that courts were even established in the days of Noah, the judges of which were Shem, Abraham, Isaac, and Amram, continuing until Moses. He, in turn, established a court of seventy judges, and from that time the Supreme High Court was of that number (seventy-one, including Moses), and thereafter supreme courts of twenty-three, and courts of three, were established at all times, and wherever the Jews resided; the sages of the second Temple naming these courts " great " and " small " Sanhedrin. Reifmann's reasons are gathered from the post-biblical literature, and are based upon the Bible. According to him, the three judges had to decide civil cases only, the twenty-three, criminals and capital punishments, and the seventy-one were a political body, who were to decide also the great events; as, for instance, an entire tribe, or the princes and heads of tribes. We, however, would say that the court of three had also to decide criminal cases to which capital punishment did not apply. So it seems to us, from this tract, p. 212 of the Talmud, that a stubborn and rebellious son was punished with stripes by a court of three, before being finally sentenced to death by the court of twenty-three.

Reifmann also quotes from "Midrash Aggada," that before prophesying a prophet was obliged to get permission from the Sanhedrin, who previously tried him whether he was a true prophet or not We may here add that this contradicts the Talmud, for it says that to recognize a true prophet was by demanding a sign, p. 260, and if the prophet would have been obliged to get the permission of the Sanhedrin, this would certainly be mentioned in the Talmud instead.

This is as much as we have to say in regard to the time and name, and that the Sanhedrin ceased about forty years previous to the destruction of the Temple. At the same time we would call the attention of the readers to the fact that this tract distinguishes itself from all others in Halakha as well as in Haggada. Aside from the many strange explanations of the verses of Scripture, which are not used in other extracts, it says plainly that there are numerous laws written in the Pentateuch which have never occurred, and never will occur, but that they were written merely for study. The Haggada also distinguishes in taking the power to judge upon the Bible personages if they are to have a share in the world to come, and also in criticism of their acts, even of the most holy of them. This is self-evident that the later commentaries, and especially the cabbalists, interpreted the Haggada after their ways. We, however, have translated it almost literally, with an effort to make it in some respects intelligible to the general reader, and have also added footnotes, where we deemed it necessary. And we may say that the real student will find much pleasure if he will devote his special attention to this tract.

For this purpose we have made from this celebrated tract a double volume, as we deem it will please the readers and the students, and will also equalize the size of the volumes.

M. L. R.

September 16, 1902.

CONTENTS.

CHAPTER I.

CHAPTER II.

CHAPTER III.

CHAPTER IV.

CHAPTER V.

CHAPTER VI.

CHAPTER VII.

CHAPTER VIII.

CHAPTER IX.

CHAPTER X.

CHAPTER XI.

SYNOPSIS OF SUBJECTS

OF

TRACT SANHEDRIN (SUPREME COUNCIL).

CHAPTER I.

MISHNA *I.* To which cases judges are needed to decide, and to which commoners; which three, five, twenty-three, and seventy-one. The Great Sanhedrin consisted of seventy-one, and the Small of twenty-three. How many a city should contain, that it should be fit for a supreme council. If one were known to the majority of the people as an expert, he alone might decide civil cases. A permission from the Exilarch holds good for the whole country (of Babylon and also for Palestine); from the Prince in Palestine, for the whole of Palestine and Syria only: he may teach the law, decide civil cases, and may also decide upon the blemishes of first-born animals. He (a priest) saw a divorced woman and married her, and with this he annulled his priesthood. He erred in his opinion—*e.g.*, there were two, Tanaim and two Amoraim who differed in a case, and he decided the case according to one. There are three Tanaim who differ concerning arbitration. When the decision is already given in accordance with the strict law, an arbitration cannot take place. May or may not a judge say, "I do not want to decide this case"? and under what circumstances? Is mediation a meritorious act, or is it only permitted? There were many who used to say maxims of morality, and Samuel found that they were only repetitions of verses in the Scriptures. "Say unto wisdom, Thou art my sister," means, if the thing is certain to you as that it is prohibited for you to marry your sister, then you may say it; but not otherwise. If one appoints a judge who is not fit to be such, he is considered as if he were to plant a grove in Israel. The court shall not listen to the claims of one party in the absence of the other (in civil cases). "You shall judge righteously" means, you shall deliberate the case carefully, and make it just in your mind, and only thereafter may you give your decision: "For the judgment belongeth to God." The Holy One, blessed be He, said: "It is the least for the wicked to take away money from one and give it to another illegally," etc. Is warning needed to a scholar? Where is the hint that collusive witnesses are to be punished with stripes? Punishment of stripes is not applied to those who do no manual labor. The numbers three, five, and seven—to what have they a similarity?

CHAPTER II.

CHAPTER III.

CHAPTER IV.

MISHNAS *I.* TO *III.* Cases coming before the court, the witnesses thereof must be examined and investigated. What difference is there between civil and criminal? The following from (a) to (g). Biblically there is no difference between civil and criminal cases concerning investigations. But why is it enacted that civil cases do not need investigation? " Justice, only justice, shalt thou pursue," means that one shall follow to the city of a celebrated judge, etc. What has the court first to say to the advantage of the defense in criminal cases? If one has tried a case, and made liable him who is not, or *vice versa*, etc. Tudus the physician testified that not one cow or one swine was sent from Alexandria in Egypt of which the womb was not removed. If one was found guilty by the court, and thereafter one come, saying : I know a defense for him, etc. So long as the fire in the stove burns, cut off all that you want to roast, and roast it. (*I.e.*, when you are studying a thing, consider it thoroughly to prevent questions.) All who take part in the discussion may explain their reasons, until one of the accusers shall yield to one of the defenders. In the neighborhood of R. Johanan there was one who was blind who used to judge cases, etc. From the time of Moses until the time of Rabbi, we do not find one man who was unique in· the possession of wisdom, riches, and glory, etc. One may teach his disciple, and at the same time may judge in association with him in criminal cases. In ten things civil cases differ from criminal cases. All are competent to judge civil cases. But not all of them are competent to judge criminal cases. The Sanhedrin sat in a half-circle in order that they could see each other, etc. The Torah has testified that we are such a kind of people that even a fence of lilies is sufficient for us, and will never be broken. How were the witnesses awestruck in criminal cases? A human being stamps many coins with one stamp, and all of them are alike; but the Holy One, blessed be He, has stamped every man with the stamp of Adam the first, and, nevertheless, not one of them is like the other. Although the court of the Sanhedrin existed no longer, the punishment of the four kinds of death prescribed in the Scripture was not abolished by Heaven. Adam the first was created singly, and why? That disbelievers should not say there were many Creators in heaven, etc. In three things one is different from his neighbor—in voice, etc., ...   97–114

CHAPTER V.

MISHNA *I.* The court used to examine the witnesses with seven inquiries, etc. Should one of the witnesses say, "I have something to say in behalf of the defendant," or one of the disciples, "I have something to say to the disadvantage of the defendant," the court silences him. Why not say that eight queries are necessary in the examination? Viz., how many minutes are there in the hour? Do you recognize this man as the murderer of him who was slain? Was he a heathen or an Israelite? Have you warned him? Did he accept the warning? etc. Whence do we deduce that the warning is prescribed biblically? Witnesses who testified in case of a betrothed woman, if they be found collusive, are not to be put to death. What is the difference between examination? etc. Until what time may the benediction of the moon be pronounced? If Israel should have only the meritorious act of receiving the glory of their heavenly Father once a month, it would be sufficient. They do not drink wine. And why not? In civil cases the court may say: The case becomes old, etc.,   .   .   115–125

CHAPTER VI.

MISHNAS *I.* TO *IV.* If the conclusion was to condemn, the guilty one was taken out immediately to be stoned. A herald goes before him, heralding: So and so, etc. One stands with a flag. I doubt who had to bear the cost of the flag and horse mentioned in the Mishna, etc. If one of the disciples said, "I have something to say in behalf of the defendant," and thereafter he became dumb? He who is modest, the verse considers him as if he should

CHAPTER VII.

etc., meaning to include the heathen, who are warned of blasphemy. Ten commandments were commanded to Israel in Marah ; seven of them are those which were accepted by the descendants of Noah. For transgression of these commandments a descendant of Noah is put to death, viz., adultery, bloodshed, and blasphemy. A descendant of Noah may be put to death by the decision of one judge, by the testimony of one witness, etc. Every relationship for which the punishment of the courts of Israel is death, a descendant of Noah is warned of it; but all other relationships, the punishment of which is not death, are permissible to them. He who raises his hand to his neighbor, although he has not as yet struck him, is called wicked. "Flesh in which its life is, which is its blood, shall ye not eat," [Gen. ix. 4] means any member of the animal, while it is still alive. We do not find any case where what is forbidden to the descendants of Noah should be allowed to the Israelites. An unclean thing never came from heaven. There is no difference if one hears it from the blasphemer himself or from the witness who heard it from the blasphemer—he must rend his garments . . 164–187

etc. Punishment with the sword applies to a murderer and to the men of a misled town. If one pressed down a person while he is in water, or in fire, preventing him from coming out, he is guilty, etc. If one bound a person, and he died thereafter of hunger, he is not guilty of a capital crime. If, however, he put him in a sunny place, and he died because of the sun, he is guilty. Ball-players—if one threw a ball with the intention of killing some one, he is to be put to death, and if it was unintentional, he is to be exiled, etc. All agree that if one kills a person whose windpipe and larynx (gullet) are cut or whose skull is fractured, he is free (for it is considered as if he attacked a dead man). If one strikes a person with a stone or with his fists, and he was diagnosed (by the physicians of the court) to die, and thereafter he improved, etc. Capital punishment does not apply to one who intended to kill an animal and killed a man, an idolater and killed an Israelite, etc.; but it does apply to one who intended to strike a person on the loins with an article which was sufficient for this purpose, and he strikes him to death on his heart, etc. A murderer mixed up among others—all of them are free, etc. If it happen that the persons sentenced to deaths of different kinds, and are so mixed that it is not known who comes under this kind of death and who under another, all of them must be executed with the more lenient death. If one committed a crime which deserves two kinds of death, he must be tried for the more rigorous one. Ezek. xviii. must not be taken literally, but "the mountains he eateth not" means that he does not live upon the reward of the meritorious acts done by his parents; "his eyes he lifteth not up to the idols" means that he never walked overbearingly, etc., . 222-238

CHAPTER X.

CHAPTER XI.

it not named after him? The angel who rules the souls after their departure from this world is named Dumah. Hiskiah, who has eight names, shall take revenge on Sanherib, who also has eight names. Hiskiah's (king of Judah) whole meal consisted of a litter of herbs. Pharaoh, who personally blasphemed, was also punished by Heaven. Sanherib, who blasphemed through a messenger, was also punished through a messenger. Ten trips had the wicked made on that day, etc., as it reads [II Kings, x. 28 to 32]. There was one day more appointed for the punishment of the iniquity of Nob. And the astrologers told Sanherib, etc. If the judgment is postponed over one night there is hope that it will be abolished entirely. The legend how Abishai saved King David from Yishbi's hand at Nob. Sanherib, when he came to attack, brought with him forty-five thousand princes with their concubines in golden carriages, etc. See pages 293-296, the many legends concerning Sanherib. Be careful with the children of the Gentiles, as it happens very often wisdom emanates from them. That the day on which Achaz died consisted of only two hours. And when Heskiah became sick and thereafter recovered, the Holy One returned the ten hours to that day, etc. Three hundred mules loaded with iron saws which cut iron were given to Nebusaradan by Nebuchadnezzar while going to attack Jerusalem. Nebusaradan was a true proselyte, from the descendants of Sissera were such who studied the law in Jerusalem, and from the descendants of Sanherib were such who taught the Torah among a majority of Israelites, etc. Have you heard when the fallen son will come? etc. In his Sabbatic period when the son of David will appear in the first year there will be fulfilled, etc. The generation in which the son of David will come, young men will make pale the faces of the old, etc. The world will continue for six thousand years, the first two thousand of which was a chaos, etc. There are no less than thirty-six upright in every generation who receive the appearance of the Shekinah. All the appointed times for the appearance of the Messiah have already ceased. And it depends only on repentance and good deeds. Jerusalem will not be redeemed but by charity. What the Messiah told to Jehoshua ben Levi : Ben David will not arrive until Rome shall have dominated, etc. Discussion concerning the name of the Messiah. The cock said to the bat, I look out for the light because the light is mine (I see it), but for what purpose do you wait for it? The days of the Messiah will be as from the day of creation until now. " He hath despised the word of God," means he who learned the Torah but does not teach it. He who learned the Torah and does not repeat it is similar to him who sows but does not harvest, etc. Has not Moses written something better than : And Lotan's sister was Thimna, etc. ? Who is meant by the term epicurian ? What good have the rabbis done for us? They have never permitted us to eat a crow, and they have not prohibited us to eat a dove, etc. The measure with which man measures will be measured out to him—i.e., as a man deals he will be dealt with. A good woman is a good gift; she may be given to one who fears God. A bad woman is leprosy to her husband, etc. One may ask the fortune tellers who tell fortunes by certain oils or eggs. But it is not advisable to do so, because they often lie. Support me, and I will bear the statement of Aqiba, my disciple, who says : " Pleased are chastisements," etc. Three men (biblical personages) came with indirectness, etc. What means, "and he lifted up his hands"? He took off his phylacteries in his presence. (See footnote, page 323.) The legends concerning Jeroboam,

TRACT SANHEDRIN (SUPREME COUNCIL).

CHAPTER I.

MISHNA *I.* : To decide upon the following cases, three persons are needed (the Gemara explains for which common and for which judges): Civil cases, robbery, wounds, whole damages and half, double amount and four and five fold payments; * and the same in the case of forcing, seducing, and libel (*i.e.*, an evil name, Deut. xxii. 19). So is the decree of R. Meir.

The sages, however, maintain: In the last case (libel) twenty-three are needed, as this is not a civil case, but a crime which may bring capital punishment. In the case of stripes, three. In the name of R. Ishmael, however, it was said: Twenty-three are needed. To the intercalation of a month and to proclaim a leap year, three. So is the decree of R. Meir.

Rabban Simeon b. Gamaliel maintains: It begins with three persons and is discussed by five, and the decision is rendered by seven If, however, it was decided by three, their decision holds good.

The elders who had to lay their hands upon sacrifices [Lev.

---

* All this is explained in Tract Baba Kama.

iv. 15], and also in the case of the heifer [Deut. xxi. 3]—according to R. Simeon, three are needed, and according to R. Jehudah, five. At the performance of the ceremony of Halitzah and denial, three; to appraise the value of the plants of the fourth year (which must be redeemed), and the second tithe, of which the value in money is to be appraised, three; to appraise the value of consecrated articles, three; in cases of Arakhin (vows of value, men or articles), if movable property, three—according to R. Jehudah, one of them must be a priest; and if real estate, ten, and one of them a priest; and likewise to appraise the estimated value of men [Lev. xxvii.].

Crimes (which may bring capital punishment), twenty-three; in the case of Lev. xx. 15, twenty-three, as verse 16 reads: "Then shalt thou kill the woman and the beast"; and also in the preceding verse: "The beast also shall ye slay." And the same is the case with the stoning of an ox, of which it reads [Ex. xxi. 29]: "The ox shall be stoned, and the owner . . . be put to death"—which means, as for the death of its owner twenty-three are needed, so also for the stoning of the ox.

The wolf, the lion, the bear, the tiger, the bardls,* and the serpent are killed by the judgment of twenty-three. R. Eliezer, however, maintains: Every one who hastens to kill them is rewarded. But R. Aqiba says: Twenty-three are needed.

A whole tribe, or a false prophet, or a high-priest, if they have to be judged for a crime which may bring capital punishment, a court of seventy-one judges is needed. The same number of judges is needed to decide upon battles which are not commanded by the Scriptures, and also for enlarging the city of Jerusalem by annexing its suburbs or free land; and the same is the case if it is necessary to enlarge the courtyard of the Temple. Also, the same number of judges is needed for appointing supreme councils to each tribe. A misled town [Deut. xii. 14] must also be condemned by seventy-one. However, a town which stands on the boundary cannot be condemned; nor three of them at one time at any place, but only one, or two.

The Great (Sanhedrin) consisted of seventy-one, and the small of twenty-three. Whence do we deduce that the great council must be of seventy-one? From [Num. xi. 16]: "Gather unto me seventy men." And add Moses, who was the head of them— hence seventy-one? And whence do we deduce that a small one must be twenty-three? From [ibid. xxxv. 24 and 25]: "The

---

* According to some, the hyena; to others, another sort of a preying beast.

congregation shall judge "; " And the congregation shall save."*
We see that one congregation judges, and the other congregation saves—hence there are twenty; as a congregation consists
of no less than ten persons, and this is deduced from [ibid. xiv.
27], " To this evil congregation," which was of the ten spies,
except Joshua and Caleb.   And whence do we deduce that three
more are needed ?   From [Ex. xxiii. 2]: " Thou shalt not follow
a multitude to do evil"—from which we infer that you shall
follow them to do good.   But if so, why is it written at the end
of the same verse, " Incline after the majority, to wrest judgment"?†   This means, the inclination to free the man must
not be similar to the inclination to condemn; as to condemn
a majority of *two* is needed, while to free, the majority of *one*
suffices.   And a court must not consist of an even number, as,
if their opinion is halved, no verdict can be established; therefore one more must be added.   Hence it is of twenty-three.

How many shall a city contain that it shall be fit for a
supreme council ?   One hundred and twenty families.   R. Nehemiah, however, maintains: Two hundred and thirty—so that each
of them should be the head of ten families, as we do not find in
the Bible rulers of less than ten.

GEMARA: Are not robbery and wounds civil cases ?   Said
R. Abuhu: The Mishna means to explain the term " civil
cases " by robbery and wounds; but to the admitting of debts
or loans, three judges are not needed.   And that so it should
be understood, both expressions were needed; as, if it stated
civil cases only, it would include loans, etc. ; and if the expression " robbery," etc., only, one might also say the same is the
case with loans, etc. ; and the expression " robbery," etc., is
because the main point wherein three judges are prescribed by
the Scriptures is in cases of robbery [Ex. xxii. 7]: " Shall the
master of the house be brought unto the judges."   And concerning wounds, it is the same whether a wound be in one's
body or in his pocket (money), and therefore it begins with civil
cases, and explains that cases like robbery are meant, and not
common ones, etc.   But whence are common loans excluded,
that they do not need three ?   Did not R. Abubu say: If two
persons have judged in a matter of civil law, all agree that their

---

* Leeser translates, " to deliver," the meaning of which is to save, as it is
adopted in the original text.

† Leeser's translation here is incorrect, not only according to the Talmud, but
also to the *punctuation* of the verse.

judgment is of no value? Therefore we must say that the Mishna means to exclude loans and admission of debts—to exclude from three *established* judges; but three common men are needed. And the reason is what R. Hanina said: Biblically, investigation is needed of crimes as well as of civil cases. As it is written [Lev. xxiv. 22]: "One manner of judicial law shall ye have." But why was it said that civil cases do not need investigation? In order not to lock the door to borrowers. And Rabha explained this statement as meaning that in two kinds of civil cases—loans, etc.—three common people are needed; but in cases of robbery, etc., three established judges. And R. Aha b. R. Ekha said: Biblically, even one is fit to decide civil cases, as it is written [ibid. xix. 15]: "In righteousness shalt thou judge thy neighbor." But the rabbis enacted three, in order to prevent men of the market, who are ignorant of law, to undertake to judge cases. But is it not the same with three common men? Are they not men of the market? If three undertake to judge a case, it is highly probable that at least one of them knows something of law. But if so, let two who should make an error in judging not be responsible? If this should be enacted, then all the market people would undertake to decide upon things.

But what is the difference between Rabha and R. Aha b. R. Ekha (according to both, three common men are needed in cases of common loans, etc.)? They differ in the following, which was said by Samuel: If two commoners have decided upon loan cases, their decision is to be respected; but they are considered an impertinent Beth Din. Rabha does not hold with Samuel, and maintains: Their decision must not be respected. And R. Aha holds with him (Samuel).

"*Whole damages and half,*" etc. Are not damages the same as wounds (both are to be paid)? Because it has to state half damages, it mentions also whole damages. Are not half damages also the same? The Mishna teaches concerning money which is to be collected according to the strict law and that which is only a fine. But this is correct only as to him who says that half damages are a fine; but as to him who says half damages are strict law, what can be said? Because it has to state about the double amount, and four and five fold, which are more than the amount damaged, it mentions also half damages, which is less; and as half is mentioned, it mentions also the whole.

Whence do we deduce that three are needed? From what the rabbis taught. It treats [Ex. xxii. 7 and 8] three times of judges; hence three are needed. So said R. Yachiha. R. Jonathan, however, maintains: The first expression "judges," as the beginning, must not be taken into consideration, as it is needed for itself, and therefore only the two expressions "judges," mentioned after, are to be counted, and the third one is added only because we do not establish a court of an even number (as said above).

The rabbis taught: Civil cases are to be discussed by three. Rabbi, however, said: It is discussed by five, so that the final decision should be by three. But even when there are three, is not the final decision made by two? He means to say, because the conclusion must be of three judges. This explanation was ridiculed by R. Abuhu, saying: On such a theory, then the great Supreme Council ought to be one hundred and forty-one, to the end that the final conclusion should be made by seventy-one; and of a small council there ought to be forty-five, so that the conclusion should be made by twenty-three. And therefore we must say, as the Scripture reads, "Gather unto me seventy," it means the seventy ought to be at the time established. And the same is it in the case above cited, "the congregation shall judge, and the congregation shall save," meaning that at the time of judging there shall be ten. And in the same way are to be interpreted the just cited verses 7 and 8, that the plaintiff has to bring his case before three only. Therefore it may be said that the reason of Rabbi's decision is that because in the first verse is written, "The judges may condemn," as in the last, three is meant, so is it with the word Elohim, mentioned before, which means judges, also two is meant, which makes four; and one is added, so that they shall not be an even number—hence five. The rabbis do not care for this, as the term which is translated, "They may condemn," is written in the singular, and is only read in the plural.

The rabbis taught: Civil cases are decided by three; but if one is known to the majority of the people as an expert, he alone may decide. Said R. Na'hman: e.g., I decide cases alone, without consulting any other rabbis. And so also said R. Hyya.

The schoolmen propounded a question: What does R. Na'hman mean by saying: As, for instance, I? Does he mean similar to him, who knew the laws traditionally and by common sense, and was also so empowered by the Exilarch; but if there was one who was equal to him in wisdom, but had no permission, his decision must not be respected? Or does he mean to say, if one were equal to him in wisdom he might so do without permission? Come and hear: Mar Zutra, the son of R. Na'hman, made an error in one of his decisions, and came to question R. Joseph whether he must make good the error. To which he answered: If he was appointed by the parties as a judge, he had not to pay; if not, he must pay. Infer from this that he who is appointed by the parties may so do even without permission from a higher court.

Said Rabh: If one wants to decide cases, and not be responsible in case of an error, he shall get permission from the Exilarch. And so also said Samuel.

It is certain that here in Babylon a permission from the Exilarch holds good for the whole country; and the same is the case from the Prince in Palestine, for the whole of Palestine and Syria. And it is also certain that if one has a permission from the Exilarch, he may practise in Palestine. As the following Boraitha states: The sceptre shall not depart from Judah. These are the exilarchs of Babylon, who rule over Israel with their sceptres. "And a lawgiver," etc., [Gen. xlix. 10] means the grandsons of Hillel, who are teaching the Torah among the majority of the people. The question, however, is, if with the permission of the princes they may judge in Babylon?

Come and hear: Rabba b. Hana had decided a case and erred, and came to question R. Hyya whether he had to pay. To which he answered: If the parties appointed you as a judge, you have nothing to pay; but if not, you have. Now, as Rabba b. Hana had permission from Palestine, and would be obliged to pay if not appointed, it is to be inferred that the permission from Palestine did not hold good in Babylon. But is it not a fact that Rabba b. R. Huna, when he would quarrel with the house of the Exilarch, used to say: I did not take any permission from you, but from my father, who had it from Rabh, and the latter from R. Hyya, and the latter from Rabbi? This was concerning worldly affairs only. But if the permission of Palestine does not hold good for Babylon, why did Rabba b. Hana take it? For the cities which are situated on the boundary of Palestine. How was the case when he took the permission? When he was about to descend from Palestine to Babylon, R. Hyya said to Rabbi: My brother's son, Rabba b. Hana, descends to Babylon. And Rabbi answered: He may teach the law, decide civil cases, and may also decide upon the blemishes of first-born animals which are prohibited to be slaughtered without a blemish on their body.*

When Rabh was about to go to Babylon, R. Hyya said to Rabbi: The son of my sister goes to Babylon.   Said Rabbi: He may teach the law, decide cases, but not about blemishes of the first-born of animals.

Why did R. Hyya name the first " my brother's son " and the second " my sister's son " ?   And lest one say that so was the case, did not the master say: Abu, Hana, Shila, Marta, and R. Hyya all were the sons of Abba b. Aha Kharsala of Khaphri ?   (Hence Rabh, who was Abu's son, was also his brother's son—why did he say " my sister's " ?)

Rabh, who was his brother's and also his sister's son (on his mother's side), he named him " the son of my sister "; but Rabba b. Hana was the son of his brother only.   And if you wish, it may be said that R. Hyya named him " my sister's," because of his great wisdom.   As it is written [Prov. vii. 4] " Say unto wisdom, Thou art my sister."   But why should Rabh not be permitted to decide about blemishes ?   Was he not wise enough for this ?   Is it not a fact that he was wiser than any of his contemporaries ?   Or was he not acquainted enough with the kind of blemishes ?   Did not Rabh say: I have dwelt eighteen months with a pasturer of cattle to learn the blemishes which are temporary, and those which remain forever ?   This was done that Rabba b. Hana should be respected, as Rabh was highly respected even without that.   And if you wish, it might be said that because of the fact itself, that Rabh was an expert concerning blemishes, it was not allowed to him to practise, for the reason that Rabh would allow such blemishes as other experts were not aware of, and people who should see that would act likewise, relying upon Rabh, so that they would finally allow the animal which had a temporary blemish to be slaughtered.

It is said above: " Rabbi said: He shall teach law."   To what purpose was this said ?   Does such a scholar as Rabh need such a permission for teaching ?   This was said because of the

---

* The first-born of cattle which might be legally eaten, and also of an ass, had biblically to be submitted to the priest when the Temple was in existence ; but after the destruction of the Temple they had to be raised until a blemish on their bodies appeared.   But what kind of a blemish made them fit for slaughtering ?   They had to be examined by an expert who understood blemishes, and was familiar with the entire law ; and a permission was needed for the expert.

following case: It happened that Rabbi went into a certain place and saw that they kneaded dough without offering a sample for legal purity. And to the question why they did so, their answer was: There was a disciple who taught: Water of *Bzein* (swamp) does not make articles subject to defilement. In reality, however, the expression was: "Mee Beizim," which means eggs; and they took it for Bzein, and acted accordingly. And therefore it was taught: A decree was enacted that a disciple should not teach unless he had the permission of his master.

Tanchun, the son of R. Ami, happened to be in the city of Hthar, and lectured: One may wet wheat and pound for peeling on Passover. And they said to him: Is not there here R. Mani of the city of Zur, who is a great scholar, and there is a Boraitha: A disciple must not decide a Halakha at the place of his master, unless distant from him three parsas—which distance Israel took when travelling in the desert. And he answered: I was not aware of this.

R. Hyya saw a man standing in a cemetery, and said to him: Are you not the son of so and so, who was a priest? He said: Yea, but my father was one of those who follow their eyes. He saw a divorced woman and married her, and with this he annulled the priesthood.

It is certain, when one takes a permission to give judgment in part, that it holds good (as so it was with Rabh). But how is it if the permission was conditionally for a certain time? Come and hear what R. Johanan said to R. Shauman: You have our permission until you shall return to us.

The text says: Samuel said: If it was decided by two, their decision is valid; but they are called an impertinent Beth Din. R. Na'hman repeated this Halakha, and Rabha objected from the following: If two are defending and two are accusing, and one says, "I do not know how to decide," judges must be added; now, if it were as you say, that the decision of two is valid, let, then, the decision of the two hold good? There it is different, as they start with the intention that it should be decided by three. He then objected to him from the following: Rabban Simeon b. Gamaliel said: Judgment in accordance with the strict law must be decided by three. In an arbitration, however, two suffice; and the strength of the mediation is greater than that of the law; as, if there were two who had decided a case in accordance with the law, although they were appointed by the parties, they (the parties) may retract. But if a mediation was made by the arbitrators, no retraction can take place. And lest one say that the rabbis differ with R. Simeon, did not R. Abuhu say: All agree that a decision passed by two is valueless? And he answered: Do you oppose one man to another (Abuhu may say so, and Samuel otherwise)?

R. Abba objected to R. Abuhu from the following: If one has decided upon a case—freed the guilty, or pronounced guilty the innocent, or decided unclean a thing which is clean, or *vice versa*, the act is valid and he must pay from his pocket. (Hence we see that even the decision of one is respected.) This Boraitha speaks of when the parties had appointed him for this purpose. But if so, why must he pay? It means, if they tell him: We appoint you to decide this case in accordance with the biblical law.

Said R. Safras to R. Abba: Let us see what was the error. If the error was that he decided against a Mishna, did not R. Shesheth say in the name of R. Assi that he who made an error as to a Mishna might retract from his decision? Hence such a decision is not valid, and he has not to pay from his pocket. Therefore it must be said that it means he erred in his opinion. How is this to be understood? Said R. Papa: *E.g.*, there were two Tanaim and two Amoraim who differed in a case, and it was not decided with whom the Halakha prevailed. However, the world practised according to one party, and he had decided the case according to the other party; and this could be called erring in one's opinion.

Shall we assume that in that case in which Samuel and R. Ahuhu differ, the Tanaim of the following Boraitha also differ: Arbitrating must be done by three persons. So is the decree of R. Meir. The sages, however, maintain: One is sufficient? The schoolmen who heard this thought that all agree that arbitration is similar to a strict law, and therefore they assumed that the point of their difference was: R. Meir holds three are needed, and the sages that two suffice. Nay, all agree that a strict law must be decided by three, and the point of their differing is: Whether arbitration must be similar to a strict law: according to one it must, and according to the other it must not.

Shall we assume that there are three Tanaim who differ concerning arbitration? One holds: Three are needed; the second, two; and the third, that even one is sufficient. Said R. Aha b. R. Ekba, according to others R. Yema b. Chlamia: He who says two are needed holds that even one is sufficient; and only to the end that they should be able to testify to this case as witnesses did he say two. Said R. Ashi: Infer from this that an arbitration does not need a sudarium; for if it should be necessary, why should not the one who maintains that three are needed be satisfied with two and a sudarium? The Halakha, however, prevails: An arbitration needs a sudarium.

The rabbis taught: Even as a strict law needs three, so is it with arbitration. However, when the decision is already given in accordance with the strict law, an arbitration cannot take place. R. Eliezer, the son of R. Jose the Galilean, used to say: It is prohibited to mediate, and he who should do so sins; and he who praises the mediators despises the law, as it is written [Ps. x. 3]: "The robber blesseth himself when he hath despised the Lord." But it may be taken as a rule that the strict law shall bore the mountain, as it is written [Deut. i. 17]: "The judgment belongs to God." And so was it said by Moses our master. But Aaron (his brother) loved peace, ran after it, and used to make peace among the people, as it is written [Mal. ii. 6]: "The law of truth was in his mouth, and falsehood was not found on his lips; in peace and equity he walked with me, and many did he turn away from iniquity." And R. Jehoshua b. Karha also said: Arbitration is a meritorious act, as it is written [Zech. viii. 16]: "With truth and the judgment of peace, judge ye in your gates." How is this to be understood? Usually, when there is judgment, there is no peace; and *vice versa*. It must then be said that an arbitration is a judgment which makes peace. So also was it said about David [II Sam. viii. 16]: "And David did what was just and charitable * unto all his people."

Here, also, "just" and "charitable" do not correspond; as if just, it could not be called charitable, and *vice versa*. Say, then, it means arbitration, which contains both.

The first Tana, however, who said above that arbitration is prohibited, explains the passage thus: He, David, judged in accordance with the strict law—he acquitted him who was right, and made responsible him who was so, according to the law; but when he saw that the culpable one was poor and could not pay, he used to pay from his pocket. Hence he did judgment to one and charity to the other. Rabbi, however, could not agree with such an explanation, because of the expression,

---

* *Zdakha* is the term in Hebrew, which means also charity.

" unto all his people "; and according to the above explanation, it ought to be " to the poor." Therefore said he: Although he did not pay from his pocket, it was counted as a charitable act that he delivered a theft out of the hands of the defendant.

R. Simeon b. Menasia said: If two persons brought a case before you, before you have heard their claims, and even thereafter, but you are still not aware to whom the strict law inclines, you may say to them: Go and mediate among yourselves. But after you are aware who is right according to the strict law, you must not advise them to mediate, as it is written [Prov. xvii. 14]: " As one letteth loose (a stream) of water, so is the beginning of strife; therefore before it be enkindled, leave off the contest "; which means, before it be enkindled you may advise a mediation, but not after you know with whom the law is. Similar to this is: If two persons came with a case before you, one being mighty (who can harm you) and the other common, you may say to them, " I am not fit to judge between you," so long as you have not heard their claims; or even thereafter, not knowing as yet to whom the law inclines. But you must not say so after you are aware; as it is written [Deut. i. 17]: " Ye shall not be afraid of any man."

R. Jehoshua b. Karha said: Whence do we deduce that if a disciple were present when a case came before his master, and saw a defence for the poor and an accusation for the rich (which his master might overlook), he must not keep silence? From the verse just cited. R. Hanin said: One must not keep in his words out of respect for any one; and witnesses also must be aware for whom they testify, and for whom their testimony goes. And who is he who will punish them for bearing false witness? As it is written [Deut. xix. 17]: " Then shall both the men who have the controversy stand before the Lord." And the judge must also be aware of same, as it is written [Ps. lxxxii. 1]: " God standeth in the congregation of God; in the midst of judges doth he judge." And so also it reads [II. Chron. xix. 6], which was said by the king Jehoshaphat: " Look (well) at what ye are doing; because not for man are ye to judge, but for the Lord."

And should the judge say: Why should I take the trouble and the responsibility to myself?—therefore it is written at the end of this verse: " Who is with you in pronouncing judgment." Hence the judge has to decide according to what he sees with his eyes.

What is to be understood by final judgment ? Said R. Jehudah in the name of Rabh: When the judge is able to pronounce:
You, so and so, are guilty, and you, so and so, are right. Said
Rabh: The Halakha prevails with R. Jehoshua b. Karha. Is
that so ? Was not R. Huna a disciple of Rabh, and his custom
was to question the parties of a case before him: Do you desire
strict law, or arbitration ? Hence we see that he did not begin
with mediation; and R. Jehoshua said that mediation is a
meritorious act. R. Jehoshua, with his statement, means also to
say: Ask the parties which they like better. But if so, it is the
same as what the first Tana said (*i.e.*, it is prohibited to arbitrate
after the conclusion, but not before the case is begun) ? The
difference between them is—according to R. Jehoshua it is a
meritorious act; and according to the first Tana it is only a permission for the judge, but not meritorious. But then it is the
same as R. Simeon b. Menasia said. There is also a difference,
as according to the latter we must not advise an arbitration after
hearing the claim, which is not according to the former. All
the Tanaim mentioned above differ with R. Thn'hum b. Hnilai,
who said: The above-cited verse [Ps. x.] was said concerning
the golden calf [Ex. xxxii. 5]: "And when Aaron saw this."
What did he see ? Said R. Benjamin b. Jeptheth in the name
of R. Elazar: He saw Chur, who was killed by the people. And
he thought: "If I do not listen to them, they will do likewise
with me, and will commit a sin, as written [Lam. ii. 20]: 'Shall
there be slain in the sanctuary of the Lord the priest and the
prophet ?' And they will have no remedy. It is better for
them that I should make the golden calf, and to that probably
there will be a remedy by repenting."

There was one who used to say: It is well for him who is
silent while being reproved; and if he is accustomed to do so,
it prevents a hundred evil things which he might have to overcome through quarrelling. Said R. Samuel to R. Jehudah: This
man only repeats what is already written in the above-cited
verse [Prov. xvii. 14].* There was another who used to say:
A thief is not killed for stealing two or three times (*i.e.*, do not
wonder if the punishment does not occur at once, as finally
it will come). And Samuel said to R. Jehudah: This is
also repeating the verse [Amos, ii. 5]: "Thus hath said the

---

* It is inferred from the term in Hebrew, "Reshit Madun," which is not
translatable into English.

Lord, For three transgressions of Israel, and for four, will I not turn away their punishment."

There was another who used to say: Into seven pits does the man of peace fall and come out, and the wicked does not come out from the first into which he falls. And to this also said Samuel to R. Jehudah: It is a repetition of the verse, Prov. xxiv. 16: " For though the righteous were to fall seven times, he will rise up again "; and should the wicked fall in one,* he will not rise again.

There was another who used to say: If the court levied on one's mantle for a bet to his neighbor, he might chant a song and go on his way. And to this the same said to the same: This also is to be understood from [Ex. xviii. 23]: " The whole of this people will come to its place in peace."

There was another who used to say: She slumbers, and the basket which was placed on her head fell down. And also to this said Samuel: The same is understood of [Eccl. x. 18]: " Through slothful hands the rafters will sink," etc. And there was another who used to say: The man on whom I relied raises his fist against me. To which Samuel referred [Ps. xli. 10]: " Yea, even the man that should have sought my welfare, in whom I trusted, who eateth my bread, hath lifted up his heel against me."

There was one more who used to say: When love was strong, we—I and my wife—could place ourselves on the flat of a sword. Now, when love is gone, a bed of sixty ells is not sufficient for us. To which R. Huna said: We can see this from the Scriptures in [Ex. xxv. 22]: " I will speak with thee from above the cover." And a Boraitha states that the ark measured nine spans, and the cover one; hence, altogether, it measured ten. Also in [I Kings vi. 2]: " . . . house which was built . . . sixty cubits in length." And finally we read [Is. lxvi. 1]: " . . . where is there a house that ye can build unto me ?" (*I.e.*, when the Tabernacle was built, ten spans sufficed, and at the exile no house in the world could be found in which the Shekinah would rest.)

R. Samuel b. Na'hmani in the name of Jonathan said: A judge who judges truth to his fellow-men makes the Shekinah to rest in Israel; as the above-cited Psalm lxxxii. 1 reads: " God

---

* The end of the verse, " but the wicked shall stumble into misfortune," is not found in the Scriptures. This is one of several places which shows that at that time in the Bible was another text.

standeth in the congregation of God; in the midst of judges
doth he judge." And those who do the contrary influence the
Shekinah to leave, as it is written [ibid. xii. 6]: " Because of
the oppression of the poor, because of the sighing of the needy,
now will I arise, saith the Lord."

The same said again in the name of the same authority: A
judge who takes away from one and gives to another, against
the law, the Holy One, blessed be He, (in revenge) will take
souls from his house. Thus it is read [Prov. xxii. 22, 23]:
" Rob not the poor because he is poor, neither crush the afflicted
in the gate; for the Lord will plead their cause, and despoil the
life of those that despoil them."

And he said again, in the name of the same authority: A
judge should always consider as if a sword lay between his shoulders and Gehenna was open under him. As·it is written [Solo-
mon's Song, iii. 7, 8]: " Behold, it is the bed which is Solomon's; sixty valiant men are round about it, of the valiant ones
of Israel. All of them are girded with the sword, are expert in
war; every one hath his sword upon his thigh, because of the
terror in the night—which means the terror of Gehenna, which
is equal to the night.

R. Jashyha, according to others R. Na'hman b. Itz'hak,
lectured: It is written [Jer. xxi. 12]: " O house of David, thus
hath said the Lord: Exercise justice on (every) morning, and
deliver him that is robbed out of the hand of the oppressor."
Do, then, people judge only in the morning, and not during the
entire day ? It means, if the thing which you decide is clear to
you as the morning, then do so; but if not, do not. R. Hyya
b. Abba in the name of R. Jonathan, however, said: This is inferred from [Prov. vii. 4]: " Say unto wisdom, Thou art my
sister," which means, if the thing is as certain to you as that it
is prohibited for you to marry your sister, then you may say it,
but not otherwise.

R. Jehoshua b. Levi said: If there are ten judges discussing
about one case, the collar lies upon the neck of all of them.
But is that not self-evident ? It means even a disciple who is
sitting before his master (although the result does not depend
upon him).

R. Huna used to gather ten disciples of the college when a
case came before him, saying: In case of error, let them also
have sawings of the beam. And R. Ashi, when it happened
that there was the carcass of a slaughtered animal to examine if

it was legal, used to gather all the slaughterers of the city, for the above-said purpose.

When R. Dimi came from Palestine, he said: R. Na'hman b. Kohen lectured: It is written [ibid. xxix. 4]: "A king will through the exercise of justice establish (the welfare of) a land; but one that loveth gifts overthroweth it"; meaning, if the judge is like unto a king, who needs not the favor of any one, he is establishing the land; but if like unto a priest who goes around the barns asking for heave-offering, he overthroweth it. The house of the Prince had appointed a judge who was ignorant, and it was said to Jehudah b. Na'hman, the interpreter of Resh Lakish: Go and be his interpreter. He bent himself to hear what was said for interpretation; but the judge said nothing. Jehudah then exclaimed: Woe unto him that saith to the wood, "Awake!" "Rouse up!" to the dumb' stone. Shall this teach? Behold, it is overlaid with gold and silver, and no breath whatever is in its bosom [Hab. ii. 19]. And the Holy One, blessed be He, will punish his appointer, as the following verse reads: "But the Lord is in his holy temple: be silent before him, all the earth."

Resh Lakish said: If one appoints a judge who is not fit to be such, he is considered as if he were to plant a grove in Israel. As it is written [Deut. xvi. 18]: "Judges and officers shalt thou appoint unto thyself"; and ibid. 21 it reads: "Thou shalt not plant unto thyself a grove—any tree." R. Ashi added: And if this were done in places where scholars are to be found, it is considered as if one should do it at the altar, as the cited verse continues: "near the altar of the Lord thy God."

It is written [Ex. xx. 23]: "Gods of silver and gods of gold," etc. Is it only prohibited from gods of silver, and of wood we may? Said R. Ashi: This means the judge who is appointed by means of silver and gold. Rabh, when he went to sit on the bench, used to say: By my own will I go to be slain (*i.e.*, if I make an error I shall be punished for it), without attending the needs of my house; and I enter, clear the court, and I pray that the departing should be like the entering (as he came without sin, so should he depart). And when he saw the crowd run after him, he used to say: "Though his exaltation should mount up to the heavens, and his head should reach unto the clouds, yet when he but turneth round will he vanish for ever" [Job, xx. 6, 7] (to quiet his excitement).

Mar Zutra the Pious, when he was carried on the shoulders

of his followers on the Sabbaths before the festivals (each Sabbath before the three festivals they used to preach festival laws), he used to say [Prov. xxvii. 24]: " For property endureth not forever, nor doth the crown remain for all generations."

Bar Kapara lectured: Whence do we deduce what the rabbis said: Be deliberate concerning judgment ? From [Ex. xx. 23]: " Neither shalt thou go up by steps upon my altar"; and the next verse is : " These are the laws of justice."

R. Eliezer said: Whence do we know that the judge should not step upon the heads of the whole people (the hearers of the lectures used to sit on the floor during the lectures, and one who passed among them appeared as if he were stepping on their heads) ? From the same cited verse. It treats: Thou shalt set before them the laws of justice; it ought to be: Thou shalt teach them ? Said R. Jeremiah, and according to others R. Hyya b. Abba: It means the preparation of things belonging to judgment: the cane, the strap, the cornet, and the sandal. As R. Huna, when he used to go on the bench, used to say: Bring here all the things above mentioned.

It is written [Deut. i. 16]: " And I commanded your judges at that time." This was a warning to the judges that they should be careful with the cane and straps, which were in their hands to punish them who rebelled. Farther on it is written: " Hear the causes between your brethren and judge righteously." Said R. Hanina: This is a warning to the court that it shall not listen to the claims of one party in the absence of the other (in civil cases); and the same warning is to one of the parties—he shall not explain his claim in the absence of his opponent. " You shall judge righteously " means, you shall deliberate the case carefully, and make it just in your mind, and only thereafter you may give your decision.

It is written: " Between a man and his brother, and his stranger." Said R. Jehudah: It means, even between a house and its attic. (I.e., if it were an inheritance, the judge must not say: You both need dwellings—what is the difference, if one take the house and one the attic ? But he must appraise the value of each and then give his decision. " And his stranger " means, if you hire your house to a stranger for a dwelling, it cannot be said: What is the difference, if I give him an oven or a stove ? But you must give him according to the conditions. So R. Jehudah. Farther on it reads: " Ye shall not recognize (respect) persons in judgment." According to R. Jehudah, it means: You shall not recognize him if he is your friend; and according to R. Elazar, it means: You shall not recognize him as strange to you, if he is your enemy.

The host of Rabh had to try a case before Rabh, and when he entered he said to Rabh: Do you remember that you are my guest? And he answered: Yea, but why? And he said: I have a case to try. Rejoined Rabh: I am unfit to be a judge for your case (because you reminded me that you favored me some time ago). And he appointed R. Kahana to judge the case. R. Kahana, however, had seen that he relied too much upon Rabh, so that he would not listen to him. He then said to him: If you listen to my decision, well and good; and if not, I will put Rabh out of your mind (i.e., I will put you under the ban). It reads farther on: " The small as well as the great shall ye hear." Said Resh Lakish: It means, you shall treat a case of one peruta with the same care and mind as you would treat a case involving a hundred manas. To what purpose was this said? Is this not self-evident? It means, if two cases come before you, one of a peruta and one of one hundred manas, you shall not say: It is a small case, and I will see to it after.

" Ye shall not be afraid of any man; for the judgment belongeth to God." Said R. Hama b. R. Hanina: The Holy One, blessed be He, said: " It is the least for the wicked to take away money from one and give it to another illegally"; but they are troubling me that I shall return the money to its owner. " And I commanded you at that time." Above it reads: " I commanded your judges." Said R. Elazar in the name of R. Simlai: This was a warning for the congregation, that they should respect their judges; incidentally, also, a warning to the judges that they should bear with the congregation. To what extent? Said R. Hana, according to others R. Sabbathi: Even [Num. xi. 12] " as a nursing father beareth the sucking child."

It treats [Deut. xxxi. 23]: " Thou must bring this people," etc. And in verse 7 it is written: " Thou must go with." Said R. Johanan: Moses said to Joshua: You and the elders shall rule over them; but the Holy One, blessed be He, said: " *Thou* shalt bring them (i.e., thou alone), because there must be one ruler to a generation, and not two or many.

There is a Boraitha: A summons must be by the consent of three judges. And this is in accordance with Rabha, who said: If the messenger of the court had summoned one in the

2

name of one of the three judges who are in the court, the summons is nothing unless he state it is in the name of all the three
judges, provided it was not a court day; but on a court day he
has to mention nothing.

"*Double amount.*" R. Na'hman b. R. Hisda sent a message to R. Na'hman b. Jacob: Let the master teach us. In
cases of fine, how many persons are needed? [What was the
question—does not the Mishna state three? The question was,
whether one judge, who is an expert, may do this, or not?]
And the answer was: This is stated in our Mishna, in the double
amount, and four and five fold—three. And it cannot be said
it means three common men; for your grandfather said in the
name of Rabh: Even ten commoners are illegal to decide cases
of fine. Hence the Mishna means judges, of whom, nevertheless, three are needed.

"*It may bring capital punishment.*" And what is it (meanwhile his claim is money—why should three not be sufficient)?
Said Ula: The point of their differing is, if an evil tongue is to
be feared (*i.e.*, while he comes to the court complaining about
his wife, witnesses may come and testify that she had indeed
sinned; and then it is a crime of capital punishment). According to R. Meir, the fear of such is not to be taken into consideration; and according to the rabbis, it is. Rabha, however,
maintains: The fear of an evil tongue is not taken into consideration by all of the parties; but the point of their difference is,
if the honor of the first should be respected or not. And it
treats that twenty-three were gathered for that case, and the
husband claimed that he would bring witnesses that his wife
had sinned. But thereafter he could not bring witnesses, and
the case remained as a claim for money only, and then the
twenty departed. And he asked them to decide at least his
civil claim. According to R. Meir, this case, as a money matter, might be tried by three; but according to the rabbis, we
must respect the honor of the judges gathered, and therefore
even in the latter case all the twenty-three have to take part.

An objection was raised from a Boraitha which states: The
sages said: If the claim was money, then three suffice; but if
a crime which could bring capital punishment, then twenty-
three are needed. And this is correct only according to Rabba's
statement, viz.: If the beginning of the claim was money, then
three; and if the beginning was crime, then twenty-three. But
according to Ula's it is contradictory.

Said Rabha: I and the lion of our society, who is R. Hyya b. Abbim, have thus explained this: The Mishna treats of a case in which the husband brought witnesses that his wife had sinned, and his father-in-law brought witnesses who proved the first collusive. And his claim against the husband was money; and therefore three sufficed. But in a case where crime is charged, twenty-three are necessary.

Abayi, however, maintains: All agree that an evil tongue is to be feared; and they also agree that the honor of the first must be respected. The Mishna, however, speaks of a case in which the warning was as to capital punishment, but not stoning. (*I.e.*, as will be explained in the proper place, one should not be put to death for a crime of which he was not warned that the punishment for it was death; and according to some, the warning must be: The punishment for such a crime is such and such a death. And as the punishment of adultery is stoning, and she was warned only of death in general, according to him who holds that the warning must state the kind of death, in this case no capital punishment can occur.) And this is in accordance with R. Jehudah, who said elsewhere: One is not put to death unless he was informed in the warning what kind of death he should die.

R. Papa maintains: It speaks of a scholarly woman who was aware of what kind of punishment pertained to such a thing; and the point of their differing is, if to a scholar warning is needed. And R. Ashi maintains: The warning was as to stripes, instead of capital punishment; and the point of their differing is, if a trial involving stripes needs twenty-three, in accordance with the opinion of R. Ishmael, or not.* And Rabhina maintains: It speaks of when one of the witnesses was found a relative, or incompetent to be a witness; and the point of their difference is, if the testimony of the other witnesses should be ignored because of the incompetent one, or not (explained at length in Tract Maccoth). And if you wish, it can be said that it speaks of when one was warned by some others, but not by the witnesses; and there are some of the Tanaim who hold that the warning holds good only when it was made by the witnesses. And it might also be said that the witnesses contradicted one another, at the cross-examination, concerning certain unimportant things (*e.g.*, how he and she were dressed when the crime was com-

---

* All this will be explained in the proper place in succeeding volumes.

mitted); but they did not contradict each other concerning the important thing (*e.g.*, the date and hour). And there is a difference between Tanaim whether such a contradiction is to be taken into consideration, or not?

R. Joseph said: If the husband brought witnesses that she had sinned, and the father brought witnesses who proved them collusive, the witnesses of the husband are put to death, but do not pay the prescribed fine. If, however, the husband brought a third party of witnesses, who proved collusive the second party, they are to be punished both with death and with payment of fine to the husband.

Rabha said: If witnesses testify that A had sinned with a betrothed woman, and thereafter they be found collusive, they are put to death, but do not pay the fine; if, however, they testified that A had sinned with the daughter of B, who was betrothed, they pay the fine also. And the same is the case if they testify that one had connection with an ox, and they were found collusive; if, however, they testify with the ox of so and so, they have to pay the fine to the owner of the ox also. But to what purpose did he state the other case—is it not the same as the first? Because he himself was in doubt concerning the following case: If one testified that so and so had connection with *my* ox, should he be trusted or not? Shall we say that only a testimony which incriminates one's self is not to be trusted—because one is kin to himself and cannot make himself wicked, but in a case where one's property is involved, we do not say that he is kin to his money, and therefore he should not be trusted. After deliberating, however, he decided that the testifying concerning his ox should be trusted, as the latter case is not taken into consideration.

"*The cases of stripes*," etc. Whence is this deduced? Said R. Huna: It is written [Deut. xxv. 1]: "And they judge them," which is plural, and no less than two; and as a court must not be of an even number, one is to be added—hence it is three. In the same verse it reads: "And they justify . . . and they condemn," which is also plural, and no less than two —hence two and two are four, and with the three mentioned above it is seven?

The latter terms are needed for that which Ula said: Where is to be found a hint in the Scriptures concerning collusive witnesses? [A hint—does it not read (ibid. xix. 19): "Then shall ye do unto him as he had purposed to do unto his brother"?

Where is the hint that collusive witnesses are to be punished with stripes?] From the above-cited terms, " and they shall justify . . . condemn the wicked: Then shall it be, if the guilty man deserve to be beaten," etc., which is not to be understood as meaning the court only, as the words, " they shall justify the righteous," would be superfluous in that case. And therefore it is to be explained thus: If there were witnesses who had made the righteous guilty, and thereafter other witnesses came and justified the righteous who were indeed right, and made guilty the witnesses who accused them; then, if the former were to be punished with stripes, if found guilty, the same punishment is to be meted to the guilty witnesses.

But is there not a negative commandment in Ex. xx. 16: " Thou shalt not bear false witness"? This negative commandment is counted among those who do no manual labor; and for the transgression of such, punishment of stripes is not applied.

"In the name of Ishmael it was said," etc. What is his reason? Said Abayi: The analogy of expression, Rosha (guilty). It reads [Deut. xxv. 2]: " Guilty man," and [Num. xxxv. 31]: " Who is guilty of death." As in case of death, twenty-three are needed, the same is the case with stripes. Rabha, however, maintains: His reason is simple, as stripes take the place of that. Said R. Aha, the son of Rabha, to R. Ashi: If so is the case, why must he be examined by the court to see if he can stand the forty stripes? Let him be beaten without any examination; and if he cannot stand them, let him die. And he answered: It reads [Deut. xxv. 3]: " And thy brother be rendered vile before thy eyes." Hence if you beat, you must beat one who is still alive, but not a dead body. If so (said R. Aha again), why does a Boraitha state that if the examination shows that he can stand only twenty, he is beaten with that number, which can be made a multiple of three, say eighteen only? Let him receive twenty-one; and if he cannot receive the last stripe let him die, as the last stripe was on a body which was still alive (*i.e.*, thrice seven are twenty-one, and as he would not die by twenty according to the examination, the twenty-one would still be on a live body). Rejoined R. Ashi: The verse reads: " Thy brother thus rendered vile before thy eyes," which means that after the stripes he shall still be thy brother, which would not be the case if he died while being beaten.

" To the intercalary month," etc. It does not state for the

consideration of the intercalary, nor does it state for the consecration of the month; but for the intercalary itself, why are three needed ? Let it be not consecrated at the thirtieth day, and it will become intercalary by itself (*i.e.*, if the thirty-first day be consecrated as the first of the next month, the past month will be intercalary with one day). Said Abayi: Read: For the consecration of the month. And so also we have learned in a Tosephtha: For the consecration of the month and the proclamation of a leap year, three. So is the decree of R. Meir. Said Rabha: You say: Read " for the consecration "; but it is stated " the intercalary." Therefore, he maintains, the consecration in the additional day (*e.g.*, the thirtieth) must be by three; but after the day is over, no consecration is needed. And it is in accordance with R. Elazar b. Zadok, who said (Rosh Hashana, p. 1): If the moon was not seen at the usual time, no consecration is needed, as it was already consecrated by heaven. R. Na'hman says: The consecration after the thirtieth day must be by three; but at the thirtieth no consecration takes place at all.

And it is in accordance with Plimi, who says in the following Boraitha: When the moon is seen at her usual time, no consecration is needed; but if not at the usual time, then it must be consecrated. R. Ashi, however, maintains: It is to be understood, the consideration if the month should be intercalary, and the expression " to intercalary " means the consideration of it. And because it needs to teach to proclaim a leap year, it says also intercalary. Hence only to the consideration, but not to the consecration, which is in accordance with R. Eliezer, who said: A month must not be consecrated at any time, as it is written [Lev. xxv. 10]: " Ye shall hallow the fiftieth year," from which we infer that a year may be consecrated, but not months.

" *Rabban Simeon Gamaliel,* " etc. There is a Boraitha: How was it said by R. Simeon b. Gamaliel that it began with three, was discussed by five, and concluded by seven ? Thus: If one of the three says it must be considered, and the other two say it is not needed, then the individual's opinion is abandoned. If, however, *vice versa*, two more must be added to discuss the matter; and then, if two say it needs, and three say no, the majority is considered. And if *vice versa*, then two more must be added, and the decision is according to the majority.

The numbers three, five, and seven, to what have they a

similarity ?   R. Itz'hak b. Na'hmani and one of his colleagues, who was R. Simeon b. Pazi, and according to others just the reverse, differ.   One said that the three were taken from the three verses specifying the blessings of the priests (Num. vi. 24, 25, 26).   And the other said: Three from the "three door-keepers" mentioned in II Kings, xxv. 18; and five, from [ibid. ·19]: "The five men of those that could come into the king's presence"; and the seven from "the seven princes of Persia and Media" [Esther, i. 14].

R. Joseph taught the same as the latter, and Abayi questioned him: Why did not the master explain this to us before now ?   To which he answered: I was not aware that you needed the explanation.   Has it happened that you questioned me, and I would not answer ?

The rabbis taught: A year must not be intercalated with one month, except by them who are invited for it by the Nashi.   It happened with Rabban Gamaliel, who commanded that seven persons should be invited for the morrow in his attic, for the purpose of the intercalation of the year, that on the morrow, when he came, he found eight persons, and said: He who was not invited shall leave.   Samuel the Little then arose and said: I am the one who was not invited.   I came here, not to take part in the intercalation, but to get experience in the practice of this ceremony.   To which the former answered: Sit down, my son; sit down.   All the years which have to be intercalated might be done by you.   But so was the decision of the sages, that such must be done only by the persons who were invited. (Says the Gemara:) In reality, it was not Samuel the Little, but some other, and he did so only not to bring shame upon his colleague.   It happened that as Rabbi was lecturing he perceived the odor of garlic, and he said: He who has eaten garlic shall leave.   R. Hyya then rose and left the place; and every one, seeing R. Hyya go out, did the same.   On the morrow R. Simeon, the son of Rabbi, met R. Hyya, and questioned him: Was it you who disturbed my father yesterday ?   And he answered: Save God!   Such a thing would not be done in Israel by myself. And from whom did R. Hyya learn this ?   From R. Meir, as is stated in the following Boraitha: It happened with a woman who came to the college of R. Meir, saying: One of you has be-trothed me, but I do not know who it was.   Then R. Meir arose and wrote her a divorce, and handed it to her; and after him, all the people in the college did likewise.   And from whom did

R. Meir learn this? From Samuel the Little; and Samuel the Little from Shechanyah b. Yechiel, who said to Ezra [Ezra, x. 2]: "We have indeed trespassed against our God, and have brought home strange wives of the nations of the land; yet now there is hope in Israel concerning this thing." And he, Shechanyah, learned this from Jehoshua b. Nun, of whom it is said [Josh. vii. 10]: "Get thee up; wherefore liest thou upon thy face? Israel hath sinned," etc.

The rabbis taught: Since the death of the last prophets, Haggai, Zechariah, and Malachi, the Holy Spirit has left Israel; nevertheless they were still used to a heavenly voice. It happened once that they had a meeting in the attic of the house of Guriah, in the city of Jericho, and a heavenly voice was heard: Among these people there is one who is worthy that the Shekinah should rest upon him; but his generation is not fit. And the sages turned their eyes on Hillel the Elder. And when he departed, they lamented him. "Woe, pious! Woe, modesty! O thou disciple of Ezra." The same happened again when they had a meeting in an attic in the city of Yamnia, and the heavenly voice said: Among these people is one worthy that the Shekinah should rest upon him, but his generation is not fit. And the rabbis turned their eyes on Samuel the Little. When he departed, he also was lamented: "Woe, pious! Woe, modesty! O thou disciple of Hillel!"

The rabbis taught: A year must not be intercalated without the Prince's consent. It happened once that Rabban Gamaliel went to one ruler in Syria, and remained there longer than was expected; and the sages had intercalated the year on the condition that Rabban Gamaliel should agree; and then, when he came, he said, "I agree," and the year was intercalated without any other ceremony.

The rabbis taught: A leap year should not be made unless necessary, because of the spoiled roads, bridges requiring to be repaired, and because of the ovens where the paschal lambs were to be roasted, and they were not yet dry; and for them who reside in exile, and had left their places for Jerusalem to offer the paschal lamb, but could not reach in such a short time; but not if there was still snow or cold, and also not for them who resided in exile and had not as yet left their places for Jerusalem.

The rabbis taught: A leap year should not be made because of the kids, lambs, and pigeons which are too young. But this may be taken as a support. How so? Said R. Janai in the name of R. Simeon b. Gamaliel: We inform you that the pigeons are still soft, and the lambs still thin, and the time of spring has not yet arrived; and it has pleased me to add to this year thirty days. An objection was raised from the following Boraitha: How much is to be added to a leap year? Thirty days. R. Simeon b. Gamaliel said: One month of twenty-nine days. Said R. Papa: If they wish, they can make it with thirty days; and if they wish, with one month of twenty-nine days. Come and see the difference between the old, mighty generation and that of the new, modest one. There is a Boraitha: It happened with Rabban Gamaliel, who used to sit on a step in the court of the Temple, that Johanan his scribe was standing before him, and three pieces of parchment were lying before him. And he told him: Take one parchment, and write to our brethren in Upper Galilee and to our brethren in Lower Galilee: May your peace be increased! We inform you that the time has come to separate tithe of the mounds of olives. And take another piece of parchment, and write to our Southern brethren: May your peace be increased! We inform you that the time has come to separate tithe of the garden sheaves. And take the third one, and write to our brethren in exile in Babylon, and to our brethren in Media, and to all other Israelites who are scattered in exile: May your peace be increased everlastingly! We inform you that the pigeons are soft, and lambs thin, and the time of spring has not yet come, and it pleases me and my colleagues to add to this year thirty days. (Hence Gamaliel wrote: " pleased me and my colleagues"; and Simeon his son did not mention his colleagues.) (Says the Gemara:) Perhaps this happened after R. Gamaliel was discharged and reappointed, as then he became more modest.

The rabbis taught: For the following three things a leap year is made: because of the late arrival of spring; of the unripeness of tree-products; and for the late arrival of Thkhupha (the equinox).* When two of the three things occur, the year is made intercalary; but not if one of them. And when one of the reasons is spring, all rejoiced. And R. Simeon b. Gamaliel said: When Thkhupha (the equinox) was the reason. And the schoolmen questioned: How is he to be understood? Does he mean that they rejoiced when the Thkhupha (the equinox) was

---

* See Rosh Hashana, p. 12, second edition.

one of the reasons, or does he mean to say that if it was the reason it suffices to make the year intercalate even without other reasons? The question remains undecided.

. The rabbis taught: For the following three lands the leap year was made: Judea, Galilee, and the other side of the Jordan. For two of them, but not for one. If it happened that Judea was one of them, all rejoiced, because the offer of the omer (as the first of the harvest) was brought only from the land of Judea.

The rabbis taught: The year is to be made intercalary only in the land of Judea; but if it was made already in Galilee, their act is valid. However, Hananiah, the man of Anni, has testified that if the leap year was made in Galilee it was not considered. And R. Jehudah b. R. Simeon b. Pazi said: The reason of Hananiah is [Deut. xii. 5]: "Even unto his habitation shall ye refrain," which means, all your repairing should be only in the habitation of the Omnipotent.

The rabbis taught: A leap year is to be made only during the day-time, and if it was done in the night it is not intercalate. And the same is the case with the consecration of the month; it holds good in the day-time, and not in the night.

The rabbis taught: A leap year must not be made in the years of famine. And there is a Boraitha: R. Meir used to say: It is written [II Kings, iv. 42]: "And there came a man from Ba'al-shalishah, and brought unto the man of God bread of the firstfruits, twenty loaves of barley-bread," etc. And we know by tradition that the city of Ba'al-shalishah was the most fruitful city in the whole land of Israel, in which the fruit became ripe previous to all other cities; and nevertheless at that time it was not ripe, but only one kind of grain; and not wheat, but barley, as so it reads. And lest one say it was before the time the omer was to be brought, therefore it is written at the end of this verse: "Give it unto the people, that they may eat." Hence, under such circumstances, that year ought to have been intercalary. And why was it not made so by Elisha? Because it was a year of famine, and every one went to the barns in order to get something to eat, and therefore it was not intercalated.

The rabbis taught: The year must not be intercalary before Rosh Hashana (i.e., no meeting must be appointed to discuss upon the necessity of an additional month in the next year). Even if it were so done, it is not to be taken into consideration. However, if circumstances compelled them to do so, they may do it immediately after Rosh Hashana; but the additional month must be no other one than Adar. Is that so ? Was not a message sent to Rabha: A couple came from the city of Lecarte, and caught an eagle, and in their hands were found things which were made in the city of Luz (*e.g.*, Thkhalth, for Tshitzith). And by the kindness of the Merciful One, and because of their unripeness, they were redeemed, and left in peace. And the descendants of Na'hshun desired to establish one nazib (ruler) more, but the Aramaic had prevented them. However, the prominent men of the cities held a meeting, and added one ruler (nazib) in that month in which Aaron (the high-priest) died. (Hence we see that a meeting about a leap year was appointed in the month of Ab, as Aaron died in that month ?) *

The discussion, and even the establishment, may be done even before Rosh Hashana; but it must be kept secret until the day of New Year is past. But whence do we know that with the above-mentioned word " nazib " they meant " a month " ? From [I Kings, iv. 7]: " And Solomon had twelve superintendents (nazibun) . . . for the king's household, one month in the year "; but ibid. 19 reads: " Besides the one superintendent (nazib) who was in the land ? "

R. Jehudah and R. Na'hman—one said: One manager over all the superintendents. And the other maintains that this nazib was for the intercalary month.

The rabbis taught: A leap year must not be made in one year, for the next; and also three successive years must not be intercalary. R. Simeon, however, said: It happened with R. Aqiba, that he established three leap years, one after the other, while he was in prison. And he was answered: This is no evidence, as the court had established each leap year in its proper time.

The rabbis taught: A leap year must not be appointed, neither in the Sabbatic year nor in the following year. But when were they used to be established ? On the eve of the Sabbatic year. The house of Rabban Gamaliel, however, used to appoint it for the year following the Sabbatic.

The rabbis taught: No appointment of a leap year must be because of defilement. R. Jehudah, however, maintains it may,

---

* This riddle was sent at the time when it was prohibited by the Roman government to establish a leap year, and even to discuss about it. Therefore the message was sent as a riddle so as to be unintelligible to those not concerned.

and adds: It happened with King Hezekiah, who had established such because of defilement, and thereafter he prayed for
forgiveness. As it is written [II Chron. xxx. 18]: " For a large
portion of the people, even many out of Ephraim and Manas-
seh, Issachar, and Zebulun had not cleansed themselves, but ate
the Passover not as it is written. However, Hezekiah prayed
for them, saying: " The Lord, who is good, will grant pardon
for this."

R. Simeon said: If they had established it because of defilement, it is intercalary; and Hezekiah prayed for forgiveness
because the law dictates that only the month of Adar shall be
intercalary. He, however, intercalated the month Nissin. R.
Simeon b. Jehudah, however, said in the name of R. Simeon:
He prayed for forgiveness because he seduced Israel to establish
a second passover.

The master said: He intercalated the month of Nissin. Did
he not hold the tradition [Ex. xii. 2]: "This month shall be
unto you the chief of months," which means Nissin; and it is
written, *this* is Nissin, but no other month shall be named
Nissin? He erred in that which is said in the name of Samuel:
In the thirtieth day of Adar no intercalary month must be
appointed, because this day was fit that it should be the first
of Nissin. And he, Hezekiah, did not hold this theory. There
is also a Boraitha which states: In the thirtieth day of Adar no
month must be intercalated because it is fit to be the first of
Nissin.

. But how is it if, notwithstanding this, it was established on
that day? Said Ula: Then the month must not be consecrated
on that day. But how is it if it was consecrated also? According to Rabha, the consecration abolishes the intercalary; and
according to R. Na'hman, both hold good—the intercalary and
the consecration. Said Rabha to R. Na'hman: Let us see!
From Purim to Passover are thirty days; and on Purim we
begin to lecture about the law of Passover. Now, if they should
appoint another Adar on the thirtieth day after the lectures of
Passover were already heard, people would not believe then that
another month was appointed, and so they would use leavened
bread on Passover. And he answered: Why, they would believe, as they know the establishment of a leap year depends on
counting; and they would say that it was not as yet clear to the
rabbis—the reckoning of this year—until the thirtieth day of
Adar arrived.

R. Jehudah in the name of Samuel said: A leap year must not be established unless the Thkhupha was less with a greater part of the month, which are sixteen days. So is the decree of R. Jehudah. R. Jose, however, said: Twenty-one days. And both took their reference from [Ex. xxxiv. 22]: And the feast of ingathering at the closing (Thkhuphat—equinox) of the year. One holds that the whole feast should be in the new Thkhuphat; and the other holds that it is sufficient if a few days of the feast should occur in the new Thkhuphat. How is this to be understood? If they hold that the day in which the Thkhupha occurs is counted to the past Thkhuphat, why, then, is it necessary for R. Jehudah that the Thkhuphat shall be less with sixteen, and to R. Jose with twenty-one days? Even if it would be less with fifteen days, according to R. Jehudah, and twenty days, according to R. Jose, the whole festival will not be on the new Thkhuphat according to R. Jehudah, as the fifteenth day of Nissin, which is the first day of the feast, and in which the Thkhuphat occurs, is counted to the past Thkhuphat; and also according to R. Jose, if the Thkhuphat occurs on the twenty-first day, which is counted to the past, not one of the festival days would occur on the new Thkhuphat, as the festival begins on the fifteenth, and the seventh ends with the twenty-first. Therefore it must be said, of the day in which the Thkhuphat occurs, both R. Jehudah and R. Jose count it as the beginning of the new Thkhuphat.*

" *Laying the hand of the elders upon sacrifices.*" The rabbis taught: It is written [Lev. iv. 15]: " And the elders of the congregation shall lay their hands," etc. (The expression in Hebrew is, " Vsomkhu Ziqnye Hoedha "—literally, " and they shall lay," " the elders," " of the congregation.") From the expression Hoedha, which means the congregation, instead of elders of the congregation, it is deduced that it means the prominent of the congregation, and from the plurality of Vsomkhu (" and they shall lay," which means no less than two) and the plurality of the elders, who are also two, it is deduced four persons; and as the number of the court must not be even, one is added—hence it makes five. So is the decree of R. Jehudah. R. Simeon, however, maintains: There is only one

---

* The detailed explanation of all this would take too much space. However, it will be understood by those who know the order of the Jewish calendar. Although in our work it is of no importance, we hope that the reader will have an idea of it from our text, without the detailed explanation and the discussion following, omitted.

plurality in the elders, who are two, and one is added for the purpose mentioned above, making three only. And there is a Boraitha: To laying the hand upon the elders, and laying the hands of the elders upon the sacrifices, three are needed. What does this mean? Said R. Johanan: Laying the hand upon the elders means, to give one the degree of Rabbi: Said Abayi to R. Jose: Whence do we deduce this? From [Num. xxvii. 23]: "And he laid his hand upon him," etc. Then let one be sufficient, as Moses was only one person; and lest one say that Moses took the place of the Large Sanhedrin, who were seventy-one, then say that to confer a degree seventy-one are needed? This difficulty remains.

Said R. Aha b. Rabha to R. Ashi: Do we lay the hands upon the man to whom we want to give such a degree? And he answered: We support him with that, that we name him Rabbi and give him the permission to judge about fines upon them who deserve it.

Is it indeed so—that one man cannot bestow a degree? Did not R. Jehudah in the name of Rab say: Behold, the memory of that person shall remain blessed forever—I mean, R. Jehudah b. Baba, as, if not ben Baba, the law of fines would be forgotten from Israel. It happened once that the government passed an evil decree upon Israel, that he who bestowed a degree should be put to death, and the same should be done with him who received the degree. The city where the degree was conferred should be destroyed, and even the boundaries which were used while giving the degree should be torn out. Jehudah b. Baba then went and sat between two great mountains, and between two large cities—between the two suburban limits of the cities of Usha and Sprehen—and conferred the degree of Rabbi on five elders; and they were: R. Meir, R. Jehudah, R. Simeon, R. Jose, and R. Elazar b. Shamuas. According to R. Ivia, there was a sixth: R. Nehomai. When the enemy got wind of it, Jehudah said to them: My children, run away. And to their question: Rabbi, what will become of you? he answered: I shall remain before them as a stone which cannot be moved. It was said that three hundred iron spears were put by the enemy into his body, making it as a sieve. (Hence we see that even one person only is authorized to give a degree?) There were some other persons with him, but they were not mentioned, because of the honor of Jehudah b. Baba. Was indeed Meir elevated by Jehuda? Did not Rabha b. Hanah say in the name of Johanan that R. Aqiba gave the degree to R. Meir? Yea, R. Aqiba did so, but it was not accepted; and from R. Jehudah b. Baba he accepted.

R. Jehoshua b. Levi said: The custom of giving degrees must not be used out of Palestine. What does he mean? Shall we assume that loss of fines should not be judged at all out of Palestine? This is not so, as there is a Mishna: Sanhedrins are to be established in Palestine as well as in other places out of Palestine. He means that one must receive his degree in Palestine only.

It is certain that a degree of Rabbi is not considered when the bestower is out of and the receiver is in Palestine. But how is it if the bestower is in Palestine and the receiver is out? Come and hear: R. Johanan was troubled for R. Shaman b. Aba, who was not present and could not receive the degree R. Johanan wished to honor him with. R. Simeon b. Zerud and his colleague Jonathan b. Ekhmai, according to others *vice versa*—one of them who was present they supported with a degree, and the one who was not did not receive such.

R. Hanina and R. Hoseah were two about whom R. Johanan troubled himself very much, to honor them with the degrees they deserved, but was always prevented, whereat he was very sorry. Said they to him: Let master not worry, as we are descendants of the house of Eli. And R. Samuel b. Na'hman in the name of R. Jonathan said: Whence is it deduced that the descendants of Eli are prevented by Heaven from receiving degrees? From [I Sam. ii. 32]: "And there shall not be an elder in thy house in all times"—which cannot be meant literally —"an old man," as it is written [ibid. 33]: "And all the increase of thy house shall die as (vigorous) men." Hence it means a *degree* of an elder (scholar).

R. Zera used to hide himself so as not to be honored with a degree, because of R. Elazar's statement: Be always misty, in order to have a better existence. Thereafter, when he heard another statement of the same authority, "One is not raised to a great authority unless all his sins are forgiven by Heaven," then he went to receive a degree. When he was graduated as a rabbi, his followers sang for him thus: "There is no dyeing, no polishing, no painting, and nevertheless it is handsome and full of grace." When Ami and Assi were graduated as rabbis, likewise people sang of them thus: "Of such men—of such people—appoint rabbis for us, but not from the sermonisers";

and according to others, "not steel-hearted and impudent men."

R. Abubu, when he came from college in the court of the Zaiser, the matrons of Zaiser's house used to sing for him: "Great man of his people! ruler of his nation! candle of light! may thy coming be welcomed in peace."

"*Case of the heifer.*" The rabbis taught [Deut. xxi. 2]: "Then shall thy elders and thy judges go forth," etc. Elders, two, and judges, two, are four, etc. (will be translated in Tract Souta, as the proper place).

"*Plants of the fourth year and second tithe,*" etc. The rabbis taught: What is to be considered second tithe of which the value is not known? Rotten fruit, sour wine, and rusty coins. They also taught: Such second tithe must be redeemed by the appraisement of three buyers who all know the price of such stock; but not by three laymen who do not know the exact price. Among the buyers may be a Gentile, and also the owner of the stock. And R. Jeremiah questioned: How is it if the three were partners? Come and hear: One and his two wives may redeem the second tithe of which the value is not known. Hence it is allowed. This is no support, as this Boraitha may speak of such as were apart in business. *E.g.,* R. Papa and his wife, the daughter of Aba of Sura (who used to do business for herself).

"*Consecrated articles,*" etc. Our Mishna is not in accordance with R. Eliezer b. Jacob of the following Boraitha, who said: Even for a small fork of the sanctuary, ten persons are needed to appraise the value for redeeming. Said R. Papa to Abayi: R. Eliezer is correct that it needs ten, as he may hold with the statement of Samuel, who said: Priests are ten times mentioned in the portion which speaks of consecrated things. But whence did the rabbis take three? This difficulty remains.

"*Arakhin . . . movable property.*" What are they? R. Giddle in the name of Rabh said: If one vows, the value of this utensil is to be consecrated, then it must be appraised for its value, and he must pay. R. Hisda, however, said in the name of Abayi: It means, if one vows his own value, and appoints movable property for the collection. R. Abuhu said: If one vows his own value for the treasurer of the priests, when he came to collect, if he collects from movable property, three suffice to appraise it; but if from real estate, ten are needed. Said R. Aha of Diphthi to Rabhina: It is correct that three are needed to appraise articles which are to be redeemed from the sanctuary; but why are three needed for bringing into the sanctuary? And he answered: It is common sense. What is the difference between bringing in and taking out? The reason of appraisement is because an error can occur by which the sanctuary would suffer; and this can take place in both taking out and bringing in.

"*A priest*," etc. Said R. Papa to Abayi: It is correct that R. Jehudah requires that one of them should be a Cohen, as in that portion a Cohen is mentioned; but what is the reason of the rabbis, who do not require him—and for what purpose is a Cohen mentioned, according to them? This difficulty remains.

"*By ten, and one of them a priest*," etc. Whence is all this deduced? Said Samuel: In this portion the word Cohenim is mentioned ten times, and only one of them is needed for itself; and all the others are considered as an exclusion after an exclusion, as to which there is a rule that such comes to add something. And therefore we add nine Israelites to one Cohen. R. Huna b. R. Nathan opposed, saying: Why not say: Add five Israelites to five Cohenim? This difficulty also remains.

"*The value of men*," etc. But does, then, a man become consecrated? Said R. Abuhu: If one vows, the money he is worth (not according to age, which is prescribed biblically) must be appraised as if he were a slave sold on the market; and a slave is equal to real estate. Therefore it needs ten: R. Abim questioned: How is it if one vows the value of his hair, and it should be cut off? Shall we say that things which ought to be cut off are considered as already cut, and movable, and the appraisement needs three only; or, so long as it is attached to the body, it is considered as the body itself, and ten are needed? Come and hear: If one consecrated his slave, no transgression is committed by using him for work. R. Simeon b. Gamaliel said: If one uses his hair, it is a transgression: And we are aware that he speaks when the hair in question is still attached to the body and is ready to be cut off. Hence there is a difference of opinion among the Tanaim.

"*The stoning of an ox . . . and the owner put to death.*" Said Abayi to Rabha: Whence do we know this verse means to equal the judgment of the ox to that of its owner? Perhaps it is meant literally—that its owner also shall be put to death? Said Hezekiah, and so also was it taught by his school: It is written [Num. xxxv. 21]: "He who smites him shall be put to death, for he is a murderer." From which we infer that only when he himself smote is he to be put to death: but he is not to be killed for the death by his ox.

"*The wolf, the lion,*" etc. Said Resh Lakish: This is in case they have killed some one; but if not, it is not a meritorious act to kill them. [Hence we see that he holds that these beasts can be considered the property of one who domesticates them.] R. Johanan, however, maintains: In any case, it is a meritorious act to kill them. [Hence he holds that they cannot be domesticated, and are considered ownerless.]

There is an objection from our Mishna: R. Eliezer says: Every one who hastens to kill them is rewarded—which is correct according to R. Johanan, who may explain the word "rewarded"—with the skin of the animal; but according to Resh Lakish, who said, only when they have killed, there is a rule that when so it was, the rabbis considered them as if they were already sentenced to death by the court, and in such a case it is prohibited to derive any benefit from them. What, then, means Eliezer by the expression " he is rewarded " ? It means that he will be rewarded by Heaven. There is a Boraitha in accordance with Resh Lakish, as follows: An ox, as well as other animals or wild beasts which kill, must be judged by twenty-three. R. Eliezer, however, maintains: An ox which has killed, by twenty-three; but as to all wild beasts, he who hastens to kill them will be rewarded by Heaven.

"*R. Aqiba says,*" etc. Is it not the same as the first Tana ? They differ in the case of a serpent.

" *A whole tribe,*" etc. Let us see what sin a whole tribe may commit. Shall we assume that it has violated the Sabbath ? We know that there is a difference between an individual and a majority only in the case of idolatry; but in the other commandments there is no difference, according to the Scripture. And if it means that the whole tribe was accused of idolatry, and they should be judged as a majority, then our Mishna is neither in accordance with R. Jashiah nor with R. Jonathan of the following Boraitha: How many people must be in the city which shall be misled ? From ten to one hundred. So is the decree of R. Jashiah. R. Jonathan, however, maintains: From one hundred up to the majority of the tribe. Now we see that even Jonathan says the majority, but not the whole tribe. Said R. Mathna: It means the Prince of the tribe only. As R. Ada b. Ahaba explains [Ex. xviii. 22]: " Every great matter " means, the matter of a great man; so also here, by the whole tribe is meant the head of it.   Rabhina, however, said: The Mishna speaks of a case in which the whole tribe was accused of idolatry, your difficulty being, do we then judge them as a majority? We may say, Yea! although their punishment is similar to that of an individual who is to be stoned.   And this is in accordance with R. Hama b. Jose, who said in the name of R. Oseah: It is written [Deut. xvii. 5]: "Then shalt thou bring forth that man or that woman who has committed this wicked thing, unto thy gates"—which means only an individual, but not the whole city, to thy gates.   The same is the case with a whole tribe; only an individual can be brought to the gates to be stoned, but not the whole tribe.   (Hence they are judged by seventy-one, as a majority.)

"*False prophet,*" etc.   Whence is this deduced?   Said R. Jose b. Hanina: From an analogy of expression—"presume" —which is to be found in the case of a false prophet [Deut. xviii. 20] and in the case of a rebelling elder [ibid. xvii. 12].   As in the latter case seventy-two are needed, so also in the former. But is not the expression "presumptuously" used in the cited verse concerning death, of which the verse reads; and death is judged by seventy-three only?   Therefore said Resh Lakish: The analogy is in the expression "Dobhor,"which is mentioned in both the verses cited.

"*High-priest,*" etc.   Whence is this deduced?   Said Ada b. Ahaba: From the above-cited Ex. xviii. 22, which is explained as the matter of a great man.

"*To decide upon battles,*" etc.   Whence is this deduced? Said R. Abuhu: From [Num. xxvii. 21]: "And before Elazar the priest shall he stand . . . he and all the children of Israel with him, and all the congregation."   "He" means the king.   "All Israel with him" means the priest who was anointed to be the leader of the war.   "And all the congregation" means the Sanhedrin.   But perhaps the cited verse means that only for the just-mentioned persons the Urim is allowed to be used; but not for common men.   And the question, Wherefrom is it taken that seventy-one are needed to decide about battles? remains. Therefore it must be said, as R. Aha b. Bizna in the name of R. Simeon the Pious said: A harp was placed over the bed of David, and when midnight arrived a north wind used to blow in it, so that the harp would play by itself and awake David, who used to get up and occupy himself with the Torah until the

morning star arose. And thereafter the sages of Israel used to
enter to him, saying: Lord our king, thy nation Israel needs
food. And to his answer: Go, then, and make business among
yourselves, they answered him: A handful of food can never
satisfy a lion, and a pit can never be filled with the earth taken
out from it. Whereupon David decided: They shall go to a
battle. Then they consulted Achithophel, took also advice from
the Sanhedrin, and asked the Urim, etc.

R. Joseph said: Whence do we know from the Scripture
that such was the custom? From [I Chron. xxvii. 34]: "And
after Achithophel (came) Yehoyada, the son of Benayahu, and
Ebyathar; and the captain of the king's army was Joab. Achithophel was the counsellor, as it reads [II Sam. xvi. 23]: "And
the counsel of Achithophel, which he counselled in those days."
Yehoyada means the Sanhedrin, as it is written of his father
Benayahu [I Chron. xviii. 17]: "And Benayahu, the son of
Yehoyada, was over the Kerethites and the Pelethites," which
means the Sanhedrin, to whom Yehoyada his son was the head
after Benayahu. And why was the Sanhedrin named Kerethites
and Pelethites? Because the literal meaning of the two terms
in Hebrew is "cutting" and "wonder"; and the Sanhedrin,
with their decisions, used to cut off and do wonderful things.
"And Ebyathar" means the Urim Vethumim; and then comes
"the captain of the king's army, Joab," which means war. And
R. Itz'hak b. Ada, and according to others B. Abudimi, said
that [Ps. lvii. 9] "Awake, psaltery and harp, I will wake up the
morning dawn," is a support to R. Aha b. Bizna's statement.

"*For enlarging the city*," etc. Whence is this deduced?
Said R. Shimi b. Hyya: From [Ex. xxv. 9]: "In accordance
with all that I show thee, the pattern of the tabernacle, and the
pattern of all instruments thereof, even so shall ye make it"—
which means, so shall ye do in the later generations. Rabha
objected from the following: "All the utensils which were made
by Moses, the anointment sanctified them; however, the utensils
which were made after him, the using of them for service consecrated them." And why? Apply, "So shall ye do," etc.,
to the utensils also; they shall need anointment in the later
generations also? With this it is different, as [Num. vii. 1]:
"And had anointed them, and sanctified them," means them
with anointment, but not those which should be made in a later
generation. But how is it inferred from the passage that for the
utensils made in the later generations anointing is prohibited?

Said R. Papa: It is written [ibid. iv. 12]: " Wherewith they minister in the sanctuary." We see, then, that the passage makes them sanctified by ministering with them.

" *Appointing supreme councils,*" etc. This is taken from Moses, who had established the first Sanhedrin; and the person of Moses is equalized to seventy-one of them.

The rabbis taught: Whence do we know it is a duty to appoint judges ? From [Deut. xvi. 18]: " Judges and officers," etc. But whence do we know that it is a duty to appoint them to each tribe ? From [ibid., ibid.]: " Throughout thy tribes." (From this verse is deduced that judges as well as officers are to be appointed to each tribe.) R. Jehudah maintains: It was also necessary to appoint one who should rule over all the judges; as this verse reads, " Shalt thou appoint," which means that the Great Sanhedrin, who ruled all the judges in the lower houses, should be appointed by them. R. Simeon b. Gamaliel said: It reads: " Throughout thy tribes, and they shall judge," which means, it is a meritorious act to appoint judges to a tribe from its own people.

" *To condemn a misled town,*" etc. Whence is this deduced ? From [ibid. xvii. 5]: " Then shalt thou bring forth that man," etc. An individual you may bring to thy gates, but not the whole city, as said above by R. Hama b. Joseph (here mentioned Hyya, instead of Hama).

" *Town on the boundary,*" etc. Why so ? Because it reads, " From thy midst," but not from a boundary.

" *Nor three of them,*" etc. Because it is written [ibid. xiii. 13]: " *One* of thy cities." But why two ? Because of the word " cities."

The rabbis taught: One, but not three. But perhaps one, and not two ? Because it reads cities, two are meant. Hence with the term one, one, not three, is meant. Rabh used to say at one time that for one court it is not allowed to make three, but for two or three courts it is allowed; and at another time he said that it is not allowed to do so, even in several courts ? And the reason is, that Israel must not be made bald-headed. Said Resh Lakish: This is said only in one country; but in several countries, it may. R. Johanan, however, is of the opinion that even then it must not, for the reason that the land should not be bald-headed. There is a Boraitha in accordance with R. Johanan: Three misled cities must not be made in the land of Israel; two, however, may—*e.g.*, one in Judea and one in

Galilee; but not two in Judea, nor two in Galilee. And if it were near to the boundary, even one must not be proclaimed misled; for, should it come to the ears of the heathens, they might destroy the whole land of Israel. But why not deduce it from the passage which states "from thy midst," and not from the boundary? This is in accordance with R. Simeon, who used to explain the reasons of what is stated in the Scriptures.

"*The Great Sanhedrin,*" etc. What is the reason of the rabbis, who said that Moses was as head of them? Because it reads [Num. xi. 16]: "And they shall stand there with *thee*," which means, and thou shalt remain with them. R. Jehudah, who says seventy only, maintains: It was necessary for Moses to remain with them, that the Shekinah should rest upon them.

The rabbis taught: It is written [ibid. xi. 26]: "And there remained two men in the camp." According to some, it means that their names remained in the urn. As, at the time the Holy One, blessed be He, said to Moses: Gather unto me seventy men of the elders of Israel, he thought: How shall I do it? Shall I appoint six of each tribe? Then there will be two more. Or shall I take five of each? Then there will be ten less. Or shall I appoint from two tribes five only, while from the others six each? Then will I bring jealousy among the tribes. So he chose six from each, and wrote on seventy tickets "Zaqan" (elder), and two he left blank; then mixed, and put all of them into the urn. Then he said: Go, each, and take your ticket. To those who drew "elder," he said: You are already sanctified by Heaven. But those who drew the blanks had no claim, as such was their lot.

Similar was the case from [ibid. iii. 47]: "Thou shalt take five shekels apiece for the poll." And to this Moses also said: How shall I do it? If I should say to one, "Give the shekels," he may answer, "The Levite has already redeemed me." Therefore he wrote on twenty-two thousand tickets "Levite"; and on two hundred and seventy-three he wrote "five shekels," mixed them, put them in the urn, and told the people: Each shall draw his ticket. To the one who drew "Levite" he said: You are free, as the Levite has redeemed you. And he who drew five shekels was told to pay the amount and go.

R. Simeon, however, said: Not their names remained in the urn, but themselves remained in the camp in doubt, saying: We are not worthy of such a high appointment. And the Holy One, blessed be He, said: Because ye were modest, I will increase your grace. And what grace was increased to them? All the seventy had prophesied once, and ceased; but these two did not cease to prophesy. And what was their prophecy? They said : Moses shall die, and Joshua shall bring Israel to his land. Aba Hanin, however, said in the name of R. Elazar: They prophesied about the quail, saying, "Come up, quail. Come up, quail." And R. Na'hman said: About Gog and Magog they prophesied, as it is written [Ezek. xxxviii. 17]: " Then hath said the Lord Eternal: Art thou (not) he of whom I have spoken in ancient days through means of my servants the prophets of Israel, who prophesied in those days (*Shanim*) years, that I would bring thee against them?" Do not read *Shanim*, but *Shnaim*, which means two. And who were the two who had prophesied at one period, with one and the same prophecy? Eldad and Medad.

It is correct in respect to him who said above that their prophecy was, " Moses shall die," what is written [Num. xi. 28]: " My lord Moses, forbid them." But in respect to them who said they prophesied about other things, why, then, should they be forbidden? Because it was not seemly for them thus to prophesy in the presence of Moses. What is meant by the words, " forbid them " ? He meant to say: Appoint them, they shall occupy themselves with the needs of the congregation, and they will be destroyed by themselves.

Whence do we know that three more are needed, as, after all, sentence of guilt by a majority of two cannot take place; as, if eleven defend and twelve accuse, then there is only a majority of one; and if ten defend and thirteen accuse, there is a majority of three? Said R. Abuhu: Such a case can be only when there is a necessity to add more judges according to all. (*I.e.*, in case eleven accuse and the same number defend, and one of them says: I am in doubt. And in such a case all agree that judges must be added, as the one who is in doubt cannot be counted; and then two more are to be added. And if the two who were added also accuse, there is a majority of two.) And such also can be found in the Great Sanhedrin, in accordance with R. Jehudah, who said: There was an even number of seventy. R. Abuhu says again: In case more judges are to be added, an even number may be made in the Small Sanhedrin also. Is this not self-evident? Lest one say that the one who says he is in doubt is counted, and if thereafter he gives a reason for his decision after deliberating he may be listened to, he comes to teach us that as from the time he is in doubt he is not to be counted at all, so after the deliberation he may not be listened to.

R. Kahana said: If all the persons of the Sanhedrin are accusing, the defendant becomes free. Why so ? Because there is a tradition that such a trial must be postponed for one night, as perhaps some defence may be found for him; but if all accuse him, it is not to be supposed that some will find any defence for him over night, and therefore they are no longer competent to decide in his suit.

R. Johanan said: The persons who are chosen to be members of the Sanhedrin must be tall, men of wisdom, of good appearance, and of a considerable age; and, also, they should understand something in cases of witchcraft; and they must also know seventy languages, so that they shall not need to hear a case through an interpreter. R. Jehudah in the name of Rabh said: In a city in which there are not to be found two persons who can speak seventy languages, and one who can understand them although he cannot speak, Sanhedrin must not be established. In the city of Bethar were three; and in the city of Yamiam were four, namely: R. Eliezer, R. Jehoshua, R. Aqiba, and Simeon of Tehmon their disciple, who was not of age to become a rabbi.

An objection was raised from the following: A Sanhedrin in which three of them could speak seventy languages was considered a wise one; and if four, it was considered the highest one. We see, then, that three who could speak were needed ? Rabh holds with the Tana of the following Boraitha: If two, it is a wise one; and if three, it is the highest one.

There is a rule that, where there is to be found throughout the Talmud the expression " the man who learned in the presence of the sages," Levi before Rabbi is meant; and where the expression, " discussed before the sages," Simeon b. Azi, Simeon b. Zoma, Hanan the Egyptian, and Hayanya b. Hkhinai are meant. R. Na'hman b. Itz'hak taught five persons—the four mentioned above, and the fifth was Simeon of Tehmon. Where it is mentioned, " our Masters in Babylon," Rabh and Samuel are meant; " our Masters in Palestine," R. Abbi is meant; " the judges of the Exile," Karna is meant; " the judges of Palestine," R. Ami and R. Assi; " the judges of Pumbeditha," R.

Papa b. Samuel; "the judges of Nahardea," R. Ada b. Minumi; "the elders of Sura," R. Huna and R. Hisda; "the elders of Pumbeditha," R. Jehudah and R. Eina; "the geniuses of Pumbeditha," Eiphah and Abimi sons of Rabha; "the Amoraim of Pumbeditha," Rabba and R. Joseph; "the Amoraim of Nahardea," R. Hama. If it is said "the Nhardlaien taught," Rami b. Berokha is meant. But was it not said by Huna himself: "It was said in the college"? Therefore it must be said that "Hamnuna" is meant. "It was said in Palestine," R. Jeremiah is meant; "a message was sent from Palestine," R. Jose b. Hanina is meant. And where it is said, "it was ridiculed in Palestine," R. Elazar is meant. But do we not find a message was sent from Palestine: According to R. Jose b. Hanina it is so and so? Hence R. Jose b. Hanina cannot be meant in the expression, "there is a message from Palestine"? Therefore it must be reversed. Where it is said, "a message from Palestine," R. Elazar is meant; and "it was ridiculed in Palestine," R. Jose b. Hanina is meant.

"*How many shall a city . . . one hundred and twenty,*" etc. What is the reason of that number? Twenty-three of the. Small Sanhedrin, and three rows of twenty-three each (hearers), make ninety-two; and ten idle men, who must always be in the houses of prayer and learning, make one hundred and two; and two scribes, two sextons, two parties for defendant and plaintiff, two witnesses, and two men who may be able to prove the witnesses collusive, and still two more who could prove the last ones collusive—hence in the total there are one hundred and fourteen. There is a Boraitha that in a city in which the following ten things do not exist, it is not advisable for a scholar to reside, and they are: Five persons to execute what the court decides; a treasury of charity (which is collected by two and distributed by three); a prayer-house, a bath-house, lavatories, a physician, a barber, a scribe, and a teacher for children. And according to others it was said in the name of R. Aqiba: In the city should be several kinds of fruit, as the consuming of fruit enlightens the eyes.

"*R. Nehemiah,*" etc. There is a Boraitha: Rabbi said: Two hundred and seventy-seven. And there is another: Rabbi said: Two hundred and seventy-eight. And there is no contradiction, as one Boraitha is in accordance with R. Jehudah, who needs only seventy for the Great Sanhedrin.

The rabbis taught: It is written [Ex. xviii. 21]: "And place these over them, as rulers of thousands, rulers of hundreds, rulers of fifties, and rulers of tens." Rulers of thousands were six hundred; rulers of hundreds were six thousand; rulers of fifties, twelve thousand; and rulers of tens, sixty thousand. Hence the total number of the officers in Israel were seventy-eight thousand and six hundred.

CHAPTER II.

MISHNA *I.*: The high-priest may judge and may be judged; he may be a witness and may be witnessed against; he may perform the ceremony of Halitzah, and the same may be done to his wife if he dies childless, or his brother may marry his wife in such a case. He, however, must not marry his brother's wife when his brother dies childless—because it is forbidden for a high-priest to marry a widow. If a death occurs in his family, he must not accompany the coffin; but if the coffin with those accompanying it are no longer visible in the street, he goes after them. And so with other streets—when they are not visible, he may enter the street, etc.; and in such manner he may follow the coffin to the gate of the city. So is the decree of R. Meir. R. Jehudah, however, maintains: He must not leave the Temple at all, as it reads [Lev. xxi. 12]: "And out of the sanctuary shall he not go."

When he, the high-priest, condoled with others, it was usual that the people went one after another, and the superintendent of the priests would place him between himself and the people (so that he could say a word of condolence to every one of them); but when he was being condoled with, the people used to say to him: We shall be your atonement (*i.e.*, to us shall occur what ought to occur to you), and his answer was: You shall be blessed by Heaven. And at the condoling meal, all the people were placed on the floor, but he sat on a chair.

A king must not judge, and he is not judged; he must not be a witness, nor be witnessed against. The ceremony of Halitzah does not exist for him, nor for his wife. He does not marry his childless brother's wife, and his brother must not marry his wife.   R. Jehudah, however, maintains: If he was willing to give Halitzah or to marry his brother's wife, he may be remembered among the good.   And he was told: Even if he is willing, he must not be listened to.

His widow must not remarry.   R. Jehudah said: A king may marry the widow of a king, as so we found with David, who married the widow of Saul; as it reads [II Sam. xii. 8]: " And I gave unto thee the house of thy master, and (put) the wives of thy master into thy bosom."

GEMARA: Is it not self-evident that the high-priest may judge ?   It was stated, because it was necessary to say that he may be judged.   But this is also self-evident; as if it were not permitted to judge him, how could he judge ?   Is it not written [Zeph. ii. 1]:" Gather yourselves," which Resh Lakish explained in Middle Gate (p. 287): " Correct yourself first, and then correct others " ?   Therefore we must say, because in the latter part it was necessary to teach that a king must not judge or be judged, it teaches also that the high-priest may judge and be judged. And if you wish, it may be said that it came to teach us what is stated in the following Boraitha: A high-priest who killed a person—if intentionally, he may be killed; and if unintentionally, he may be sent into exile: he transgresses a positive and a negative commandment, and is also, concerning other laws, considered as a commoner in every respect.

Intentionally—he may be killed.   Is this not self-evident ? It was necessary to state, if unintentionally, he might be sent into exile.   But is this also not self-evident ?   Nay!   One may consider, because it reads [Num. xxxv. 28]: " He shall remain until the death of the high-priest," that he who has a remedy to return to his land by the death of the high-priest shall be sent into exile; but he who has no such remedy should not; and there is a Mishna: He who kills a high-priest, or a high-priest who has killed a person, is not returned from the city of refuge for everlasting, and therefore he should not be exiled—it comes to teach us that it is not so.   But perhaps it should be so ? There is another verse [Deut. xix. 3]: " Every man-slayer," which includes a high-priest.

The Boraitha states: He transgresses a positive and negative commandment.   Must he, then, transgress ?   It means to say that if it happened he should transgress a positive and a negative commandment, he is considered a commoner in every respect.

"*Be a witness, and witnessed against,*" etc.   May he be a witness ? Have we not learned in the following Boraitha: It reads [Deut. xxii. 1]: "And withdraw thyself."   There are cases from which one may withdraw himself, and there are others from which he may not.   How so ?   *E.g.*, a priest who sees a lost thing lying in a cemetery is not obliged to pick it up for the purpose of returning it; or if there were an old, respectable man, and it was not in accordance with his honor to bother with such a thing, or even if one's time is more valuable than the value of the lost thing, he may withdraw himself.   Hence it is self-evident that it is not fit for a high-priest to go and witness. Why, then, should he be obliged ?   Said R. Joseph: He may be a witness in a case that concerns the king.   But does not our Mishna state "that a king must not be a witness, and not be witnessed against " ?   Therefore said R. Zera: He may be witness in the case of a prince, the son of the king.   A prince—is he not considered a commoner in all respects concerning the law ?   Say he may witness before the king.   But have we not learned that the king must not be a member of the Sanhedrin; and also that both the king and the high-priest must not take part in the discussion about a leap year ?   For the honor of the high-priest, the king comes and remains with the Sanhedrin until the testifying of the high-priest ends, and then both depart; and the Sanhedrin themselves deliberate and decide the matter.

The text states that a king must not be a member of the Sanhedrin, nor a king and a high-priest engage in the discussion about a leap year.   The first is deduced from [Ex. xxiii. 2].* And the second—a king—because he would not like to add a month to the year, because of the increase of the wages of the military; and a high-priest, because of the cold (*i.e.*, it is prescribed by the Scriptures to take during the Day of Atonement legal baths five times in cold water, and by adding a month, the month of Tishri would fall when in a usual year is the month of Cheshvi, which is much colder than Tishri).

Said R. Papa: Infer from this that the seasons of the year follow the usual months, and not according to the intercalary month.   Is that so ?   We know that it happened, three pasturers

---

* How it is deduced from this verse it is impossible to express in any living language.   Even in the Hebrew we have to make from the word Rebh—literally, "quarrel"—the word Rab—literally, "great," and to intepret the passage in another fashion altogether.   It would therefore be of no use to insert the verse as it is usually translated.

were standing and conversing in the presence of rabbis thus: One of them said: If there were enough heat so that the wheat which was sown in the beginning of the month, and the barley which was sown recently, should sprout, the month could be named Adar; and if not, it remains Shbat. The second said: If in the morning there is such a cold that the ox trembles from it, and in the middle of the day he should hide himself in the shadow of a fig tree, the month may be considered Adar; and if not, it remains Shbat. And the third said: If the winter has already lost its strength, and the air you blow from your mouth moderates the cold brought by the east wind, it is Adar; and if not, it remains Shbat. And as that year was not so in any of these cases, the rabbis intercalated it. Hence we see that the intercalary comes because of the cold, and not *vice versa?*

How can you conceive that the rabbis had relied upon the pasturers to intercalate a year? They relied upon their own reckoning, and the gossip of the pasturers was considered as a support only.

" *He may perform the ceremony of Halitzah,*" etc. The Mishna makes no difference if the widow was from betrothal or from marriage. And this can be correct only with a marriage, as there is a positive commandment that a high-priest must marry a virgin, and a negative commandment that he must not marry a widow; while to marry the wife of his childless brother is a positive commandment only, which cannot invalidate a positive and a negative commandment. But if the widow was from betrothal, she is still a virgin; there remains only one negative commandment, he shall not take a widow. And there is a rule that a positive commandment invalidates a negative commandment? The positive commandment applies only to the first intercourse, but not thereafter, upon which the negative commandments rest. And if the first were allowed, he would come to commit a transgression thereafter, and therefore it is prohibited. And so also a Boraitha states.

" *If death happens,*" etc. The rabbis taught: " He shall not leave the sanctuary" means he shall not go with them, but he may go out after them. How so? " When they are not visible in the street, he may appear," etc.

" *To the gate of the city,*" etc. Is not R. Jehudah correct with his statement? R. Meir may answer: According to your theory, he must not leave the Temple for home? You must then explain this passage, that it means that he must not go out from his sanctuary; and while he goes after them, when they are no longer visible, he will not come in contact with the corpse. R. Jehudah, however, fears that because of his sorrow it may happen that when he shall accompany them he will come in contact with the corpse, and violate his sanctity.

"*Condole with others,*" etc. The rabbis taught: When he goes in the row to condole with others, his vice and the ex-high-priest are placed at his right, and the head of the priest's family at the mourners'; and all other people are placed at his left. But when he stands in the row to be condoled with by others, the vice only is placed at his right, but not the ex-high-priest, as he may be dejected, thinking that the ex-priest sees a revenge in him.

Said R. Papa: From the Boraitha three things are to be inferred: (*a*) That the vice and superintendent are identical; (*b*) that the mourners stand and the people pass by; and (*c*) that the mourners are placed at the left side of the condolers.

The rabbis taught: Formerly the custom was for the mourners to stand and the people to pass by; but there were two families in Jerusalem who had quarrelled, one saying: I must pass first. according to my dignity; and the other said: I must pass first: Therefore it was enacted that the people should stand and the mourners pass. Said Rami b. Aba: R. Jose reëstablished the old custom that the mourners shall stand and people pass, in the city of Sephorias. And he said also: The same enacted in the same city that a woman should not go into the street with her child following her, but that she should follow the child, because of an accident that happened. (Rashi explained: It happened that immoral men had stolen a child who was following its mother, and put it in a house; and while she was crying and searching for it, they said to her: Come with us and we will show it to you. And while doing so, she was assaulted.) He also said: The same enacted in Sephorias that women should talk to each other while they were at their toilet, for the purpose that men should not intrude.

R. Menashia b. Evath said : I questioned R. Jashiah the Great in the cemetery of Huzl, and he told me that a row is not less than ten persons, not counting the mourners, who must not be among them; and there is no difference if the mourners stand and the people pass, or *vice versa*.

"*Being condoled with,*" etc. The schoolmen questioned: What did he say when he condoled with others ? And they were answered from a Boraitha, which states: He used to say: Be comforted.

"*A king must not judge,*" etc.   Said R. Joseph: This is concerning the kings of Israel; but the kings of the house of David are judged and judge.   As it is written [Jer. xxi. 12]: "O house of David, thus said the Lord: Exercise justice on every morning."   We see that they did judge; and if they were not to be judged, how could they judge?—as is said above by Resh Lakish. And what is the reason it is prohibited to the kings of Israel? Because an unfortunate thing happened as follows: The slave of King Janai murdered a person; and Simeon b. Cheta'h said to the sages: Notwithstanding that he is the slave of the king, he must be tried.   They sent to the king: Your slave has killed a man.   And Janai sent his slave to them to be tried.   However, they sent to him: You also must appear before the court. As it is written [Ex. xxi. 29]: "Warning has been given to its owner"—which means the owner of the ox must appear at the time the ox is tried.   He then came and took a seat.   Said Simeon b. Cheta'h: King Janai, arise, so that the witnesses shall testify while you stand; yet not for us do you rise, but for Him who said a word, and the world was created.   As it reads [Deut. xix. 17]: "Stand before the Lord."   And the king answered: It must not be as you say, but as the majority of your colleagues shall decide.   Simeon then turned to his right, but his colleagues cast their eyes upon the floor without any answer; and the same did his colleagues at his left.   Simeon then exclaimed: You are all troubled in mind (disconcerted)!   May the One who rules minds take revenge upon you.   Gabriel came then and smote them to the floor, that they died.   And at that time it was enacted that a king should neither judge nor be judged, neither be a witness nor be witnessed against.

"*If he was willing to give Halitzah,*" etc.   This is not so? Did not R. Ashi say: Even he who holds that if a prince has relinquished his honor it holds good, agrees that if a king does so his honor is not relinquished.   As it is written [Deut. xvii. 15]: "Set a king over you"—which means, that respect (fear) for the king should always be before thy eyes (*i.e.*, and in the ceremony of Halitzah the woman takes off his shoe, and spits before him, which is a disgrace for a king, and must not be done even if he is willing)?   R. Jehudah, however, maintains: Where there is a biblical commandment, it is different.

"*His widow must not remarry,*" etc.   There is a Boraitha:

The sages answered R. Jehudah: The verse you refer to means, the woman who was ordained to him by the king, Saul; and they were Merab and Michal, his daughters.

The disciples of R. Jose questioned their master: How could David marry two sisters while they were both living? And he answered them: He married Michal after the death of Merab. And R. Jose said so in accordance with his theory in the following Boraitha, which states: He, R. Jose, used to lecture about passages in the Scriptures which were obscure, namely: It reads [II Sam. xxi. 8]: " And the king took the two sons of Rizpah, the daughter of Ayah, whom she had born unto Saul, Armoni and Mephibosheth; and the five sons of Michal, the daughter of Saul, whom she had borne * to Adriel, the son of Barzillai the Meholathite." But was Michal given to Adriel? Was she not given to Palti b. Layish? It reads [I Sam. xxv. 44]: " But Saul had given Michal his daughter, David's wife, to Palti, the son of Layish." Hence the Scripture equalizes the betrothing of Merab to Adriel to the betrothing of Michal to Palti b. Layish; as the betrothing of Michal to Palti was a sin (for she was already the wife of David, and according to the law a second betrothing is not considered at all), so also was the betrothing of Merab to Adriel a sin (for she was already David's wife). R. Jesh b. Karha, however, maintains: The betrothal of Merab to David was by an error. As it is written [II Sam. iii. 14]: " Give up to me my wife Michal, whom I espoused," etc. But what would he say to that passage which reads, "the five sons of Michal, the daughter of Saul"? He might say: Did, then, Michal bear them? Was it not Merab who bore them, whereas Michal merely brought them up? But they bore the name of Michal, because the Scripture considers the one who brings up an orphan as if it were born to him.

R. Hanina says: This is inferred from [Ruth, iv. 17]: " There hath been a son born unto Naomi," etc. Did, then, Naomi bear him? Was it not, in fact, Ruth who bore him? Therefore we must say that, though Ruth bore him, he was nevertheless named after Naomi, because she brought him up. R. Eleaser said: From [Ps. lxxvii. 16]: " The sons of Jacob and Joseph. Selah." Were they, then, born to Joseph, and not to

---

* Leeser translates " brought up," according to the sense. The term in the Bible, however, is the same as in the first part of this verse; therefore the question in the text.

Jacob? They were born to Jacob, but Joseph fed them, and therefore they were named after him.

R. Samuel b. Nahmeni in the name of R. Jonathan said: He who teaches the Torah to the son of his neighbor, the Scripture considers him as if he were born to him. As it is written [Num. iii. 1]: "And these are the generations of Aaron and Moses"; and the following verse reads: "And these are the names of the sons of Aaron." It is only to say that they were born to Aaron and Moses taught them, and therefore they were named after him.

It is written [Is. xxix. 22]: "Therefore thus hath said the Lord unto the house of Jacob, he who hath redeemed Abraham." Where do we find that Jacob redeemed Abraham? Said R. Jehudah: He redeemed him from the affliction of bringing up his children. (*I.e.*, Abraham was promised by the Lord that He would multiply his children, and so the affliction of bringing them up was to lie upon Abraham; but, in fact, it was Jacob who was afflicted by bringing them up.—Rashi.) And this is what is written [ibid.]: "Not now shall Jacob be ashamed, and not now shall his face be made pale"—which means, he shall not be ashamed of his father and his face shall not become pale because of his grandfather.

In the Scripture there is written in some places "Palti," in other places "Paltiel." Said R. Johanan: His name was Palti; and why was he named Palti-El? "For God saved him from sin" (*i.e.*, "Polat" in Hebrew means "to break through" and "El" means God, and according to tradition Palti did not live with Michal [although he slept with her in one bed], because of her betrothal to David). Said R. Johanan: The strength of Joseph was moderation on the part of Boas, and the strength of the latter was moderation on the part of Palti. "The strength of Joseph was moderation on the part of Boas"—as it is written [Ruth, iii. 8]: "And it came to pass at midnight, that the man became terrified," etc. And Rabh said: His body became as soft as (boiled) turnip heads. "And the strength of the latter was the moderation of Palti"—as with Boas it occurred only on one night, and with Palti it was continually. The same said again: It is written [Prov. xxxi. 29]: "Many daughters have done virtuously, but thou excellest them all." "Many daughters" means Joseph and Boas. "That feareth the Lord shall indeed be praised" [ibid. 30] means Palti b. Layish. R. Samuel b. Nahmeni in the name of R. Jonathan said [ibid. 30]: "False is grace" means Joseph; "and beauty vain" means Boas"; "... that feareth the Lord" means Palti b. Layish. According to others, "False is the grace" means the generation of Moses, "and vain is the beauty" means the generation of Joshua; "... that feareth the Lord" means the generation of Hezkiah. And still according to others, "False is the grace" means the generation of Moses and Joshua, "and vain is the beauty" means the generation of Hezkiah; "... fear of the Lord," etc., means the generation of R. Jehudah b. Elii. As it was said: In the time of that rabbi six disciples had covered themselves with one garment (as they were very poor), and occupied themselves with the study of the Torah.

MISHNA *II*.: If a death occurs in the house of the king, he must not leave the gate of the palace. R. Jehudah, however, maintains: If he is willing to accompany the coffin, he may do so, as we find that David accompanied the coffin of Abner [II Sam. iii. 31]: "And King David walked behind the bier." But he was told that David did so only to appease the spirit of the people. And at the condoling meal all the people are placed on the floor and he is seated on the dais.

GEMARA: The rabbis taught: In those places where it is customary for women to follow a coffin, they may do so; and where it is customary for them to precede the coffin, they have to do accordingly. R. Jehudah, however, maintains that women must always precede the coffin, as we find in the case of David, who followed the coffin, as in the above-cited verse in the Mishna. And he was told that this was only to appease the spirit of the people. And they were appeased, because David used to go from the men to the women and from the women to the men for this purpose. As it is written [ibid. 37]: "And all the people and all Israel understood on that day that it had not been of the king." Rabha lectured: It is written [ibid. 35]: "And all the people came to cause David to eat food while it was yet day." (The term "to cause" is expressed in Hebrew *Le habroth*, and according to him it was written *Le hakhbroth*. The first term means food and the second means to destroy— *Korath*); from which it is to be inferred that in the beginning the people came to destroy him because of the death of Abner, but after he had appeased them they caused him to eat.*

---

* In the Scripture which is before us there is nothing of the kind. However, we have remarked several times that their text of the Scripture was different from ours. And so also is it remarked in a foot-note in the Wilna edition, 1895.

Said R. Jehudah in the name of Rabh: Why was Abner punished ? Because he ought to have warned Saul he should not kill the priest of Nob, and he did not do so. R. Itz'hak, however, maintains: He did warn, but was not listened to. And both infer this from the following verses [ibid. 33, 34]: " And the king lamented over Abner, and said, O that Abner had to die as the worthless dieth ! Thy hands were not bound and thy feet were not put in fetters . . . " The one who said that he did not warn interprets thus: "Thy hands were not bound and thy feet were not put in fetters." Why didst thou not warn ? And he who said that he did, but was not listened to, interprets it thus: " O that Abner should die as the worthless dieth ! Thy hands were not bound . . . " And thou didst warn Saul. Why, then, " as one falleth before men of wickedness art thou fallen " ? But according to the latter, that he did warn—why was Abner punished ? Said R. Na'hman b. Itz'hak: Because he postponed the kingdom of David for two years and a half.

MISHNA *III.*: And he (the king) declares a war which is not commanded in the Scripture, after consultation with the court of twenty-one judges. He may also establish a way in private property, and nobody has a right to protest against it. The way of a king has no limit. When the military take plunder from the enemy, they must transfer it to the king, and he takes his share first.

GEMARA: Was not this already taught in the first Mishna of this tract: A court of seventy-one judges is needed to decide upon battles which are not commanded, etc. ? Because it teaches of other things which belong to the king, this is also repeated. R. Jehudah in the name of Samuel said: All which is written in I Samuel, viii. in that portion relating to a king, the king is allowed to do. Rabh, however, maintains that the whole portion was not said except to warn them. The above Amoraim differ in the same respect as the Tanaim of the following Boraitha: It is written [Deut. xvii. 15]: " Set a king over thee," etc. According to R. Jose, all that is written concerning a king in Samuel, the king is allowed to do. R. Jehudah, however, maintains that the whole portion is written only to frighten them, as the expression, " to set a king over thee," means that the fear of the king shall be always upon you. And thus R. Jehudah used to say: There are three positive commandments which Israel was commanded at the time they entered Palestine, viz.: They shall appoint a king; they shall destroy the descendants of Amalek; and they shall build a temple. R. N'hurai, however, says: The whole portion was said only because they murmured against Samuel, requesting a king. As it is written [ibid., ibid. 14] "And thou sayest, I wish to set a king over me," etc.

There is a Boraitha: R. Eliezer said: The elders of that generation rightly asked Samuel for a king. As it reads [I Sam. viii. 5]: "Appoint for us a king to judge us like all the nations." But the commoners who were among them degraded the case. As it reads [ibid., ibid. 20]: "That we also may ourselves be like all the nations; and that our king may judge us, and go out before us, and fight our battles."

There is another Boraitha: R. Jose said: Three positive commandments Israel was commanded when they entered Palestine, viz.: They shall appoint a king; they shall destroy the descendants of Amalek; and they shall build a temple. But it was not known which was the first. However, from [Ex. xvii. 16], "And he said, Because the Lord hath sworn on his throne that the Lord will have war with Amalek from generation to generation," it is to be inferred that the commandment relating to the king was first, because the word "throne" implies a king. As it is written [I Chron. xxix. 23]: "Then sat Solomon on the throne of the Lord as king." But it was still unknown which should be first, the case of Amalek or the temple. But from [Deut. xii. 10], "He will give you rest from all your enemies . . . and then shall it be that the place," etc., it is to be inferred that the cutting off of the nation of Amalek was to be first. And so was it with David. As it reads [II Sam. vii. 1]: "And it came to pass, when the king dwelt in his house, and the Lord had given him rest," etc., he spake then to Nathan the prophet about the Temple.

The rabbis taught: The treasures of kings which are plundered in time of war belong to the king only; all other plunder, however, half to the king and half to the people. Said Abayi to R. Dimi, according to others to R. Aha: It is correct that the treasures of kings belong to the king, as so it is customary. But from where do we know that other plunder is half to the king, etc.? From [I Chron. xxix. 22]: "And they anointed him unto the Lord as chief ruler, and Zadok as priest." We see, then, that he compares the ruler to Zadok. As in the case of Zadok the high-priest, a half belongs to him and a half to his brother, the same is the case with the ruler. And wherefrom do you know that in the case of Zadok it is so? From the following Boraitha: Rabbi said: It reads [Lev. xxiv. 9]: "And it shall belong to Aaron and to his sons," meaning half to Aaron and half to his sons.

MISHNA *IV.*: He (the king) must not marry more than eighteen wives. R. Jehudah, however, maintains: He may marry as many as he likes, provided that they shall not turn his heart away. And R. Simeon maintains: Even one wife, should she be liable to turn his heart away, he must not marry her. And the verse which reads, "Neither shall he take to himself many wives," means even when they were similar to Abigail.

GEMARA: Shall we assume that R. Jehudah takes account of the reason mentioned in the Scriptures and R. Simeon does not? Have we not heard elsewhere just the reverse? A widow must not be pledged, no matter if she be rich or poor. As it is written [Deut. xxiv. 17]: "Thou shalt not take in pledge the raiment of a widow." So is the decree of R. Jehudah. R. Simeon, however, maintains: If she be rich she may be pledged, but when she is poor she must not be pledged. And one is obliged to return the pledge to her. And to the question: How is this to be understood? it was said thus: If you take a pledge from her, you are obliged, biblically, to return it every evening, and by this act she will get a bad name, etc. Hence we see that R. Jehudah does not take account of the reason mentioned in the Scriptures (as there it is written: "You shall return to him; as if not, he will not have whereupon to sleep," which treats only of the poor, and R. Jehudah's theory is that even a rich person must not be pledged)? R. Jehudah does not take account of the reason in all other cases. But here it is different, as the verse itself explains the reason—that "his heart shall not be turned away." And R. Simeon may also say: Do we not take account in all other cases of the reason? Why, then, does the Scripture give the reason here? Let it say, "He shall not marry many wives," and we would understand the reason that it is because of his heart. And as the reason is mentioned, it is for the purpose that even if only one, and she is liable to "turn his heart away," he must not marry her.

The number eighteen mentioned in the Mishna, whence is it deduced? From [II Sam. iii. 2–5]: "And there were born unto David sons in Hebron: And his first-born was Amnon, of Achinoam the Yizreelitess; and his second was Kilab, of Abigayil the wife of Nabal the Carmelite; and the third, Abshalom, the son of Maachah the daughter of Thalmai the king of Geshur; and the fourth, Adonijah, the son of Chaggith; and the fifth, Shephatyah, the son of Abital; and the sixth, Yithream by Eglah, David's wife. These were born unto David in Hebron." And the prophet said [ibid., ibid. xii. 8]: "And if this be too little, I could bestow on thee yet many more like these." *

Now let us see! The number of the wives mentioned in the Scriptures is six. "Like this" is six more, "and like this" is again six more, of which the total is eighteen. But was not Michal his wife, who is not mentioned? Said Rabh: Eglah is identical with Michal. And why was she named Eglah? Because he liked her with the liking of a cow for her new-born calf. And so also it reads in Judges, xiv. 18: "And he said unto them, If he had not ploughed with my heifer," etc. (from which we see that he names the wife heifer or calf).† But had, then, Michal children? Is it not written [II Sam. vi. 23]: "And Michal the daughter of Saul had no child," etc.? Said R. Hisda: She had no children after that time (mentioned in the Scripture), but previous to this she had children. But is it not written [ibid. v. 13]: "And David took yet more concubines and wives out of Jerusalem." (Hence it is to be supposed that he married more than eighteen.) Nay, he married more, to fulfil the number of eighteen. What are wives, and what are concubines? Said R. Jehudah: Wives are married by betrothal and marriage contract; concubines are without both of them.

R. Jehudah in the name of Rabh says: Four hundred children were born to David by the handsome women whom he took captive (i.e., those mentioned in Deut. xxi. 11). All of them had never cut their hair. They were placed in golden carra. And in time of war they were placed with the chief officers of the military, and they were the mighty soldiers in David's army. The same said again in the name of the same authority: Thamar was a daughter of one of the above-mentioned handsome women. As it reads [II Sam. xiii. 13]: "But now, O speak, I pray thee, unto the king; for he will not withhold me from thee." And if she were really his daughter, how could she say that the king would allow a sister to marry her brother? Infer from this that she was one of the children borne by one of the above-mentioned handsome women. It reads [ibid. 3-10]: "But Amnon had a

---

* The term in Hebrew is " Khohino ve Khohino "—literally, " like this and like this." Hence the analogy in text.

† Eglah is, literally, " a calf."

friend . . . and Yonadab was a very shrewd man." Said
R. Jehudah in the name of Rabh: He was shrewd to advise
evil. It reads [ibid. 19]: "And Thamar put ashes on her head,
and the garment of divers colors which was on her she rent."
There is a Boraitha in the name of R. Jehoshua b. Karha:
From that which happened to Thamar, a great safeguard was decreed by the sages, as it was said: If it so happened to daughters
of kings, so much the more could it happen to daughters of
commoners; and if to the chaste, so much the more to the lewd.
And therefore said R. Jehudah in the name of Rabh: At that
time a decree was made that one must not stay with a married
woman alone, nor with a single one. Is that so ? Is this not
prohibited biblically ? As R. Johanan in the name of R. Simeon
b. Johozadek said: Where do we find a hint in the Scriptures
that one must not stay alone with a married woman ? [Deut.
xiii. 7]: "If thy brother, the son of thy mother . . . should
entice thee." Does, then, only a brother from the mother's
side entice, and not a brother from the father's side ? It is but
to say that only a son may stay alone with his mother, but it is
not allowed for anyone besides to stay alone with a married
woman. (Hence it is biblical ?) Say that at that time it was
decreed that one must not stay alone even with a single
woman.

It is written [I Kings, i. 5]: "And Adoniyah the son of
Chaggith exalted himself, saying, I shall be king." Said R.
Jehudah in the name of Rabh: Infer from this that he wanted
to place the crown on his head and could not. (Rashi explains
this that there was a band of gold in the crown which fitted the
descendants of David who had an indentation in their heads
which Adoniyah had not.) It is written further: "And he
procured himself a chariot and horsemen, and fifty men who ran
before him." What is there exceptional in this for a prince ?
Said R. Jehudah in the name of Rabh: The milt of all of them
was taken out (so that it should be easy for them to run), and
also the flesh of the soles of their feet was cut off.

MISHNA *V.*: He (the king) must not acquire many horses
—only sufficient for his chariots; and also he must not acquire
more gold and silver than to pay the military. He must also
write the Holy Scrolls for himself; when he goes to war he must
bear them with him; when he enters the city they must be with
him, and the same when he sits judging the people; and when
he takes his meals they must be placed opposite him. As it is

written [Deut. xvii. 19]: "And it shall be with him, and he shall read therein all the days of his life."

GEMARA: The rabbis taught: He shall not acquire many horses, and lest one say even those which are needed for his chariots, therefore it is written "for himself," from which it is to be inferred that for the chariots he may; but if so, what, then, is meant by "he shall not acquire many horses"? It means horses which should remain idle. And whence do we deduce that even one horse which is idle is under the negative commandment, "He shall not acquire many horses"? For it is written there [ibid., ibid. 16], "in order to acquire many horses." Is it not said above of even one horse, and it is idle, that he transgresses the commandment, "He shall not acquire many horses"? Why is it written "in order to acquire," etc.? That he should be responsible for the transgressing of the above commandment for each horse which is idle. But how would it be if in the Scripture were not mentioned "for himself"—he would not be allowed even for the chariots? Is this possible? Then, it could be explained, he should have the exact number needed, but not more.

"*Much gold and silver,*" etc. The rabbis taught: It is written: "He shall not acquire much gold and silver"—lest one say not even sufficient for paying the military, therefore it is written "for himself." But how would it be if this were not written—he would not be allowed, even for paying the military. Is that possible? Then, it could be explained that he should have the exact amount, but not more. Now, as we see that from the words "for himself" things are inferred, what do you infer from the same words which are written concerning wives? This excludes commoners, who are allowed to take as many as they please.

R. Jehudah propounded a contradiction in the following verses [I Kings, v. 6]: "And Solomon had forty thousand stalls for the horses for his chariots, and twelve thousand horsemen"; and [II Chron. ix. 25]: "And Solomon had four thousand stalls for horses and chariots, and twelve thousand whom he quartered in the cities for chariots, and near the king at Jerusalem." How is it to be understood? If there were forty thousand stables, every one of them contained four thousand stalls; and if it were only four thousand stables, then each contained forty thousand stalls. R. Itz'hak propounded the following contradiction: It reads [I Kings, x. 21]: "None were of silver; it was not *in the least* valued in the days of Solomon "; and [ibid. 27]: " And the king rendered the silver in Jerusalem *like stones*." (Hence it had some value?) This presents no difficulty. The first verse speaks of before Solomon married the daughter of Pharaoh, and the second after this.

R. Itz'hak said: (Here is repeated from Tract Sabbath, 1st ed., page 109, in the name of R. Jehudah. See paragraph there —same rabbi.)

The same said again: Why does not the Scripture explain the reason of its law? Because in two verses it was so done, and the greatest men of a generation stumbled because of them. They are, " he shall not acquire many wives," for the purpose that they should not " turn his heart away." And King Solomon said: I shall take many wives, and my heart shall not be turned away. However [I Kings, xi. 4]: " And it came to pass . . . that his wives turned away his heart." And the same was the case with the horses, of which he said: I shall acquire many, and shall not return to Egypt. However [ibid. x. 29]: " And a chariot-team came up and went out of Egypt," etc.

" *Write the Holy Scrolls.*" There is a Boraitha: He must not suffice himself with those left by his parents. Rabba said: It is a meritorious act for one to write the Holy Scrolls at his own expense, though they were left to him by his parents. As it is written [Deut. xxxi. 19]: " Now therefore write this song." Abayi objected from our Mishna: " He shall write the Holy Scrolls for himself," and must not suffice himself with those of his parents. And this speaks only of a king, but not of a commoner. Our Mishna treats of two Holy Scrolls, as it is explained in the following Boraitha: It is written [ibid. xvii. 18]: " He shall write for himself a copy of this law," which means that he must write for himself two Holy Scrolls, one which he must bear with him wherever he goes, and one which shall remain in his treasury. The one he has to bear with him he shall write in the form of an amulet, and place it on his arm. However, he must not enter with it a bath or toilet house. As it is written [ibid., ibid. 19]: " And it shall be with him and he shall read," which means it shall be with him in those places where it is allowed to read it, but not in those where it is not.

Mar Zutra, according to others Mar Uqba, said: " Originally the Torah was given to Israel in Hebrew characters and in the Hebrew language; the second time it was given to Israel in Ezra's time, but in Assyrian characters and in the Aramaic language; finally the Assyrian characters and the Hebrew language were selected for Israel, and the Hebrew characters and the Aramaic language were left to the Hediotim (Idiots). Who are meant by Idiots? Said R. Hisda: The Samaritans. What is meant by Hebrew characters? Said R. Hisda: The Libnuah characters.*

There is a Boraitha: R. Jose said: Ezra was worthy that the Torah should be given through him, if Moses had not preceded him. Concerning Moses it reads [Ex. xix. 3]: "And Moses went up unto God"; and concerning Ezra it reads [Ezra, vii. 6]: "This Ezra went up." The term "went up" concerning Moses means to receive the Torah, the same being meant by the same expression concerning Ezra. Farther on it is written [Deut. iv. 14]: "And me the Lord commanded at that time to teach you statutes and ordinances." And it is also written [Ezra, vii. 10]: "For Ezra had directed his heart to inquire into the law of the Lord and to do it, and to teach in Israel statutes and ordinances." And although the Torah was not given through him, the characters of it were changed through him. As it is written [ibid. iv. 7]: "And the writing of the letter was written in Aramaic, and interpreted in Aramaic." And it is also written [Dan. v. 8]: "They were not able to read the writing, nor to make its interpretation." (Hence we see that the new characters the Aramaic people could not read.) And why are they named Assyrian? Because they were brought from the country of Assyria.

There is another Boraitha: Rabbi said: In the very beginning the Torah was given to Israel in the Assyrian characters, but after they had sinned it was turned over to them as a dasher. However, after they repented, it was returned to them. As it is written [Zech. ix. 12]: "Return you to the stronghold, ye hopeful prisoners: even to-day do I declare that I will recompense twofold unto thee." And why is it named Assyrian? Because the characters are praised above all other characters. ("Ashur" in Hebrew means "praise.") R. Simeon b. Elazar, however, said in the name of R. Eliezer b. Parta, quoting R. Elazar the Modai, that the characters were not changed at all. As it is written [Ex. xxvii. 10].† And it is also written [Book

---

* For the explanation of this passage see our " Pentateuch : Its Languages and its Characters " (pp. 14, 15). See also there who Utra or Uqba was.

† We have not inserted the verse, as the translation of it does not correspond at all.

of Esther, viii. 9]: " And to the Jews according to their writing, and according to their language." From which it is to be inferred, that as their language was not changed neither was their writing. But if so, what means the term Mishna † in the verse in Deuteronomy cited above: " He shall write a copy of this law "—the two copies of the Holy Scrolls which a king has to write, as said above: One for the treasury and one which he must bear attached to his arm. As it is written [Ps. xvi. 8]: " I have always set the Lord before me, that, being at my right hand, I might not be moved." But he who maintains that the writing was not changed at all, what does he infer from the verse just cited ? That which was said by R. Hana b. Bizna: He who praises should always think that the Shekinah is opposite him, as the cited verse reads.

MISHNA *VI.*: One must not ride on his, the king's horse, and also must not seat himself on his chair, and must not make use of his sceptre. And none must be present when he cuts his hair, and not when he is naked, and not when he is in the bath-house. As it is written: " Thou shalt set a king over thee," which means that his fear shall be always upon thee.

GEMARA: R. Jacob in the name of R. Johanan said: Abishag was allowed to Solomon but not to Adoniyah, because Solomon was a king; and to a king it is allowed to make use of the sceptre of his predecessor, but not to Adoniyah, who was a commoner. How is to be understood that which is written in I Kings, 4 : " And she became an attendant on the king"; and to her request that the king should marry her he answered: You are prohibited to me (as I have already eighteen wives). Said R. Shoman b. Aba : Come and see how hard is divorce in the eyes of the sages: So they permitted Abishag to be with David and did not allow him to divorce one of his wives in order to marry her. Said R. Eliezer: He who divorces his first wife, even the altar sheds tears on account of him. As it is written [Mal. ii. 13]: " And this do ye secondly, covering the altar of the Lord with tears, with weeping and with loud complaint, so that he turneth not any more his regard to the offering, nor receiveth it with favor at your hand." And immediately after it reads: " Yet ye say, Wherefore ? Because the Lord hath been witness between thee and the wife of thy youth, against whom thou hast indeed dealt treacherously: yet is she thy companion, and the wife of thy covenant."

---

* The term " Shana " means to "repeat," and also " change."

R. Johanan, according to others R. Elazar, said: Frequently, one's wife dies when her husband owes money and has not to pay. As it is written [Prov. xxii. 27]: " If thou have nothing to pay, why should he take away thy bed from under thee ?" The same said again: To him whose first wife dies, it is as if the Temple had been destroyed in his days. As it is written [Ezek. xxiv. 16 and 18]: " I will take away from thee the desire of thy eyes," etc. " And when I had spoken unto the people in the morning, my wife died at evening"; and [ibid. 21]: " I will profane my sanctuary, the pride of your strength, the desire of your eyes."   And R. Alexander said: To him whose wife dies, the whole world is dark for him. As it is written [Job, xviii. 6]: " The light becometh dark in his tent, and his lamp will be quenched above him."   And R. Jose b. Hanina adds: Also his steps become shortened, as immediately it reads: " His powerful steps will be narrowed."   And R. Abuhu adds: Also his advice is no more of use; as the end of the cited verse reads: " and his own counsel will cast him down."

Rabba b. Bahana said in the name of R. Johanan: It is hard for heaven to appoint marriages as it was to divide the sea; as in Ps. lxviii. 7: " God places those who are solitary in the midst of their families : he bringeth out those who are bound unto happiness." *

R. Samuel b. Na'hman said: For everything there may be an exchange, but for the wife of one's youth. As it is written [Is. liv. 6]: " And as a wife of one's youth that was rejected." R. Jehudah taught to his son R. Itz'hak: One does not find pleasure only in his first wife, as it is written [Prov. v. 18]: " Thy fountain will be blessed; and rejoice with the wife of thy youth." And to the question of his son, Whom do you mean ? he answered: *E.g.*, your mother. Is that so ? We are aware that the same read before R. Itz'hak his son [Eccl. vii. 26]: " And I find as more bitter than death the woman whose heart is snares and nets," etc. And to the question of his son, Whom do you mean ? he answered: *E.g.*, your mother. True, she was hard to him at the start, but finally she overruled herself and did all he pleased. R. Samuel b. Umaya said in the name of Rabh: A wife is similar to a piece of metal, and does not make any covenant but with him who makes her a vessel. As it is written

---

* The Talmud takes the last cited words for the exodus from Egypt, and explains : " Do not read the Hebrew term so, but otherwise," which it is impossible to give in the English version.

[Is. liv. 5]: " For thy husband is thy master," etc.   There is a
Boraitha: One dies but to his wife, and the wife dies but to her
husband.   The first is deduced from [Ruth, i. 3]: " Thereupon
died Elimelech Naomi's husband "; and the second from [Gen.
xlviii. 7]: " And as for me, when I came from Padan, Rachel
died by me."

" *Cuts his hair.*"   The rabbis taught: The king must cut his
hair every day.   As it is written {Is. xxxiii. 17]: " The king in
his beauty shall thy eyes behold."   A high-priest every eve
of Sabbath, and the commoner priest every thirty days.   Why
every eve of Sabbath?   Said R. Samuel b. Na'hman in the
name of R. Johanan: Because the watching priests are relieved
every eve of Sabbath.   And why for a commoner every thirty
days?   Because it reads [Ezek. xliv. 20]: " And their heads shall
they not shave close, nor suffer their hair to grow long: they
shall only crop (the hair of) their heads."   And there is an
analogy of expression from a Nazarite [Num. vi. 5].   As concerning a Nazarite it is thirty days, the same is the case here.
And whence do we know that for a Nazarite it is thirty days?
Said R. Mathna: It reads: Holy shall he be.   Because the
generation of *Yihiye* counts thirty (a Yod counts ten, a He, five,
and in the word *yihiye* there are two Yods and two Hes).   Said
R. Papa to Abayi: Why not explain the above-cited verse as
that they shall not be allowed to let their hair grow at all?   And
he answered: If it read: " They shall not let their hair grow,"
your explanation would be correct; but as it reads " to grow
long," it must be explained as the rabbis enact: They shall let
it grow thirty days.   (Said R. Papa again:) If so, in our time,
when there is no temple, it is to equalize the cutting of the hair
to the partaking of wine, which was prohibited to the priests
only when they had to enter the Temple (as after the case of
hair-cutting immediately follows the prohibition of the partaking
of wine).   Is that so?   Have we not learned in a Boraitha:
Rabbi said: I say that it is prohibited for the priest to drink
wine at any time whatever.   But what can I do, in that the
destruction of the Temple was their remedy: as they were forbidden to drink wine in order that they should not enter the
Temple while drunk, so, now that the Temple no longer exists,
they do not care?   Said Abayi: According to whom do the
priests drink wine in our time?   In accordance with Rabbi's
statement.

Rabbi was questioned: How was the hair-cutting of the high-priest, which it is told was done very artistically ?   And he answered: Go and see the hair-cutting of Ben Aleshe.   And there is a Boraitha: Rabbi said: Not in vain has B. Aleshe expended his money to learn the art of cutting hair: it was only to show how the high-priests used to cut their hair.

CHAPTER III.

MISHNA *I.*: Civil cases by three ; one party may select one
and so the other, and both of them select one more ; so is the
decree of R. Meir. The sages, however, maintain that the two
judges may select the third one. One party may reject the
judge of his opponent, according to R. Meir. The sages, however, say : This holds good only when the party brings evidence
that the judges selected by his opponent are relatives, or they are
unqualified for any other reason. If, however, they were qualified, or they were recognized as judges from a higher court, no
rejection is to be considered. The same is the case with the witnesses of each party, according to R. Meir, so that the rejection
of each party against the witnesses of its opponent may be taken
into consideration. The sages, however, say : Such holds good
only in the cases said above concerning the judges, but not otherwise.

GEMARA : How is to be understood the expression of the
Mishna : One party selects one, etc.? Does it mean one party
may select one court of three judges, and likewise the other; and
then both the third court, which would be altogether nine judges?
Are, then, three not sufficient? It means, if one party selects one
judge its opponent may also do so, and then both may select the
third one. And what is the reason of such a selection? It was
said in Palestine in the name of R. Zera : Because each party
selects its own judge, and both agree in the selection of the third
one, the decision will be a just one.

" *The sages, however, say,*" etc. Shall we assume that the
point of their difference is what was said by R. Jehudah in the

name of Rabh : Witnesses may not sign a document unless they are aware who will be the others; and so R. Meir does not hold this theory and the rabbis do? Nay! All hold this theory, and the point of their difference is thus: According to R. Meir, the consent of the parties is also needed; but the rabbis hold that the consent of the judges, but not of the parties, is needed.

The text reads: R. Jehudah said in the name of Rabh: Witnesses, etc. There is also a Boraitha: Pure-minded people of Jerusalem used not to sign a document unless they were aware who was the other who was to sign it, and also would not sit down to judge unless they were aware who was to be their colleague, and would also not go to a banquet unless they were aware who were invited to it.

" *Each party may reject*," etc. Has, then, one the right to reject judges? Said R. Johanan: It speaks of the little courts in Syria, where there were Gentile judges who were not recognized by the higher court. But if they were, no objection could be taken into consideration. But does not the latter part state: "and the sages, however, say . . . recognized by the court"? From which it is to be understood that their opponent R. Meir speaks even of them who were recognized? They mean to say: If not disqualified (on account of kinship or bad conduct) they are to be considered as if they were authorized judges against whom no rejection can take place.

Come and hear: The sages said to R. Mair: One cannot be trusted with any right to protest against a judge who was appointed by the majority? Read: One has no right to reject a judge who was appointed by the majority. And so we have learned in the following Boraitha: One may reject the selected judge of his opponent until he has selected a judge who was recognized by a majority. So is the decree of R. Mair. But are not witnesses considered as recognized judges, and nevertheless R. Mair said that one party may disqualify the witness of his opponent? Aye! But was it not already said by Resh Lakish: How is it possible that a holy mouth like R. Mair's should say such a thing? Therefore it must be supposed that R. Meir did not say "witnesses," but "his witness" (*i.e.*, a single witness). Let us see! What does he mean by one witness? If concerning a civil case, the law itself disqualifies him; and if concerning an oath, he is trusted by the law as if there were two witnesses. It speaks of a civil case, and the case was that previously the parties accepted him, saying that his testimony would be considered as

5

if it were testified by two. But, after all, what news did he come to teach us—that he may retract? This we have learned already in the succeeding Mishna, which states that, according to R. Mair, he may retract, to which R. Dimi b. R. Na'hman b. R. Joseph said that the Mishna speaks of when he has accepted his father as a third judge (and because biblically a father is not fit to judge in a case of his son), he may retract even if he has previously accepted him. Why not say the same in our case, because one is not fit for a civil case he may retract although he had previously accepted him? Both cases were needed, as if the case about his father only were stated one might say that because the same is fit to be a judge in other cases, therefore the rabbis maintain that no retraction is to be considered; but in the case of a commoner, who is not fit to be a judge in any case whatsoever, the retraction would hold good, even in accordance with the rabbis. And if the case of a commoner were stated, one might say that only in that case R. Meir permitted to retract. But in the other case he agrees with the rabbis, therefore both are stated.

But how would the expression of the Mishna be understood? It speaks about the judge in the singular (one may reject the *judge*, etc.), and concerning witnesses, it speaks in the plural (one may reject the *witnesses*, etc.). Hence we see that the Mishna is particular in its expression. How, then, can you say that R. Mair maintains a single witness? Said R. Elazar: It means that he—one of the parties, and also another one who does not belong to this case—come to reject this witness, as then they are two against one, and therefore the rejection holds good. But, after all, why should one of the parties have a right to reject? Is he not interested in this case, and there is a rule that the testimony of such is not to be taken into consideration. Said R. Aha b. R. Ika: The case was that he laid before the court the reason of his protest, which can be examined.

Let us see what was the reason. If, *e.g.*, robbery, it must not be listened to, as he is interested in this case. Therefore we must say that the reason was the incompetence of his family— *e.g.*, that he or his father was a bondsman, who was not as yet liberated. According to R. Mair, he may be listened to, as his testimony is against the entire family. The rabbis, however, maintain that even then he must not be listened to because of his interest in this case, and the court has not to consider his testimony at all.

When R. Dimi came from Palestine, he said in the name of

R. Johanan that the point of their difference is two parties of witnesses, *i.e.*, *e.g.*, the borrower said : " I have two parties of witnesses who will testify to my right," and brought one party of them against which the lender protests.   According to R. Mair, the protest holds good because the opponent himself confessed that he had another party.   Hence he may bring the other party, against whom no protest would be considered (and his reason is that a proof is needed to each claim, even if it is not so important that it could injure the case); and according to the rabbis, no protest must be listened to even in such a case, as they do not desire a proof to each claim.   But when there was only one party of witnesses, all agree that no rejection is considered.

Said R. Ami and R. Assi to R. Johanan : How is it if the other party of witnesses were found to be his relatives, or incompetent to be witnesses for any other reason, should the testimony of the first party be considered, or because of the incompetence of the other party, the first party also loses credit ?   Said R. Ashi : The testimony of the first party was already accepted, and therefore there is no basis to ignore their testimony because of the incompetence of the other party.   Shall we assume that R. Mair and the rabbis differ the same as Rabbi and R. Simeon b. Gamaliel differ concerning one who claims that he has bought a document and " hazakah " (Last Gate, p. 377), and in the discussion we come to the conclusion that the point of their difference is, if one must prove his words or not ?   Nay !   According to R. Simeon b. Gamaliel, they do not differ at all, and the point of their difference is according to Rabbi's statement there. R. Mair holds with Rabbi.   The rabbis, however, maintain that Rabbi does so only in case of the claim of hazakah, which is based upon the document ; but in our case, where the testimony of the witnesses is not based upon that of others, even Rabbi admits that no proof is needed.

When Rabbin came from Palestine, he said in the name of R. Johanan that the first part of our Mishna treats of incompetent witnesses but competent judges, and because they reject the witnesses the judges are also rejected ; and the latter part speaks of the reverse—that the judges were incompetent and not the witnesses, and the witnesses are rejected because of the judges. Rabha opposed : It would be correct to say that because of the incompetence of the witnesses one may reject the judges, as the case can be brought before other judges.   But how can the witnesses be rejected because of the judges?   Then the party would remain without witnesses at all. It speaks of when there was another party of witnesses. But how would it be if there were no other witnesses? Then no rejection is to be considered. Thus Rabbin said the same that R. Dimi said? The theory of " because " is the point of their difference. As to R. Dimi, the theory of because is not to be used at all, while according to Rabbin it is.

The text says: Resh Lakish said: " The holy mouth of R. Mair should say such a thing," etc. Is that so? Did not Ula say that he who saw Resh Lakish in the college saw one uprooting hills and crushing them? (Hence how could he say such a thing, which was objected to?)

Said Rabhina: Was it not said of R. Mair that he who saw him in the college had seen one uprooting *mountains* and crushing them (and nevertheless he was criticised by Resh Lakish). Therefore he (Ula) meant thus: Come and see how the sages respected each other (though Resh Lakish was such a genius, he nevertheless, in speaking of R. Mair, named him holy mouth).*

MISHNA *II.*: If one says, " I accept as a judge in this case your father or my father," or, " I accept certain three pasturers to judge our case," according to R. Mair he may retract thereafter, and according to the sages he must not. If one owes a note to a party, and the latter said to him, " Swear to me by your life, and I will be satisfied," according to R. Mair he may retract, and according to the sages he may not.

GEMARA: Said R. Dimi b. R. Na'hman b. R. Joseph: It speaks of when he has accepted his father as a third judge. Even then he may retract, according to R. Mair. Said R. Jehudah in the name of Samuel: The Tanaim of the Mishna differ in case the creditor said to the debtor: Your or my father may judge this case, and if they should acquit you, I will renounce my claim. But if the debtor said to the creditor: I trust your father, and if they shall hold me liable, I will give you the money—all agree that he may retract. R. Johanan, however, said that they differ in the latter case.

The schoolmen propounded a question: Does R. Johanan mean to say that they differ only in the latter case, but in the former, " I will renounce my claim," all agree that no retraction is to be considered; or, does he mean to say that they differ in both cases? Come and hear what Rabha said: They differ only

* Here is a repetition from Tract Sabbath, pp. 89–92, which is already translated.

if he said, " I will satisfy your claim,' but in case of " I will renounce my claim," all agree that he cannot retract.   Now let us
see ! If the question of the schoolmen is to be resolved according to Rabba's decision just mentioned, it is correct, as he is in
accordance with R. Johanan ; but if the question should be resolved that they differ in case of renouncing, etc., according to
whom would be Rabha's opinion ?   Rabha may differ with both,
and declare his own opinion.   R. Aha b. Tahlipa objected to
Rabha from the latter part of our Mishna's statement, that if he
told him to swear by his life, according to R. Mair he may retract, etc.   Does not the Mishna speak of one who is to be
acquitted with an oath, which is equal to " I renounce my
claim"?   Nay; it speaks of them who ought to swear and collect, which is equal to " I will give you."   But this was stated
already in the first part?   The Mishna teaches both cases, one in
which he is dependent upon himself and one in which he is dependent on the mind of others.   And both are needed ; as, if
there were stated the case when he is dependent upon others—
e.g., " I trust your father," etc.—one might say that only in such
a case R. Mair permits to retract, as he has not as yet made up
his mind to pay, thinking that probably he will be acquitted ; but
when he depends upon himself—e.g., " Swear by your life," etc.—
R. Mair also admits that he cannot retract.   And if this case
only were stated, one might say that in such a case only the
rabbis hold that he cannot retract ; but in case he depends upon
others, they agree with R. Mair.   Therefore both are needed.

The Tanaim of the Mishna differ in case Resh Lakish said :
the decision was not yet rendered ; but after it was, all agree that
no retraction can take place.   R. Johanan, however, maintains
that they differ in the latter case.

The schoolmen propounded a question : Does R. Johanan
mean to state that they differ in a case where the decision was
rendered, but in case the decision was not as yet rendered all agree
that a retraction can take place, or does he mean to say that they
differ in both cases ?   Come and hear what Rabha said : If one
has accepted a relative or one who is legally disqualified to be a
judge, if before the decision, his retraction holds good ; but if
after, no retraction is to be considered.   Now let us see ! If the
saying of R. Johanan is to be explained that they differ when
the retraction took place after the decision—but if before, all
agree that it holds good—Rabbi's decision is correct, as it is in
accordance with R. Johanan's explanation and in accordance

with the rabbis. But if it should be explained that they differ also in case it was before the decision, according to whom would be Rabha's decision just mentioned? Infer from this that they differ in the case after the decision; but before, all agree that a retraction holds good.

R. Na'hman b. R. Hisda sent a message to R. Na'hman b. Jacob: Let the master teach us in which case the Tanaim of our Mishna differ—after or before the decision, and with whom the Halakha prevails. And the answer was: After the decision, and the Halakha prevails with the sages. R. Ashi, however, said that the question was: Do they differ in case he said, "I will renounce my claim," or in case "I will satisfy your claim"? And the answer was: They differ in the latter case: the Halakha prevails with the sages. So was it taught in the College of Sura. In the College of Pumbeditha, however, it was taught: : R. Hanina b. Shlamiha said it was a message from the college ' to Samuel: Let the master teach us how is the law if the retraction took place before the decision, but they have made the ceremony of a sudarium? And the answer was that nothing could be changed in such a case.

MISHNA *III.*: The following are disqualified to be witnesses: Gamblers (habitual dice-players) and usurers, and those who play with flying doves; and the merchants who do business with the growth of the Sabbatic year. Said R Simeon: In the beginning they were named the gatherers of Sabbatic fruit; *i.e.*, even those who had gathered the fruit, not for business, were disqualified. However, since the demand of the government to pay duties increased, the gatherers of the Sabbatic fruit were absolved from the disqualification, and only those who did business with same were disqualified. Said R. Jehudah: Then the merchants and all the other persons named above were disqualified only when they had no other business or trade than this; but if they had, they were qualified.

GEMARA: What crime is there in dice-playing? Said Rami b. Hama: Because it is only an *asmachtha*, which does not give title. R. Shesheth, however, maintains that such is not to be considered an *asmachtha*; but they are disqualified because they do not occupy themselves with the welfare of the world—and the difference between them is if they had another business besides. As we have learned in our Mishna, according to R. Jehudah, if they have some business besides, they are qualified. Hence we see that the reason of the disqualification is because they do not occupy themselves with the welfare of the world—and this contradicts Rami b. Hama's above statement? And lest one say that R. Jehudah's opinion is only of an individual, as the rabbis differ with him, this is not so, as Jehoshua b. Levi said that in every place where R. Jehudah says "this is only," or if he says "provided," he comes only to explain the meaning of the sages, but not to differ with them; and R. Johanan maintains that when he says "this is only," he comes to explain, but when he says "provided," he means to differ. And as in our Mishna he expresses himself "this is only," all agree that he is only explaining. Hence Rami is contradicted? Do you contradict one man with another man? Each of them may have his opinion. Rami holds that they do differ, and Shesheth that they do not. Have we not learned in the following Boraitha that it does not matter if he has another business besides; he is nevertheless disqualified? The Boraitha is in accordance with R. Jehudah in the name of Tarphon of the following Boraitha: R. Jehudah said in the name of R. Tarphon, concerning a Nazarite (Tract Nazir, 34a), that wherever there is any doubt he is not deemed a Nazarite. And the same is in our case, as the gambler is not certain that he will win or lose, it cannot be considered a real business, but robbery, and therefore he is disqualified even when he has another business.

"*Usurers.*" Said Rabha: One who borrows to pay usury is also disqualified. But does not our Mishna state "usurers," which means the lenders, and not the borrowers? It means to say a loan which is usurious. There were two witnesses who testified against Bar Benetus. One said: In my presence he has given money at usury; and the other said: He has loaned to me at usury. And Rabha disqualified b. Benetus from being a witness. But how could Rabha take into consideration the testimony of him who said: I have borrowed from him at usury? Did not Rabha say that the borrower also is disqualified, because, as soon as he has borrowed at usury, he is wicked; and the Torah says: Thou shalt not bring a sinner as a witness. Rabha is in accordance with his theory elsewhere, that one is not trusted to make himself wicked. (Hence his testimony that he himself has borrowed at usury is not taken into consideration, but that part, that Benetus has loaned to him at usury, was.) There was a slaughterer who sold illegal meat in his business, and R. Na'hman disqualified him. And he let his hair and nails grow as a sign of repentance; and Na'hman was about to remove the disqualifica-

tion. Said Rabha to him: Perhaps he is deceiving you. But
what remedy can he have? As R. Aidi b. Abin said elsewhere:
For him who is suspected of selling illegal meat there is no
remedy, unless he goes to a place where he is not known and
returns a valuable lost thing, or he recognizes the illegality of
meat in his business, even if it is of great value.

"*Flying doves,*" etc. What does this mean? In this college it
was explained: If your dove should fly farther than mine (such
and such a distance), you shall take an amount of money. And
Hama b. Oushia said that it means an ἁρυω, one who uses
his doves to entice to his cot doves belonging to other cots—and
this is robbery. But to him who maintains, " If your dove shall
fly farther," etc., is this not gambling? (Why, then, is it repeated?) The Mishna teaches both cases—depending upon
himself and depending upon his dove; as if depending upon himself only were stated, one might say that, because he was sure he
would win, he offered such an amount, and he has not made up
his mind to pay the sum willingly in case of a loss, and therefore
it is considered an *asmachtha*, which does not give title. But in
the other case, where he is dependent upon his dove, in which he
is not sure, and has nevertheless offered a sum of money, it is to
be supposed that he made up his mind to pay willingly in any
event, and therefore it is not considered an *asmachtha*. And if
this latter case were stated, one might say that he did so probably because the winning of the race depends on the clapping,
and he knew better how to clap (at the pigeon race); but when
he depends upon himself, it is different. Therefore both are
stated.

An objection was raised from the following: Gamblers are
counted those who play with dice; and not only dice, but even
with the shells of nuts or pomegranates. And when is their repentance to be considered? When they break the dice and renounce this play entirely, so that they do not play even for
nothing. And usurers are counted both the lender and the borrower, and their repentance is to be considered only then when
they destroy their documents and renounce this business entirely, so that they do not take usury even from a heathen,
from whom it is biblically allowed. And among those who play
with doves, those who train doves to fly farther are counted; and
not only doves, but even other animals; and their renunciation
is considered only when they destroy their snares and renounce
the business entirely, so that they do not catch birds even in

deserts.   Among those who handle Sabbatic fruits are counted those who buy or sell, and their renunciation is considered only when they cease to do so in the next Sabbatic year.   Said R. Na'hamia: It is not sufficient that they cease to do so, but they must return the money which they derived from the sale of the fruit.   How if one say: I, so and so, have obtained two hundred zuz from the Sabbatic fruit, and I present them for charity? We see, then, that among those who play with doves, those who do so with other animals are also counted; and this can be correct only according to him who explains our Mishna: " If your dove should fly farther than mine," as the same can be done with other animals.   But to him who says an *ἀρυω*, could this be done with other animals?   Aye, this can be done with a wild ox; and it is in accordance with him who says that a wild ox may be counted among domesticated animals.

There is a Boraitha: There was added to the disqualified witnesses robbers and forcers (*i.e.*, those who take things by force, although they pay the value for them).   But is not a robber disqualified to be a witness biblically?   It means even those who do not return a found thing which was lost by a deaf-mute or by minors (which according to the strict law is not to be returned, but it was enacted that it should be returned for the sake of peace—that there should be no quarrel with their rela-tives), and as this does not occur frequently, they were not counted among the disqualified.   Thereafter, however, they were added, as, after all, they take possession of money which does not belong to them.   And the same is the case with the forcers, who were not placed among the disqualified, because this does not happen frequently.   Thereafter, however, as the rabbis saw that it became a habit, they added them also.

There is another Boraitha: There was secondly added to that category, pasturers, collectors of duty, and contractors of the government.   Pasturers were not put in this category previously, because, when it was seen that they led their animals into strange pastures, it was only occasionally; but later, when it was seen that they did it intentionally, they were also added.   And the same is the case with the collectors of duty and the contractors, as at first it was thought that they took only what belonged to them; but after investigation, when it was found that they took much more than they ought, they were added.   Said Rabha: The pasturer in question—it matters not if he is a pasturer of small cattle or of large ones.   Did Rabha indeed say so?   Did he not say that a pasturer of small cattle is disqualified only in Palestine, but not outside of it, and pasturers of large cattle even in Palestine *are* qualified? This was taught of them who raise the cattle for themselves; and if they are small cattle, they are disqualified because it was forbidden to keep small cattle in Palestine, as explained elsewhere. And so it seems to be as the previous Mishna expresses, "three pasturers," and it is to be assumed for witnesses. Nay; it means for judges, and this is to be understood from the number three. As if for witnesses, for what purpose are three needed? But if for judges, why does the Mishna express itself "pasturers"—let it state three laymen who do not know the law? It means to say that even pasturers who spend their time in uninhabited places are nevertheless qualified to judge of the appointment of the parties.

R. Jehudah said: A pasturer of whom it is not heard that he leads his cattle into strange pasture is nevertheless disqualified, but a duty collector of whom it is not said that he takes more than he ought, is qualified.

The father of R. Zera was a collector for thirteen years, and when the governor would come to that city he used to say to the scholars: Go and hide yourselves in the houses, so that the governor shall not see so many people, or he will demand from the city more taxes. And also to the other people, when he saw them crowded in the streets, he used to say: The governor is coming, and he will kill the father in presence of the son, and the son in presence of his father. And they also used to hide themselves. And when the governor came, he used to say to him: You see that there are very few people in this city. From whom, then, shall we collect so much duty? When he departed, he said: There are thirteen maes which are tied in the sheet of my bed; take and return them to so and so, as I took it from him for duty and did not use it.

"*They were named gatherers of Sabbatic fruit*," etc. What does this mean? Said R. Jehudah thus: Formerly it was said the gatherers of the fruit were qualified, but the merchants were not. But when it was seen that they used to pay the poor that they should gather the fruit for them and bring it to their houses, it was enacted that the gatherers as well as the merchants were disqualified. This explanation, however, was a difficulty to the scholars of the city of Rehaba as to the expression of our Mishna, "since the demand of the government," and according to this explanation it ought to be, "since the increase of buyers,"

and therefore they explain thus : Since the government has increased their duties [as R. Jani announced, " Go and sow in the
Sabbatic year, because of the duties "], it was enacted that the
gatherers were qualified, but not the merchants.

Hyie b. Zarssuqi and Simeon b. Jehuzdack went to intercalate a year in Essia, and Resh Lakish met them and said: I
will go with them to see how they practise.   In the meantime
he saw a man who was ploughing in the Sabbatic year, and he
said to them : Is this man a priest, who is suspected of doing
work in the Sabbatic year ?   And they answered: Probably he is
hired by a Gentile to do so.   He saw again a man who was
collecting the fluid in a vineyard and putting it back into the
bale.   And he said again : Is this man a priest, who is suspected,
etc. ?   And they answered: He who trims vines in the Sabbatic
year may say : I need the twigs to make a bale for the press.
Rejoined Resh Lakish : The heart knows whether it is done for
" ekel " (a legitimate purpose) or out of " ăkalkaloth" (perverse-
ness).   And they rejoined: He is a rebel.   When they came to
their place, they ascended to the attic and moved the steps that
he (Resh Lakish) should not ascend with them.   The latter then
came to R. Johanan and questioned him : Men who are suspected of transgressing the Sabbatic year, are they fit to establish
a leap year ?   After deliberating, however, he said: It presents
no difficulty to me, as they may be compared with the three
pasturers mentioned above (p. 46), and the rabbis recommended
them to do so, as so it should be according to their reckoning.

Afterward, however, he said to himself : There is no similarity,
as, concerning the three pasturers mentioned thereafter, the rabbis selected the right number needed for intercalation.   Here,
however, they themselves did it, and they are only a society of
wicked men who are not at all qualified to intercalate.   Said R.
Johanan: I am distressed that you called them wicked.   When
the above-mentioned rabbis came to R. Johanan, complaining that
Resh Lakish called them pasturers of cattle in the presence of R.
Johanan and he kept silent, he answered: If he were to call you
pasturers of sheep, what could I do to him?

* Ula said: One's thought for his maintenance injures him in his
study of the law (*i.e.*, because of his sorrow it remains not in his
mind for a long time, and he forgets it easily).   As it is written
[Job, v. 12]: " Who frustrateth the plans of the crafty, so that

---

* The Haggadic passage we have transferred to the last chapter of this tract, which
is all Haggadah.

their hands cannot execute their well-devised counsel." Said
Rabba, however: If he occupies himself with the Torah for the
sake of Heaven, he is not injured. As it is written [Prov. xix. 21]:
" There are many thoughts in a man's heart; but the counsel of
the Lord alone will stand firm "—which is to be explained: A
study which is for the sake of Heaven, no matter in what circumstances one is, it remains forever.*

" *Only then*," etc. Said R. Abubu in the name of R. Elazar:
The Halakha prevails with R. Jehudah. And the same said again
in the name of the same authority: All the persons mentioned
in the Mishna and in the Boraithas are disqualified only then
when their crime was announced by the court. However, concerning a pasturer, R. Aha and Rabhina differ. According to one,
even concerning him announcement is needed; and according to
the other, no announcement is needed for his disqualification.
(Says the Gemara :) It is correct, according to him who holds that
no announcement is needed, that which R. Jehudah said above,
that a pasturer is disqualified even if we are not aware of any
crime; but according to him who holds that even a pasturer
must be announced, why, then, Jehudah's decision? Because he
holds that the court has to announce of each pasturer, no matter
what he is, that he is disqualified. There was a document for a
gift which was signed by two robbers, and R. Papa b. Samuel
was about to make it valid because they were not announced by
the court. Said Rabha to him: When to a robbery which is
only rabbinical an announcement is needed, should we say that
the same is needed to a biblical robbery?

R. Na'hman said: They who accept charity from idolaters
are disqualified to be witnesses, provided they do so publicly, but
not if privately; and even publicly, they are disqualified only
then when it was possible for them to do same privately and
they do not care to disgrace themselves publicly; but if not,
one is not disqualified, as he is compelled to get a living. The
same said again: He who is suspected of adultery is qualified to
be a witness. Said R. Shesheth to him: Master, answer me.
Should a man who has forty stripes on his shoulders † be quali-

---

* Rashi gives also another interpretation to this passage ; viz., mental resolution
frequently fails, even if it is concerning the study of the Torah—*e.g.*, if one made up
his mind to finish such and such a tract in a certain time. And to this came Rabba
to say, if it was for the sake of Heaven, it would not fail, etc.

† Rashi explains this, that one who is suspected of such an offence, but cannot
be punished with the prescribed punishment because there were no legal witnesses

fied? Said Rabha: R. Na'hman admits that concerning a woman he is disqualified to be a witness. And Rabhina, according to others R. Papa, said: This is said only concerning a divorce, but concerning bringing her into the house of her husband, the suspicion does not matter. R. Na'hman said again: If one has stolen in the month of Nissan at the harvest-time, and has stolen again in the month of Tishri, he is not named a thief so that he should be disqualified, provided he was a gardener and stole a thing of little value, and if it was a thing which could be consumed without any preparation. The gardener of R. Zebid stole a kab of barley, and R. Zebid disqualified him. And also another one stole a bunch of dates, and was also disqualified.

There were undertakers who had buried a corpse on the first day of Pentecost, and R. Papa put them under the ban and disqualified them to be witnesses. However, Huna b. R. Jehoshua qualified them, and to the question of R. Papa: Are they not wicked? he answered: They thought they were doing a meritorious act. But were they not put under the ban for this transgression, and nevertheless did it again? They thought that the putting under the ban was only a kind of atonement imposed by the rabbis for violating the holiday. However, the burial act itself is meritorious, though they will have to be under the ban for a few days for violation of a holiday.

An apostate who eats illegal meat, which is identical with carcasses, because it is cheaper, all agree that he is disqualified. But if he does this not because it is cheaper, but for the purpose of angering his former brothers in faith,* according to Abayi he is disqualified and according to Rabha he is not. The reason of Abayi is because he is wicked, and the Scripture reads plainly: "Thou shalt not bring a sinner as a witness." Rabha's reason, however, is that it speaks of one wicked in money matters only. An objection was raised from the following: "The meaning of the Scripture concerning the testimony of a sinner means one who is wicked in money matters; as, for instance, robbers and perjurers. No matter if the oath was a vain one (*e.g.*, if one has sworn that a stone is a stone), or if the oath was a false one concerning money matters." Hence we see that even a vain swearer

---

or he was not warned, has nevertheless been punished with stripes, as so it is stated (Tract Kidushin, 81b).

    * Our explanation in the case of angering may be new, as we are not in accord with other commentators. However, it seems to us that this is the correct interpretation, as to which we challenge criticism.

is also disqualified? By the expression "vain swearer" is not meant as explained, but that he has sworn in vain concerning money matters—*e.g.*, A owes money to B, which was not neces- sary at all, as A has never denied it. An objection was raised from the following : " Thou shalt not bring a sinner as a witness," means one wicked in robbery—namely, robbers and usurers. Hence this Boraitha contradicts Abayi's statement. The objec- tion remains.

Shall we assume that the above Amoraim differ in the same respect as the Tanaim of the following : A collusive witness is disqualified in all law cases. So is the decree of R. Mair. R. Jose, however, maintains : Provided he was made collusive in a case of capital punishment ; but if in money matters, he is still qualified to be a witness in criminal cases? Now, shall we say that Abayi holds with R. Mair, who maintains that even from a lenient we disqualify to a rigorous one, and Rabha holds with R. Jose, who maintains that only from a rigorous case we disqualify even to a lenient one, but from lenient to rigorous we do not? Nay! In accordance with R. Jose's theory, they do not differ. But the point of their difference is concerning R. Mair's theory, as Abayi holds with him, and Rabha maintains that even R. Mair said so only concerning a collusive witness in money mat- ters, which is both wicked against man and wicked against heaven ; but in our case, where the wickedness is in heavenly things only, even R. Mair admits that he is qualified to be a wit- ness in money matters. The Halakha, however, prevails with Abayi. But was he not objected to? The Boraitha which con- tradicts Abayi is in accordance with R. Jose. But even then, is it not a rule, when R. Mair differs with R. Jose, that the Halakha prevails with the latter? In this case it was different, as the edi- tor of the Mishnayoth taught an anonymous Mishna in accord- ance with R. Mair's opinion. And where is it? This was explained in the following case : Bar Hama had slain a man and the Exilarch told Aba b. Jacob to investigate the case ; and if he really slew the man, they should make the murderer blind. (Since the Temple was destroyed, capital punishments were abolished by Israel, and therefore to make a man blind was to make him dead to the world.) And two witnesses came to testify that he surely killed the man. The defendant, however, brought two witnesses who testified against one of the witnesses. One of them said : In my presence this man stole a kab of barley ; and the other said : In my presence he stole the handle of a borer.

And the Exilarch said to him: You wish to disqualify this man to be a witness because of R. Mair's theory, but I know of the rule that the Halakha prevails with R. Jose when he differs with R. Mair; and according to R. Jose, if one was collusive in money matters, he is still qualified in criminal cases. Said R. Papa to him: This is so in other cases; but in this case it is different, as there is an anonymous Mishna in accordance with R. Mair. But which Mishna is it? Shall we assume it to be that which stated that he who is competent to judge criminal cases is competent for civil cases also, which cannot be in accordance with R. Jose, as, according to his theory, there is a witness who was made collusive in civil cases and is still competent in criminal cases? Hence it is in accordance with R. Mair. But perhaps the cited Mishna does not speak about collusive witnesses, but of such as are incompetent to be witnesses because of their family. Therefore we must say that he means our Mishna which states the following are disqualified for witnesses: Players with dice, etc.; and a Boraitha adds: And also slaves. This is the rule in all cases in which women are not allowed to be witnesses—they also are disqualified. And this cannot be in accordance with R. Jose, as he holds that they are qualified to be witnesses in criminal cases, for which women are disqualified. Hence it is in accordance with R. Mair. B. Hama then arose and kissed him, and freed him from paying duties all his life.

MISHNA *IV.*: The following are counted relatives who may not be witnesses: Brothers, brothers of father or mother, brothers-in-law, uncles by marriage from father's or mother's side, a stepfather, a father-in-law, the husband of one's wife's sister, they and their sons and their sons-in-law, and also a stepson himself —but the latter's children are qualified. Said R. Jose: This Mishna was changed by R. Aqiba. The ancient Mishna, however, was thus: One's uncle, one's first-cousin, and all those who are competent to be one's heirs and also all one's relatives at that time; but if they were relatives and thereafter became estranged, they are qualified. R. Jehudah, however, maintains that even if a daughter dies and leaves children, her husband is still considered a relative. An intimate friend, as well as a pronounced enemy, is also disqualified. Who is considered an intimate friend? The groomsman. And who is considered a pronounced enemy? The one who has not spoken to him for three days because of animosity. And the sages answered R. Jehudah: The children of Israel are not suspected of witnessing falsely because of animosity.

GEMARA: Whence is this deduced? From that which the rabbis taught. It is written [Deut. xxiv. 16]: "Fathers shall not be put to death for the children . . . for his own sin," etc. To what end is this written? If only to teach the meaning of it literally, it would not be necessary, as the end of the verse reads, "for his own sin shall every man be put to death." It must therefore be interpreted, fathers should not die by the witnessing of their children, and *vice versa.* From this is deduced fathers by sons, and *vice versa;* and so much the more fathers who are brothers are incompetent to testify for each other. But whence do we know that grandsons (cousins) are also incompetent to testify for each other? It should read, "parents shall not die because of their son." And why "sons" in the plural? To teach that their sons are not competent to testify for each other. But whence do we know that two relatives are not qualified to testify in one case even for a stranger? It should read in the singular, "and a son for his parents." And why in the plural, "and sons"? To teach that two sons are incompetent to testify in one case, even for a stranger. But from this is deduced the relatives from the father's side only. Whence, however, do we know that the same is the case with the relatives from the mother's side? From the repetition of the word "fathers" in the same verse. And as it was not necessary for the relatives on the father's side, apply it to the relatives on the mother's side. But this verse speaks of accusation. Whence do we know that the same is the case concerning advantage? From the repetition of the words, "shall not die," which were not necessary in the case of accusation. Apply it, therefore, to cases of advantage. All this, however, is said concerning criminal cases. But whence do we know that it is the same with civil cases? Hence it reads [Lev. xxiv. 22]: "One manner of judicial law," etc., meaning that all cases must be judged equally.

Rabh said: My father's brother shall not witness in my cases; he, his son, and his son-in-law. And similarly, I, for my part, will not witness in his cases, neither my son nor my son-in-law. But why? Is not one's son a grandnephew, who is a third to a father's brother, and our Mishna teaches that only a cousin is not competent, who is second to the party, but not a second-cousin, who is third to the party? The expression in our Mishna, "his son-in-law," means the son-in-law of his son, who is already a third. But if so, why does it not teach "the son of his son" (grandson)? Incidentally, the Mishna teaches us that the husband is equal to his wife.   But if so, according to whom would be the following Boraitha, taught by R. Hyya: Eight fathers, which counts twenty-four, including their sons and sons-in-law (*i.e.*, father and brother, two grandfathers, and four great-grandfathers —two from each side—and eight sons and eight sons-in-law)? And if our Mishna means the son's son-in-law, then it ought to be thirty-two, viz.: eight fathers, eight sons, eight sons-in-law, and eight grandsons.   Therefore we must say that our Mishna means his son-in-law.   And why does Rabh name him the son-in-law of his son?   Because he is not a descendant from him, but came from strangers, he is considered not of the second generation but as of the third.   But, after all, according to Rabh's saying it is a third to a second-cousin, and we are aware that Rabh holds that such is qualified to be a witness?   Therefore we must say that Rabh holds with R. Elazar, who says in the following Boraitha: Even as my father's brother cannot be a witness for me, neither his son nor his son-in-law, the same is the case with the son of my father's brother and with his son and son-in-law.   Still, this cannot serve as an answer to the objection that Rabh himself has qualified a third to a second-cousin?   Say, Rabh holds with R. Elazar only concerning his son, but differs with him concerning the son of his father's brother.   And the reason of Rabh's theory is because it reads: " Fathers shall not die because of their sons; and sons," etc.—which means the addition of one more generation.   And the reason of R. Elazar is: " For their children " means that the incompetence of the fathers shall extend to their children also.

R. Na'hman said: The brother of my mother-in-law cannot be a witness for me, and the same is the case with his son, and also with the son of the sister of my mother-in-law.   And there is also a Boraitha similar to this, viz.: The husband of one's sister, also the husband of the sister of one's father and the husband of the sister of one's mother, their sons and their sons-in-law, are also excluded from being witnesses.   Said R. Ashi: While we were with Ula we questioned him: How is it concerning the brother of one's father-in-law and his son, and also concerning the son of the sister of his father-in-law?   And he answered: This we have learned in a Boraitha: One's brothers, the brother of one's father and of one's mother, they, their sons and their sons-in-law—all are incompetent.

It happened that Rabh was going to buy parchments, and he was questioned: May one be a witness to his stepson's wife?   The

6

answer to this question was, according to the College of Sura, that
the husband is the same as his wife; and according to the College
of Pumbeditha, the answer was that the wife is the same as her
husband—which means that he is considered as if he were really
her father-in-law. And as Huna in the name of Rabh said:
Whence do we know that the woman is considered to be the same
as her husband? From [Lev. xviii. 14]: "She is thy aunt." Is
she indeed his aunt? Is she not the wife of his uncle only? We
see, then, that the wife is considered the same as her husband.

"*A stepfather . . . his son and son-in-law.*" Is not his
son a brother of the party from the mother's side? Said R. Jeremiah: It means the brother of his brother—*e.g.*, the son of his
stepfather from another wife. R. Hisda, however, qualified such
a person. When he was questioned: Was he not aware of Jeremiah's explanation of our Mishna just mentioned? He answered:
I do not care for it. But if so, it is his brother. The Mishna
teaches concerning a brother from the father's side, and also
from the mother's side. R. Hisda said the father of the groom
and the father of the bride may be witnesses for each other, as
their relation is similar to the relation of a cork to a barrel only,
which cannot be counted relationship. Rabba b. b. Hana said:
One may be a witness for his betrothed, but not for his wife.
Said Rabhina: Provided he testified against her; but if his testimony is in her behalf, he is not trusted. In reality, however,
(says the Gemara,) there is no difference: One is not trusted in
any case, as the reason concerning witnesses is that one is too
near in mind to his relatives; and as she is betrothed to him, he
is not fit to be a witness in any case.

The rabbis taught: One's stepson only. R. Jose says: The
husband of one's wife's sister only. And there is another Boraitha: The husband of one's wife's sister only. R. Jehudah says:
One's stepson only. How is this to be understood? Shall we assume that the Tana of the first Boraitha has mentioned only the
stepfather, but that the case is the same with the husband of one's
wife's sister? And R. Jose with his statement also does not mean
to differ, but he mentioned the latter, and the same is it also with
the former. Then our Mishna, which states, "the husband of
one's wife's sister, he, his son, and his son-in-law are excluded,"
would be neither in accordance with R. Jedudah nor with R. Jose.
Or does the Boraitha mean to say that regarding a stepfather only
is he excluded, but concerning the husband of the wife's sister, he,
with his sons, etc., is excluded; and R. Jose differs, as, according

to his opinion, the latter only is excluded, but not his sons, etc.; but a stepfather, with his sons, etc., is excluded? Then the Boraitha of R. Hyya, mentioned above, which states that there are twenty-four, would be neither in accord with R. Jose nor with R. Jehudah. Therefore we must say that the Boraitha is to be explained thus: The stepfather only is to be excluded, but concerning the husband of his wife's sister, his children are also excluded. And R. Jose came to teach that even concerning the latter he only is excluded, but not his children, and so much the more a stepfather. And then our Mishna is in accordance with R. Jehudah and the Boraitha in accordance with R. Jose. Said R. Jehudah in the name of Samuel: The Halakha prevails with R. Jose.

There was a deed of gift which was signed by two brothers-in law—*i.e.*, two husbands of two sisters—and R. Joseph was about to make it valid, based upon the decision of Samuel that the Halakha prevails with R. Jose. Said Abayi to him: Whence do you know that Samuel meant R. Jose of our Mishna, who quali-fied the husband of one's wife's sister? Perhaps he meant R. Jose of the Boraitha who disqualified him. This could not be supposed, as Samuel said, *e.g.*, I and Pinchas, who are brothers and brothers-in-law—but if only brothers-in-law, they are qualified. And Abayi rejoined: It is still uncertain, as perhaps Samuel meant to say: Because Pinchas was the husband of his wife's sister. Therefore said R. Joseph to the beneficiary: Acquire title to this gift by the testimony of the witnesses who were present when the gift was transferred to you, in accordance with R. Aba's decision. Said Abayi again: But did not Aba admit that if there was a forgery in the deed while writing, it is invalid even in the latter case? And R. Joseph said to the beneficiary: Go! you see people do not allow me to transfer it to you.

" *R. Jehudah said,*" etc. Said Thn'hum in the name of Tabla in the name of Bruna, quoting Rabha: The Halakha prevails with R. Jehudah. Rabha, however, in the name of R. Na'hman, and also Rabba b. b. Hana in the name of R. Johanan, said: The Halakha does not prevail with him: There were some others who taught the saying of Rabba with regard to the following: Thus lectured R. Jose the Galilean: It is written [Deut. xvii. 9]: "And to the judge that may be in those days." Was it neces-sary to state thus? Can it then be supposed that one should go to a judge that is not in his days? Therefore it is to be ex-plained that it means that the judge was previously a relative of his, and that thereafter he became estranged. And to this said Rabba, etc., the Halakha prevails with R. Jose the Galilean.

The sons of Mar Uqba's father-in-law were relatives, and became thereafter estranged. And they had a case, and came with it to his court. He, however, exclaimed: I am disqualified from being your judge. They then rejoined: Is it because you hold with R. Jehudah? We will bring you a letter from Palestine stating that the Halakha does not prevail with him. Rejoined he: I myself know that I am not attached to you with wax, and my saying that I am disqualified to judge you is because I know that your custom is not to listen to my decision.

"*A friend is a groomsman.*" But how long shall this friendship hold? R. Aba in the name of R. Jeremiah, quoting Rabh, said: All the seven days of the wedding. The rabbis, however, in the name of Rabha said that after the first day the friendship is no longer considered, and he is qualified.

"*An enemy,*" etc. The rabbis taught: It reads [Num. xxxv. 23]: "He was not his enemy and did not seek his harm"—which means, he who is not one's enemy may be a witness and he who does not seek one's harm may be his judge. This is concerning an enemy. And whence do we know that the same is the case with a friend? Read, then, "and he is not his enemy and not his friend"—and then he may be a witness; and if he does not seek his harm and not his welfare, then he may be his judge. But is it, then, written a friend? This is common sense. Why not an enemy? Because his mind is far from doing any good to him; and the same is it with a friend, whose mind is near to do all that he can in his behalf. The rabbis, however, infer from this two things: one concerning a judge and the other that which we have learned in the following Boraitha: R. Jose b. R. Jehudah said: From the verse, "he is not his enemy and does not seek his harm," is to be inferred that if two scholars have animosity toward each other they must not judge in a case together.

MISHNA *V.*: How were the witnesses examined? They were brought into separate chambers and were frightened to tell the truth. And then all except the eldest were told to go out, and he questioned: How do you know that A owes money to B? And if his answer was: "Because A himself told me that he owes him," or, "C told me that such was the case," he said nothing, unless he testified that, in the presence of myself and my colleague, A confessed that he owed to B two hundred zuz: and then the second witness is brought in and they examine him, and if both testimonies correspond the court discusses about the case. If two of the judges acquit and one makes him liable, he is acquitted; and if *vice versa*, he is liable. If, however, one acquits and the other makes him liable, and the third one says, " I don't know," then judges must be added. And the same is the case if there were five, and two of them were against two, while the fifth was doubtful. After the conclusion of the judges is arrived at, they are told to enter, and the eldest of the judges announces, " You, R, are acquitted," or, " You, A, are liable." And whence do we know that one of the judges must not say : I was in favor of the defendant, but my colleagues were against, and I could not help it, as they were the majority. As to this it reads [Lev. xix. 16] : " Thou shalt not go up and down as a talebearer among thy people"; and it reads also [Prov. xi. 13] : " He that walketh about as a talebearer revealeth secrets."

GEMARA : How were the witnesses frightened ? Said R. Jehudah. Thus [ibid. xxv. 14] : " Like clouds and wind without rain, so is a man that vaunteth falsely of a gift " (*i.e.*, that because of false witnesses, even though it is cloudy, the rain is withheld), Said Rabha : This is no frightening, as they may think what people say, even seven years of famine do not pass the gate of a specialist. " Therefore," said he, " it was said to them [ibid., ibid. 18] : ' A battle-axe, and a sword, and a sharpened arrow is a man that testifieth as a false witness against his neighbor.' " And R. Ashi maintains that even this is not sufficient, as they may think, even in time of a pest one does not die before his time. Therefore said he : I was told by Nathan b. Mar Zutra that they were frightened that false witnesses were disgraced even in the eyes of those who hired them. As it reads [I Kings, xxi. 10] : " And set two men, sons of Belial, opposite to him, and let them bear false witness against him," etc.

"'*A*' *himself told me*," etc. This is a support to R. Jehudah, who said in the name of Rabh : If one wants the case to be recognized by the court, he must insist that the debtor shall say : Ye shall be my witnesses. And so also was taught by Hyya b. Aba in the name of R. Johanan. And there is also a Boraitha as follows : (A said to B :) " I have a mana with you," and he answered, " Yea." On the morrow A asked him, "Give it to me," and B said it was only a joke, he is free. And not this only, but even if A has had two witnesses hidden under a fence (so that B could not see them), and questioned him : " Have I a mana with you ? " and B answered, " Yea." And to the question,

"Would you like to confess before witnesses?" B answers, "I am afraid, if I do so, you will summon me to the court"; and on the morrow A asks B to give him the mana, and his answer is, "It was only a joke," he is not liable. However, one must not defend a seducer. A seducer! Who has mentioned this term? The Boraitha is not complete, and should read thus: If, however, B does not defend himself, the court must not question him; perhaps it was a joke. But in criminal cases, a similar question must be asked by the court, although he has not so defended himself, except in the case of a seducer. And why? Said R. Hama b. Hanina: From the lecture of R. Hyya b. Aba I understand that it is because it reads [Deut. xiii. 9]: "Nor shall thy eye look with pity on him, nor shalt thou conceal it for him."

Said Abayi: All that is said above is, provided the defendant claims, "It was a joke"; but if he claims, "I have never confessed," he must be considered a liar and is liable. R. Papa b. R. Aha b. Ada, however, maintains: In the case of a joke, people do not remember their confession, and therefore even such a claim must be investigated.

There was one who had hidden witnesses under the curtains of his bed, and he said to his debtor, "Have I a mana with you?" and he answered, "Yea." And he questioned him again, "May the people who are here sleeping or awake be witnesses?" and he answered, "No." And when the case came before R. Kahana, he said: He cannot be liable, as he said no. A similar case happened with one who had hidden witnesses in a grave, and to the question, "May the living and the dead be witnesses?" he answered, "No." And when the case came before Resh Lakish, he acquitted him. Rabhina, according to others R. Papi, said: The decision of R. Jehudah that it must be said by the party, "Ye are my witnesses," is no matter whether it is said by the lender in the presence of the borrower and he keeps silent, or by the debtor himself. And this is inferred from that which was said above, that the debtor had answered the question with *no;* but if he should remain silent, he would be liable. There was one who was named by the people "the man who has against him a whole kab of promissory notes." And when he heard this, he exclaimed: Do I owe to anyone but B and C? The latter then summoned him before the court of R. Na'hman, and R. Na'hman decided that the above exclamation could not be taken as evidence, as it might be that he said so for the purpose that people should not think him too rich. There was another one who was named "the mouse who lies on dinars," and at the time he was dying he said: A and B are my creditors. After his death the creditors summoned his heirs before R. Ismael b. R. Jose, and he made the heirs pay, for the reason that, if he said so while in good health, it might be supposed that he did so for the purpose mentioned above, but this could not apply to a man who was dying. The heirs, however, only paid the half, and were summoned for the other half in the court of R. Hyya, who decided, as it is supposed that one may say so for the purpose that he shall not appear too rich, so it may be said that the deceased did so that his children should not appear too rich. The heirs then demanded what they had already paid, to which R. Hyya answered: It was decided long ago by a sage, and the decision must remain.

If one has confessed before two witnesses and they have made the ceremony of a sudarium, they may write it down; but if there was no sudarium, it must not be written. If he has, however, confessed before three without a sudarium, according to Rabh it may, and according to R. Assi it must not, be written. However, there was such a case before Rabh, and he took into consideration R. Assi's decision.

R. Ada b. Ahba said: Such a document of confession is dependent upon circumstances. If the people were gathered by themselves and he confessed before them, then it must not be written; but if he himself caused the gathering, it may. Rabha, however, is of the opinion that even in the latter case it must not be written unless he said to them, " I accept you as my judges"; and Mar b. R. Ashi maintains that even then a judgment is not to be written unless they appoint a place, and summon him to the court.

It is certain, when one has confessed with the ceremony of a sudarium in cases of movable property, that a judgment may be written, but not otherwise. But how is it with real estate—without a sudarium? According to Ameimar it may not, and according to Mar Zutra it may be written. And so the Halakha prevails. It happened that Rabhina came to the city of Damhariah, and R. Dimi b. R. Huna of the same city questioned him: How is the law if the confession was for movable property which is still in full possession of the parties? And he answered: Then it is considered as real estate. R. Ashi, however, maintains that so long as the creditor has not collected it, it is to be considered as money, because if the possessor would like to sell it, he could do so even after the confession, which is not the case in real estate.

There was a document of confession in which it was not written: " He (the debtor) has said to us, 'Write a document, sign it, and give it to him' (the creditor)," and both Abayi and Rabha decided that this case was similar to that of Resh Lakish, who decided that witnesses would not sign a document unless they were aware that the person who told them to sign was of age; the same is the case here, they would not sign it unless he said to them, " Sign and give." R. Papi, according to others R. Huna b. Joshua, opposed: Is there a thing of which we, the judges, are not sure, and the scribes are? Therefore the scribes of Abayi and of Rabha were questioned, and they were aware of the law, when it must be written and when not. There was another document of confession in which the memoranda, and all the versions which are needed thereto, were written correctly, but the words, " in the presence of us three," were missing, and the document was signed by two only. And Rabhina was about to say that this case was similar to that of Resh Lakish mentioned above; but R. Nathan b. Ami said to him: Thus was it said in the name of Rabha: In such a case it may be feared that it was an error by the court—i.e., they thought that such might be done by two. Said R. Na'hman b. Itz'hak; If in the document was written, " we the Beth Din," although it was signed by two, it is valid without any investigation. But perhaps it was written by an impudent Beth Din of two, of which, according to Samuel, the decision is to be considered, but they are named impudent (and the Halakha does not so prevail). The case was that the document read, "the Beth Din appointed by R. Ashi." Still, perhaps the same holds with Samuel. It means that it was written: Our master, Ashi, thus said.

The rabbis taught: If one said: " I have seen your deceased father hide money in a certain place, saying this belongs to so and so," or, " The money is for second tithe," if this place is to be found in this house, he said nothing. If, however, the place was in a field, where the witness could take it without being prevented, his testimony is to be considered, this being the rule in such a case. If he is able to take it himself without notifying, his word is to be trusted, but not otherwise. Moreover, if they themselves saw their father hide money in a chest, or the like, and he said to them, " This money belongs to so and so," or, " It is for second tithe," if it looks as if he told this as his last will, he is to be trusted; but if it appears that he desires to deceive them, then his words are not to be considered. The same is the case if one became harassed, searching for the money which his father left for him, and he dreamed that the sum was of such and such an amount and was placed in a certain place, but it was for second tithe. Such a case happened, and the sages decided that the caprices of dreams are not to be taken into any consideration.

"*If two of the judges acquit*," etc. But how is the judgment to be written? According to R. Johanan, "So and so is acquitted," and according to Resh Lakish, "Such and such judges acquitted, and such hold him liable." R. Elazar, however, says it should be written, "From the discussion of the judges, the decision is that such is acquitted." And what is the difference? The tale-bearing. According to R. Johanan it must not be written who acquits and who holds liable, as this would appear like tale-bearing; and according to Resh Lakish, it must be written, as, if not, it would appear like a unanimous verdict, and it would look as though they had lied; and R. Elazar's decision is: To prevent vainglory it may be written, "From their discussion, the decision is that the defendant is acquitted," in which there is no talebearing and it does not appear unanimous.

"*Are told to enter.*" Who? Shall we assume the parties? It is not stated the parties, but the witnesses, must go out. You must then say that the witnesses are told to enter, and this would not be in accordance with R. Nathan of the following Boraitha: The testimony of the witnesses is not to be conjoined unless both witnesses have seen the case together. R. Jehoshua b. Karha, however, maintains that, even if they have seen one after the other, their testimony is not to be approved by the court unless they both testify together. R. Nathan, however, maintains that the court may hear the testimony of one to-day, and on the morrow from the other one, when he appears. Hence, according to him, both witnesses may not be present? The Mishna means the parties, and it is in accordance with R. Nehemiah, who said in the following Boraitha: So was the custom of the pure-minded in Jerusalem. They let the parties enter, listened to their claims, and thereafter let the witnesses enter, listened to their testimony, and told all of them to go out, and then discussed the matter.

The text says that their testimony is not conjoined, etc. What is the point of their difference? If you wish, it may be said common sense. If, for instance, one testifies that he has seen A borrow a mana from B, and on the morrow the other witness testifies that he has seen A borrow a mana from B, one may say, *e.g.*, C has seen one mana and D has seen another mana. Hence their testimony cannot be conjoined according to the first Tana of the Boraitha; but according to R. Jehoshua b. Karha it may be conjoined, as both admit that A owes a mana to B. This is common sense. And if you wish, they differ in the meaning of the verse [Lev. v. 1]: "And he is a witness," etc. And there is a Boraitha: It reads [Deut. xix. 15] : " There shall not rise up one single witness against." Why is it written " single "? This is a rule for every case in which is mentioned " a witness," that it means two, and the term single is expressed because their testimony is to be considered only then when they saw it together. So is the explanation of the first Tana. B. Karha, however, gives his attention to the verse cited [Lev. v.]: "And he is a witness, since he either hath seen or knoweth something." Hence it matters not whether they have seen together or singly. And what is the point of difference between R. Nathan and the first Tana? Also, if you wish, it is common sense; and if you wish, in the explanation of the Scripture. " Common sense "—usually one witness is brought not to make the defendant pay, but to make him liable for an oath. Hence, if their testimony does not come together, it cannot be conjoined to make the defendant pay. Such is the meaning of the first Tana. But Nathan maintains: Even when they come together, does, then, their testimony go out from one mouth? They testify one after the other, and we conjoin them. The same is the case when they come on two days. " In the explanation of the Scripture " [ibid., ibid.] : " If he do not tell it, and thus bear his iniquity." And both the first Tana and Nathan hold with the opponents of B. Karha, that both witnesses have to see the case together. And the point of their difference is, if the testimony is to be similar to the seeing of the case. One holds it is : hence it cannot be conjoined if not seen together; and one holds it is not.

Simeon b. Alyaqim was anxious that the degree of Rabbi should be granted to Jose b. Hanina, but the opportunity did not present itself. One day they were sitting before R. Johanan, and the latter questioned : Is there one here who knows if the Halakha prevails with B. Karha or not? And B. Alyaqim pointed to Jose b. Hanina, saying: He knows. Johanan then said: Then let him tell. But B. Alyaqim, however, rejoined: Let the master give him the degree of Rabbi, and then he will tell. And he did so,

and then said to him : My son, tell me just so as you have heard.
And he answered : I have heard that B. Karha yielded to R.
Nathan. Rejoined R. Johanan : Is that what it was necessary
for me to know ? Is it not self-evident that B. Karha could not
demand that they should testify together, as he does not desire
that the seeing shall be together ? Nevertheless, since you have
already ascended to the degree of Rabbi, it may remain with you.
And R. Zera said : Infer from this act that if a great man gives
a degree, even conditionally, it remains forever.   .

Hyya b. Abin in the name of Rabh said : The Halakha prevails with Jehoshua b. Karha concerning real estate, as well as
movable property. Ula, however, maintains : It prevails with
him concerning real estate only. Said Abayi to Hyya : You say
that the Halakha prevails. Is there one who differs with him ?
Did not Aba say in the name of R. Huna, quoting Rabh : The
sages yield to B. Karha concerning the testimony as to real
estate. And so also taught Idi b. Abin in the Section Damages,
taught by the College of Karna : The sages yield to B. Karha concerning the testimony as to a first-born, as to real estate, as to
hazakah, and concerning the signs of maturity—for a male as
well as for a female ? You contradict one person with another.
People may hold different opinions. Said R. Joseph : I say in
the name of Ula that the Halakha prevails with B. Karha
concerning real estate, as well as movable property. However,
the rabbis who came from the city of Mehuza say in the name of
Zera, quoting Rabh : Concerning real estate, but not concerning
movable property. And Rabh is in accordance with his theory
elsewhere, that a confession after a confession, or a confession
after a loan, may be conjoined ; but a loan after a loan, or a loan
after a confession, do not conjoin. (*I.e.*, if one says, " In my presence A confessed on Monday that he owed a mana to B " ; and
the second witness says, " In my presence A confessed on Tuesday that he owed a mana to B," they may be conjoined. And
the same is the case if one says, " On Monday A borrowed from
B a mana in my presence," and the other witness testifies, " In
my presence A confessed on Tuesday that he owed a mana to B."
But if one testifies that in his presence A made a loan to B on
Monday, and the other testifies that the same was done on Tuesday, they are not to be conjoined, as they may be two different
manas. And the same is the case if one testify that A confessed
on Monday that he owed a mana to B, and the other testified
that B had made a loan to A on Tuesday.)

Na'hman b. Itz'hak met Huna b. R. Jehoshua, and questioned him thus : Let us see why the testimony of a loan after a loan is not to be conjoined. Because the loan which one witness has seen may not be the same which the other saw. Why, then, not say the same concerning a confession? Say, the confession of Tuesday was not the same as that of Monday? The answer was: He speaks of when he said to the last witness, " The mana which I confess before you is the same as that which I confessed yesterday before so and so." But even then, the second witness only knows this, but not the first. It means that after he has confessed before the second he goes again to the first witness, telling him, " The mana which I confessed before you, I did so also before so and so." Rejoined Na'hman : Let your mind be at rest, for you have set my mind at rest. And Huna asked him: What was the trouble? Because I had heard that Rabha, and according to others R. Shesheth, swung an axe at it (i.e., disproved the opinion), saying: Is this not similar to a confession after a loan? Which means that he said in his confession, " I confess before you that I owe a mana to so and so, which I borrowed yesterday in the presence of so and so." Hence it was already said once by Rabh. Why, then, the repetition? Rejoined Huna : This is what I have heard of your people—when they tear out trees, they plant them again (i.e., you answer questions, and then object to them again). The sages of Nahardea, however, say that, no matter if it is a confession after a confession, a loan after a confession, or a loan after a loan, they are to be conjoined, as they hold with B. Karha.

R. Jehudah said : Witnesses in civil cases who contradict one another in unimportant investigations are to be considered. Said Rabha : It seems that he meant that the contradiction was that one said the purse in which the mana was given was a black one and the other said it was a white one. But if one says that the loan was with old coins and the other said it was with new ones, they are not to be conjoined. But is such a contradiction not to be taken into consideration even in criminal cases? Did not R. Hisda say that if one testifies that he killed him with a sword and the other with an axe, it is not to be considered ; but if one says the murdered or the murderer was dressed in white, while the other testifies that he was dressed in black, their testimony holds good? And the answer was: Do you contradict one scholar with another? Each may have his own opinion. The Nahardeans, however, maintain that even if one testifies old coins and the other new, they are nevertheless to be conjoined; and this is because they hold with B. Karha. But have you then heard B. Karha say that they may be conjoined even when they contradict each other? Therefore we must say that the Nahardeans hold with the Tana of the following Boraitha: R. Simeon b. Elazar said: The schools of Shamai and Hillel do not differ, if there were two parties of witnesses. If one party testifies that he owes him two hundred, and one party testifies one hundred, the latter amount is to be collected, as in the testimony of two hundred one hundred is certainly included. In what they do differ is that, if among one party of witnesses was this contradiction (*i.e.*, one says that he owes two and the other one hundred), according to the school of Shamai the whole party must be disqualified, because one of them is surely a liar; and according to the school of Hillel they are not, as both admit that he owes one hundred (and so the Nahardeans, be it old or new coins, both admit that he owes a mana). Suppose one testifies that he borrowed a barrel of wine and the other of oil. Such a case came before Ami, and he made him liable to pay the value of a barrel of wine, as a barrel of oil amounts to twice as much as a barrel of wine. But according to whom was his decision? Is it in accordance with R. Simeon b. Elazar? He said so, because in the amount of two hundred a hundred is surely included; but did he say so in such a case as that of the barrels? The case was that they testified not for the barrels themselves, but for the value (*i.e.*, one testified that he owed him the amount of a barrel of wine and the other the amount of a barrel of oil, which is twice as much).

Suppose one of the witnesses says the law was made in the first attic, and the other says in the second attic. Said R. Hanina: Such a case came before a rabbi, and he conjoined their testimony.

"*And whence do we know that one of the judges must not say?*" The rabbis taught: Whence do we know that one of the judges, when he is going out, must not say, "I was in favor of the defendant, but my colleagues were against, and I could not help it, as they were the majority"? To this it reads [Lev. xix. 16]: "Thou shalt not go up and down as a talebearer among thy people"; and it reads also [Prov. xi. 13]: "He that walketh about as a talebearer revealeth secrets." There was a disciple of whom there was a rumor that he told a secret thing which was taught in the college, after twenty-two years, and R. Ami drove him out of the college, saying: This man is telling secrets.

MISHNA *VI.*: So long as the defendant brings evidence to his advantage, the decision may be nullified by the court. If he was told: "All the evidence which you have, you may bring before the court within thirty days," if he found such within thirty days, it affects the decision, but after that it does not. Exclaimed R. Simeon b. Gamaliel: But what should the man do who could not find such within thirty days, but found it after? If he was told to bring witnesses, and he said, "I have none"; "Bring any other evidence," and he said, "I have none," and after the time had elapsed he brought evidence and found also witnesses, it is as nothing. And to this also R. Simeon b. Gamaliel exclaimed: What should this defendant do if he was not aware that there were witnesses and evidence? However, if, after he said "I have no witnesses," seeing that he is about to be liable, he says, "Bring in so and so to testify in this case," or he takes out from under his girdle a new evidence, it counts nothing (even according to R. Simeon).

GEMARA: Said Rabba b. R. Hana: The Halakha prevails with R. Simeon. And the same says again: The Halakha does not prevail with the sages. Is this not self-evident? If it prevails with R. Simeon, it cannot prevail with the sages? One might say the Halakha prevails with R. Simeon to start with; but if some have done in accordance with the sages, it should remain so. He comes to teach us that even if it was so done, it must be changed.

"*If he was told to bring witnesses,*" etc. Said Rabba b. R. Hana in the name of R. Johanan: The Halakha prevails with the sages. And the same said again: The Halakha does not prevail with R. Simeon b. Gamaliel. Is this not self-evident—that if the Halakha prevails with the sages it cannot prevail with R. Simeon? He comes to teach us that only in this case the Halakha does not prevail with R. Simeon, but in all other cases it does; and this is to deny what Rabba b. b. Hana said in the name of R. Johanan, that everywhere R. Simeon b. Gamaliel is mentioned in the Mishnayoth the Halakha prevails with him, etc. (Last Gate, p. 388). There was a young man who was summoned to the court before R. Na'hman, and he asked him: "Have you no witnesses?" and he answered: "No." "Have you some other evidence?" and he answered: "No." And R. Na'hman made him liable. The young man went and wept; and some people heard him cry, and said: We know something in your behalf in the case of your father. Said R. Na'hman: "In such a case even the rabbis would admit that the young man was not acquainted with the business of his father and therefore the new evidence is to be taken into consideration." There was a woman with whom a document was deposited and she gave it away to some one, saying: "I am aware that this document is already paid," and R. Na'hman did not believe her. Said Rabha to him: Why should she not be trusted? Should she desire to tell a lie, she could burn it. And R. Na'hman answered: Inasmuch as it was approved by the court and known that it was deposited with her, the supposition that if she wanted to lie she could burn it does not apply. And Rabha objected to R. Na'hman from the following: A receipt which was signed by witnesses may be approved by its signer. If, however, there were no witnesses, but he was coming out from a depository; or the receipt was written on the document after the signature of the witness (which was in the hands of the creditor), it is valid. Hence we see that a depository is to be trusted. This objection remains. When R. Samuel b. Jehudah came from Palestine, he said in the name of R. Johanan: The defendant has always a right to bring evidence against the decision of the court, unless all his claims are concluded and he himself confesses that he has no more witnesses nor any other evidence. However, even after this, if witnesses arrived from the sea countries, or the box of documents of his father was deposited with a stranger who has returned it after he was found liable, it may be taken into consideration to change the first decision. When R. Dimi came from Palestine, he said in the name of R. Johanan: If one is summoning a party who says, "I want my case to be brought before the assembly of sages," while the plaintiff says, "It is sufficient that it be tried in the court of this city," the plaintiff may be compelled to follow the defendant to the assembly. Said R. Elazar: Rabbi, is it right that, if the plaintiff claims one mana from the defendant, he shall spend another mana to go with him to the assembly? Therefore the reverse must be done: The defendant should be compelled to bring the case before the court in that city. It was taught also in the name of R. Saphra: If two men were cruel to one another, and one of them insisted, "We shall try our case here," while the other says, "Let us go to the assembly," the latter must be compelled to try his case in that city. However, if there was a necessity to question the assembly, they might write and send it in writing. And also, if the defendant demands, "Write down the reason why you accused me, and give it to me," he may be listened to.   In the case of a widow whose husband dies childless and she has to marry his brother, she is obliged to go to that place where the brother is to be found (that he should marry her or perform the ceremony of Halitzah).   And to what distance? Said R. Ami: Even from Tiberias to Sephorius.   Said R. Kahana: Whence is this deduced?   From the Scripture [Deut. xxv. 8]: "The elders of *his* city "; of his, but not of hers.   Said Ameimar: The Halakha prevails that one may be compelled to go to the assembly (and there try his case).   Said R. Ashi to him: But did not R. Elazar say : He may be compelled to try his case in that city? This is when the borrower said thus to the lender ; but if the lender claims so, we apply to him [Prov. xxii. 7]: "The borrower is servant to the man that lendeth."

A message was sent from Palestine to Mar Uqba: To him to whom the world is light as to the son of Bathiah (it means to Moses), peace may be granted.   Uqban the Babylonian complained before us that Jeremiah his brother destroyed his way (*i. e.*, he has treated me badly, through which I have lost my money), and we have decided that he shall be compelled to appear before us in the city of Tiberias.   (How is this to be understood?   Thus:) They said to him : You may try him.   If he will listen to you, well and good ; and if not, you must compel him to see us in the city of Tiberias.   Said R. Ashi: This was a case of fine, and in Babylon they are not allowed to try cases of fine; and that which they said to Mar Uqba, "You shall try him," etc., was only to honor him.

CHAPTER IV.

MISHNA *I.*: Cases coming before the court, be they civil or criminal, the witnesses thereof must be examined and investigated. As it is written [Lev. iv. 22] : "One manner of judicial law shall ye have." But what difference is there between civil and criminal cases? It is the following : (a) The former cases are to be tried by three, and the latter by twenty-three judges. (b) In the former the discussion may commence either with the accusation or with the defence, while the latter must commence with the defence and not with the accusation. (c) In the former case one voice suffices either to accuse or to acquit, and in the latter he is acquitted by one voice, while to condemn two are needed. (d) In the former the judge who proclaimed his view either to advantage or to disadvantage may, after deliberating, announce his view to the contrary. In the latter, however, he may do so only to acquit, but not to condemn. (e) In civil cases the whole body of the court may defend or accuse, while in criminal cases all of them may acquit, but the whole body must not accuse. (f) The former may be discussed in the daytime and the decision rendered at night, while in the latter the decision must be in the daytime. But if they did not come to a conclusion on the same day, they have to postpone it to the morrow. (g) The decision concerning the former may be reached on the same day either to one's advantage or to his disadvantage, while in the latter the decision may be rendered on the same day to free him, but not to condemn him until the next day ; and, therefore, cases of capital punishment must not be begun on the eve of Sabbath or of a legal holiday. In civil cases,

7   97

and regarding defilement and purity, they begin by asking the opinion of the eldest, while in criminal cases they begin with those who are sitting on the side.

All are qualified to judge civil cases, but not every one is qualified to judge criminal cases; as to the latter—only priests, Levites, and Israelites who may legally marry daughters of priests.

GEMARA: Are investigation and examination indeed needed in civil cases? If so, there is a contradiction from the following Tosephta: A document of which the date shows the first of Nissan in a Sabbatical year and witnesses came, saying, "How can you testify in favor of this document—were you not with us at the same date mentioned in the document in such and such a place?" The document as well as the witnesses are valid, as it is to be supposed that they might have written the document after the date mentioned therein. Hence if investigation and examination are needed, why should they be valid because of the above reason? Would not the investigation show if it were so or not. But according to this theory, how is to be understood the following Mishna: Promissory notes which were written at an earlier date are invalid. However, if they were written at a later date, they are. Now, if an investigation in civil cases is needed, why should that which was written at a later date be valid? (The investigation would show that the witnesses who signed the document were not present when the loan was made, as it was signed at an earlier date. Hence the loan which was made earlier is to be considered a verbal loan, which does not collect from encumbered estates, and the note should be considered a forgery?) This presents no difficulty, the objection mentioned applying more to the statement of the Boraitha, as it speaks of a Sabbatical year, in which people do not usually lend money because of the law [Deut. xv. 2] of that year, and nevertheless it makes valid that which was written in the month of Nissan, because the above-mentioned law concerning promissory notes applies only at the end of the year. However, the contradiction to our Mishna remains!

R. Hanina said: Biblically there is no difference between civil and criminal cases concerning investigations, as it reads, "One manner of judicial law," etc. But why was it enacted that civil cases do not need investigation? So as not to close the door to borrowers. (And our Mishna, which states that it is needed, was taught *before the enactment ;* and the Boraitha cited *after the enactment.*) But if so, let the judge who made an error in the decision of the case not be responsible? If this should be enacted, so much the more would the door be closed to borrowers. Rabha, however, maintains that our Mishna treats of fine cases and the Boraitha of loan cases. However, both were taught after the above-mentioned enactment. And R. Papa maintains that both treat of loan cases. But our Mishna speaks of a case which appears to the court unfair ; and to such, investigation is needed. The Boraitha speaks of non-suspicious cases. And this is in accordance with Resh Lakish, who used to propound a contradiction to the following : It reads [Lev. xix. 15] : " In righteousness shalt thou judge thy neighbor "; and Deut. xvi. 20 reads : " Justice, only justice, shalt thou pursue," from which it is to be understood that an investigation is needed ? And he answered that the first verse speaks of an ordinary case and the second of a suspicious one. R. Ashi, however, maintains that the above answer of R. Papa, concerning the contradiction from the Mishna, holds good. However, the supposed contradiction of the verse is to be explained that the first speaks of a strict law and the second of an arbitration, as the following Boraitha states : " Justice, only justice," etc., one word means strict law and the other means arbitration. How so ? If, *e.g.*, two boats are plying on a river and they meet each other, if both try to pass where there is not room, both would be lost ; but if one passes after the other, both would be saved. And the same is the case with two camels passing the steps of Beth Chorin, which met each other. If both tried to pass together, both would fall ; but if one after the other, both would be saved. Then the strict law is that the unloaded one should wait, and the loaded one pass ; or, if one was near to the dangerous place and the other far off, the nearer one has to pass ; but if both were loaded, or if both were at the same distance, then arbitration must be used as to which one has to pay to the other for loss of time.

The rabbis taught : " Justice, only justice, shalt thou pursue," means that one shall follow to the city of a celebrated judge, *e.g.*, at Luda, after R. Elazar ; at Brur-Heil, after Rabban Johanan b. Zakkai. [There is a Boraitha : (At the time the government had forbidden circumcisions and weddings, they made use of hand-mills to announce a circumcision.) Then, if one heard the sound of a bandmill in the city of Burni, he understood that there was a ceremony of circumcision in that city ; and if one saw many lights in Bene Heil, he understood that there was a wedding banquet in that city].

There is another Boraitha interpreting the cited verse thus: You should always trouble yourself to follow after the sages in assembly, as, for instance, after R. Elazar at Luda; after R. Johanan b. Zakkai at Brur-Heil; after Jehoshua at Pekiein; after Rabban Gamaliel at Jamnia; after Aqiba at Bene Braq; after Matia at Rome; after Hanania b. Thrduin at Sikhni; after Jose at Sephorius; after Jehudah b. Bathyra at Nzibin; after Hanina, the nephew of Jehoshua, in exile; after Rabbi at Beth-Shearin; and (when the Temple was in existence) after the sages at their assembly in the chamber of the Temple.

" *With the accusation or with the defence.*" But what has the court first to say to the advantage of the defence in criminal cases? Said R. Jehudah: The court may ask the witness: " Whence do we know that it was as you say?" But from such an interrogation the witness will become dejected, and will refrain from saying anything. [But let him be dejected? Have we not learned in a Boraitha, R. Simon b. Eleazar said: The witnesses may be transferred from one place to another that they shall become dejected and retract from their statement if it was not true? What comparison is this? There they become dejected by themselves; but here, if you say to them, " Whence do we know that what you say is true?" *you* cause them to be dejected.] Therefore said Ula: The court questioned the other party, " Have you other witnesses to make collusive the witnesses of your opponents?" Said Rabba to him: Is this what you call *beginning with the defence?* With this saying you begin by accusing witnesses of the other party. Therefore said he: The court may say to the other party, " Have you other witnesses who may contradict the witnesses of your opponent?" R. Kahna says: The court may say, " From your testimony it seems that the defendant may be acquitted"; and thereafter they discuss the matter. Both Abayi and Rabha say: The court may say to the defendant, " Do not fear; if you have not committed the crime, nothing will be done to you." And R. Ashi said: The beginning should be with the announcement of the court: Every one who knows of a defence concerning the defendant may come to tell it before the court. There is a Boraitha in accordance with Abayi and Rabha as follows: It reads [Num. v. 19]: " If thou hast not gone aside to uncleanness behind thy husband, then be thou free." Said Rabbi: Infer from this that in criminal cases the beginning must be with the defence (as it is written first, " then be thou free ").

"May after deliberating . . . announce to the contrary."
There is a contradiction from the following: If one has tried a
case and made liable him who is not, or *vice versa ;* has purified a thing which is unclean, or *vice versa,* his decision holds
good, but he has to pay for his error from his own pocket.
(Hence we see that he must not retract?)   Said R. Joseph: This
presents no difficulty.   A judge who was appointed by the
court, if he made an error, he must pay for it; but if he was appointed by the parties only, he has not.   But is there not a
Boraitha: If he was appointed by the court, he has not to pay?
Said R. Na'hman: The just cited Boraitha treats of when there
was a superior judge to him, who ignores his decision; therefore
he is free from paying, as the superior judge decides it properly.
But if there is no superior and his decision remains, then he
must pay for his error.   R. Shesheth, however, maintains: It
depends in what the error was made.   If he erred in that which
is plainly taught in a Mishna, then he has not to pay, because
his decision will not be executed ; but if he erred in his opinion,
then he has to suffer.   So did he hear from R. Assi.   Rabhina
questioned R. Ashi: Is it the same even if he has erred in that
which was taught in the Boraithas of R. Hyya and R. Oshia?
And he answered: Yea.   And how is it if he erred in that which
was said by Rabh and Samuel?   And he answered: Yea.   And
how is it if he erred in that which was said by you and me?
And he rejoined: What, then, are we?   Are we splitting wood
or gathering splinters in the forest!   How is to be understood,
"erred in his opinion"?   (See the answer in Chapter I., page
9, line 21.)

R. Hamnuna objected to R. Shesheth from the following: It
happened that a cow of which the womb had been removed was
brought before R. Tarphon, and he made the owner give it to the
dogs.   However, a similar case came before the sages in Jamnia,
and they made it valid, because Tudus the physician testified
that not one cow or one swine was sent out from Alexandria in
Egypt of which the womb was not removed, for the purpose that
they should not bring forth offspring.   And R. Tarphon exclaimed thus: O Tarphon, thy ass is gone! (*I.e.,* I have to sell
my ass to pay for the error.)   Said R. Aqiba to him: You are
free, as there is a rule that a judge who is appointed by the majority has not to pay for his error.   Now, if an error in that
which was taught in a Mishna does not hold good and must be
redecided, why does not Aqiba say: You have erred against a

Mishna? R. Aqiba meant to say both—first: You have erred against a Mishna; and secondly: Even if you erred in your own opinion you would also be free, because you were chosen by the majority.

Said R. Na'hman b. Itz'hak to Rabha: How could R. Hamnuna object to Shesheth from the case of the cow? Did not Tarphon give it to the dogs? Hence the cow was no longer in existence, and it could not be redecided. Hamnuna meant to say thus: If the decision should be that the case of one who erred against a Mishna is not to be redecided, it is correct that Tarphon was afraid that he must pay, and R. Aqiba told him that he must not, because he was a recognized judge. But if the Halakha is that in such a case it must be redecided, let Aqiba say to him: How would it be if the cow were still in existence—your decision would not remain and the cow would be declared valid? The same is the case even now that it is not in existence, as you did not yourself give it to the dogs: You had only decided that it was invalid, and as your decision does not count, the owner of the cow, himself, has to suffer for his act.

R. Hisda, however, explains our Mishna that it means: If the judge himself took from the one who was liable in his eyes and gave to his opponent, only then must he pay from his pocket, but not otherwise. But this would be correct in one case only—namely, if he had made liable the just, then we could say that he took from the just and gave to his opponent. But how could this be done in the second case, in which he has acquitted the one who was liable, as he only said to him: You are not liable? His decision, "You are free," is counted as if he would take with his hand and give to him. But if so, how is to be understood the following statement of the Mishna, that the judge may retract from this view, no matter if it is concerning defence or accusation, as this can be explained only in case he said to the just, "You are liable," but did not collect from him, as then he may retract and say, "You are not liable"? But in case he made liable a just man, how could such a case take place, if not by the decision, "You are free"? And it is said above that such a decision is considered as if he would take from one party and give to the other: hence, after such, no retraction can take place. Our Mishna, with its expression, "whether in defence or in accusation," means to say that with the acquittal of one party the other party is accused; namely, a retraction may take place in behalf of one who was erroneously made liable but it was not as yet collected, although it is a disadvantage to his opponent, but in case he has acquitted the one who is liable he has to pay from his pocket.   But if so, then in criminal cases a retraction could take place only when it is in behalf of the defendant, but at the same time his opponent is not accused.   And this can be said if the criminal case was a violation of Sabbath or a case of adultery ; but in case of murder, how can such be found ?   But how, if there is a retraction that he is not guilty of slaying a person, who is accused ?   It may be said the relatives of the person murdered ; as biblically, if the relatives of the person murdered took revenge on the murderer and slew him, he is freed ; and by the retraction from guilty to not guilty, if the relative should put his hand on the murderer, he would be accused.   But could such a thing be supposed ?   You mean to say, because perhaps the relative of the person murdered will take revenge, therefore no retraction shall take place and the defendant shall be put to death.   And secondly, does not the Mishna state, whether concerning defence or accusation ?   This difficulty remains.   Rabhina, however, says : Even in case he has acquitted the one liable, it may also be found that the judge did it with his hand—namely, in case he had a pledge and the judge took it away from him and transferred it to the borrower.

"*Criminal cases*," etc.   The rabbis taught : Whence do we know that if one was found guilty by the court, and thereafter one came, saying : I know a defence for him, that the case may be retried ?   Because it reads [Ex. xxiii. 7] : " Him who hath been declared innocent and righteous, thou shalt not slay."   Read : Him who was declared innocent even by one person, you shall not slay (without a reinvestigation).   And whence do we know concerning the one who was acquitted by the court, and thereafter one says, " I know of a fact which will make him guilty," that he must not be listened to ?   From the same cited verse : " Him who hath been declared righteous, ye shall not slay."   Said R. Shimi b. Ashi.   And just the reverse may be done with a seducer, as the Scripture reads [Deut. xiii. 9] : " You shall not have any pity," etc.   R. Kahana infers this from [ibid., ibid. 10] : " You shall surely kill him," etc.

R. Zera questioned R. Shesheth : Whence do we know that the same law applies to them who are to be punished with exile ? And the answer was : From an analogy of the expression " murder," which is to be found in both cases.   And whence do we know that the same is the case with them that are to be punished

with stripes? From an analogy of the expression " wicked," which
is to be found in both cases. And so also is it plainly stated in
a Boraitha.

" *But not to condemn.*" Said Hyya b. Aba in the name of
R. Johanan : Provided he has erred in a thing which the Sadduceans oppose ; but if they admit, it must read so plainly in
the Scripture. And such a decision is not to be taken in consideration at all, as schoolchildren are aware of it ; it must be
retried. The same Hyya questioned R. Johanan : How is it if
we err in a case of adultery? And he answered : So long as the
fire in the stove burns, cut off all that you want to roast, and
roast it. (*I.e.*, when you are studying a thing, consider it thoroughly to prevent questions. You have heard from me that, in
a thing which the Sadduceans admit, his decision is not counted.
Is not adultery one of these ?)

" *All of them,*" etc. Does the Mishna mean that even the
witness who had accused him may also thereafter defend him?
Then our Mishna is in accordance with R. Jose b. Jehudah, and
not in accordance with the rabbis of the following Boraitha: It
is written [Num. xxxv. 30] : " But one witness shall not testify
against any person to cause him to die." It means whether to
defend or to accuse. Jose b. Jehudah, however, maintains that
he may testify to defend, but not to accuse. (Hence our Mishna
is not in accordance with him.) Said R. Papa : Our Mishna,
with its expression *all*, means to add one of the disciples who sat
in a row before the judges, and such may make use of his opinion
according to all.

What is the reason of R. Jose's statement? Because it reads
" to cause him to die," we infer that only to accuse he must
not testify, but to defend he may. But if so, why do the rabbis
differ? Said Resh Lakish : Because it appears that the witness is
interested in this case. And what do the rabbis infer from the
words " to cause him to die "? They apply this to one of the
disciples, as we have learned in the following Boraitha : If one
of the witnesses says : " I have something to say in defence
of the defendant," whence do we know that he must not be
listened to? From the verse cited : " One witness shall not testify." And whence do we know, if one of the disciples say, " I
have something to say to the disadvantage of the defendant,"
that he must also not be listened to? From the same : " One
shall not testify to cause him to die."

" *Only to acquit, but not to condemn.*" Said Rabh : This is

said only at the time they discuss this matter ; but at the time
of the conclusion he may change his views from defence to
accusation also.   An objection was raised from the following:
" On the morrow they arise early and come to the court.   He
who defended has to say : I defended yesterday and am of the
same opinion to-day.   And he who accused has also to say: I
accused, and am of the same opinion to-day.   However, he who
had accused may change his view to defence, while this is not
allowed to him who defended."   Now, on the morrow it is time
for the conclusion, and it nevertheless states that the defendant
may not change his view?   According to this theory, no discussion is to be prolonged on the morrow; and this is certainly not
so.   Hence the Boraitha means that he must not do so at the
time of discussion.

Come and hear another objection : " All who take part in the
discussion may explain their reasons, until one of the accusers
shall yield to one of the defenders (and then the majority of one
will suffice to acquit)."   Now, if you say that one may change
his view from defence to accusation, why does not the Boraitha
state, "or to the contrary "?   It is simply because the Tana of
the Boraitha does not care to repeat a matter of accusation.

Come and hear another objection : " R. Jose b. Hanina said:
If one of the disciples has defended and dies at the time of the
conclusion, his view should be considered as if he were still alive."
And why ?   Let it be said that if he were alive he might retract
from his view?   This is no objection, as in reality he did not retract.   But how can you explain that the decision of R. Jose b.
Hanina may correspond with Rabb's statement?   Was not a
message sent from Palestine as follows: R. Jose's statement
denies our master's (Rabh's) statement?   Nay, the message was
just the contrary: R. Jose's statement does not deny the statement of our master in Babylon.

" Discussed in the daytime," etc.   Whence is this deduced?
Said R. Aha b. Papa: From [Ex. xviii. 22]: " And let them
judge the people at all times."   But how is it to be inferred from
this that the conclusion must not be at night, and the discussion
may?   This is in accordance with Rabha, who has propounded
a contradiction from the just cited verse to that of Deut. xxi. 16:
" Then shall it be, on the day* when he divideth . . . what

* In Leeser's version it is not mentioned "on the day," notwithstanding that the
text so reads, which, according to the sense, may mean "the time."   The Talmud,
however, takes it literally.

he hath"—on the day, "but not at any time"? And the answer was that the beginning of the trial must be in the daytime,
but the conclusion may be even at night-time in civil cases. Our
Mishna is not in accordance with R. Mair of the following
Boraitha: It reads [ibid., ibid. 5]: "Every controversy and every
plague."* What have plagues to do with controversies? The
Scripture compares controversies to plagues, in order to apply the
law of the latter to the former. As concerning plagues it must
be in the daytime [Lev. xiii. 14]: "But on the day," etc., the
same is the case with controversies. And also as, concerning
plagues, it cannot be judged by one who is blind, as the priest
must see the signs, the same is the case with controversies. And
also the law concerning controversies, which must not be judged
by relatives, applies to plagues—that the priest must not be a
relative of him who has the plague.

In the neighborhood of R. Johanan there was one who was
blind who used to judge cases, and R. Johanan did not protest.
But could R. Johanan be silent in such a matter? Is it not
against his own decision? Did not he himself declare that the
Halakha always prevails with an anonymous Mishna, and there
is one which states: Every one who is qualified to judge is also
qualified to be a witness? However, there are some who are
qualified to witness, but not to judge; and the same R. Johanan
has declared that it means one who is blind of one eye, who is
qualified to witness, but not to judge. Hence one who is blind,
who is disqualified to be a witness because he cannot see, ought
also to be disqualified to judge? R. Johanan found another
anonymous Mishna for his basis, namely : "Civil cases may be
discussed in the daytime and the conclusion at night," which is
the same as a case of one who is blind. But why does he give
preference to the latter Mishna, and not to the first? If you
wish, it may be said because the latter treats of a majority, while
the first treats of an individual. And if you wish, it is because
the latter is taught concerning the laws of trying cases.

"*If they did not come to a conclusion,*" etc. Whence is this
deduced? Said Shini b. Hyya: From [Num. xxv. 4]: "Take
all the heads of the people and hang them up before the Lord in
the face of the sun." If people have sinned, wherein have the
heads of the people sinned, that they should be hanged? Said
R. Jehudah in the name of Rabh: Thus said the Holy One,
blessed be He, to Moses: "Take the heads of the people, and set

* Leeser's translation does not correspond.

them at separate places, that they shall judge the guilty ones
and hang them in the face of the sun (which means in the daytime)." And why in separate places? Shall we assume, because
two capital punishments must not be decided on one and the
same day? Did not R. Hisda say that this is said only when
capital punishments are of different kinds, but if of one kind they
may? Therefore it must be said : To hasten the execution of
the guilty, that the anger of Heaven shall cease.

" *They have to postpone it until the morrow.*" Whence is this
deduced? Said R. Hanina : From [Is. i. 21] : " Righteousness
lodged therein ; but now murderers "—which means, formerly
they used to postpone the condemnation for a night, and now
that they are not doing so they are considered murderers.

" *Must not be begun on the eve of Sabbath,*" etc. Why so?
Because it could not be done otherwise ; as, if they should begin
and finish on the eve of Sabbath, perhaps they would need to
condemn him, and then they would have to postpone it over
night. And to conclude the case on Sabbath and to execute on
the same day, the execution does not violate the Sabbath ; and
should it be executed at night, after Sabbath the law requires,
" in the face of the sun " ; and should the conclusion be on Sabbath and the execution on the following day, then it would be
torture for the guilty one, which is not allowed. Should they
begin on the eve of Sabbath and conclude on the day after Sabbath, then they are liable to forget the reasons. Although there
were two scribes who used to write down the discussions—the
defence as well as the accusation—they wrote only what was
said, but could not write the heart of the man. And, therefore,
it was impossible otherwise.

" *They used to ask the opinion,*" etc. Said Rabh : I used to be
among the judges of the court of Rabbi, and they used to begin
the question of opinions with me. But does not the Mishna
state that they have to begin with the eldest? Said Rabba b.
Rabba, according to others Hillel b. Wals : It was different in
the court of Rabbi, as in all cases they used to begin from those
who were sitting at the side. The same said again : From the
time of Moses until the time of Rabbi we do not find one man
who was unique in the possession of wisdom, riches, and glory.
Is this so? Was it not so with Jehoshua? Nay, there was
Elazar the high-priest, who was equal to him. But was not
Pinchas such a man? Nay, there were the elders who ruled with
him. But was there not King Saul, of whom the same could be

said? Nay, there was Samuel. But did not Samuel die before
Saul? It means, all the years of his life. But was not David
such a man? There was Era of Ja'ir. He also departed before
him. It means, also, all the years of his life. Was not King
Solomon such a man? There was Shimi b. Geara. But did not
Samuel slay him? It means, all the years of his life. Was there
not Hezekiah? There was Shbna. Was there not Ezra? There
was Nehemiah. Said R. Ada b. Ahbah: I can add thus: From
the time of Rabbi until the time of R. Ashi there is also not to
be found a man who was unique in all that is said above. But
was there not Huna b. Nathan? R. Huna was under the influence of R. Ashi.

" *Criminal cases they began from those sitting at the side.* "
Whence is this deduced? Said R. Aha b. Papa: It is written
[Ex. xxiii. 3]: "Neither shalt thou speak in a cause." (The term
for "cause" is "rib," literally "quarrel," and "rab" means
"great.") Do not read "rib," but "rab," which means: You
shall not contradict one who is greater than you. Rabba b. b.
Hana in the name of R. Johanan said: This is inferred from
[I Sam. xxv. 13]: "Gird ye on every man his sword, and they
girded on every man his sword; and David also girded on his
sword." (We see that first it was done by the people and afterwards by the master.)

Rabh said: One may teach his disciple, and at the same time
may judge in association with him in criminal cases. An objection was raised from the following concerning purification and
defilement. A father with his son, or a master with his disciple,
are counted as two voices. However, in civil cases, in criminal
cases concerning stripes, in consecration of the month and in the
establishment of leap year, a father with his son, or a master with
his teacher, is counted as one voice only. (Hence we see that
the master with his disciple cannot judge together in criminal
cases, so that they should be counted two.) Rabh speaks of such
disciples as R. Kahana and R. Assi, who needed only Rabh's tradition, but not his sagacity, to equalize things.

R. Abuhu said: In ten things civil cases differ from criminal
cases. However, all of them do not apply to the case of an ox
which is to be stoned, except as to the number of judges, twenty-
three being needed, similar to all other criminal cases. But
whence is this deduced? Said R. Aha b. Papa: From [Ex. xxiii.
6]: "Thou shalt not wrest the judgment of thy poor in his
cause"; *i.e.*, thou shalt not wrest the case of thy poor, but thou

mayst wrest the case of the stoning of an ox. (And as this law does not apply to the stoning of an ox, so do not apply the other laws except the one of the twenty-three judges mentioned above.) But are there not some other things in which criminal cases differ from civil? Have we not learned in a Boraitha that among the Sanhedrin must not be any one of great seniority, a castrate, and those who have no children? R. Jehudah also adds to these a cruel man.

"*All are competent to judge civil cases.*" What does the Mishna mean by the expression "all"? Said R. Jehudah. To add a bastard. But this was taught already in the above-mentioned Boraitha, that all who are competent to judge criminal cases are competent for civil cases. However, there are those who are competent for civil cases but not for criminal. And in our discussion we have debated: "What does it mean by all who are competent?" The same R. Jehudah said: It means to add a bastard. One means to add a proselyte and the other means to add a bastard; and both cases are necessary to be stated. For if a proselyte only were stated, one might say, it is because he is eligible to marry a daughter of an Israelite; but a bastard, who is not allowed to do so, is not competent. And if a bastard only were stated, one might say, because, after all, he is a descendant of an Israelite; but a proselyte, who is a descendant of a heathen, is not competent. Therefore both statements are necessary.

"*But not all of them are competent to judge criminal cases.*" What is the reason? That which was taught by R. Joseph: As the court must be select in its uprightness, so it must be select in all other things—without any blemish. And R. Ameimar said: Where is there to be found an allusion to this in the Scripture? In [Solomon's Song, xiv. 7]: "Thou art altogether beautiful, my beloved, and there is no blemish on thee." But perhaps it means literally that the judges shall be without any bodily blemish? Said R. Aha b. Jacob: It reads [Num. xi. 16]: "And they shall stand there *with thee*"—which means those who are equal to thee (*i.e.*, in birth, but not a proselyte and a bastard). But perhaps there is a difference, because of the glory of the Shekinah. Therefore said R. Na'hman b. Itz'hak: This is inferred from [Ex. xviii. 22]: "When they shall bear with thee." This means they shall be equal to thee in birth.

MISHNA *II.*: The Sanhedrin sat in a half-circle in order that they could see each other. Two scribes of the judges stood before them, one on the right and one on the left, and they wrote down the reasons of the accuser and of the defender.   According to R. Jehudah there were three—one who wrote down the reasons of the accuser and one the reasons of the defender, and one the reasons of both.   And before them sat three rows of scholars (disciples).   To every one of them his seat was known.   If it was necessary to add a judge, one from the first row was elevated, and one from the second came and took the latter's place, and one from the third took the place of this one ; and for the place in the third row one of the standing people was selected, but he did not take the same seat as the one departed occupied, but that to which he was entitled.

GEMARA : Whence is this deduced?   Said R. Aha b. Hanina : From [Solomon's Song, vii. 3] : "Thy navel is like a round goblet which lacketh not the mixed wine."   By " navel " is meant   the   Sanhedrin.   And why were they named navel? Because they used to sit in the middle of the world (according to the Talmud, Jerusalem was the middle of the world and the Temple was in the centre of Jerusalem), and also protected the whole world.   And why were they named a " round goblet "? Because the Sanhedrin sat in a circle : " Which lacketh not the mixed wine "—*i.e.*, if one wished to leave, it must be seen that besides him twenty-three remained, and if there were less, he must not.   " Thy body is like a heap of wheat fenced about with lilies," means that as from a heap of wheat all derive benefit, so all were pleased to hear the reasons given by the Sanhedrin in their discussions.   " Fenced about with lilies " means that even a fence of lilies was not broken by them to go out of it.   This is what was said by a certain Minn to R. Kahana : Your law permits a man to stay alone with his wife during the days of her menstruation.   Is it possible that flax and fire should be together and should not burn?   And he answered : The Torah has testified that we are such a kind of people that even a fence of lilies is sufficient for us, and will never be broken.   Resh Lakish said : This is inferred from ibid. vi. 72, which means that even thy vain fellows are full of meritorious acts—like the pomegranate.*   R. Zera said : From [Gen. xxvii. 27] : " And he smelled the smell of his garments," etc.   Do not read " bgadov," which means dress, but "bagdov," which means his transgressor.   There were ὕβριον †

* It is useless to quote the passage, as its translation does not correspond with the saying of Resh Lakish at all.

† We have translated in accordance with Schönhack's Dictionary, as it seems to us correct.

(insolent fellows) in the neighborhood of R. Zera, who nevertheless associated with them and showed them respect, to the end
that they should repent. The rabbis, however, were not satisfied with this. But after the soul of R. Zera had gone to its
resting-place the above-mentioned people took this to heart,
saying: Hitherto there was the little man who prayed for us,
but now who will do so? And they repented and became good.

" *Three rows*," etc. Said Abayi: Infer from this that if one
left his place, all in the row had to change their places. But could
one not protest, saying: Hitherto I have sat in front, and now
you place me in the back? Said Abayi: To such a protest he
was answered: There is a parable that it is better for one to be
the tail of a lion than the head of a fox.

MISHNA *III.*: How were the witnesses awestruck in criminal cases? They were brought in and warned: Perhaps your
testimony is based only on a supposition, or on hearsay, or on that
of another witness, or you have had it from a trustworthy man ; or
perhaps you are not aware that finally we will investigate the
matter by examination and cross-examination. You may also be
aware of the fact that there is no similarity between civil and
criminal cases. In civil cases one may repay the money damage
and he is atoned ; but in criminal cases the blood of the person
executed, and of his descendants to the end of all generations,
clings to the originator of his execution. So do we find in the
case of Cain, who slew his brother. It reads [Gen. iv. 10] : " The
voice of the 'bloods' of thy brother are crying unto me from
the ground." It does not read " blood," but " bloods," which
means his blood and the blood of his descendants. [According
to others it reads " bloods " in the plural, because his blood was
scattered all over the trees and stones.] Therefore the man was
created singly, to teach that he who destroys one soul of a human
being, the Scripture considers him as if he should destroy a whole
world, and him who saves one soul of Israel, the Scripture considers him as if he should save a whole world. And also because
of peace among creatures, so that one should not say: My
grandfather was greater than yours ; and also that the heretic
shall not say: There are many creators in heaven ; and also to
proclaim the glory of the Holy One, blessed be He. For a human
being stamps many coins with one stamp, and all of them are
alike ; but the King of the kings of kings, the Holy One, blessed
be He, has stamped every man with the stamp of Adam the First,
and nevertheless not one of them is like the other. Therefore

every man may say: The world was created for my sake, hence I must be upright, just, etc. Should you (witnesses) say: Why should we take so much trouble upon ourselves? To this it is written [Lev. v. 1]: "And he is a witness, since he hath seen or knoweth something; if he do not tell it, and thus bear his iniquity." And should you say: After all, why should the blood of this man cling to us? To this it is written [Prov. xi. 10]: "When the wicked perish, there is joyful shouting."

GEMARA: The rabbis taught: What means a supposition? The court may say to them: Although you saw that one ran after his companion to a ruin and you ran after them, and found a sword in his hand from which the blood dripped, and you also saw the one killed move convulsively, you saw nothing (so long as he did not kill him in your presence).

There is a Boraitha: Simeon b. Shetha said: May I not live to see the consolation of our people if I did not see one who ran after his companion to a ruin, and I ran after him, and saw a sword in his hand from which blood dripped, and the one killed moved convulsively, and I said to him: You wicked one, who has slain this man—I or you? But what can I do that your blood is not legally in my hands, as it reads [Deut. xvii. 6]: "Upon the evidence of two . . . be put to death." But He who knows the thoughts of man shall take revenge on this man who has slain his companion. It was said that both (Simeon and the murderer) had not moved before a snake came and stung the guilty one that he died.

But was this man liable to be killed by a snake? Did not R. Joseph say, and so also taught the disciples of Hiskia: Since the Temple was destroyed, although the court of the Sanhedrin existed no longer, the punishment of the four kinds of death prescribed in the Scripture was not abolished by Heaven—as, e.g., he who is liable to be stoned finds his death by falling from a roof or by being trodden down by a wild beast; he who is liable to be burned finds his death by fire or by the bite of a snake; he who is liable to be slain by the sword falls into the hand of the government, which slays him, or he comes to death by the sword of murderers; and he who ought to be hanged finds his death by drowning in the river or by diphtheritis. (But the murderer is only to be slain, and not burned?) This man was liable to be burned for another crime; and the master said elsewhere that he who is guilty of two crimes is to be punished by the heavier death.

"*Supposition.*" We see that a supposition does not hold good in the case of crimes.   Does it hold good in civil cases? And if yea, it would be in accordance with R. Aha, who said in the " Last Gate " that if there was a biting camel among camels and a killed camel was found at its side, it might be taken for a certainty that it had killed him and its owner was liable.   But according to this theory, if there was a witness who heard this by hearsay from another, which is not considered in criminal cases, it should be considered in civil.   Does not the Mishna state that if he said, " The defendant has confessed to me that he owes," etc.; or, " So and so told me that he owes him," he said nothing? Hence if such does not hold good in civil cases, why should this be repeated concerning criminal cases?   Therefore we must say that, notwithstanding that such a testimony is not considered in civil cases, they nevertheless warned them in criminal cases. The same is the case with the above-mentioned case of supposition.

" *You shall be aware*," etc.   R. Jehudah b. Ahia said: Infer from the verse cited in the Mishna that Cain made wounds and gashes on the body of his brother Abel, as he did not know by what member the soul departed until he reached his neck.   The same said again: From that time when the earth opened its mouth to receive the blood of Abel, it has not again opened.   As it is written [Is. xxiv. 16]: " From the edge of the earth," etc. Hence it reads " from the edge," but not " from the mouth." Hiskia, his brother, however, objected to him from [Num. xvi. 32]: " And the earth opened her mouth," etc.   And he answered: It opened for disadvantage, but not for advantage. The above said again in the name of the same authority: Exile atones for only half of a sin, but not for all of it, as it reads [Gen. iv. 14]: " And I shall be a fugitive and vagabond on the earth," etc.; and [ibid. 16]: " And dwelt in the land of Nod " (vagabond).   Hence half of his sin was atoned.*

" *Therefore after them man was created singly.*"   The rabbis taught: Adam the first was created singly, and why?   That disbelievers should not say there were many Creators in Heaven. And another reason is because of the upright and the wicked, that the upright should not say: We are descendants of an upright man ; and the wicked should not say : We are descendants of a wicked one (hence we are not to be blamed).   There is another reason : Because of families, that they should not quarrel, saying:

---

* Here come Haggadah, which we have transferred to the Haggadic part of this tract.

8

Our parents were better than yours. As we see that when only one man was created there are quarrels of rank, how much the more if many original Adams had been created. Still another reason : Because of robbers and forcers. As even now, when he was created singly, there are robbers and forcers although they are all from one father, how much the more would there be robbers and forcers if they were from different parents.

"*To save the glory*," etc. The rabbis taught : To save the glory of the King of the king of kings, the Holy One, blessed be he ! A human being stamps many coins and all are alike, but the Holy One, blessed be He, has stamped every man with the stamp of Adam the First, and nevertheless not one is like his neighbor. As it reads [Job, xxxviii. 14] : "She is changed as the sealing-clay ; and (all things) stand as though newly clad." And why are not the faces of men alike ? Because one might see a nice dwelling or a handsome woman, and say : It is mine. As it reads [ibid. 15] : "And from the wicked is their light withdrawn, and the high-raised arm is broken."

There is a Boraitha :   R. Mair used to say : In three things one is different from his neighbor—in voice, in face, and in mind : in voice and in face, because of adultery ; and in mind, because of robbers. (*I.e.*, if one were to know the mind of his neighbor, he would know of all his treasures and mysteries and would rob him of them.*)

---

* Here also are a few pages of Haggadah, which we have transferred to the Haggadic chapter.

CHAPTER V.

RULES AND REGULATIONS CONCERNING PRELIMINARY QUERIES, EX-
AMINATION, AND CROSS-EXAMINATION IN CRIMINAL CASES.
WHAT MAY OR MAY NOT BE CONSIDERED A CONTRADICTION OF
WITNESSES. HOW IS IT IF A DISCIPLE NOT BELONGING TO THE
JUDGES SAYS: "I HAVE SOMETHING TO SAY TO HIS ADVANTAGE
OR DISADVANTAGE"? BY WHAT MAJORITY ONE MAY BE AC-
QUITTED AND BY WHAT ACCUSED; AND TO WHAT NUMBER
JUDGES MAY BE ADDED, IF THEY CANNOT COME TO ANY CONCLU-
SION.

MISHNA *I.*: The court used to examine the witnesses with
the following seven inquiries: (a) In what Sabbatic period?
(b) In what year of the latter? (c) In what month? (d) On
what date of the month? (e) On what day? (f) At what hour?
(g) And in what place? R. Jose, however, maintains: "Only
on what day? At what hour? In what place?" And also: Did
you know this man? Did you warn him?

If the crime was idolatry, they were questioned which idols
they worshipped and what kind of worship? He who is more
particular and who enlarges the examination is praiseworthy. It
happened that Ben Sakkai had examined the witnesses concerning the kind and the size of the figs of a certain fig tree which
was connected with the crime.

What is the difference between examination and queries?
In the latter, even if only one answered, "I don't know," the
complaint is dismissed; while in examination, if one of the witnesses, and even two, claim that they did not know, their testimony holds good. In both cases, however, if they contradict
each other, their testimony is ignored. If one says, "It happened on the second of the month," and the second says, "on
the third of it," their testimony holds good, as it is to be supposed that to one was known the intercalation of the last month
and to the other it was not. However, if one says "on the
third" and the other says "on the fifth of the month," their testimony is ignored. If one says "in the second hour" and the
other says "in the third," it holds good; but if one says "in the

third" and the other "in the fifth hour of that day," it is ignored. R. Jehudah, however, maintains that it still holds good;
but if one says "in the fifth hour" and the other says "in
the seventh," even according to R. Jehudah it is ignored, as in
the fifth hour the sun is in the east, while in the seventh hour
it is already in the west.

After one witness was examined they let the second enter
and examined him. And if their testimony correspond, the
discussion begins with the defence. Should one of the witnesses
say, " I have something to say in behalf of the defendant, or one
of the disciples, " I have something to say to the disadvantage of
the defendant," the court silences him. If, however, one of the
disciples says, " I have something to say in his behalf," they take
him out of his place, and set him among them, and he remains there
the whole day; and if his words are reasonable, he is listened to.
Furthermore, if the defendant says, " I have something to say in
my behalf," he is to be listened to if there is something in his
defence. If the judges find a good reason to acquit him, they do
so immediately; and if not, they postpone the trial to the morrow. The judges then go out in pairs, and eat something—not
much, but do not drink wine the whole day. They continue their
discussion (outside of the court) all night, and on the morrow
they come early to the court. He who was among the defenders
says: I defended yesterday, and am still of the same opinion.
The same is it with the accuser—he has to say : I accused, and
am still of the same opinion. The one who has accused may retract from his statement of yesterday, to the advantage of the
defendant. This is not allowed to him who has defended. If
some of them erred in their statements, the scribes of the judges
remind them of it. And again, if the conclusion is to the advantage of the defendant they free him immediately; and if not,
they arise to be numbered. If twelve of them acquit and eleven
accuse, he is acquitted. But if twelve accuse and eleven acquit,
and even if eleven accuse and eleven acquit, but the twenty-third
says, " I am in doubt"; even if twenty-two are for acquitting or
accusing and one says, " I don't know," judges are to be added.
And to what number? Two and two, till the whole number
reaches seventy-one. And then if thirty-six acquit and thirty-
five condemn, he is acquitted; but if *vice versa*, the discussion is prolonged until one of the accusers accepts the opinion
of the acquitters.

GEMARA : Whence is all this deduced? Said R. Jehudah :

From Deut. xiii. 15: "Then shalt thou inquire and make search, and ask diligently." And it reads also [ibid. xvii. 4]: "And it be told thee, and thou hearest of it, thou shalt inquire diligently '; and also [ibid. xix. 18]: "And the judges shall inquire diligently." But perhaps the Scripture does not require seven queries in one case, and it is meant literally (namely, in the crime of a misled town three queries, and concerning idolatry two, and the same also concerning collusive witnesses; as in the former searching is mentioned three times and in the latter searching is mentioned twice). As if seven in one case were needed, let the Scripture state all the above cases together, and then all other criminal cases would be inferred from this. Because searching is mentioned in all three cases above, we infer one from the other, so as to apply everything which is in one case to the others. But the law concerning those cases is not similar, as the case of a misled town cannot be equalized to the other two cases, as they are punished only in their body, but not in their estate; while in the case of a misled town all its estates must be destroyed. Neither can idolatry be equalized to the two cases, as the latter are put to death by the sword, while an idolater is to be stoned. And the case of collusive witnesses is also in one respect more rigorous than the others, as they are put to death withont warning? One is inferred from the other, because of the analogy of the expression "diligently," which is to be found in all the cases, and would be superflous if it were not written for that purpose. And to such an analogy, which comes from a superfluous expression, an objection is not to be made. Hence we infer the case which is to be punished with hanging by an *a fortiori* conclusion, from those which are to be punished by stoning or by the sword; and those by burning, by an *a fortiori* conclusion from those by stoning, etc. But such an *a fortiori* conclusion would be correct if all of the rabbis agreed that stoning is a more rigorous death than all the others. But there are some who hold that burning is more rigorous. Hence, according to them, the above *a fortiori* conclusion could not he drawn. Therefore said R. Jehudah: The seven queries of examination are inferred from [ibid. xiii. 15]: "And behold, if it be true—the thing is certain," which term is again repeated in ibid. xvii. 4. The words "certain" and "true," which are repeated, make four, and in the above three cases "searching" is mentioned seven times. These altogether make eleven, of which seven are to be taken for the seven queries, three of them for an analogy, and the one which remains applies to that case of which the punishment is burning, in accordance with R. Simeon's theory that burning is more rigorous. And concerning the rabbis, who hold that ston-ing is more rigorous, it does not matter if a thing which is to be inferred by the drawing of an *a 'fortiori* conclusion is neverthe-less mentioned in the Scripture.

R. Abuhu ridiculed this statement. Why not say that the superfluous word of the eleven in question is to teach that eight queries are necessary in the examination? Eight queries! What is this? How many minutes are there in the hour? And so, also, a Boraitha states that queries were used. But such a ques-tion is correct, according to Abayi, who said that R. Mair main-tains that one is not liable to err in the minutes at all, or in a few minutes. But according to him, after R. Jehudah, who main-tains that one is liable to err in a half hour, and according to Rabha, who maintains that one can err even in a whole hour, what should be the eighth query? "What period of the jubilee year?" However, he who maintains that the eleventh word mentioned above is applied to something else, maintains that the latter query is not necessary, as they were already questioned: What period of the Sabbatic year?

"*R. Jose said,*" etc. There is a Boraitha: R. Jose said to the sages: According to your theory, if a witness came before the court testifying, "Yesterday this man killed some one," may he be questioned in what period of the Sabbatic year, or in what year, month, and on what day of the month? And he was answered: The same as, according to your theory, that the queries should be: On what day, at what hour, and in what place? How is it if one testifies before the court, "This man has just killed a man"? Nevertheless the above queries are put to him: On what day, and at what hour? Hence, although not necessary, nevertheless he is to be questioned in accordance with the theory of R. Simeon b. Elazar, who maintains that the examination should be made severe, that the witnesses may lose heart in case they do not tell the truth. The same is the case with the other queries—they have to be put although it is not necessary. R. Jose, however, may say: Usually the case is not tried just after the crime is committed, and therefore it is very seldom that the witness has to say: He killed him just now. However, one or a few days after the crime has been committed, it frequently happens that the case is tried.

"*Do you know this man?*" etc. The rabbis taught: The

query was: Do you recognize this man as the murderer of him who was slain? Was he a heathen or an Israelite? Have you warned him? Did he accept the warning? Did he answer in spite of this? Did he commit the crime just after he was warned? And if the crime was idolatry : Which idol has he worshipped— the idol Peor or Markulis? How did he worship it? Did he sacrifice an animal or incense to it, or pour out wine for it, or bow himself down before it?

Ula said : Whence do we deduce that the warning is prescribed biblically? From [Lev. xx. 17] : "And if a man take his sister, the daughter of his father, or the daughter of his mother, and see her nakedness." Is he guilty because he has seen it? It must therefore be said that it means he is aware of the crime (*i.e.*, aware that she is his sister and that it is a crime). Hence the same is it with all other crimes—that he is not to be sentenced unless he was aware that it was a crime ; and to be certain that he was aware, it can only be through warning. And as this verse speaks of a crime for which he is punished with ' korath," which means through Heaven, to which warning is not applied, apply to it the punishment of stripes. The school of Hiskia deduces it from [Ex. xxi. 14] : "But if a man come presumptuously upon his neighbor, to slay him with guile," which means it was presumptuously done even after he was warned. The school of R. Ismael inferred this from [Num. xv. 33] : "And they that find him gathering sticks," which means that after they warned him he still gathered the sticks. And the school of Rabbi deduced this from [Deut. xxii. 24] : " Because he had done violence." *
And all of them are needed; as if it were stated only in the case of his sister, as to which it was explained that it means the punishment of stripes, one might say that this applies only to stripes, but not to capital punishment. Therefore the cited verse in Ex. xxi. And if the two only were stated, one might say that it applies only to a kind of death which is more lenient than stoning, but to the punishment of stoning, which is very rigorous, it does not apply. Therefore all are needed.

The Boraitha states : Did he answer in spite of this? Whence do we know this? Said Rabha, and according to others Hiskia :

---

* The expression in Hebrew is *al dbar asher enah*, etc.—literally, "the thing which he has violated," etc.; and it should be written " because he has violated," without the term "dbar" (thing). The Talmud takes the term "dbar," which means "thing," and which if punctuated "dibur" means "talk," to mean that he was *told* it was a crime and he did not listen.

From [ibid. xvii. 6]: "Shall he that is worthy of death be put to death," which means, provided he answered, "I will do this even should it cause my death."

R. Hanan said: Witnesses who testified in case of a betrothed woman, if they be found collusive, are not to be put to death, as they may say: Our intention was to make it unlawful for her to be his wife only, but not that she should be put to death. But did they not warn her? It speaks of when they did not. But in such a case it is self-evident, as without warning she is not to be put to death. He speaks of a scholarly woman, and this is in accordance with R. Jose b. Jehudah, who said in the follow-ing Boraitha: Warning does not apply to a scholar, as the pur-pose of warning is only to recognize if the perpetrator of the crime did it while he was not aware that such was a crime, or he did it although he was aware; and as a scholar is aware of this crime, no warning is needed. And as they are not to be put to death, she also is exempted from death, as the Scripture requires that the collusive witnesses should be punished with the same punishment as the perpetrator of the crime, if it were true; and as they claim that they intended only to make it unlawful for her to be the wife of her betrothed, such a punishment is not appli-cable to the witnesses, and therefore she also is acquitted.

R. Hisda said: If one of the witnesses testifies that he slew him with a sword and the other says "with a razor," it is not admis-sible. But if one says that the murderer or the one murdered was dressed in white, and the other testifies, "He was in black," it is to be considered admissible. An objection was raised from the following: "It should exactly correspond," means that if one testi-fies that he slew him with a sword and the other with a razor, or if one says that he was dressed in black and the other that he was dressed in white, it does not? R. Hisda explains this Boraitha, that it means if both have testified that he strangled him with a muffler, and one said "It was a white one," and the other said "It was a black one." Come and hear another objection: If one says, "He wore black sandals," and the other says, "white ones," it is not considered corresponding? Also this Boraitha may be explained that he kicked him with his sandals and killed him. Come and hear another objection from our Mishna: It happened that Ben Sakkai examined the witnesses . . . of a certain fig tree? Said R. Jose: Do you want to contradict a man from Ben Sakkai's theory? He was of the opinion that there is no difference between examination and query, and his

theory is individual. Who was Ben Sakkai? Shall we assume
that it means Rabban Johanan ben Sakkai? Was he, then,
among the Sanhedrin? Is there not a Boraitha that the age of
R. Johanan was one hundred and twenty: the first forty years
he was engaged in business, the middle forty he studied, and the
last forty he taught? And there is another Boraitha: Forty
years before the Temple· was destroyed, the Sanhedrin was
exiled from the chamber of the Temple to a store. And R.
Itz'hak b. Abudimi explained that it means that from that time
the Sanhedrin did not try cases of capital punishment. And
there is also a Mishna which states that after the Temple was
destroyed R. Johanan ben Sakkai enacted, etc. Hence we see
that during forty years of his life there were no cases of capital
punishment in the court of the Sanhedrin, and it cannot be that
the examination in question was made by him. Therefore it
must be said that this Ben Sakkai was some one else. And so
it seems to be, as if it were R. Johanan b. Sakkai, how is it possible that Rabbi, the editor of the Mishnayoth, should name him
Ben Sakkai only. But have we not learned in a Boraitha: It
happened that *R. Johanan b. Sakkai* examined . . . the
kind of figs? Therefore it must be said that at that time he was
a disciple who was sitting in the row before the Sanhedrin, and
he said something which was accepted by the Sanhedrin, and
therefore it was established in his name. Hence while he was as
yet a student he was named Ben Sakkai; and afterwards, when
he began to teach, he was named Rabban Johanan. And the
Mishna which mentioned him by the name of Ben Sakkai did so
because when this happened he was·still Ben Sakkai; the Boraitha, however, mentioned him by his name of the latter period.

"*What is the difference between examination?*" etc. How is
to be understood: If two claim, etc.? Is it not self-evident
that if the testimony holds good when one says, "I don't know,"
the same is the case also when two say so? Said R. Shesheth:
This statement applies to the first part—namely, if the investigation shows that two of them are aware and the third says, "I
don't know," even then their testimony is ignored; and it is in
accordance with R. Aqiba, who compares three witnesses to two.
As with two, if there is a difference in their testimony, the case
is to be dismissed, the same is it with three, if even only one of
them says, "I don't know." Said Rabba: How can such an explanation hold good? Does not the Mishna state that their
testimony holds good? Therefore said he: It is to be ex-

plained just in the reverse. Even concerning queries, if two witnesses are aware, but the third one says, " I don't know," their testimony holds good; and it is not in accordance with R. Aqiba.

R. Kahana and R. Saphra used to learn the Tract Sanhedrin in the college of Rabba, and when Rami b. Hama met them, he questioned them : What new have you found in the Tract San-bedrin, as taught by Rabba? And they rejoined : And how would it be if we had learned Tract Sanhedrin other than at Rabba's college—would you ask us for any news? It must be that there is some difficulty to you in this tract. Tell us, then, what it is. And he answered : The statement of the Mishna, which makes a difference between queries and examination—the reason for which is unknown to me. Are not both prescribed biblically? And they answered : What comparison is this? In the inquiry, if one said, " I don't know," their testimony is an-nulled, because the witnesses of such a testimony cannot be made collusive. And there is a rule that such a testimony is not to be taken into consideration ; while in examination, if one said, " I don't know," their testimony still holds good. Hence they re-main legal witnesses who can be made collusive. Rejoined he : If it is so, then you have brought with you very great news. Rejoined they : Because of the kindness of you, master, not to object to us, it may be named good news ; but if you were to use your sagacity to object to us, we would have nothing to say.

"*The intercalation of the month*," etc. Until what date of the current month should the supposition of the ignorance of the intercalation of the last month hold good? Said R. Aha b. Hanina in the name of R. Assi, quoting R. Johanan : Until the greater part of the month is passed (*i.e., e.g.*, if one says, " It was on the twentieth of the month," and the other says, " on the twenty-first," the supposition of the intercalation is not to be taken into consideration, and their testimony is annulled). Said Rabha : This we infer also from our Mishna, which states that, if one says " on the third," and the other " on the fifth," their testimony is ignored. And if the intercalation were taken into consideration, why not say that one of the witnesses was aware of two intercala-tions (*i.e.*, from the last two months), and the other was not aware of it? Hence the reason must be, because one may not be aware of it during the first half of the month, but in the second half it is impossible that he has not heard of it. (Says the Gemara:) This, however, is not to be taken as a support, as it may be said that one is not aware of it even during the second half of the month. And the reason why the Mishna does not say that he was not aware of two intercalations is because, usually, each intercalation was announced by blowing in the cornet; and it could happen that one might overhear one blowing, but not two.

R. Aha b. Hanina said again in the name of the same authority: Until what time may the benediction of the moon be pronounced? Until it becomes more round. But until what date? R. Jacob b. Bibi in the name of R. Jehudah said: Until the seventh. And the sages of Nahardea said: Until the sixteenth. And the basis of both is R. Johanan's statement. They differ, however, in the explanation of it. According to R. Jehudah, his expression, "until it becomes more round," means when it is already half; and according to the others, R. Johanan means a full moon. Said R. Aha of Diphthi to Rabhina: Let one pronounce, after the time of the month's benediction has elapsed, the benediction of "Who is good, and does good to the world," And he answered: Do we then pronounce the benediction of "Blessed is He who judges true" when the moon diminishes, so that we shall pronounce the blessing, "Who is good," etc., after the full moon? But why not pronounce both? Because to a custom no such benedictions are used. The same said again in the name of the same authority: He who pronounces the benediction of the moon in time is considered as if he had received the glory of the Shekinah. And this is deduced from the analogy of the expression "zeh" mentioned in Ex. xiii. 2 and ibid. xv. 2.

In the school of R. Ismael it was taught: If Israel should have only the meritorious act of receiving the glory of their heavenly Father once a month, it would be sufficient. Said Abayi: Therefore we must pronounce the above benediction standing. Miramar and Mar Zutra used to stand shoulder to shoulder, pronouncing this benediction. Said R. Aha to R. Ashi: In the West they used to pronounce the benediction, "Blessed be He who renews the moon." And he answered: Such a blessing our women also pronounce. We, however, have adopted that which was composed by R. Jehudah: "Blessed be He who with His words has created the heavens, and with the breath of his mouth all their hosts, to whom he gave order and time, that they should not change His command; and they rejoice and are happy in doing the will of their creator. They work truthfully,

and what is done through them is truth." *   And to the moon
He commanded that she renew herself every month, and that she
should be a crown and a guide to the people who were selected
by Him from their birth.   It is a symbol to the children of
Israel that, finally, they also will be renewed like unto her (the
moon), and they will praise their Creator, his name, and the glory
of His kingdom.   Blessed be Thou, Eternal, who dost renew the
moon.

[R. Aha b. Hanina in the name of R. Assi, quoting R.
Johanan, said: With whom can you fight a war of the Torah?
With him who posesses bundles of Mishnayoth.   And R. Joseph,
who was a master in Mishnayoth, applied to himself (Prov. xiv.
4): " But the abundance of harvests is (only) through the strength
of the ox." †]

"*If one says, 'in the second hour,'*" etc.   Said R. Shimi b.
Ashi: This is only when they differ concerning the hour; but if
one says, "It was before sunrise," and the other says, "It was
after," their testimony is to be ignored.   Is this not self-evident?
I.e., even if one says, " It was before sunrise," and the other says,
" At the sunrise."   Is this also not self-evident?   Lest one say
that the one who says it was before the rising of the sun stood
at such a place that he could not see it well, he comes to teach us
that it is not so.

"*The whole day,*" etc.   The whole day only?   Have we not
learned in a Boraitha that if they accepted his reasons he remains
with them all the time ; but if his reasons were not accepted, he
nevertheless remains there the whole day to the end that his
descent should not be a disgrace to him?   Said Abayi: Explain,
then, our Mishna that he remains there the whole day if his
reasons were not accepted.

"*They do not drink wine,*" etc.   And why not?   Said R.
Aha b. Hanina: Because of [Prov. xxxi. 4]: "Nor for *rausnim*
(princes) strong drink."   By " rausnim " is meant that those who
occupy themselves with *raus* (secrets) of the world should not
drink strong drinks.

---

* This benediction, which is copied in the prayer books, is not exact as in the
original Talmud.   And also not of that which was copied by Hananiel, but of that
which was copied by Asher.   And there is a great difference in the translation.   We,
however, have translated according to that of the Talmud, as so is our method.

† It is unknown to us why the passage in the text is inserted here ; it also quotes a
verse from Prov. xxiv., which does not correspond.   However, according to our
method, we could not omit it.

"*The opinion of the acquitter.*" But how is it if he does not accept it? Said R. Aha, and so also R. Johanan: They have to acquit him. Said R. Papa to Abayi: If so, why was he not acquitted previously when they (were still twenty-three)? And he answered: So said R. Johanan: Because they should not leave the court disputing, According to others the answer was: R. Jose of the following Boraitha holds with you. As there is no addition to the court of seventy-one, so there is no addition to the court of twenty-three (but if there is no majority for condemning, the defendant is freed).

The rabbis taught: In civil cases the court may say: The case becomes old. But this cannot be said in criminal cases. What does this mean? If it means it becomes so old that it is hard to reach a conclusion, and that therefore it must be postponed, then the reverse should be the case. It means, in criminal cases they must postpone it, as perhaps they will find some defence, but not in civil. Said Huna b. Monoach in the name of Aha b. Ika: Reverse the Mishna. R. Ashi, however, said: The Mishna must not be reversed, as the expression "become old" means that the matter has received a thorough discussion and may not be further prolonged. An objection was raised from the following: The oldest of the judges may proclaim the case old. And this is correct according to the explanation of R. Ashi, as such a proclamation belongs to the oldest. But according to the first explanation, should the oldest blame himself? Nay, it would be a disgrace if some one else should say this to him. But if he himself proclaims this, there is no disgrace. According to others, it was questioned: How could the oldest praise himself, saying that the matter has become so clear that objection cannot be made? Is it not written [Prov. xxvii. 2]: "Let another man praise thee, and not thy own mouth." With a trial it is different, as it rests upon the shoulders of the oldest; for the Mishna states: After the conclusion, the oldest of the judges proclaims: "You, so and so, are acquitted"; or, "You, so and so, are guilty."

RULES AND REGULATIONS CONCERNING THE EXECUTION BY STON-
ING AND THE MANNER OF HERALDING. HOW THE CRIMINAL
WAS URGED TO CONFESS BEFORE DEATH. THE STRIPPING OFF
BEFORE DEATH OF THE DRESS OF A MALE AND OF A FEMALE.
THE HANGING AFTER STONING, AND HOW IT WAS PERFORMED.

MISHNA *I.*: If the conclusion was to condemn, the guilty
one was taken out immediately to be stoned. The place where
he had to be executed was outside of the court, as it reads [Lev.
xxiv. 13]: "Lead forth the blasphemer." One stood at the gate
of the court with a flag in his hand, and one who rode on a horse
stood so far distant that he could see the signal of the flag in case
there were any. And then if one came before the court, saying,
"I have something to say in his defence," the man raised up the
flag, and he who was on horseback rushed and stopped the pro-
cession; and even if the guilty one himself says, "I have something new to say in my defence," he is to be brought back to the
court, even four and five times, provided there is something in it
which is worthy of consideration. And then, if the court finds that
he is not guilty, he is acquitted, and if not, he is taken back to be
stoned. And a herald goes before him, heralding: So and so, the
son of so and so, is taken to be stoned, because he committed
such and such a crime, and A and B are his witnesses. Every
one who knows something in his defence may come and tell it
before he is executed.

GEMARA: Was, then, the place of execution outside of the
court only? Does not a Boraitha state that it was outside of all
the three camps (when they were in the desert), and when they
were in the cities the place of execution was outside of them?
Yea! it is as you say, and the expression of the Mishna, "outside
of the court," means that if it happened that the court took
its place outside of the three camps or outside of the towns,
even then the place of execution must be outside of the court,
for the purpose that it should not appear that the court itself
executed him, or for the purpose that there should be a proces-

sion, to give time to one who might have some defence for the guilty.

Whence is this deduced?   From that which the rabbis taught: It reads: "Lead out the blasphemer to without the camp," meaning out of all the three camps.   But perhaps only out of one camp?   There is an analogy of the expression "camp" which is mentioned here, with that in the case of the burning bullocks [ibid. iv. 20]: "And he shall carry forth the bullock to without the camp, and burn him"; and as there it means outside of all three camps, as explained elsewhere, the same is the case here. R. Papa, however, maintains that this is to be inferred from the following: Let us see.   Moses sat in the camp of the Levites, and the Merciful One said to him: "Lead out the blasphemer to without the camp."   Hence, out of the camp of the Levites. And thereafter it reads [ibid. xxiv. 23]: "And they led forth the blasphemer to without the camp, and they stoned him," which means out of the camp of the Israelites.

But is not the verse necessary in itself, to state that it was done as Moses commanded?   This is written plainly farther on: "And the children of Israel did as the Lord had commanded Moses."   But to what purpose is it written, "they have stoned him with stones?"   It is already written they did it, and it is self-evident that they stoned him?   It is needed, as we have learned in the following Boraitha: It reads, "they stoned him with a stone," which means him—his body—but not his garments; i.e., they had to undress him before the execution. "With a stone" means that if he dies by the first stone no others are needed.   In Num. xv. 35 it reads: "With stones," in the plural.   And both expressions are needed, as if it were stated only in the singular, one might say that one stone should be thrown, and should it not cause death, no other stones must be thrown; and if it were mentioned in the plural only, one might say that many stones are needed to start with.   Therefore both are stated.*

But how could R. Papa differ from the Boraitha mentioned above?   Does not the Tana state it was said so?   Hence the analogy of expression was traditional, to which an Amora had no right to object.   The Tana meant to say that if there were not a verse it could be inferred from the analogy; but inasmuch as there is a verse, the analogy is not necessary.   R. Ashi said

* Leeser translates all the verses in the plural ; in the text, however, in Leviticus it is in the singular and in Numbers in the plural.

that from the same cited verse this is inferred. Let us see! Moses was in the camp of the Levites, and the Merciful One commanded him: "Lead out the blasphemer," etc.—meaning from the camp of the Levites. "Out of the camp," means the camp of Israel.

"*One stands with a flag,*" etc. R. Huna said: "I am certain that the stone with which the executed was stoned, as well as the tree upon which he was hanged, the sword with which he was slain, and also the cloth with which he was choked must be at the expense of the congregation. However, I doubt who had to bear the cost of the flag and the horse mentioned in the Mishna. The defendant, as they are provided only for his sake, or the congregation, because they are obliged to do all they can to save him? I am in doubt also as to that which was said by R. Hyya to R. Ashi in the name of R. Hisda. When one was going to be killed, they used to put a grain of frankincense in a goblet of wine and gave him to drink, so that he should become dazed. As it is written [Prov. xxxi. 6]: "Give strong drink unto him that is ready to perish, and wine unto those who have an embittered soul." And there is a Boraitha that the wine and the frankincense were donated by the respectable women of Jerusalem. Now, if it happened that they were not donated, who must bear the expense? Says the Gemara concerning the latter: Common sense dictates, at the expense of the congregation, as the verse reads "give," which means the congregation.

R. Aha b. Huna questioned R. Shesheth: How would it be if one of the disciples said, "I have something to say in behalf of the defendant," and thereafter he became dumb? Gestured R. Shesheth, saying: Then we would have to consider that there was some one at the other end of the world who had some defence for him. But, after all, it was said by the disciple that he had a defence, and when he became dumb, would it not be right for the court to investigate again—perhaps they would find out what he meant? Come and hear that which was said above by R. Jose b. Hanina: If one of the disciples who defended him at the time of the discussion dies, it will be seen at the time of the conclusion whether he is still alive and defends him. Hence we see that if he has already defended, and he says: "I have something to say in his defence," and he becomes dumb before he gives his reasons, it is not to be taken into consideration. Rejoined R. Aha: Notwithstanding that it is certain to you that R. Jose meant when his defence was already made by him, but not otherwise, it is still a question to me.   For perhaps R. Jose said so because it is usual, if one has something to say, that he says it immediately; but if it happened that he became dumb before telling the reasons, it might be that even R. Jose would admit that the court must look the matter up again.

"*Which is worthy of consideration,*" etc.   Does the Mishna mean that for the first two times it must be examined while he is yet at his place—if there is something, etc.?   Have we not learned in a Boraitha, that the first two times he is to be brought back to the court, even if he does not give a good reason; and only at the third time it is to be examined if there is something in his defence before he is taken back?   Said R. Papa: I interpret it that the Mishna means after the second time.   But who decides whether it is a good reason or not?   Said Abayi: After the second time the court appoints a pair of the rabbis to follow him, and if he has something to say, they examine him and decide if there is a good reason to take him back or not.   But why should not the same rabbis be appointed previously, so that even at the first time he should not be brought back unless the rabbis found a good reason?   Because he is affrighted he cannot say at the beginning all he wishes to say.

"*Such and such a crime,*" etc.   Said Abayi: "The herald must also proclaim the day, the hour, and the place, for the purpose that perhaps there will be found some people who know that the witnesses were not in that place on that day or at that hour, and they will come to make them collusive.

"*The herald goes before him,*" etc.   It means only when he is already sentenced, but not before.   R. Jehoshua b. Levi said: Him who repents and mortifies his passions after they have taken a firm hold of him, and he confesses before Heaven, the verse considers him as if he should glorify the Holy One, blessed be He, in both this world and the world to come.   As it is written [Ps. l. 23]: "Whoso offereth thanksgiving, glorifieth me."*   The same said again: When the Temple was in existence, if one brought a burnt-offering the reward for such was with him; a meat-offering, the reward of such was with him: but him who is modest, the verse considers him as if he should sacrifice all the sacrifices mentioned in the Scripture.   As it reads [ibid. li. 19]: "The sacrifices of God are a broken

---

* The term in Hebrew is "zobeach touhda yichabdon'ni"—literally, "He who slaughters thanks-offering, glorifieth me"; and as the last word is written with a double Nun instead of one, he infers both worlds.

9

spirit." Furthermore, his praying is never despised, as it reads farther on : " A broken and a contrite heart, O God, wilt thou not despise."

MISHNA *II.* : When he (the guilty one) was far from the place of execution—a distance of ten ells—he was told to con_fess, as so is the custom, that all who are to be executed should confess, and they who do so have a share in the world to come. And so do we find with Achan, to whom Joshua said: " My son, give . . . and make confession." And [ibid., ibid. 20] Achan answered Jehoshua: " Truly, I have sinned, and thus and thus have I done." And whence do we know that he was atoned after his confession? From [ibid., ibid. 25]: " And Joshua said, How hast thou troubled us! So shall the Lord trouble thee this day." *This day*—but not in the world to come. However, if the guilty one does not know how to confess, he is told to say : My death shall atone for all my sins. R. Jehudah said : If he knew that he was innocent of this crime, he might say : My death shall atone for all my sins, except this one. And R. Jehudah was answered : If it were so, all those who were to be executed would say so, to the end that they should be innocent in the eyes of the people.

The rabbis taught : In the verse cited—in what Jehoshua said to Achan—the term "na" is used, and "na" means "I pray." At the time the Holy One, blessed be He, saw [Joshua, vii. 11] : " Israel hath sinned," Jehoshua said before Him : " Lord of the Universe, who has sinned?" To which He answered: "Am I a talebarer, to tell you who. Go and draw lots." And he did so, and the lot fell on Achan. And he said to him : Joshua, do you accuse me on account of a lot? Thou and Elazar, who are the greatest of this generation, if I were to draw lots between thee and him, to one of you the lot would fall. And Jehoshua re-joined : I pray thee, do not discredit the decision of the lots, as the land of Israel will be divided by lots. As it is written [Num. xxvi. 55] : " Through the lot shall the land be divided." " Give confession!" Said Rabhina : He bribes him with words. We want of you only the confession. Give the confession, and you will be free: And Achan answered Jehoshua, and said : " Truly, I have indeed sinned against the Lord the God of Israel, and thus and thus have I done." Said R. Assi in the name of R. Hanina : Infer from this that Achan had committed a similar crime trice—twice in the days of Moses and once in the day of Jehoshua. As it reads : " And thus and thus I have done."

R. Johanan in the name of R. Elazar b. Simeon said: Five times—four in the time of Moses and once in the time of Jehoshua. As it reads: "I have sinned, and thus and thus I have done." But why was he not punished until the last crime? Said R. Johanan in the name of the same authority: Because Israel was not punished for crimes which were committed secretly until they passed the Jordan.

On this point the Tanaim differ. It is written [Deut. xxix. 28]: "The secret things belong unto the Lord our God, but those things which are publicly known belong unto us and to our children for ever, to do all the words of this law." Why are the words "unto us and to our children" and the Ayin of the "ad" pointed? To teach that they were not punished for secret crimes until they passed the Jordan. So is the decree of R. Jehudah. Said to him R. Nehemiah: Where is the place in which it is written that they were punished for secret crimes at any time? Is it not written in the cited verse, "forever?" Say, then, as they were not punished for secret crimes, so they were not punished for crimes which were done publicly until they passed the Jordan. But why was Achan punished—his crime was in secret? Because his wife and children were aware of it. "Israel hath sinned!" Said R. Abbah b. Zabda: Although he had sinned he was still called an Israelite. And said R. Abbah: This is what people say: "A myrtle which stands between thorns is still a myrtle," and so it is named. In Joshua, vii. 11, five times is "gam" (also) written in the cited verse: Infer from this that he had transgressed all that is written in the five books of Moses.

The Exilarch said to R. Huna: It reads [ibid., ibid. 24]: "And Joshua took Achan the son of Zerach, and the silver, and the mantle, and the wedge of gold, and his sons, and his daughters, and his ox, and his ass, and his sheep, and his tent, and all that he had; and all Israel were with him, and they brought them up unto the valley of Achor." Yea! he had sinned; but wherein had his sons and daughters sinned? And he answered: According to your theory, what had all Israel to do with this? Hence it was only to terrify them. The same was it with his sons and daughters. It reads farther on: "And all Israel burned them with fire and stoned them with stones." * Were they, then, pun-

---

* Leeser has translated this improperly. The real translation is thus: "And all Israel stoned him with a stone, and they burnt them with fire and stoned them with stones. Hence the supposition of Rabbina.

ished with both? Said Rabhina: That which was fit for burning, *e.g.*, silver, gold, and garments, was burned, and those which
were fit for stoning, *e.g.*, oxen and other cattle—were stoned·
It reads [ibid., ibid. 21]: "I saw among the spoil a handsome
Babylonish mantle, and two hundred shekels of silver." Rabh
said: A silk mantle; and Samuel said: A σαραβαλλα. It
reads farther on [ibid., ibid. 23]: "And as they laid them out
before the Lord." Said R. Na'hman: Joshua cast them down
before the Lord, saying: Lord of the Universe, were these little
things worth that the majority of the Sanhedrin should be killed
on account of them? It reads [ibid., ibid., 5]: "And the men of
Ai smote of them about thirty and six men." There is a Boraitha: Thirty-six men were slain. So said R. Jehudah. Said
R. Nehemiah, to him: "Is it, then, written thirty-six? It reads,
"about," and it means that only Joer b. Menasseh, who was
equal to the majority of the Sanhedrin, was put to death.

R. Na'hman said in the name of Rabh: It reads [Prov. xviii.
23]: "The poor speaketh entreatingly, but the rich answereth
roughly." "The poor speaketh," means Moses; and "the rich,"
etc., means Joshua: But why? Is it because he cast them down
before the Lord and said: "Little things," etc.? Did not Pinchas
do the same? As it reads [Ps. cvi. 30]: "Then stood up Phinehas,"
etc. It ought to be written, "vayitpalel," which means, "and
he prayed," instead of "vayiphalel (debated). Infer from this
that he had debated with his Creator. He cast them before the
Lord, saying: "Lord of the Universe, were they, then, worthy
that on account of them twenty-four thousand persons of Israel
should fall?"—as it reads [Num. xxv. 9]. So·said R. Elazar.
And if because of [Joshua, vii. 7]: "Wherefore hast thou caused
this people to pass over the Jordan?"—did not Moses say
similar to this [Ex. v. 22]: "Wherefore hast thou let so much
evil come upon this people?" Therefore it must be said,
because Joshua said at the end of the above-cited verse (7):
"Would that we had been content, and dwelt on the other side
of the Jordan." It reads [ibid., ibid. 10]: "Get the eup," etc.
R. Shilla lectured: The Holy One, blessed be He, said to him:
Thou thyself hast transgressed more than Israel, as I have commanded [Deut. xxvii. 4]: "And it shall be so, as soon as ye are
gone above the Jordan, that ye shall set up these stones," and ye
went a distance of sixty miles before ye did this.

After Shilla went away, Rabh appointed an interpreter and
lectured: It reads [Joshua, xi. 15]: "As the Lord had com-

manded Moses and his servant, so did Moses command Joshua, and so did Joshua; he left nothing undone of all that the Lord commanded Moses." But why is it written, "Get thee up?" It means that the Lord said to him: "Thou thyself hast caused all the evils, because thou didst excommunicate the goods of Jericho, and no crime would have been committed if thou hadst not done so." And this is what is written [ibid. viii. 2]: "Only its spoil and its cattle shall ye take for booty unto yourselves." It reads [ibid. v. 13, 14]: "And it came to pass, when Joshua was by Jericho . . . And he said, No; for as a captain of the host of the Lord, am I now come. And Joshua fell on his face to the earth," etc. How could Joshua do so? Did not R. Johanan say: One must not greet a stranger, with peace in the middle of the night, as perhaps he is a demon, and so much the more must he not bow before him? There it was different, as he said: I am a captain of the Lord. But perhaps he lied? We have a tradition that even the demons do not pronounce the name of the Lord in vain. And then the angel said to him: "Yesterday you abolished the presenting of the daily eve-offering, and to-day you abolished the studying of the law." And to the question, "For which of the two transgressions hast thou come?" he answered: For that of to-day. Hence it reads [ibid. viii. 18]: "And Joshua went that night into the midst of the valley." And R. Johanan said: Infer from this that he had occupied himself the whole night with the deepness of Halakhoth.* Samuel b. Unya in the name of Rabh said: The study of the Torah is greater than the sacrifices of the daily offerings, as the angel said: For that of to-day.

Abayi said to R. Dimi: It reads [Prov. xxv.]: "Do not proceed to a contest hastily, lest (thou know not) what thou wilt have to do at its end, when thy neighbor has put thee to confusion. Carry on thy cause with thy neighbor; but lay not open the secret of another." How do the people of the West explain this passage? And he answered: At the time the Holy One, blessed be He, said to Ezekiel [Ezek. xvi. 3]: "And thou shalt say . . . thy father was an Emorite and thy mother was a Hittite," the arguing spirit (Gabriel) before the Holy One, blessed be He, said: "Lord of the Universe, if Abraham and Sarah should come and stand before thee, and thou saidst to them this, they should become ashamed." "Carry on thy cause with thy

---

* The term in Hebrew, "emek," has two meanings—"valley" and "deep." Hence the explanation of R. Johanan.

neighbor; but lay not open the secret of another." Had he, then (Gabriel) a right to say such a thing? Yea! As R. Jose b. Hanina said: Gabriel has three names—Piskon, Aitmun, Zigoron. *Piskon* means that he argues before Heaven for Israel's sake; *Aitmun* means that he restrains the sin of Israel; *Zigoron* means that when he concludes his defence for Israel and it does not have any effect, none of the other angels would attempt any further defence, being certain that none would accomplish anything if Gabriel had not done so.

It reads [Job xxxvi. 19]: "Hast thou prepared thy prayer before thy trouble came?"* said R. Elazar: One should always proceed with prayer before trouble comes. As if Abraham had not proceeded with his prayer until the trouble between Bith-El and the city of Ai, not one of Israel would have remained alive when the trouble happened at the city of Ai. Resh Lakish said: He who strengthens himself with prayer on the face of the earth has no enemies on the face of Heaven. R. Johanan said: One should always pray mercy, that all shall support his strength to pray, and he should not have enemies to accuse him in Heaven.

"*Atoned after confession*," etc. The rabbis taught: Whence do we know that his confession has made atonement for him from Joshua: "How hast thou troubled us! so shall the Lord trouble thee this day." *This day*, but not in the world to come. And it is also written [1 Chron. ii. 6]: "And the sons of Zerach: Zimri and Ethan, and Heman and Calcol and Dara, in all five." To what purpose is it written "in all five"? It means all five have a share in the world to come. Here it reads "Zimri," and in Joshua he is named Achan. Rabh and Samuel—according to one, his name was Akhan. And why is he named Zimri? Because his acts were according to Zimri of the Pentateuch. And according to the other his name was Zimri. And why is he named Akhan (circle)? Because he caused the sins of Israel to rest upon them like a circle.

"*To the end that they should be innocent*," etc. But what harm could he do, if he should say so? He could cast suspicion on the court and the witnesses. The rabbis taught: It happened with one who was going to be executed, that he said: If I am guilty of this crime, my death shall not atone for all my sins. And if I am innocent of this crime, my death shall atone for all

---

* We translate according to the Talmud. Leeser's translation, among others, does not correspond.

my sins, and I have nothing against the court and all Israel; but to the witnesses I do not surrender my innocence, and they shall not be atoned for, for ever. When the sages heard this, they said: It is impossible to bring him back, as the sentence is already rendered; but he shall be executed, and the collar shall rest upon the neck of the witnesses. Is this not self-evident—for who could trust such a man? The case was, that the witnesses retracted from their first statement. But even then, what did it amount to? Is there not a rule that after testimony has been made and accepted no retraction can take place? The case was, that they gave a good reason for their retraction, and nevertheless they were not listened to. (So did it happen with the contractor Bar Mayon.) *

---

* Rashi thus explains this: It happened with a contractor, who was wicked, that he died and was to be buried on the same day as a great man in Israel. And all the inhabitants of the city came to take part in the funeral of the latter, and the relatives of the contractor were also occupied in bearing the coffin of the contractor in the same street, following after the coffin of the great man. Suddenly, however, enemies fell upon them, and all of them left the coffins and ran away, except one disciple, who did not leave the coffin of his master. Thereafter, when they returned, people exchanged the coffin of the contractor for that of the great man, notwithstanding the disciple's cry that it was an error, and buried the contractor with great honor instead of the great man; and the relatives of the contractor buried the scholar. And the disciple was much grieved because his master was buried in such disgrace and the contractor with such honor. Finally his master appeared to him in a dream, and counselled him not to grieve, saying: Come with me and I will show you my glory in the garden of Eden, and also the place of that wicked man in Gehenna. And the reason why I was punished was because I was present when a scholar was disgraced, and I did not protest. And the contractor prepared a banquet for the governor of his country, and as the governor did not appear he donated the banquet to the poor of the city, and this was his reward. And to the question of the disciple: Till when shall this man be in Gehenna? The answer: Until Simeon b. Shetha shall die and take his place. And what is the sin of b. Shetha? There are many Israelitish women who occupy themselves with witchcraft in the city of Askalon, and Simeon b. Shetha, who is the head of the court, does not seize them. On the morrow this disciple told this to Simeon b. Shetha. And he selected eighty tall young men, gave to every one a big pitcher which contained a mantle, to the end that it should be kept dry, as that day was a rainy day, and told them that they should be careful to complete the task, as there were eighty witches, and every one of them had to lift up one woman, as then they could not employ any more witchcraft. He then visited the witches at their palace, leaving the young men outside. And to the question who he was and what he wanted, he answered: I am a witch, and am come to try how far you are skilled in it. And they said to him: What can you do? To which he answered: To-day is a rainy day, but nevertheless I can bring you eighty young men, all of whom are wrapped in dry mantles. And they said to him: Bring them in. He went out, and at his hint they took out the mantles from the pitchers, wrapped themselves in them, and entered. Each of them lifted up a woman; and so they overcame them, took them out, and all of them were hanged. Their relatives, how-

MISHNA *III.*: When he came to four ells from the place of execution, he was stripped of his garments. If a male, he was covered in front; and if a female, she was covered on both sides. So said R. Jehudah. The sages, however, say: A male was stoned while naked, but not a female.

GEMARA: The rabbis taught: If it was a male, he was covered a little in front, but a female was covered in the greater part of the front and back. So said R. Jehudah. But the sages say: Only a male was stoned while naked, but not a female. And what is their reason? [Lev. xxiv. 14]: " And all the congregation shall stone him." And what does it mean? It cannot be said " him," but not " her " (a female), as it reads [Deut. xvii. 5]: " Then shalt thou bring forth that man or that woman," and therefore it must be said, it means him without his garments, but her with her garments. Hence he is to be stoned while naked, but not a female. R. Na'hman in the name of Rabba b. Abuhu said: (The reason why a woman was not stripped is because it reads [Lev. xix. 18]: " Thou shalt love thy neighbor as thyself," which means, in case he is sentenced to death, select for him a decent death, that he shall not be disgraced.*)

MISHNA *IV.*: The stoning-place was two heights of a man. One of the witnesses pushed him on his thighs (that he should fall with the back to the surface), but if he fell face down, he had to be turned over. If he died from the effects of the first fall, nothing more was to be done. If not, the second witness took a stone and thrust it against his heart. If he died, nothing more was to be done; but if not, all who were standing by had to throw stones on him. Thus [Deut. xvii. 7]: " The hand of the witnesses shall be first upon him, to put him to death, and the hand of all the people at the last."

GEMARA: There is a Boraitha: With his own height he was

---

ever, who grieved over them, plotted against Simeon's son, and two of them plotted together that their false testimony concerning a crime which results in capital punishment should correspond, and so testified before the court, and he was condemned. And when he was brought to be executed, he said : If I am guilty of this crime, etc. After the witnesses heard this they retracted, and gave the execution of the women as a reason for their false testimony ; and nevertheless he was executed. This legend is to be found in the Palestine Talmud—Tract Hagigah, Chapter II.—with many changes ; and according to the Aruch, the name of this contractor mentioned was Bar Mayon.

* In the text there is repeated here a contradiction from Tract Souteh, its proper place, which we therefore omit.

thrown down from the height of three men.   Was such a height
necessary?   Does not a Mishna in First Gate state that as a
pit which causes death is of ten spans, so all other heights which
may cause death must be no less than ten spans.   Hence the
height of ten spans is sufficient?   Said R. Na'hman in the name
of Rabba b. Abuhu: From the above-cited verse [Lev. xix.],
it is inferred that a decent death must be selected for him.   If
so, why not from a still higher place?   Because his body would
be mangled.

"*One of the witnesses pushed him*," etc.   The rabbis taught:
Whence do we know that he must be pushed?   From [Ex. xix.
13]: "But he shall surely be stoned, or shot through."   From
the term "yorauh yeyoreh," which means pushing.   And
whence do we know that he must be stoned?   From the term
"soqueul."   And whence do we know with both stoning and
pushing?   Therefore it reads "soquoul yisoquel auyorauh yeyoreh."   And whence do we know that when he died from
pushing nothing more was to be done?   From "au," which
means "or."   And because the term is future, we infer that
the same shall be in later generations.

"*Took a stone*," etc.   Took!   Have we not learned in a
Boraitha: R. Simeon b. Elazar said: There was a heavy stone,
which two men had to carry, and this he took and thrust against
his heart, and if he died he fulfilled his duty.   (Hence if two
men had to carry it, it could not be taken by one.)   He lifted
it up with the support of his comrade, and then he alone threw
it, that the blow should be stronger.

"*To throw stones*," etc.   Is there not a Boraitha: It never
happened that he did not die from the hand of the witnesses, so
that one should need to throw another stone?   Does, then, the
Mishna state that it was so done?   It states, "should it be
necessary."

The master said: "There was a stone," etc.   But does not
a Boraitha state that the stone with which he was stoned, as
well as the tree upon which he was hanged, or the sword with
which he was killed, or the muffler with which he was choked,
must be buried with him?   It means that before it was buried
they prepared another like it, which remained.   But is there
not another Boraitha which states that the above things were
not buried with the one executed?   Said R. Papa: It does not
mean that it was buried just with him, but near him, at a distance of four ells.

Samuel said: If before the execution the hands of the witnesses were cut off, he becomes free from death, because the
commandment, " the hand of the witnesses should be on him
first," cannot be fulfilled.   But if so, should witnesses who have
no hands be disqualified?   There it is different, as the verse
reads, " the hand of the witnesses," which means that when they
testified they had hands.   An objection was raised from the following: Every one, of whom two witnesses testify that he was
sentenced at such and such a court, and A and B were his witnesses, he is to be put to death.   Hence we see that in any case
he is executed?   Samuel may explain the Boraitha that it means
that the witnesses themselves testified that they were witnesses
in the former court.   But is it indeed needed that it should be
done as the verse dictates?   Is there not a Boraitha: It reads
[Num. xxxv. 21]: " He that smote him shall surely be put to
death; (for) he is a murderer."   We know that one is to be
put to death by that which applies to him; but whence do we
know that if it is impossible that he should be killed by that
which applies to him, he is nevertheless to be executed by any
death which is possible?   From the verse cited, " he shall surely
die," which means in any case?   That case is different, as it
reads, " he shall surely die."   But let all other cases be inferred
from it?   Because the verse cited, which speaks of a murder,
and the verse which speaks of the avenger of the one murdered, are two verses which dictate one and the same thing
(death), and there is a rule that from two such verses nothing
is to be inferred.   What verse of the avenger is meant?   [Ibid.,
ibid, 19]: " The avenger of the blood himself shall slay."   Infer from this that it is a meritorious ʼact for the avenger to do
so himself.   And whence do we know that if the murdered one
had none such, that the court is obliged to appoint one?   From
the end of the verse, "when he meeteth him, shall he slay him?"
Said Mar the elder b. R. Hisda to R. Ashi: How can one say
that it is not needed as the verse dictates?   Does not Mishna 5
in Chapter viii. of this tract state that it must be done just as the
verse dictates, and it is deduced from the Scripture.   With the
verse cited in the Mishna in question it is different, as that verse
is altogether superfluous, and is written only so that it should
be done just as it dictates.   But does not a Boraitha say in the
eleventh chapter, concerning a misled town, that if there was
not a main street in this city, according to R. Ismael such is not
to be recognized as a misled town, as the verse dictates, " You

shall gather all its goods in the main street," and according to R. Aqiba a main street should be made? We see, then, that they differ only if such should be made or not, but both agree that it must be done just as the verse dictates? In this case Tanaim differ, as a Mishna in Tract Negaim (xiv. 9) states: If he (referring to Lev. xiv. 25) lacked the thumbs of his right hand and foot, or the right ear, he can never be purified. R. Eliezer, however, said: It may be done at the place they are lacking. And R. Simeon said: It shall be placed on the left one.

MISHNA *V.*: All who are stoned are also hanged. So is the decree of R. Eliezer. The sages, however said: Only a blasphemer and an idolater are hanged (but no others). A male is hanged with his face toward the people, and a female with her face toward a tree. So R. Eliezer. The sages, however, say: A male is hanged, but not a female. Said R. Eliezer to them: Did not Simeon b. Shetha hang females in the city of Askalon? And he was answered: He hanged eighty women in one day, and there is a rule that even two must not be sentenced in one day, if the punishment is with the same death. (Hence Simeon's act was only temporary, because of the need of that time, and nothing is to be inferred from it.)

GEMARA: The rabbis taught: It reads [Deut. xxi. 22]: " And he be put to death, and thou hang him on a tree." And lest one say: " All who are put to death must also be hanged," therefore it is written in the second verse [ibid., ibid. 23] : " For he that is hanged is a dishonor of God " (a blasphemer), and as a blasphemer is to be stoned, the same is the case with all others who are to be stoned. So R. Eliezer. The sages, however, say: that as with a blasphemer who has denied the cardinal principle of our faith (*i.e.*, he does not believe in God), the same is the case with an idolater who denies the might of God, but all others who are stoned are not to be hanged. And what is the point of their difference? According to the rabbis, when there is a general expression and an explicit statement, we infer from the general expression and from the explicit statement which comes after it. And R. Eliezer infers from additions and exclusions. According to the rabbis, " He should be put to death and hanged," is a general expression; " The dishonor of God—hangs," is an explicit statement. And if they were in one verse it might be said, that the general expression applies only to that which is in the explicit statement; viz., only those which are mentioned in that case, but no others. But as they are in two verses, we infer from these an idolater, who is equal to a blasphemer in all particulars. And according to R. Eliezer, "He shall be put to death and hanged," is considered an addition; "the dishonor of God" is considered an exclusion. And if they were in one verse, we would add an idolater only; but, seeing that they are in two verses, all the cases of stoning are to be added.

"*A male is to be hanged,*" etc. What is the reason of the rabbis? It reads, "thou hang him," which means him, but not her. And according to R. Eliezer, it means him, without his garments; and the rabbis also hold this theory. But as it reads, "And if a man has committed," etc., it means a man, but not a woman. And R. Eliezer infers from the word "man," to exclude a stubborn and rebellious son. But is there not a Boraitha which states that, according to R. Eliezer, even a stubborn and rebellious son is stoned and hanged? Therefore said R. Na'hman b. Itz'hak: R. Eliezer infers from this to include a stubborn son, and his reason is this: It reads, "If a man," meaning a man, but not a son; "committed a sin," means he is put to death, because he has already committed a sin; but a stubborn son is put to death, not because he has sinned, but because in the future he will sin. And this is an exclusion after an exclusion, of which the rule is, that it comes to add.

"*Said R. Eliezer to them,*" etc. Said R. Hisda: Two must not be judged on the same day, provided there are two kinds of death; but if there is only one kind, two may be judged. But was not the case of Simeon b. Shetha one kind of death? And nevertheless it was said to him: Two cases of capital punishment must not be judged on one day. Therefore if it was taught in the name of R. Hisda, it was thus: Provided there is one kind of death applicable to two kinds—namely, for two separate crimes; but if there was only one crime, and only one kind of death, it may. R. Ada b. Ahabah objected from the following: Two must not be judged in one day, even in the case of adultery —the two adulterers, he and she? R. Hisda explained this Boraitha, that it speaks of a daughter of a priest, and her paramour, in which case, according to the law, she is to be burned and he is to be stoned. Hence there are two different kinds of death. There is a Boraitha: R. Eliezer b. Jacob said: I have heard that the court may punish with stripes and even capital punishment, not in accordance with the biblical law—not with the intention to violate the law, but to make a safeguard for it.

So it happened with one who rode on a horse on Sabbath, at the time Palestine was under the Greeks, and this man was brought before the court, and stoned, not because he deserved such a punishment, but because it was a necessity of that time, to warn others. And it also happened that one had connection with his wife under a fig tree, and he also was brought to the court, and was punished with stripes, not because he deserved such a punishment, but because of the necessity of that time.

MISHNA *VI.*: How was one hanged? The beam was put in the earth, and it was fastened at the top, and he tied the hands of the culprit one upon the other, and hung him up. R. Jose said: The beam was not put in the earth, but the top of it was supported by the wall, and he hung him up as the butchers do, and he took him off immediately. And should he leave him over night, he transgressed a negative commandment, as it reads [Deut. xxi. 23]: "Thou shalt not leave his corpse on the tree over night, but thou shalt surely bury him on that day (for he that is hanged) is a dishonor of God," etc. How so? "Why is this man hanged?" "He is a blasphemer." Hence the name of Heaven is violated. [Said R. Mair: When a man is in trouble, in what language does the Shekinah lament over him? Qalleni meiraushi, qalleni miz'raay.* Now, if the Omnipotent grieves over the blood of the wicked which was shed, so much the more about the blood of the upright!] And not only of him who was executed it was said that he should not remain over night? But even every one who leaves unburied his corpse over night transgresses the negative commandment. However, if he left it over night for the sake of its honor, as for instance to prepare for it a coffin or shroud, he does not transgress.

The one executed was not buried in the cemetery of his parents, but two cemeteries were prepared by the court, one

---

* We cannot find in the English idiom any equivalent for this. In the German translation of the Mishna (Berlin, 1823) it is translated in accordance with Rashi. "Wie lässt sich gleichsam die Gottheit bei solcher Gelegenheit aus? Mein Kopf ist mir zu schwer! Meine Arme sind mir zu schwer!" notwithstanding that such is objected to by Rabha in the Gemara farther on, and his explanation is: As one who is in trouble says, "The world is ignominous to me." And all this is taken from the term "qillelath elohim" [Deut. xx. 23], (translated by Leeser "dishonor of God"), which one reads, "qal leth," literally, "not easy," and the other "qollal-eth," literally, "an ignominy" (according to Thosphath and Hananel). And therefore it seems to us better to give the original expression of the Mishna, without any explanation, leaving the matter to the reader, as we could not omit it, according to our method.

for those who were slain with a sword and choked, and one for those who were stoned and burned. After the flesh of the corpse was consumed, the relatives gathered the bones and buried them in their right place. And the relatives came, and greeted in peace the judges, as well as the witnesses, to show they had nothing in their heart against them, as the judgment was just. The relatives also did not lament for him loudly, but mourned in their heart.

GEMARA: The rabbis taught: If the verse read, " If a man committed a sin, he shall be hanged," we would say that he should be hanged until death occurs, as the government does; but it reads, " He shall be put to death and hanged," which means he shall be put to death and thereafter hanged. How was it done? They kept him till near sunset, condemned him, killed him, and then hanged him; one hangs him up, and the other immediately loosens the knot, as his hanging was only to fulfil the commandment.

The rabbis taught: It is written, " on a tree," from which ought to be inferred that it makes no difference if the tree was still attached to the ground or not. Therefore is it written, " Thou shalt surely bury him," from which it is to be understood that everything should be already prepared for the burying. And if the tree were still attached to the ground, it could not be considered prepared, as the tree was not as yet cut off. R. Jose, however, maintains that this verse excludes also a beam which is put in the ground, as it is not considered prepared, for the tree was not as yet taken out from the ground. But the sages say that the taking out is not to be considered.

" *Why is he hanged? Because he is a blasphemer.*" There is a Boraitha: R. Mair used to say: There is a parable. To what can this be compared? To two twin brothers, one of whom was selected for a king and the other became a robber, and was hanged at the command of the king. Now, people who saw him hanged would say that the king was hanged, and therefore the king commanded the corpse to be taken off (*i.e.*, as man was created in the image of God).

" *And not only for him who was executed,*" etc. R. Johanan in the name of R. Simeon b. Jochi said: Where is to be found an allusion to this in the Torah? In " thou shalt surely bury him." King Sabur questioned R. Hama: Whence do you deduce from the Torah that one must be buried? And the latter remained silent—without answer. Said R. Aha b. Jacob: The world is transferred into the hands of fools. Why did he not answer from the above-cited verse? Because the above is to be explained that it means a coffin and shroud are to be prepared for him. But let him say: Because all the upright were buried. This is only a custom, and not a command of the Torah. And why not say: Because the Holy One, blessed be He, buried Moses? It may be said that this also was not to change the custom. Come and hear [I Kings, xiv. 13]: "And all Israel shall mourn for him, and bury him." This, also, was not to change the custom. But is it not written [Jer. xvi. 4]: "They shall not be lamented for; nor shall they be buried"? Them Jeremiah cautioned, that with them should be a change of custom.

The schoolmen propounded a question: Is the burying because the corpse shall become disgraced if not buried, or is it because of atonement? And what is the difference? If one says, "I do not wish to be buried," if it is because of the disgrace, he must not be listened to; but if it is for atonement, he should be listened to, as he says, "I don't want any atonement." Come and hear! "Because all the upright were buried." And if the reason should be for atonement, do, then, the upright need atonement? Yea, as it reads [Eccl. vii. 20]: "For no man is so righteous upon earth that he should do always good, and never sin." Come and hear the above-cited verse about Jeroboam, in which it reads that only he should be buried. Now, if the reason is atonement, why should not the others also be buried and atoned? He who was upright ought to be buried and atoned, the others who were wicked were not worthy to be atoned. The same is the case with them who were cautioned by Jeremiah that they should not be buried, because they were not worthy of atonement.

The schoolmen propounded another question: Is the lamentation an honor for the living or for the deceased? And what is the difference? If, e.g., one says, "I do not wish to be lamented," if it is an honor for the deceased only, he may be listened to; and if for the living, he may not. Or, on the other hand, if his heirs do not want to pay the mourner, if it is an honor for the deceased, they may be compelled to pay; and if it is for the living, they may not. Come and hear [Gen. xxiii. 2]: "And Abraham came to mourn for Sarah, and to weep for her." Now, if this were only an honor for the living, should the body of Sarah have been kept till Abraham came, for his

honor? Nay! Sarah herself was pleased that Abraham should
be honored because of her. Come and hear! "All Israel shall
mourn for him." Now, if it is for the honor of the living, were,
then, the people of Jeroboam worthy to be honored? The upright are pleased that any human being should be honored on
their account. But is it not written that they shall not be
mourned for and buried? The righteous do not wish that they
shall be honored because of the wicked. Come and hear Jeremiah [xxiv. 5]: "In peace shalt thou die; and as burnings were
made for thy fathers, the former kings who were before thee
so shall they make burnings for thee; and, 'Ah Lord,' shall they
lament for thee." Now, if it is to the honor of the living, what
good can this do to Zedekiah? The prophet said to him thus:
Israel shall be honored because of thee as they were honored
because of thy parents. Come and hear! It is said elsewhere
[Ps. xv. 4]: "The despicable is despised," meaning King Hezekiah, who bore the remains of his father on a bed of ropes.
Now, if it is for the honor of the living, why did Hezekiah do
so? For the purpose that his father should have an atonement.
But has he a right to invalidate the honor of Israel because of
the atonement of his father? The people themselves were
pleased to relinquish their honor, because of the atonement of
Achaz. Come and hear what was said by Rabbi in his will: "Ye
shall not lament me in the small cities, but in the large ones."
Now, if it is for the honor of the living, why such a will? He
thought: Let the people be more honored because of me. Come
and hear the statement in our Mishna: If he left it over night
for its honor, to prepare for it a coffin and shroud, he does not
transgress. Hence we see it is to the honor of the dead? Nay,
"for his honor" means for the honor of the living. But has
one the right to leave the corpse over night, for the sake of his
own honor? Yea, as the commandment not to let the corpse
hang was because of the disgrace; but if it is not disgraced, the
honor of the living is to be considered. Come and hear another
Boraitha: If he left him over night for his honor, that his friends
in other cities should hear of his death or bring for him the
lamenting-women, or prepare for him a coffin and a shroud, he
does not transgress the negative commandment; for all he does
is for the honor of the dead? It means to say that all he does
for the sake of his own honor is not considered a disgrace for
the dead. Come and hear another Boraitha: R. Nathan said:
It is a good sign for one deceased if he was punished after his

death; namely, if he was not lamented, not buried properly, or a wild beast seized upon his corpse, or if, while carrying him to burial, rain wet the corpse.   All these are good signs that it was done for his atonement.   Hence we see that all these are to be done for the honor of the dead.   Infer from this that so it is.

"*But two cemeteries*," etc.   And why so?   Because a wicked person must not be buried with an upright one.   As R. Ahha b. Hanina said: Whence do we know that a wicked person must not be buried with an upright?   From [II Kings, xiii. 22]: "And it came to pass, as they were burying a man, that, behold, they saw the hand; and they cast down the man into the sepulchre of Elisha; and as the man came and touched the bones of Elisha, he revived, and rose up on his feet."   Said R. Papa to him: But perhaps this was done to fulfil what is mentioned [ibid. ii. 9]: "Let there be, I pray thee, a double portion of thy spirit upon me."   And as Elijahu restored only one man, so did Elisha also restore one while he was alive; and the second was restored after his death.   And he answered: If it were so, why, then, does a Boraitha state that the restored only stood upon his feet, but did not go home?   And if it were for the purpose said above, he would remain alive.   But if, as you say, Elijahu's promise was not fulfilled?   As it was said by R. Johanan: This was fulfilled with the cure of Na'hman from his leprosy, for leprosy is equal to death.   As it reads [Num. xii. 12.]: "Let her not be as a dead-born child."   And as it is prohibited to bury an upright person with a wicked, so also it is not allowed to bury a lesser wicked with a greater one.   But if so, there should have been four cemeteries.   The two cemeteries were traditional.*

The rabbis taught: They who are put to death by the gov-

* Here are omitted two pages of the text, as their contents are repeated in different places.   Much of it is already translated, and the rest will appear in the proper place.   However, the following difference of Abayi and Rabha is important—namely, according to Abayi, if one dies a usual death, while he is still wicked, without repentance, his death does not make atonement for him.   And the same is the case even if he is executed by the court, if he did not repent.   But if one were slain by the government, his death atones.   And his reason is, because the government does not always act justly in its decisions, while the court does.   But according to Rabha, even if he is executed by the court, death atones ; as, according to him, there is no comparison between a death from a usual sickness and that by an execution ; and therefore in the latter case he is atoned, but not in the former.   And Ameimar said that the Halakha prevails in accordance with Abayi, but the rabbis said that the Halakha prevails with Rabha, with which the Gemara agrees.

ernment, their estates belong to the government; and they who are killed by the court, their estates belong to their heirs. R. Jehudah, however, maintains that their estates belong to the heirs even when they are killed by the government. Said the sages to him : Is it not written [I Kings, xxi. 16] : " And it came to pass, when Achab heard that Naboth was dead, that Achab rose up to go down to the vineyard of Naboth, the Yizreelite, to inherit it "? And he answered: Achab was his brother's son and was a legal heir. But had not Naboth many sons? Rejoined R. Jehudah: He slew him and his sons. As it reads [II Kings, ix. 26] : " Surely I have seen yesterday the blood of Naboth, and the blood of his sons." The rabbis, however, maintain that the expression " sons " means those who would come out from him had he remained alive. It is correct for him who says that the estates belong to the government, as it reads [I Kings, xxi. 13] : Naboth hath blasphemed God and the king." But to him who says the estates belong to the heirs, why was it necessary to add " and the king "? But according to your theory that they belong to the heirs, why was God mentioned? You may say it was done to increase the anger of the people. For the same reason, it was also mentioned, " and the king." It is correct to him that it belongs to the government, as it is written [ibid. ii. 30] : " No; but here will I die "—which means: I do not wish to be counted among those who were killed by the government, so that my estate should belong to it. But according to him who says that it belongs to the heirs, what difference did it make to Joab? The simple one of remaining alive one hour longer. It reads [ibid, ibid. 30] : " And Benayahu brought the king word again, saying, Thus hath Joab spoken, and thus hath he answered me." Joab said to Benayahu thus: Go and tell the king: You cannot do two things with me. If you wish to slay me, you must accept for yourself the curses with which your father cursed me. And if you will not accept them, you will have to leave me alive. Farther on it is said: " Then said the king unto him, Do as he hath spoken, and fall upon him, and bury him." Said R. Jehudah in the name of Rabh: All the curses with which David cursed Joab fell on the descendants of David. They were [II Sam. iii. 29] : " And may there not fail from the house of Joab one that hath an issue, or that is a leper, or that leaneth on a crutch, or that falleth by the sword, or that lacketh bread." The first fell on Rehoboam (this is inferred from an analogy of expression which

we do not deem it necessary to translate); the second—"leper"
—on Uzziyahu. As it reads [II Chr. xxvi. 9]: "The leprosy
even broke out on his forehead." "Leaneth on a crutch"—
Azza, of whom it reads [I Kings, xv. 23]: "Nevertheless, in
the time of his old age he became diseased in his feet." And
R. Jehudah in the name of Rabh said: Podagra caught him.
Said Mar Zutra b. Na'hman to R. Na'hman: What kind of a
sickness is this? And he answered: It pains like a needle in raw
flesh. (Asked the Gemara: Wherefrom did he know this? He
himself suffered from this sickness. And if you wish, he had it
as a tradition from his master; and also, if you wish, from [Ps.
xxv. 14]: "The secret counsel of the Lord is for those that fear
him; and his covenant, to make it known to them.") Falleth
by a sword—on Josiah, as it reads [II Chr. xxxv. 23]: "And
the archers shot at king Josiah; and the king said to his servants, Carry me away, for I am sorely wounded." And R.
Jehudah said in the name of Rabh: They made his body like a
sieve. "Lacketh bread"—fell on Jechonyah [II Kings, xxv.
30]: "And his allowance was a continual allowance," etc. Said
R. Jehudah in the name of Rabh: This is what people say: It is
better for one to be cursed than to curse, as usually a curse in
vain falls upon the invoker—Rashi. Joab was brought before
the court to justify himself for the killing of Abner; and he answered that he was the revenger of the blood of Asahel. But did
not Asahel prosecute Abner? And he haid: Then he could save
himself by striking on one of the members of his body. And to
the question: Perhaps he could not do so? he answered: Did he
not strike him [II Sam. ii. 23] "On the fifth rib"? to which (according to R. Johanan) the bile and the liver are attached. Now,
if he could aim at the fifth rib, could he not do so at some other
member? The court then said: Let us leave out Abner. But
why did you kill Amassa? And he answered: He was a rebel to
the king. As it reads [ibid. xx. 5]: "So Amassa . . . he
remained longer than the set time." And he was answered:
Amassa was not a rebel, as he had a good reason for his delay.*
But you are indeed a rebel, as you were inclined to Adoniyahu
against David's will. It reads [I Kings, ii. 28]: "And the report came to Joab; for Joab had turned after Adoniyahu,
though he had not turned after Abshalom." Why is it mentioned here that he had not turned after Abshalom? Said R.

---

* In the text the reason is given, but if translated it would not sound well in
English; and, besides, it is unimportant, and therefore omitted.

Jehudah: He was inclined to turn, but did not. And why? Said R. Elazar: Because the " moisture of David " was still in a good condition. And R. Jose b. Hanina said: Because the active force of David were still in their strength. As it is said above (p. 55) in the name of Rabh: " Four hundred children," etc. All the Amoraim mentioned above differ with R. Abbah b. Kahana, who said: " If not for Joab, David would not have been able to occupy himself with the law; and if not for David, Joab would not have been able to wage the war. As it is writ-ten [II Sam. viii. 16 and 17]: " And David did what is just and right unto all his people. And Joab the son of Jeruyah was over the army." It means that, because Joab was over the army, David was able to do justice, etc.; and also *vice versa*. It reads [ibid. iii. 26]: " Who brought him back from the well of Sirah." What does " well of Sirah " mean? Said R. Abbah b. Kahana: The well means the pitcher of water which David took from under the head of Saul; and Sirah—literally " a thorn "—means the piece of cloth which David cut off from the garment of Saul, which were good reasons for Abner to reconcile Saul with David, if he should care to do so; but he did not. It reads farther on [ibid., ibid. 27]: " Joab took him aside in the gate, to speak with him in private." Said R. Johanan: He brought him before the Sanhedrin to try him for having killed his brother Asahel. And to his answer that Ashael was his persecutor, he was told as said above. It reads [I Kings, ii. 32]: " And may the Lord bring back his bloodguiltiness upon his own head, because he fell upon two men more right-eous and better than he." Better than he? Because they were commanded verbally (to kill the priests of Nob) and did not listen, and Joab was commanded in a letter to kill Uriah, and he listened. It reads farther on [ibid., ibid. 34]: " And he was buried in his own house in the wilderness." Was, then, his house in the wilderness? Said R. Jehudah in the name of Rabh: It was like a wilderness. As a desert is ownerless, and every one who wishes can derive a benefit from it, so was the house of Joab. And also as a desert is free of robbery and adultery, so was the house of Joab. It reads [I Chr. xi. 8]: " And Joab repaired the rest of the city." Said R. Jehudah: Joab supplied to the poor of that city everything to which they were accus-tomed, even little things and fishes.

CHAPTER VII.

MIHSNA *I.*: Four kinds of capital punishment are prescribed to the court by the Scriptures; viz., stoning, burning,
slaying by the sword, and choking. R. Simeon, however, maintains: Their order is: burning, stoning, choking, and slaying by
the sword. The laws of stoning are already explained above
(in the preceding chapter).

GEMARA: Rabha in the name of R. S'hora, quoting R.
Huna, said: Where the sages give an arrangement (plan of ac-
tion), one must not be particular with it, as it does not matter
if one changes the order and acts with the latter before the
former, except in the case of the seven dyes with which a spot
of menstruum is to be tested, which are mentioned in Chapter
IX., Mishna 4, of Tract Nida, of which the Mishna says: If one
tested with them not according to the order mentioned, or one
mixed all the seven together and tested with them, he has done
nothing. R. Papa the Elder in the name of Rabh said: The same
is the case in the four kinds of capital punishment mentioned in
our Mishna. As R. Simeon differs in their order, it must be
understood that the Mishna is particular in their arrangement.
But why does not R. Huna mention them? R. Huna speaks
of that in which all agree, but where there is dissension he does
not. R. Papa himself said: Also concerning the arrangement
of worshipping on the Day of Atonement (when the Temple
was in existence), as there is a Mishna (Yoma, p. 84). All the
rites on the Day of Atonement, whose order is prescribed by
the Bible . . . if they are performed in a wrong order, one
has done nothing. R. Huna, however, did not mention this.

For the reason of not changing the order prescribed by the
Scripture is because of the holiness of that day, and not because
one act is more rigorous than the other. R. Huna b. R. Jehoshua maintains that the order of the daily offerings is also not
changeable, as there is a Mishna (in Tract Thamid): *This* is the
arrangement. However, R. Huna, who did not mention it,
maintains that this is only meritorious. And the rule mentioned above in the name of R. Huna excludes also the ceremony of Halitzah, and also the dressing of the priests at their
worship in the Temple, as explained elsewhere.*

"*Stoning, burning,*" etc. Stoning is more rigorous than
burning, as blasphemers and idolaters are punished with it.
And why are these two crimes considered more rigorous than
others? Because the sinners laid their hands on the main principle of the Jewish faith (*i.e.,* disbelief and denying the power
of God). But why not say, on the contrary, that burning is
more rigorous, as it applies to the daughter of a priest who has
sinned? And why should this crime be more rigorous? Because it reads that she violates her father, which means that her
father loses his priesthood. The rabbis hold that only a married woman who was the daughter of a priest is to be burned
if she sinned; but if betrothed, stoning is applied. And because
a betrothed woman is distinguished from a married one, who
bears the name of her husband and not of her father, while a
betrothed still bears the name of her father, we see that stoning
is more rigorous. The same is also more rigorous than slaying
by the sword, because of the reason stated above. But why not
say that the sword is more rigorous, because it applies to the
men of a misled town? And what is the rigor of a misled town
—that their property is to be destroyed? It may be answered
that a misleader is always considered more criminal than those
who are seduced. And there is a Boraitha that the punishment
of a misleader is stoning. Stoning is also more rigorous than
choking. And lest one say that choking is more rigorous, as it
applies to one who strikes his father or mother, and the rigor is
because the honor of the parents is equalized with the honor of
the Omnipotent, it is inferred from the case of a daughter of a
common Israelite, who is excluded from choking, which applies
to a married daughter of the same, and is included in the category of stoning; and it is already explained above that a be-

---

* Mishnas mentioned in the text will be translated in their proper places.

trothed disgraces her father and his whole family, while the disgrace of a married one belongs more to her husband.*

Burning is more rigorous than the sword, as it applies to a sinning daughter of a priest, whose crime is more rigorous for the reason stated above.   But why not say, on the contrary: The sword is more rigorous, because it applies to a misled town, the property of which is to be destroyed?   We find the term "her father" concerning stoning, and the same term is used concerning burning.   And it is to be said: As the term "her father," used concerning stoning, is more than the sword, the same is it with the term which is used by burning—that burning is also more rigorous than the sword.

Burning is also more rigorous than choking.   This is inferred from the fact that a married daughter of a priest is excluded from choking, which applies to a married daughter of a common Israelite, and is included in the category of burning. And lest one say that choking is more rigorous, as it applies to him who has struck his father or mother, the honor of whom is equalized with the honor of the Omnipotent, it is already decided above that they who laid their hands on the main principle, etc., are considered the greatest criminals.

"*R. Simeon said,*" etc.   According to him, burning is more rigorous than stoning because it applies to a daughter of a priest who has sinned; and it is considered more criminal because her father loses his priesthood.   And he (Simeon) differs from the rabbis, who make a distinction between a betrothed and a married woman, as according to him both are punished with burning; and because the greatest criminal is punished with burning, it is to be inferred that this punishment is more rigorous than all others.†

R. Simeon also differs concerning the punishment of misleaders of a misled town, as according to him they also are punished with choking.

R. Johanan used to say: A betrothed young girl, who is the daughter of a priest, is to be stoned if she has sinned; but according to R. Simeon, she must be burned.   And the same is

---

* The text here is very complicated, and Rashi, who tries to explain it at length against his method, admits that there may be objections to it, and maintains that the reason of betrothed and married does not hold good.   But the basis is, what is said above, that stoning applies to a blasphemer, etc., who laid their hands on the main principle.   We have done our best to give an idea of the text to the reader.

† Here also is repeated why stoning is more rigorous than the two others, and the same reasons are given, which it is not necessary to repeat.

the case if she had sinned with her father. (Although, if such a case happened with a commoner, burning is applied, nevertheless she is to be stoned, according to the rabbis); as according to their theory stoning is more rigorous, and there is a rule that he who is guilty of two crimes liable to capital punishment is to be executed with the more rigorous one. And according to R. Simeon, that burning is more rigorous, she is to be put to death by that. And where do we find R. Simeon saying so? In the following Boraitha: R. Simeon said: There are already two general expressions about adultery; viz. [Lev. xx. 10]: "Then shall the adulterer be put to death, "together with the adulteress." And this applies either to a betrothed or to a married woman, with whom the daughter of a priest is certainly included. Why, then, does the Scripture distinguish a daughter of a priest [ibid. xxi. 9]: "And if the daughter of any priest profane herself by committing harlotry, her father doth she profane: with fire shall she be burnt," which makes no difference between a betrothed and a married woman? To exclude her from the punishment of a betrothed commoner, to whom stoning applies; and if married, choking applies, and puts her in the category of those who are to be burned. Now, as to the punishment of a married one, which applies to a daughter of a priest, all agree that it is more rigorous than that of a commoner; the same is the case with a betrothed one, whom the Scripture excluded from an easier punishment, for a severer one. Hence burning is more severe than stoning. However, collusive witnesses (to whom, according to the Scripture, the same must be done as to the defendant, if their testimony were true) are not excluded from that punishment which they would have to suffer if they had been found collusive in the case of a daughter of a commoner, and are punished with the death of their accused; no matter if the accused were the daughter of a commoner or of a priest; namely, if they had testified regarding a betrothed one, and thereafter were found collusive; the death which would apply to her, were she a daughter of a commoner, applies to them. And the same is the case if they had testified regarding a married one.

The rabbis taught: It reads: "And if the daughter of any priest profane herself." Lest one say that it means that she profaned herself by violating the Sabbath, Therefore it reads further, "by committing harlotry." But lest one say, even if she were single, it reads here, "her father." And the same expression is used concerning a betrothed woman; as there the sin is because of her bond to a husband, the same is the case here. It is considered a crime liable to capital punishment if she were already betrothed or married. But perhaps it means when she has sinned *with* her father, and not with some one else? Therefore it reads, " she profane," which means that she has profaned him, and not he her. Hence from the analogy of expression, father, we infer that the sin is because of her husband. But from this analogy of expression it is inferred when she was betrothed. Whence do we know that, if she was not of age and nevertheless married, or of age and betrothed or married, or even if she were already an old woman, that the same is the case? Therefore it is written: " And the daughter of any priest," which means, whatever her condition. But lest one say: It speaks only when she was married to a priest, but if to Levite or to a common Israelite, to a heathen, to a descendant of one who has profaned the priesthood, to a bastard, or to a descendant of the Gibeonites who were temple-servants, it is different? Therefore it is written: " The daughter of any priest," which means, even though she was not the wife of a priest. She is to be burned, but not her paramour. She is to be burned, and not her collusive witnesses.

R. Eliezer said: With her father, burning applies; with her father-in-law, stoning applies. How is this to be understood? Shall we assume that he means she has sinned with her father? Then why only a daughter of a priest? Is not the case the same even when she was a daughter of a common Israelite? Burning applies to committing a crime with a daughter, and stoning to the crime with a daughter-in-law. We must then say that with the expression, " with her father," he means when she was still under the control of her father; and the same is it with the expression, " with her father-in-law." Now, let us see in accordance with whom is his theory. It is not in accordance with the rabbis, as they hold that only a married woman is to be burned, but not a betrothed. It is also not in accordance with R. Simeon, as he holds that there is no difference between betrothed and married—both are to be burned. And also not in accordance with R. Ishmael, as he holds that only a betrothed is to be burned, but not one married. And he also holds that if she had committed a crime with her father-in-law, choking applies. As to this, Rabin sent a message in the name of R. Jose b. Hanina: This Boraitha is to be explained thus: It is in

accordance with the rabbis.   And the expression of R. Eliezer,
" with her father," means thus: If such a crime be punished, with
an easier death than if the crime had been committed with her
father—*e.g.*, that of a married woman, daughter of a commoner,
to whom choking applies, in her case, because she is a daughter
of a priest, the death of her father, if he should commit the crime
with her, applies to her—viz., burning.   And if such a crime by
a commoner were punished with a heavier death than if the
crime were with her father—*e.g.*, a betrothed daughter of a
commoner, to whom stoning applies, no exception is to be
made, and the punishment of her sinning with her father-in-law
applies—viz., stoning.   R. Jeremiah opposed: Does, then, the
Boraitha read " easier " and " heavier death," which it should
do according to your explanation?   " Therefore," said he, " it
must be said that R. Eliezer is in accordance with R. Ishmael;
and the expression, ' with her father,' means under the control
of her father—viz., a betrothed, not yet married, to whom
burning applies; and ' with her father-in-law ' means, literally,
if she had sinned with her father-in-law she is to be stoned, but
if with some one else choking applies."

Said Rabha: This explanation is still more complicated than
the first one, as both expressions must be explained equally:
either both are to be taken literally, or both mean " under the
control."   And therefore said Rabbhina: R. Eliezer is in accordance with the rabbis, and his decision was just the reverse.
" With her father," stoning applies, and " with her father-in-
law," burning applies.   And both expressions mean " under
the control."   And although a betrothed woman is no longer
considered under the control of her father, he so expressed himself because of the latter expression, " under the control of her
father-in-law."

Said R. Na'hman in the name of Rabha b. Abuhu, quoting
Rabh: The Halakha prevails according to the message which
was sent by Rabbin in the name of R. Jose b. Hanina.   Said R.
Joseph: Do you come to teach a Halakha which will be used
only then when the Messiah shall appear?   Said Abayi to him:
According to your theory, why should we study the section
Holiness (which treats about sacrifices, at the time when the
Temple was in existence) at all?   Is not the whole for the time
when the Messiah shall appear?   You must then say that we
must study and be rewarded for it by Heaven.   The same is the
case here.   We have to study, although it is not for use to us

at this time, and the reward will come from Heaven." Answered R. Joseph: I mean to say, may one name Halakha in the explanation of a Boraitha (*i.e.*, the message of Rabbin was only concerning the explanation of the Boraitha)? To which it may be said, that such an explanation is correct. The expression "Halakha," however, means "law," which does not correspond with his meaning.

Where do we find R. Ishmael's opinion, of which it is said above that Eliezer holds with him? In the following Boraitha: It reads, "the daughter of any priest profane," etc., speaking of a young betrothed maiden. But perhaps it means a married woman? This is not the case, as the law about adultery is already written in Lev. xx., in which a daughter of a priest is included. However, we find that the Scripture has distinguished a daughter of a commoner, and applied stoning to her, if she was betrothed and not married. The same is the case with the distinction of a priest's daughter, to whom the Scripture applies burning, meaning also when she was betrothed only. Her collusive witnesses, however, are to be punished with the same death that applies to her paramour, because it reads [Deut. xix. 19]: "Then shall ye do unto him as he had purposed to do unto his brother." "To his brother," but not to his sister. So is the decree of R. Ishmael. R. Aqiba, however, maintains: There is no difference whether she was betrothed or married, as in both cases burning applies. And to the question of R. Ishmael: Why should we make a distinction concerning a daughter of a priest, the expression for which is "Naahra" (a maiden), while the same expression is used concerning a commoner who is betrothed only? R. Aqiba rejoined: Ishmael, my brother, I infer it from the word *and*, which begins the verse —" and the daughter of any priest." Rejoined R. Ishmael: "Do you desire that this should be burned, because the Vav (which means *and*) is in your way?

Let us see! R. Ishmael infers the punishment of a priest's daughter from an analogy of expression. How does he explain the above-cited verse, "her father has she profaned"? He explains it as in the following Boraitha: R. Meir used to say: This phrase means that if, until now, their custom was to consider her father holy, from that time they consider him common; if until that time he was honored, from that time he is disgraced. As people say: "Cursed be such a man who has born such a daughter; cursed is he who has brought 'her up; cursed is he that he has such an offspring." Said R. Ashi: According to whom do we name a wicked person, "wicked, the son of a wicked," although his father was upright? In accordance with the Tana of the just-mentioned Boraitha.

MISHNA *II.*: The prescribed punishment of burning was thus: The sinner was placed in waste knee-deep. Then, placing a twisted scarf of coarse material within a soft one, they wound it around his neck. One (of the witnesses) pulled one end toward himself, the other doing the same, until he opened his mouth. Meanwhile the executioner lights (heats) the string, and thrusts it into his mouth, so that it flows down through his inwards and shrinks his entrails. To which R. Jehudah said: Should the culprit die before the string is thrust into his mouth, the law of burning has not been properly executed, and therefore his mouth must be opened forcibly with a pair of pincers. Meanwhile, the string having been lighted, is thrust into his mouth so that it may reach his intestines and shrink his entrails. R. Eliezer b. Zadok, however, said: Once a daughter of a priest, having sinned, was surrounded with fagots and burned. He was answered: The court which so decided was ignorant of the exact law.

GEMARA: What kind of a string was it? Said R. Matnah: A string of lead. And whence is this deduced? They infer this burning from the burning of the congregation of Korah. As there the souls only were burned, but the bodies remained, so also here only the soul is to be burned, but the body is to remain. R. Elazar said: They infer this burning from the burning of the sons of Aaron. As there the souls only were burned and the bodies remained, the same is the case here.

Let us see! He who infers it from the congregation of Korah, wherefrom does he know that the soul, and not the body, was burned? From [Num. xvii. 3]: "The censers of these sinners against their own souls." * Which means that the souls only were burned, but the bodies remained. And the other, who infers it from the sons of Aaron, maintains that this phrase means they were burned bodily, and the expression "own souls" means that they were liable to be burned because of their souls. And it is in accordance with Resh Lakish, who said elsewhere: It reads [Ps. xxxv., 16]: "With flattering, babbling mockers, they gnashed upon me with their teeth," which

---

* Leeser translates "own lives" according to its sense. We, however, translate it literally, according to the Talmud.

means that, because they had flattered Korah for the sake of entertainments (to which he used to invite them), the ruler of Gehenna gnashed upon them with his teeth. And he who inferred this from the sons of Aaron, wherefrom does he know that their souls only were burned, etc.? From [Lev. x. 2]: "And there went out a fire from before the Lord, and consumed them, and they died before the Lord," which means that, although they died before the Lord, they died as all others—only their corpses remained. And the other maintains that the sons of Aaron were burned bodily, and the expression, "they died," means, that the beginning was from inside the body. As we have learned in a Boraitha: Abba Jose b. Dusthai said: Two fire cords came out from the Holy of Holies chamber, and were divided into four: two of them entered the nostrils of one, and two the nostrils of the other, and burnt them. But is it not written, "and consumed them"? From which it is to be inferred "them," and not something else. Yea—"them," and not their garments.

But why should burning not be inferred from the offerings of the bullocks, which were burned bodily? Common sense dictates that a man must be inferred from man, and not from cattle: as a man sins, and one infers a man who has sinned from another man, and from him whose soul was taken for his sin to him whose soul is to be taken. But he who infers it from Korah's congregation—why did he not infer it from the sons of Aaron? Because he maintains that the sons of Aaron were burned bodily, and to infer from them would not be proper, as R. Na'hman said in the name of Rabha b. Abuhu: From the phrase "Thou shalt love thy neighbor as thyself," we deduce that one may select a decent death for the sinner. But as the theory of R. Na'hman is accepted—why, then, the analogy of expressions at all? If not for the analogy, one might say that the burning of the soul, while the body remains, is not called burning at all, and that which is written, "Thou shalt love thy neighbor," etc., could be done by increasing the fire by bundles of fagots so that he should die quickly. Therefore the analogy of expression shows that such a burning, although the body remains, is called burning.

There is a tradition that Moses and Aaron used to walk, and Nadob and Abihu followed them, and all Israel after them. And Nadob said to Abihu: When will the two old men die, and you and I be the leaders of Israel? To which the Holy One,

blessed be He, said: Time will show who will bury whom.   Said
R. Papa: This is what people say: " There are many old camels
who are laden with the skins of young ones."   R. Elazar said:
A scholar, in the eyes of a commoner, at first acquaintance (the
scholar) appears to him (the ignorant man) like a golden kithon.
However, after he holds conversation with him, he appears like
a silver kithon; if he accepts a benefit from him, he appears like
an earthen one, which, once broken, cannot be mended.

Aimretha bath Tli was the daughter of a priest, who had
sinned, and R. Hama b. Tubiah surrounded her with bundles
of twigs and burned her.   And R. Joseph, when he heard this,
said: He erred twice.   In the explanation of the Mishna, in
which, according to R. Na'hman, the sinner was burned with
lead; and (b) he was not aware of the following Boraitha: It is
written [Deut. xvii. 9]: " And thou shalt come unto the priests
the Levites, and unto the judge that may be in those days."
At that time, when the priests acted, judgments concerning
capital punishments might be rendered; but when there were no
more acting priests, no such judgment could be rendered.

" *Said Elazar b. Zadok,*" etc.   Said R. Joseph: The court in
question was of the Sadducees (who take the commandments of
the Scripture literally).   Did, indeed, Elazar say so?   And the
answer was as stated in the Mishna?   Is there not a Boraitha
which states: R. Elazar b Zadok said: I recollect, when I was
a child, being carried upon the shoulders of my father, and a
daughter of a priest, who was a sinner, was brought, and was
surrounded with bundles of twigs and burned?   To which the
sages answered: At that time you were a child, and we cannot
accept any evidence from a child?   Two such cases happened
in the days of R. Elazar, and when he was answered that no
evidence of a child is to be taken into consideration, he related
before them the other case which he saw when he was already
of age, and to this they answered him: That court was an ignorant one.

MISHNA *III.*: The prescribed punishment of slaying was
thus: He was decapitated, as was customary with the Roman
government.   R. Jehudah, however, maintains: Such a death
is repulsive.   But they put his head on the (executioner's)
block and cut it off with a butcher's hatchet.   And he was answered: There is not a more detestable death than this.

GEMARA: There is a Boraitha: R. Jehudah said to the
sages: I myself am aware that the death I explained is repul-

sive; but what can we do against the Scripture, which reads [Lev. xviii. 13] : "And in their customs shall ye not walk," etc. ? To which the rabbis answered: As this is written in the Scripture, we are not learning this from them, but they learned it from us. And should one disagree with us, then what would he say to the following Boraitha: Garments and some other valuable things may be burned on the grave of kings, for the sake of their honor. And this custom is not considered the custom of the Amalekites. And why? It is because it is mentioned in the Scripture [Jer. xxxiv. 5] : "And as burnings were made for thy father," etc., we do not learn from them. The same is the case here.

Let us see! In the succeeding chapter, there is a Mishna: The following are slain with a sword: a murderer, and the men of a misled town. It is correct, "a misled town," as it is plainly written [Deut. xiii. 16], "with the edge of a sword." But whence do we know that the same is the case with a murderer? From the following Boraitha: It reads [Ex. xxi. 20] : "And if a man smite his servant or maid with a rod, and he die under his hand, it shall be surely avenged." And as we do not know what " revenge " means; therefore it is written [Lev. xxvi. 25] : "And I will bring unto you the sword avenging." Hence avenge means with a sword.

But whence do we know that they decapitated him—perhaps they killed him with the sword in another part of the body? It reads, "with the edge of a sword," which excludes stabbing. But perhaps it means splitting the head. It is already inferred by Rabha b. Abuhu from the phrase: " Thou shalt love thy neighbor as thyself," that one must select a decent death. But all this speaks of when one has slain a bondman. Whence do we know that the same is the case with a freeman (whose punishment is death in general, and there is a rule that wherever the kind of death is not mentioned, it means choking)? This cannot be, as an *a fortiori* conclusion is to be drawn: A slave, who is less in value than a freeman, if one kills him, he is punished with slaying by the sword (which is more rigorous than choking); if one kills a freeman, so much the more should he be punished with a more rigorous death. But this would be correct only to him who holds that the sword is more rigorous than choking. But to him who holds the contrary, what can be said? He infers this from another verse, as is stated in the following Boraitha: It is written [Deut. xxi. 9] : "And thou

shalt put away (the guilt of) the innocent blood from the midst
of thee." From this we see that all shedders of blood are compared to the heifer in that connection. And lest one say that
as the heifer is killed with a butcher's knife toward the back
part of the neck, the same shall be done with all other shedders
of blood, it is already inferred above that a decent death must be
selected.

MISHNA *IV.*: The prescribed punishment of choking was
thus: The sinner was placed in waste knee-deep. Then, placing
a twisted scarf of coarse material within a soft one, they wound
it around his neck. One (of the witnesses) pulled one end toward himself, the other doing the same, until the soul of the
culprit departed.

GEMARA: The rabbis taught: It reads [Lev. xx. 10]:
" And if there be a man "—" man " means to exclude a minor,
" Who committeth adultery with a man's wife "—" man's wife "
means to exclude the wife of a minor (whose marriage is not
considered). ." With his neighbor's wife " means to exclude
those people who live with their wives in common.* [Ibid.]:
" Then shall the adulterer be put to death " means choking.
But perhaps it means some other kind of death which is prescribed by the Scripture? It was said that wherever it is written in the Torah " death," without specifying which, you must
not apply a rigorous one, but an easier one (and choking is the
easiest of all the kinds of death mentioned in the Torah). So
is the decree of R. Jashiah. R. Jonathan, however, maintains:
The reason is not because choking is an easier death, but because there is a tradition that in any place where death is mentioned in the Scripture, without specifying which, it is choking.
Rabbi said: The reason is because there is mentioned in the
Scripture a heavenly death [Gen. xxxviii. 10], and there is also
mentioned death from human hands. And as a heavenly death
does not leave any marks on the body of the man, the same
must it be by death from human hands. But perhaps burning
is meant, which also does not leave any signs outside of the

* The text reads, "אשת אחרים," literally, "the wife of many strangers," and
so it means. The explanation of Rashi that the word *acherim* means a Samarite, is
probably because he did not know of the existence of such a sect who live in common with their wives. It may also be that the word "Samaritan," in Rashi, was
corrected by the censor instead of "heathen" or idolator. However, this is certain,
that the expression "acherim" in the Gemara is original, and if it meant a heathen
or a Samarite, it would not hesitate to say so. It therefore seems to us, that our
translation is correct.

body? As the Scripture prescribed burning to a daughter of a priest, it is to be understood that all other sinners are not punished with the same.

It is correct that choking is to be used, according to R. Jonathan, who says that it is a tradition; and Rabbi gives the reason. But R. Joshiah, who wants only an easier death—whence does he deduce choking at all? (Such is never mentioned in the Scripture.) And perhaps there is no more than three kinds of death, and from these three the easier one must be selected, which is the sword? Said Rabha: The four kinds of death are known traditionally. And the expression of R. Jonathan, "not because it is easier," shows that he and R. Joshiah differ concerning choking, whether it is an easier death. In the same manner differ R. Simeon and the rabbis.

R. Zera said to Abayi: There are sinners who are punished with stoning, although it is not so mentioned in the Scripture. But they are inferred from an analogy of expression, "from a familiar spirit." I question you which expression of the two following is meant—"put to death," or "their blood shall be upon them"? And he answered: The latter expression, as the first is needed, "to death," which is explained above (page 000).

MISHNA *V*.: To the following sinners stoning applies: viz., one who has had connection with his mother, with his father's wife, with his daughter-in-law, with a human male, or with cattle; and the same is the case with a woman who uncovers herself before cattle; with a blasphemer; an idolater, he who sacrifices one of his children to Moloch; one that occupies himself with familiar spirits; a wizard; one who violates the Sabbath; one who curses his father or mother; one who has assaulted a betrothed damsel; a seducer who has seduced men to worship idols, and the one who misleads a whole town; a witch (male or female); a stubborn and rebellious son.

One who has had connection with his mother is guilty of transgressing two negative commandments—the negative commandment as to his mother and the negative commandment as to his father's wife. R. Jehudah, however, maintains: He is guilty only for his mother. One who has connection with his stepmother is also guilty in respect to two negative commandments—the commandment of adultery and the separate commandment as to his father's wife. There is no difference if he has done it while his father was still alive or after his death; and there is also no difference if she was only betrothed to his father, or already married. One that commits a crime with his daughter-in-law transgresses also two commandments—adultery and of the separate commandment of his son's wife. And there is also no difference if it was done while his son was still alive or after his death, after her betrothal or after marriage.

GEMARA: There is a Boraitha: R. Jehudah said: "If his father had married his mother illegally; he transgresses only the commandment as to "mother" and not as to "his father's wife." And the expression illegally means that by marrying, he has transgressed a negative commandment which is not punished capitally or with korath. As to such, even according to the rabbis, such a marriage is not considered at all. But to death which is only of a negative commandment—*e.g.*, a widow to a high-priest—according to the rabbis the marriage is considered, and according to R. Jehudah it is not, as he holds with R. Aqiba, who is of the same opinion. R. Oushia objected: There is a Mishna in Yebamoth [Chap. II., 3]: "Owing to other legal prohibitions, or on account of the holiness of station" [ibid. ix.]. By "legal prohibitions" (to marry as above mentioned) are meant the secondary degrees of relationship prohibited by the rabbins as to intermarriage. Those prohibited to intermarry on account of holiness of station are a widow to a high-priest; a woman who had been divorced or performed the ceremony of Halitzah; who had (unlawfully) been married to an ordinary priest. To which a Boraitha adds: R. Jehudah changes the expression, viz., by "legal prohibition," a widow to a high-priest, etc., is meant; and "on account of holiness of station," the secondary degrees of relationship, etc., are meant. Hence we see that R. Jehudah changes the expression only, but nevertheless the ceremony of Halitzah is required. And if it were in accordance with R. Aqiba (that a marriage within secondary degrees is not considered at all), why, then, the ceremony of Halitzah? R. Jehudah collected only the expressions which ought to be in accordance with the opinion of the first Tana, but he himself does not require anything of that kind.

When R. Itz'hak came from Palestine, he taught just as our Mishna teaches, viz.: R. Jehudah said: He is guilty only concerning the negative commandment as to the mother. And what is the reason? Said Abayi: Because it reads [ibid. xviii. 7]: "She is thy mother," which means: You have to make him guilty only because of his mother, but not because of the wife of his father. But why do the rabbis make him guilty concerning two commandments? Do they not hold this theory? The rabbis apply this expression to that which was said by R. Shesha b. R. Idi, which is stated farther on. But does not R. Jehudah also hold the theory of R. Shesha? Hence, his theory cannot be inferred from it. Therefore said R. Aha b. Iki: It reads [ibid. 7] : " She is thy mother, thou shalt not uncover her nakedness," meaning, " for one nakedness you can make her guilty, but not for two." But if so, why does not R. Jehudah differ concerning a daughter-in-law, who is guilty, according to our Mishna, as to two commandments? It then must be said, because there is one body, although there are two transgressions, he is culpable only for one, as it reads, " her nakedness." The same should be the case concerning the mother? Therefore said Rabha: R. Jehudah holds: At the beginning of the verse, " the nakedness of thy father " means " thy father's wife." And that it means thus he infers from an analogy of expression, as stated farther on. And " father's wife " means that there is no difference whether she is his mother or not. But whence do we know that it is the same with his mother, who is not his father's wife? Therefore it is written: " She is thy mother, thou shalt not uncover her nakedness." Hence only for the crime as to the mother you make him guilty, but not as to that of his father's wife.

There is a Boraitha according to Rabha: "A man " means to exclude a minor [Lev. xxii.] : " That lieth with his father's wife " means that there is no difference whether she is his mother or not. But whence do we know that the same is the case with his mother who is not his father's wife? Therefore it reads: " His father's nakedness," which is pleonastic,* and is written only for the purpose of an analogy of expression. " Both of them shall be put to death " means by stoning—but perhaps with some other death? It is written here: " Their blood shall be upon them "; and in the case of " familiar spirits " there is also the same expression. And as concerning the latter stoning is plainly applied by the Scripture, the same is the case here. But here we have heard only of the punishment. Whence do we know of the warning? Therefore it is written: " The nakedness of thy father," etc., which means of " thy father's wife." But perhaps it means literally the father himself? It is written here, " The nakedness of thy father thou shalt not un-

---

* For the explanation of a pleonastic term we refer the reader to Mielziner's " Introduction to the Talmud " (page 150).

cover," and there it is written, " The nakedness of his father he had uncovered." As the latter means his wife, so does the former. And from the expression " his father's wife," it is inferred, whether his mother or not. But whence do we know as to his mother who is not his father's wife? Therefore it is written, " the nakedness of thy mother," etc. But this is only in the warning in which the Scripture has equalized the mother who is not his father's wife with her who is. But whence do we know that the punishment is also equal? From the analogy of the expressions: " the nakedness of thy father thou shalt not uncover," and it reads also: " He has uncovered the nakedness of his father." And so as in the warning it is equalized with the mother who is the wife of his father and with her who is not, the same holds good concerning the punishment. " She is thy mother " means, you can make her guilty only for the crime as mother, but not for the crime as father's wife. But the rabbis, who do not use the above analogy of expression, whence do they deduce the punishment of a mother who is not the wife of one's father? Said R. Shesha b. R. Idi: It reads: " *She* is thy mother," which means that the Scripture equalized the mother who is not the wife of his father with her who is.

" *Who had connection with his daughter-in-law.*" But let him be guilty also because of the wife of his son? Said Abayi: The verse begins with his daughter-in-law and ends with the wife of his son—to teach that " daughter-in-law " and " wife of his son " are one and the same.

MISHNA *V.*: One who had connection with a human male or with an animal, and also a human female who uncovers herself before a male animal, are punished with stoning. And should one say: If man has sinned, what is the fault of the animal? Because a misfortune has happened to a human being through it, therefore says the verse: " It shall be stoned." There is also another explanation; viz., should it happen that people saw the animal passing the street, they would say: On account of it so and so was stoned.

GEMARA: A human male—whence is deduced? That which the rabbis taught: " A man " means to exclude a minor; " with a male," of any age whatever or a minor. " As they lie *

---

* The term "as they lie," translated by Leeser, is not correct, as it reads "mishkhbey," which is plural and means "lyings," from which the Gemara infers that there are two lyings regarding a woman.

with a woman " means to say that with a woman there are two
kinds of lyings, one usual and one unusual; and one is guilty
as to both.   Said R. Ishmael: This verse came to teach that
which was just mentioned, as if not for this teaching it would
be pleonastic, for regarding a male there is only one kind of
connection.   " Both of them have committed an abomination,
they shall be put to death "—by stoning, but perhaps by some
other death.   Therefore it is written: " Their blood shall be
upon them."   And the same expression is used concerning " a
familiar spirit," etc.   And as the punishment of the latter is
known to be stoning, the same applies here.   From this we
have heard the punishment.   Whence is the warning?   [Ibid.
xviii. 22] : " And with a man shalt thou not lie as with a woman;
it is an abomination.'   But this is a warning only to him who
has done so.   But whence is the warning to them with whom
the connection was made?   As to this it reads [Deut. xxiii. 18] :
" There shall not be a courtesan of the sons of Israel "; and
also [I Kings, xiv. 24] : " And courtesans also were in the land
.   .   .   the Lord had driven out."   So R. Ishmael.   R. Aqiba,
however, said: " It was not necessary to have another verse
warning him with whom the connection was made, as this is
inferred from the same verse, which may apply also to the latter
by some change in pronunciation.

Concerning animals, whence is this deduced?   The rabbis
taught: From Lev. xx. 15.   " A man " excludes a minor; " with
an animal," it makes no difference whether it was a large or a
small one; " shall be put to death " means stoning—but perhaps some other kind of death?   It reads here (ibid.) " tha-
bargu " (ye shall kill), and in Deut. xiii. 10, " thahargenu "
(thou shalt kill).   And as there the punishment is stoning, as it
reads plainly in ibid. 11, the same is the case here.   Here, however, we have learned only the punishment to the man.   But
whence do we know that the animal with which the crime was
done is also to be killed in the same manner?   It reads [Ex.
xxii. 18] : " Whosoever lieth with a beast shall surely be put to
death," which was not necessary for the man, as there is another verse cited above.   Apply it, therefore, to the beast.
From this we have learned the punishment for both.   But
whence is the warning?   From the above-cited verse [Lev.
xviii. 23].   But this is only a warning to the man, and whence
the warning concerning the animal?   From Deut. xxiii. 18.
(Here are repeated the cited verses in the name of R. Ishmael,

and also in the name of R. Aqiba, that it is not necessary, as in the above verses there is a warning for both.*)

MISHNA *VI.*: A blasphemer is not guilty, unless he mentioned the proper name of God (Jehovah). Said R. Jehoshua b. Karha: Through the entire trial the witnesses are examined pseudonymously—*i.e.* (the blasphemer said): "Jose shall be beaten by Jose." (Rashi explains that the name Jose was selected because it contains four letters, as does the proper name of the Lord.) When the examination was ended, the culprit was not executed on the testimony under the pseudonym; but all are told to leave the room except the witnesses, and the oldest of them is instructed: "Tell what you heard exactly." And he does so. The judges then arise, and rend their garments, and they are not to be mended. The second witness then says: I heard exactly the same as he told. And so also says the third witness.

GEMARA: There is a Boraitha: One is not guilty unless he blesses (*i.e.*, curses) the Holy Name by the Holy Name (as illustrated in the Mishna): "Jose shall be beaten by Jose." And whence is this deduced? Said Samuel: From Lev. xxiv. 16, of which the term in Hebrew is "we-nauquib shem," which means, "when he has cursed with the name." And whence do we know that the term "nauquib" means cursing? From [Num. xxiv. 8]: "How shall I curse," etc. And the warning as to this is [Ex. xxii. 27]: "Thou shalt not revile Elohim." But does not "nauquib" mean "hole"? Why, then, not so say—*i.e.*, suppose one wrote the Holy Name on a piece of parchment and tore it, the term "we-yiqaub" [II Kings, xii. 10]? meaning he "bored a hole in its lid"—and the warning as to which should be from [Deut. xii. 3, 4]: "Ye shall destroy their name out of the same place. Ye shall not do so to the Lord," etc. It was said above if the Name should be cursed by the Name, which is not the case here. But perhaps the term "nauquib" is meant as plainly expressed, as the same is used in Num. i. 17, "which are expressed by name" (*i.e.*, it was forbidden to

---

* We deem it expedient not to translate about two pages of the text preceding the next Mishna, treating of miserable crimes with men and animals, and giving the discussion with questions and answers. it would be undesirable to express in the English language. However. it seems to us important to give the opinion of Rabh: "A minor who was over nine years and one day is guilty, and may be punished the same as one of age, if he commit a crime with man, or an animal of any kind and age." (And there is a Boraitha which agrees with him.) This is all that we think proper to take from the text.

express the name Jehovah in any case whatever, except in that
of the high-priest in *his* worshipping on the Day of Atonement
when the temple was in existence; and even then, when the
people heard this expression, they used to fall upon their faces).
And the warnings should be from [Deut. vi. 13]: " The Lord
thy God shalt thou fear " (which means to pronounce His
name). This does not hold good, firstly because, as said above,
it must be by the Name; and secondly, a warning of a positive
commandment cannot be counted as a warning. And if you
wish, it may be said because it is so written plainly [Lev. xxiv.
11]: " The son of the Israelitish woman pronounced (*we-
yiqaub*) the holy name and blasphemed." Hence this term is
used to blaspheme. But perhaps one is not guilty unless he
did both—expressed the name and blasphemed? This cannot
be supposed, as farther on it reads [ibid. 14]: " Lead forth the
blasphemer," and the expression " nauquib " is not mentioned.
Hence it is one and the same.

The rabbis taught: It reads: " any man whatsoever," etc.,
meaning to include the heathen, who are warned of blasphemy
the same as an Israelite. And they are to be executed by the
sword, as wherever it is mentioned in the Scripture concerning
death to the children of Noah, it means by the sword, and not
otherwise. But is this inferred from the verse cited? Is it not
stated farther on that such is inferred from a verse in Genesis?
Said R. Itz'hak of Navha: This verse is needed to include the
pseudonyms. And it is in accordance with R. Mair of the following Boraitha: Any man whatsoever that blasphemeth his
God shall bear his sin. To what purpose is this written? It
reads earlier [ibid. 16]: " But he that pronounced the name of
the Lord (with blasphemy) shall be put to death "? Because
from this one might say that he is not guilty, unless he has done
so with the unique proper Name, but not with the pseudonyms.
Therefore it reads in the cited verse (15), " his God "—no difference between proper and pseudonym. So is the decree of
R. Mair. The sages, however, maintain: For the unique proper
Name death is the punishment; and for the pseudonyms it is
only a warning by a negative commandment, and the punishment is as for the transgression of a negative commandment.
(Says the Gemara:) Itz'hak of Navha differs with R. Maisha,
who said: One of the children of Noah, who blasphemed God
by any of His pseudonyms whatsoever is guilty, and is put to
death, even according to the rabbis.

The rabbis taught: Seven commandments were given to the children of Noah, and they are: Concerning judges, blasphemy, idolatry, adultery, bloodshed, robbery, and that they must not eat of the member of a body while the animal is still alive. R. Hananiah b. Gamaliel said: Also of the blood of the same. R. Hidka said: Also castration was forbidden to them. R. Simeon said: Also witchcraft. And R. Jose said: All that is said in the portion on witchcraft is forbidden to a descendant of Noah. As it reads [Deut. xviii. 10-12]: "There shall not be found among thee any one who causeth his son or his daughter to pass through the fire, one who useth divination, one who is an observer of times, or an enchanter, or a conjurer, or a charmer, or a consulter with familiar spirits, or a wizard, or who inquireth of the dead. For an abomination unto the Lord are all that do these things; and on account of these abominations the Lord thy God doth drive them out from before thee." And as there is no punishment without preceding warning, hence they were commanded not to do all this. R. Elazar said: Also Kilaim. I mean to say, the descendants of Noah are allowed to dress themselves with a mixture of wool and flax; and also sow different kinds of seeds together (which are forbidden to the Israelites); but they are forbidden to gender different kinds of animals and to graft two kinds of trees together.

Whence is all this deduced? Said R. Johanan: From Genesis ii. 16.* Were the descendants of Noah indeed commanded concerning judges? Is there not a Boraitha: *Ten commandments* were commanded to Israel in Marah; seven of them are those which were accepted by the descendants of Noah, and three were added to them: viz., judges, Sabbath, and to honor father and mother. Judges—as it is written [Ex. xv. 25]: "There he made for them a statute and an ordinance," etc. And concerning Sabbath and the honor of parents it reads [Deut. v. 12 and 16]: "As the Lord thy God hath *commanded thee.*" And R. Jehudah said: "As he hath commanded thee in Marah." Said R. Aha b. Jacob: This means that Israel was commanded to establish courts of justice in every district and

---

* It would be of no use to quote the verse, as every word in it is used for an analogy of expression of the Hebrew terms. There, is besides, a difference of opinion among the Amoraim, which expression is to be used for an analogy, and what it means; and to translate it all, we would have to fill our page with Hebrew words and their explanations. After all, it would be of no importance, as the fact that to the children of Noah seven commandments were given is traditional.

city; and the children of Noah were commanded concerning judges in general only.   But is there not a Boraitha: As Israel was commanded to establish judges in every city and district, so also were the children of Noah commanded?   Said Rabha: The Tana of the Boraitha cited above is in accordance with the school of Manasheh, which excluded from the seven commandments judges and blasphemy, and included castration and kilaim.   Thus was it taught in the school of Manasheh: Seven commandments were the descendants of Noah commanded: Concerning idolatry, adultery, bloodshed, robbery, a member of a living animal, castration, and kilaim.   R. Jehudah, however, said: Adam the First was commanded as to idolatry only, as it reads [Gen. ii. 16]: " And the Lord commanded the man " *i.e.*, the Lord commanded him about the law of God (that he should not be exchanged for another).   R. Jehudah b. Bathyra said: Also as to blasphemy.   And there are some others who say, also concerning judges.

According to whom is that which was said by R. Jehudah in the name of Rabh: God said to Adam: I am God, thou shalt not blaspheme me.   I am God, thou shalt not exchange me for an idol.   I am God, the fear of me shall be always upon thee? According to the " some others " just mentioned.   (The expression " the fear of me," etc., means to appoint judges who shall punish them who transgress my commandments.)

Said R. Joseph: It was said in the college: For transgression of the following three commandments a descendant of Noah is put to death: viz., adultery, bloodshed, and blasphemy.   R. Shesheth opposed: It is correct concerning bloodshed, as it reads [Gen. ix. 6]: " Whoso sheddeth man's blood, by man shall his blood be shed."   But whence do you deduce the two others?   And should you say that it is inferred from bloodshed, then why not infer all the seven?   And if you infer it from "any man whatsoever," then idolatry is also inferred from same? Therefore said he: In the college it was said: For four they are but not put to death?   Said R. Na'hman b. Itz'hak: It means ant of Noah indeed put to death because of idolatry?   Have we not learned in a Boraitha concerning idolatry, if for such a crime one is put to death by the court of Israel, the descendants of Noah are warned of it?   Hence they are only warned, but not put to death?   Said R. Na'hman b. Itz'hak: It means that they are warned if they should commit this they will be put to death.   R. Huna and R. Jehudah and also all other dis-

ciples of Rabh say: For each case of the seven commandments
a descendant of Noah is to be killed.   As the Scripture prescribed death for one, it shall serve as an example for the others.

When R. Dimi came from Palestine, he said in the name of
R. Elazar, quoting R. Hanina: A descendant of Noah who has
separated a female slave to one of his male slaves, and thereafter
had connection with her, is to be put to death for this crime.
A similarity to this in the crime of bloodshed was not taught.
Said Abayi: If such a similarity is to be found, it may be in
that which we have learned in the following Boraitha: R. Jonathan b. Saul said: If one runs after his neighbor to kill him, and
the one who flees could save himself by injuring one of the
members of his pursuer, and he did not so, but killed him, it is
a crime of bloodshed and he is put to death for it.*   R. Jacob
b. Aha found a writing in a Haggadic book written by the college of Rabh, thus: A descendant of Noah may be put to death
by the decision of one judge, by the testimony of one witness,
and although he was not warned previously.   However, the
testimony must be from a man, and not from a woman; and the
testimony holds good even if given by one of his relatives.   In
the name of R. Ishmael it was said: He is put to death even for
killing an embryo.   Whence is this deduced?   Said R. Jehudah:
From [Gen. ix. 5]: " Your blood, however, on which your lives
depend, will I require," meaning even by one judge.   " At the
hand of every beast " means even without warning; " at the
hand of man " means even with one witness; " at the hand of
every man " means of a man but not of a woman; " brother "
means even when the witness was a relative.   And the reason of
R. Ishmael is [ibid. 6]: " Whoso sheddeth man's blood in man,†
his blood shall be shed."   What is meant by " a man in man,"
if not an embryo, which is in the entrails of his mother?   And
the first Tana, who holds that a descendant of Noah is not
guilty for an embryo, is in accordance with the school of Manasheh, which maintains that every death which is mentioned
regarding the descendants of Noah is choking; and he explains
the above-cited verse " in man shall his blood be shed," that it
means choking, from which death occurs inside of the body as
illustrated above.   R. Hamnuna objected: Does, then, the com-

* We do not understand this similarity, although Rashi in his commentary tries
to explain it at length.   It is so complicated as to be untranslatable into English.

† The term in Hebrew is " be-adam," literally, " in the man "; Leeser, however, translates according to the sense.

mandment of bloodshed not apply to a woman? Is it not written [Gen. xviii. 19]: "For I know him, that he will command his sons and his household after him"? And by the "household" it means the woman, as the sons are already mentioned? He objected, and he himself answered: It reads farther on, "that they shall keep the way of the Lord, to do righteousness and justice.' It means that he shall command his sons to appoint judges for justice and his household to do righteousness and charity.

Said R. Ibiah the Elder to R. Papa: Say, then, that a woman who is a descendant of Noah shall not be put to death if she has killed a man; as it reads "from the hand of a man," which means not from the hand of a woman? And he answered: So said R. Jehudah: It reads, "Whoso sheddeth the blood of a human," etc., which means any human whatsoever. (Said R. Ibiah again: "Say, then, that a female descendant of Noah should not be punished if she sinned, as it reads [ibid. ii. 24]: "Therefore doth a man leave his father and his mother"—a man, and not a woman. And he answered: So said R. Jehudah: It reads further, "and they become one flesh"; and with this the verse associates them to be equal in every respect.)

The rabbis taught: It should read "a man." Why is it written "any man whatsoever"? To include heathens in the warning of adultery, as well as Israelites. But was it not said above that in the seven commandments which were given to the descendants of Noah adultery is included? Said R. Johanan: It is needed for such a relationship which they do not recognize, but the Israelites do; e.g., a betrothed woman before marriage, whom they consider as single. And if it happened that a heathen should sin with a woman betrothed of an Israelite, he is to be tried in the courts of the Israelites. But if he sins with a married woman, he may be tried in his own courts—the punishment of which is by the sword, and not choking. But is there not a Boraitha: A heathen who has sinned with a betrothed woman is to be stoned; and if with a married, choked? Hence he is tried in the Israelitish courts, as in his own courts he would be slain by the sword. Said R. Na'hman b. Itz'hak: By the term married woman is meant that the ceremony of marriage was performed, but her husband had not as yet had any connection with her; and such a marriage their courts do not consider, and the bride is still deemed single. Therefore he is to be tried in the courts of Israel, and punished with their prescribed death. And so taught R. Haninah: The law of the heathen considers the wife of a man only after their connection, but not after the ceremony of marriage.

There is a Boraitha in accordance with R. Johanan: Every relationship for which the punishment of the courts of Israel is death, a descendant of Noah is warned of it; but all other relationships, the punishment of which is not death, are permissible to them. So is the decree of R. Mair. The sages, however, say: There are many relationships which in our courts are not punished with death, nevertheless the descendants of Noah are warned of them. If it happens that one of the latter has committed a crime with a daughter of Israel, which is considered adultery in the courts of the Israelites, but not in the courts of the heathens, he is to be tried in the courts of Israel. But if such a crime is considered adultery also in the courts of the heathen, he may be tried in their own courts. However, we do not find a case which would be a crime for Israelites and not for heathens, except that of a betrothed woman (as said above). But why does the Boraitha not count the case of a married woman—by the ceremony of marriage only—which is a crime according to our law, and not according to their law? The Boraitha is in accordance with the school of Manasheh: The death of the descendants of Noah is also choking. Hence it makes no difference in which court he should be tried.*

Resh Lakish said: He who raises his hand to strike his neighbor, although he has not as yet struck him, is called wicked. As it is written [Ex. ii. 13]: "And he said to the wicked one, wherefore smitest thou thy fellow?" It does not read, "why hast thou smitten," but "why smitest thou." Hence he is called wicked even if he only raises his hand to strike. Zeairi in the name of R. Hanina said: He is named sinner. As it reads [I Sam. ii. 16]: "If not, I will take it by force." And immediately after it reads: "The sin of the young men was very great." R. Huna said: If one has the habit of raising his hand against man, his arm may be cut off. As it reads [Job, xxxviii. 15]: "And the high-raised arm should be broken."† (And R. Huna acted according to his theory, and

* The text farther on discusses about a proselyte, whose mother embraces Judaism when he was yet an embryo—which relationship is allowed to him and which not; also if a heathen is allowed to marry his daughter; if a slave may marry his sister or daughter, etc.—all of which, as we deem it not fit for translation, we omit.

† Leeser's translation does not correspond.

cut off the arm of a man whose habit was to strike men with it.) R. Elazar said: There is no remedy for such a man, but burial. As it is written [ibid. xxii. 8] : " But as for the man of a strong arm, for him is the land." He said again: Only one who has a strong arm may obtain land (as usually there is much trouble to keep away cattle and all other animals which harm the growth, and also to preserve it from thieves, etc.). Resh Lakish said again: It reads [Prov. xii. 11]: " He that tilleth * his ground will be satisfied with bread." It means, when one makes himself a slave to the earth, he may be satisfied with bread, but not otherwise.

The Boraitha states: R. Hananiah b. Gamaliel, etc. The rabbis taught: It reads [Gen. ix. 4] : " But flesh in which its life is, which is its blood, shall ye not eat." This means any member of the animal, while it is still alive. And Haninah b. Gamaliel said: Also the blood of same. And his reason is that the verse is to be read thus: Flesh in which its life is, ye shall not eat, and blood in which its life is, ye shall not eat. The rabbis, however, maintain that blood is here mentioned to teach that other animals, as reptiles, are allowed to a descendant of Noah. Similar to this, it reads [Deut. xii. 23] : " Only be firm, so as not to eat the blood; for the blood is its life," which the rabbis explain as meaning the blood of the veins, by which the soul departs.

For what purpose is it written concerning the descendants of Noah, and thereafter repeated in the laws which were given on Mount Sinai? It is as R. Jose b. Hanina said: Every commandment which was given to the descendants of Noah, and thereafter repeated in the laws given on Mount Sinai, applies to both Israel and the descendants of Noah. And that which was given to the descendants of Noah, and not repeated, applies to Israel only. However, we have only one case [Gen. xxxii. 33] which was commanded before the laws were given on Mount Sinai, which was not repeated, and applies only to Israel, according to R. Jehudah's theory (in Tracts Chulin, Chap. vii., which will be explained there).

The master said: A commandment which was repeated on Sinai is for both. Why not the contrary—because it was repeated on Sinai, it must be said it was given to Israel only? Al-

---

* The term in Hebrew is " obed "; literally, " worshipped," and also " works up" ; and *ebed* means " a slave." Hence his analogy.

though idolatry was repeated on Sinai, as we find that the descendants of Noah were already punished for idolatry, therefore it applies to both. He says further that that which was given to the descendants of Noah and not repeated is for Israel only. Why not the contrary—because it was not repeated, it applies to the descendants of Noah and not to Israel? Because we do not find any case where it is forbidden to the descendants of Noah and allowed to the Israelites, a commandment which was given to the children of Noah and repeated on Sinai applies to both. Is there not circumcision? [Gen. xvii.] : " And God said unto Abraham: But thou, for thy part, shalt keep my covenant "; and it reads also [Lev. xii. 3] : " And on the eighth day shall the flesh of his foreskin be circumcised." And nevertheless it applies to Israel only, and not to the descendants of Noah? The verse just cited was needed to permit the circumcision to be done on Sabbath; as the term " on the eighth day " means even on Sabbath. And if you wish, it may be said that circumcision was given to Abraham especially. As it reads [Gen. xvii.] : " But thou, for thy part, shalt keep my covenant: thou, and thy seed after thee, in their generations "—which means "thou and thy children," but not some other man's. But according to this, let the descendants of Ishmael be obliged to circumcise? It reads [ibid. xxi. 12] : " For *in* Isaac shall thy seed be called." But if so, let this obligation be for the children of Esau also? It reads " in Isaac," but not the whole of Isaac, which means to exclude the descendants of Esau. R. Oushia opposed: Let, then, the children of Kturah not be obliged to circumcision. And R. Jose b. Abin or R. Jose b. Hanina said: From [ibid. xvii. 14] : " He hath broken my covenant " is understood even the sons of Kturah.

R. Jehudah said in the name of Rabh: Adam the First was not permitted to eat meat. As it reads [ibid. i. 29, 30] : " To you it shall be for food, and to every beast of the field," meaning, but not the beasts to you. However, after the descendants of Noah came, he permitted them. As it reads [ibid. ix. 3] : " Every moving thing that liveth shall be yours for food: even as the green herbs have I given you all things." And lest one say that they may be eaten while still alive, therefore it reads: " But flesh in which its life is, which is its blood, shall ye not eat." And lest one say that this forbids also reptiles, the term " but " excludes them. How is this to be understood? Said R. Huna: It reads " his blood," which means of animals in which the blood is separated from the flesh, and excludes reptiles, of which the blood is not separated from their flesh.

There was an objection to that which was said that Adam the First was not allowed to eat meat, from that which Jehudah b. Bathyra said (Vol. IX., p. 7): "Adam the First was sitting in the garden of Eden, and the angels served him with roasted meat," etc.   Hence he was allowed?   And the answer was that with meat which came from heaven it is different.   And the question is, was there any meat which came from heaven?   It was answered: Yea!   As it happened to R. Simeon b. Chalafta, who, being on the road, met lions, which were stirred against him; and a miracle occurred, and two legs fell from heaven, one of which the lions consumed, and the other one remained. Simeon then took it, brought it into the college, and questioned if it was allowed to eat it.   And he was answered: An unclean thing never came from heaven.   And R. Zera questioned R. Abuhu: How is it if such should come from heaven in the form of an ass?   And he was scolded for this question thus: Was it not decided long ago that no unclean thing descends from heaven?

"R. Simeon said: Also witchcraft."   What is his reason?   It reads [Ex. xxii. 17]: "Thou shalt not suffer a witch to live"; and farther on: "Whosoever lieth with a beast shall surely be put to death"—which applies also to the descendants of Noah. And as this applies to them, the same is the case with the first verse.   R. Elazar said: Kilaim!   Whence is this deduced? Said Samuel: From [Lev. xix. 19]: "My statutes shall ye keep," which means the "statutes which I stated long ago" (long ago, to the descendants of Noah).   "Thy cattle shalt thou not let gender with a diverse kind; thy field shalt thou not sow with mingled seeds."   And as concerning cattle "gender" is prohibited, so concerning fields grafting is prohibited; and as the prohibition of the first applies to every place—in Palestine and outside of it—the same is the case with the fields. But if so, why not explain [ibid., ibid. 37]: "Ye shall therefore observe all my statutes, and all my ordinances," in the same way: "my statutes which I stated long ago"?   Nay!   "You shall therefore observe my statutes" means which I have now given to you.   But in the above-cited verse, which begins, "my statutes ye shall observe," it must be said the statutes which are already stated.

"Said R. Jehoshua b. Karha,' etc.   Said R. Aha b. Jacob:

Infer from this that one is not guilty unless he blesses (curses) the Name which contains four letters, but not that of two letters (e.g., a Jud and Heh—" Ja "; or Aleph and Lamedh, which is " ehl." But is this not self-evident? Does not the Mishna state, e.g., " Jose . . . by Jose," which contains four letters? Lest one say that this is only an example, but not in particular, he comes to teach us that it is not so. According to others, Aha b. Jacob said: Infer from this that a name which contains four letters is also considered. Is this not self-evident? The example is given, " Jose by Jose," which contains four. Lest one say that one is not guilty, unless he blesses (curses) the great Name (Rashi explains: Which contains forty-two letters—which are not known to us, and the example is not particular, he comes to teach us that it is not so).*

" *They arise.*" Whence is this deduced? Said R. Itz'hak b. Ami: From [Judges, iii. 20]: " And Ehud came unto him; and he was sitting in the summer upper chamber, which was for himself alone. And Ehud said: I have a word of God unto thee. And he arose out of his chair.' Is there not to be drawn an *a fortiori* conclusion—Eglon, the king of Moab, who was a heathen, to whom the God of Israel was known only by a pseudonym, rose up from his chair when he heard the Name of God: An Israelite, hearing the great Name, so much the more must he arise?

" *Rend,*" etc. Whence is this deduced? From [II Kings, xviii. 37]: " Then came Elyakim the son of Chilkiyah, who was superintendent over the house, and Shebuah the scribe, and Yoach the son of Assaph the recorder, to Hezekiah, with their clothes rent; and they told unto him the words of Rabshakeh."

" *Not to be mended.*" Whence is this deduced? Said R. Abuhu: From an analogy of expression—" rent." It reads here: " With their clothes rent "; and [ibid. ii. 12]: " And Elisha saw it, and he cried, My father, my father, the chariot of Israel, and their horsemen. And he saw him no more; and he took hold of his clothes and rent them in two pieces." Why the word " pieces "? Is it not self-evident that when he rent them in two, they became pieces? Hence this term means that they should remain pieces and never be mended.

---

* It is almost the first time that we have translated against our method, announced in the third of the explanatory remarks on back of title pages, the reason of which we hope the reader will understand.

The rabbis taught: There is no difference if one hears it from the blasphemer 'himself or from the witness who heard it from the blasphemer—he must rend his garments. However, the witnesses themselves are not obliged to rend their garments again, as they already did so when they heard the blasphemy. But supposing they have already rent? Do they not hear this now? Hence they should rend again? This cannot be supposed, as it reads [ibid., ibid., 19]: "And it came to pass, when King Hezekiah heard it, that he rent his clothes." Hence Hezekiah rent, but they who told him did not rend again.

R. Jehudah said in the name of Samuel: If one hears a blasphemy from the mouth of a heathen, he is not obliged to rend his garments. And should one say: Why did they rend when they heard it from Rabshakeh?—he was not a 'heathen, but an apostate Jew. The same said again in the name of the same authority: Garments must be rent only upon the unique proper Name, but not upon a pseudonym. And he differs from R. Hyya in both his decisions, as R. Hyya said: If one hears a blasphemy in our times, he is not obliged to rend; for if one should say he is obliged, then all garments would be full of rents. Now, who are the blasphemers—Israelites? Are they so bold as to blaspheme God? Hence he means heathens. And are, then, the heathen aware of the unique proper Name? Hence he means a pseudonym. And nevertheless he says, " in our times," from which we understand that in previous times it was obligatory to rend upon a pseudonym also. Infer from this that so it was.

" *The second witness says: I heard exactly the same,*" etc. Said Resh Lakish: Infer from this that in civil cases, as well as in criminal, if one of the witnesses says: " I have heard just the same," and does not repeat what he has heard, it is lawful. And that which the court used to require from the witnesses, that each of them should explain how the case was, is only a higher standard which the rabbis have enacted. In the case of blasphemy, however, in which it is impossible that the second witness should repeat, they leaned on the biblical law. As, if it were biblically illegal, how could it be supposed that because it is forbidden to repeat, a man should be put to death?

" *And so also says the third witness.*" This anonymous Mishna is in accordance with R. Aqiba, who compares three witnesses to two.

MISHNA *VII.*: He is considered an idolater who worships

it with its proper * worship; and even if he only sacrifices, smokes incense, or pours wine.   He is also so considered if he bows himself to it, or accepts it as a god, even without any other act.   And also if he only says: Thou art my god.   However, he who arms, kisses, wipes the dirt, sprinkles water, washes, anoints, dresses, or shoes it, transgresses a negative command-ment [Ex. xx. 5].   He who vows or determines in its name transgresses also a negative commandment [ibid. xxiii. 13]. He who uncovers himself before Baal Peor, and commits a nuisance (is guilty, for) this is the mode of worshipping him; also, he who casts a stone on a *merculis* (*hermaeon*)—that is the way of worshipping it (and he is guilty).

GEMARA: Whence is this deduced?   The rabbis taught: It is written [Ex. xxii. 19]: He that sacrificeth unto any god, save unto the Lord only, shall be utterly destroyed.   If the word " any " were omitted from this verse, I would say it speaks of one who sacrifices animals outside of the sanctuary; but as the word is written, it is to explain that it means: who sacrifices to any idol.   From this, however, we infer sacrificing only.   But whence do we know that the same is the case with smoking incense or pouring wine?   From the words " unto the Lord only," which would be superfluous if they do not mean: all the kinds of worshipping the Lord—if he has done it to an idol, he is guilty.   Now, as sacrificing is included in the worshipping of the Eternal, and nevertheless specified, it is to be assumed that it comes to teach that one is guilty for that kind of wor-shipping which takes place inside of the sanctuary.   Whence, then, do we know that bowing is also considered?   From [Deut. xvii. 3]: " And he hath gone and served other gods and bowed† himself to them "; and [ibid., ibid. 5]: it reads: " Then shalt thou bring forth that man," etc.   But from this we know the punishment—whence is the warning?   [Ex. xxxiv. 14]: " For thou shalt bow thyself to no other god."   And lest one say that arming, kissing, shoeing are also included to be crimes subject to capital punishment, as they are to be inferred from bowing, therefore sacrificing was specified, to show that noth-ing is to be inferred from bowing, and also to teach that as a distinction is made concerning the worshipping inside of the sanctuary, the same is the case with all other worshippings which are used inside—if with such one has worshipped an idol,

---

* This is explained in the Gemara by R. Jeremiah.
† Leeser has omitted this ; we do not know the reason why.

he is liable to a capital punishment.   However, bowing is out of this rule and stands alone.

The master said: If not for the word " any," I would say it speaks of sacrificing out of the sanctuary.   But is not such a crime under the category of Korath?   Should one say that it is when he was not warned, but if he was, capital punishment applies, he comes to teach us that it is not so.

Said Rabha b. R. Hanan to Abayi: Why not say that from bowing " all kinds of worshipping " is to be inferred, and the specification of sacrificing is needed for itself, to teach that an intention of worshipping an idol with any future act, although one does not intend it by the first act, is considered worship; *e.g.*, if one slaughters a cow with the intention of sprinkling its blood, or of burning its fat before the idol, although with the slaughtering he does not worship it, it is nevertheless considered, and it is prohibited to derive any benefit from the cow, according to Johanan?   But according to Resh Lakish the cow is permissible for use, as he does not hold this theory.   And the reason of R. Johanan is because he infers it from the worshipping inside, as to which a future intention, *e.g.*, to sprinkle the blood on the morrow—makes invalid the whole sacrifice. The same is the case with an outside act, as illustrated here.

Said R. Aha of Difti to Rabhina: According to Rabha b. R. Hanan, who said to Abayi: Why not say that from bowing all kinds of worshipping are to be inferred?   What, then, would he exclude from the passage which reads [Deut. xii. 30] : " How did these nations serve their god? "   And lest one say that one who uncovers himself for such idols as are worshipped with sacrifices is excluded, this may be inferred from bowing: as the act of bowing is an honor to the idol, so are all kinds of worship which are in order to honor.   But uncovering, which is a disgrace, is not considered a worship?   Say—to exclude the one who uncovers himself for Merculis.   And lest one say that as the kind of worship of Merculis is a disgrace, the same shall be the case with the disgrace of uncovering, it comes to teach us that it is not so.   But did not R. Elazar say: Whence do we know that if one sacrifices an animal to Merculis he is guilty? From [Lev. xvii. 7] : " So that they shall offer no more their sacrifices unto evil spirits," which is not needed for itself, as this is already written elsewhere?   Apply it, therefore, to bringing an offering to an idol of which the kind of worshipping is not sacrificing.   Now, as from bowing is inferred all kinds of worshipping which are of honor, so one is liable if he did it for any idol, whatsoever be the kind of its worship. Why, then, does R. Eliezer need the above-cited verse? He means to say: Even if he had sacrificed to Merculis, not as an honor but for dishonor, he is nevertheless liable for the transgression of the negative commandment cited above.

It happened to Hamnuna that he lost his oxen, and while searching for them Rabha met him, and propounded to him a contradiction from the two following Mishnayoth: In our Mishna it is stated: " He who *worships* idols," from which is to be inferred only worshipping, but not *saying*. And there is another Mishna, farther on, which states: He who says: " I will worship," or " I will go to worship," or " We will go to worship"—is already considered an idolater. And he answered: Our Mishna means that he said: I do not accept this idol as a god unless by worshipping. Said R. Joseph to him: You are saying this as if it were your own opinion. Do you ignore the Tanaim who differ on this point in the following Boraitha: If one says: " Come ye and worship me, for I am a god," R. Mair makes him guilty as a seducer, and R. Jehudah frees him. However, if there were some who had already worshipped him, all agree that he is guilty. Thus it reads [Ex. xx. 4]: " Thou shalt not make unto thyself," etc., which means also, " Thou shalt not make thyself for an image." But the point of their difference is that he was not as yet worshipped. R. Mair makes him guilty because, according to his opinion, talking is to be taken into consideration; and according to R. Jehudah it is not. Hence we see that Tanaim differ on this point? After deliberating, however, said R. Joseph: What I said was not correct; as we find in the following Boraitha that R. Jehudah also makes one guilty for talking: R. Jehudah said: One is not guilty unless he says: " I will worship," or " I will go and worship," or " We will go and worship." And the point of their difference in the Boraitha cited above is thus: If one who is a seducer for himself (*i.e.*, " Worship me "), and there were some people who said, " Yea," according to R. Mair he is considered a seducer because there were some people who answered, " Yea " ; and according to R. Jehudah this is not considered, as their answer, " Yea," is only a joke. They ridicule him, saying: Are you not a man like us? And the Mishnayoth, which contradict each other, are to be explained thus: Our Mishna, which states " who worshipped," treats if he who was seduced, listened and worshipped him, he is guilty; because if an individual made up his mind to worship him, it is to be presumed that he will not retract.   And the other Mishna treats of when many people were seduced and worshipped him, it is not to be considered, as it is to be supposed that they will reconsider, see-ing there is nothing in him, and will retract.   And R. Joseph said: Whence did I take my theory?   From [Deut. xiii. 9] : " Then shalt thou not consent unto him, nor shalt thou hearken unto him."   From which it is to be understood that if he did listen, and consented unto him, he is culpable.   Abayi objected to him: Is there indeed a difference between an individual who was seduced and a majority?   Is there not a Boraitha: It reads [ibid., ibid. 7] : " If thy brother, the son of thy mother, should entice thee," means that there is no difference between an indi-vidual and a majority, if they were seduced?   And the verse which excluded an individual from a majority, is to make more rigorous his body—viz., to be stoned—and lenient concerning his property, which remains for his heirs; and excluded also a majority from an individual, to make more lenient their bodies —viz., slaying by the sword—and rigorous concerning their property, which must be burned.   Hence we see that only on this point is there a difference between them, but on all other points they are equal.   And therefore he explains the two con-tradictory Mishnayoth, that one speaks of when he has se-duced himself—therefore he is not culpable unless he wor-shipped, as from his talk only, it is supposed that he will retract after deliberating.   And that Mishna which makes him culpable for talking only, speaks of when he was seduced by others, as it is not to be supposed that he will retract.   On the contrary, as they are many, it is highly probable that he will be inclined to them.   And Abayi also infers his theory from the above-cited verse, " If he did not consent," etc., from which it is to be understood that if he did, he is culpable.   Rabha, however, maintains that both Mishnayoth speak of when he was seduced by others, but one treats of when the seducers said to him: " So does the idol eat, so does it drink, so does it good, and so does it harm " ; and the other one treats of when he was not so in-formed.   And he adds: Whence do I deduce my theory?   From [ibid., ibid. 8]: "Some of the gods of the nations which are round about you, that are nigh unto thee," etc.   To what purpose is it written?   Is there a difference if the idols were near to him or far from him?   It must be explained that the verse means thus: From the nature of the idols which are near to thee, thou mayst understand the nature of those which are far from thee. (*I.e.*, usually a seducer comes to tell one from such as are not known to him, and relates before him all the good of the idol, and so seduces him to worship. Hence he said to him: " So does it eat, so does it drink," etc.) R. Ashi maintains: The Mishna which makes one guilty for talking treats of an apostate, who is guilty for talking, as such would not retract after it is seen that such is his habit." Rabhina, however, said: Both Mishnayoth speak of an Israelite, not of an apostate, and they do not differ at all, as the first Mishna says, " who worshipped," and the second states not only " worship," but if he says, " I will," he is also culpable.

It was taught: If one worship an idol because he loves it, or because he fears it, according to Abayi he is culpable, and according to Rabha he is free. The former said so because, after all, he has worshipped it, and therefore he is guilty; and the latter maintains: He is guilty only when he accepts it as a god; but when this is no longer the case, he is free.

Said Abayi: I take my theory from our Mishna, which states, " If one worship," etc., " sacrifice," etc. Now, as the Mishna explains farther on all the kinds of worshipping, the term " worshipped," without specifying the kind, means for love or for fear. Rabha, however, maintains that the Mishna is to be explained as by R. Jeremiah. Said Abayi: I may infer my theory from the following Boraitha: It reads: " Thou shalt not bow thyself to them "—but thou mayst bow thyself to a man who is equal to thee. But lest one say, " Even if the man were worshipped like Haman?" therefore it reads: " Thou shalt not worship them." Now, Haman was worshipped for fear. We see, then, that such a worship is considered. Rabha, however, explains the Boraitha: Like Haman, who established himself as an idol, but not like him who was worshipped only for fear. And Abayi said again: I infer my theory from the following Boraitha: The anointed priest for war may bring an offering, if he acted unintentionally concerning idolatry. So is the decree of Rabbi. Now, let us see! What means, " he acted unintentionally "? Shall we assume that he thought, of a house of idolatry, that it was a synagogue, and bowed himself? Then why should he bring an offering—his heart was toward Heaven? We must then say that he saw an image and bowed himself. Now, if he accepted it as a god, then he has acted intention-

ally and should be put to death.   But if he has not accepted it
as a god, but bowed himself—*e.g.*, for the honor of the king
who was with him?   Then it cannot be considered a sin at all,
even to the extent of bringing an offering.   We must then say
that "unintentionally" means for love or for fear.   Rabha,
however, maintains that his error was that he thought that
such a thing was allowed.

R. Zakkai taught in the presence of R. Johanan: If one has
sarificed, smoked incense, poured wine, and bowed himself before an idol, because of one forgetfulness (that the law does not
allow it), he is liable for one sin-offering only.   And R. Johanan
answered him: Go and teach your teaching outside of the college (*i.e.*, it is nonsense).   Said R. Abba: As to the theory of R.
Zakkai, R. Jose and R. Nathan differ in the following Boraitha:
The negative commandment of kindling on Sabbath, which is
already included in the negative commandment, "Thou shalt
not do any labor," is written for the purpose of teaching that he
who kindles transgresses only a negative commandment, which
is not under the category of Korath or capital punishment, as
for all other labor on Sabbath.   And R. Nathan differs from
him (see Sabbath, p. 000).   And there is the same difference
here concerning bowing.   According to R. Jose, bowing was
specified for the purpose of showing that he who does so transgresses only a negative commandment, to which capital punishment does not apply.   And R. Nathan differs from him with
the same theory as concerning kindling.

When R. Samuel b. Jehudah came from Palestine, he said
that R. Zakkai had taught before R. Johanan thus: Concerning
Sabbath it is more rigorous than all other commandments in
one respect, and all other commandments are more rigorous
than concerning Sabbath in another respect—viz., concerning
Sabbath, if one has done two kinds of labor by one forgetfulness
(*e.g.*, he forgot that it was Sabbath), he is liable for two sin-
offerings; and in all other commandments—if, for instance, he
worshipped with two kinds by one forgetfulness—he is liable
to one sin-offering.   And in another respect the other commandments are more rigorous than concerning Sabbath; as
concerning Sabbath, if he had done any labor unintentionally
—*i.e.*, he intended to do another thing and did this—he is not
liable at all, while concerning other commandments, if such a
thing occurs, he is liable for a sin-offering.

R. Ami said: If one has worshipped by all three worships—

viz., sacrificing, smoking, and pouring—in one forgetfulness, he is liable only for one sin-offering. Said Abayi: The reason of R. Ami's theory is: Because it is written, " Ye shall not worship them," hence the Torah has included all kinds of worship into one. Did Abayi indeed say so? Has he not said: There is written in the Scripture three times " bowing," concerning idolatry: once, that one is culpable if the worship of the idol was by bowing; second, that one is culpable even if the worship of the idol was not by bowing; and the third, to distinguish it from all other worships—that one is liable for it to a capital punishment? You say once, when the usage is to worship thus. Is, then, a verse needed as to this? Is it not written plainly [Deut. xii. 30]: " How did these nations serve their gods? even so will I do likewise "? Say then, once, for such an idol as is not accustomed to be worshipped by bowing, but only occasionally; and once, for such as before which bowing is not used at all—e.g., Baal Peor; and once, to separate it for capital punishment? Hence we see that he is not in accordance with R. Ami? He said so to give a reason for R. Ami's theory, but he himself does not agree with him.

" And also if he only says, ' Thou art my god.' " R. Na'hman in the name of Rabba b. Abuhu, quoting Rabh, said: As soon as he has said, " Thou art my god," he is culpable. But what news is this? If he means capital punishment, did not the Mishna say so? He means to say that he is liable to bring a sin-offering, if this was said by an error, even according to the rabbis, who require an act. But does not a Boraitha state: One is not culpable unless by acting—e.g., sacrificing, smoking, pouring, or bowing? To which Resh Lakish said: Who is the Tana who holds that bowing is also an act? R. Aqiba, who does not require a mental act—from which it is to be understood that the rabbis do? Rabh also means to say in accordance with R. Aqiba. But is this not self-evident? Does not R. Aqiba say that even an unintentional blasphemer is also liable for a sin-offering? Lest one say that R. Aqiba holds liable a blasphemer because the punishment of korath is mentioned in the Scripture concerning him, but concerning bowing, which is not mentioned, even R. Aqiba frees him from this obligation, he comes to teach us that they are compared. As it reads [Ex. xxxii. 8]: " They have bowed themselves to it, and have sacrificed unto it," etc.

R. Johanan said: If not for the Vav in the word " he-elukha " (brought thee up) in the above-cited verse (which makes it plural and means that they also took part in the exodus from Egypt), all Israel would be liable to be destroyed. However, in this the following Tanaim differ: Anonymous teachers say: If not for the Vav in the word " he-elukha," etc. Said R. Simeon b. Johai to them: This is still worse, as there is a tradition: He who conjoins the name of Heaven with something else is to be destroyed; and therefore the Vav in " he-elukha," which makes the word plural, shows that they were fond of many gods.

" *He who arms, kisses*," etc. When Rabbin came from Palestine, he said in the name of R. Elazar that one is not punisheu with stripes for all them, unless one vows or determines in its name. But let us see! Why is one not punished for all these? Because the negative commandment is not plainly written to this effect, but was included in the negative commandment, " Thou shalt not worship them." And there is a rule that for such a commandment no stripes apply. Why, then, should stripes apply to one who vows? This commandment is also not for mental labor, but for manual. And there is a rule that concerning a commandment in which mental labor is not involved, stripes do not apply. He is in accordance with R. Jehudah, who said that for such a negative commandment stripes do apply. As we have learned in the following Boraitha: It reads [Ex. xii. 10]: " And ye shall not let anything of it remain until morning, and that which remaineth of it until morning ye shall burn with fire." Hence the Scripture came to give a positive commandment (ye shall burn) after a negative commandment (ye shall not leave), to say that for the transgression of such a negative commandment stripes do not apply. So R. Jehudah. R. Jacob, however, says: The reason why stripes do not apply is not because of that which is said by R. Jehudah, but because in this commandment no mental labor is involved, and to such no stripes apply. Hence we see that, according to R. Jehudah, even to such stripes do apply.

" *He who vows in its name*," etc. Whence is this deduced? From [Ex. xxiii. 13]: " And of the name of other gods ye shall make no mention "—which means, one must not say to his neighbor: Await me in such and such a place, where such and such an idol is to be found. " It shall not be heard out of thy mouth " means, one shall not vow or determine in its name, and shall also not cause others to do so. Another explanation to, " It shall not be heard out of thy mouth," is that it is a warn-

ing to a seducer and to a misleader.   But concerning a seducer
is it not written plainly [Deut. xiii. 12]: " And all Israel shall
hear and be afraid "?   Therefore it must be said that it is a
warning to a misleader, and also that one shall not cause others
to vow or determine in its name.   And this is a support to
Samuel's father, who said that one must not make partner-
ship with an idolater, as it may be that his partner will owe an
oath to him, and he will swear by the name of his idol.   And
the Torah says: " It shall not be heard out of thy mouth," which
means: You shall not cause others to vow in its name.

It happened once that Ula lodged in Khalmbu, and when
he came to Rabha, he asked him: " Where did the master lodge
last night? "   And he said: In Khalmbu.   Said Rabha to him:
Is it not written: " The name of other gods ye shall not mention "?   Rejoined Ula: So said R. Johanan: Every idol which
is mentioned in the Scripture, one may mention.

R. Jehudah in the name of Rabh said: It happened to a
female heathen who was very sick and vowed that if she recovered she would worship all the idols which were to be found.
And after her recovery she did so.   When she reached Baal
Peor she asked how it should be worshipped.   And she was told
that worshippers ate mangcorn, drank beer, and then uncovered
themselves in its face.   And she said: " I would rather suffer the
same sickness again than perform such a worship."   But yet the
house of Israel have not done so, as it reads [Num. xxv. 5]:
" That have been joined unto Baal Peor," which means like
the cover to a pot.   However [Deut. iv. 4]: " But ye that
cleave unto the Lord,' ètc., as a twin of dates.   A Boraitha
states: "Joined to Peor,' as a ring on the finger of a woman,
"cleave to the Lord " means, literally.

The rabbis taught: It happened to Saphta b. Als, who hired
his ass to a certain female heathen.   And when she reached the
place of Baal Peor, she said to him: "Await me here, I will
enter only for a while and come out."   And when she came out,
he also said to her: " Await me here, I will also do the same."
And to her question: " Are you not a Jew? " he answered:
" What do you care? "   He then entered, uncovered himself
and put the dirt on the nose of the idol.   And the ministers
of Peor praised him for this, saying that there was no man who
worshipped Peor as properly as he did.   The sages, however,
made him guilty for the proper worship of the idol, although
his intention was to disgrace it.   And the same is the case if he

throws a stone at Merculis, although with the intention of stoning it, he is nevertheless guilty, for so is the kind of its worship.

R. Menassah went to the city of Turta, and was told that this place is of an idol. And he took up a lump and threw it at it (the idolatrous statue). He was then told that it was Merculis, and he answered that the Mishna states " he who throws a stone at Merculis," *i.e.*, to worship. And when he came to the college he was told that the Mishna means, even if his intention was to stone it. He then said: I will go and take it up. However, he was told that it is the same transgression, for by taking one stone he makes room for another.

MISHNA *VIII.*: If one gives one of his children to Molech, he is not guilty unless he had transferred him to the servants of Molech and let him pass through the fire. If, however, he had transferred and not passed through the fire, or *vice versa*, he is not guilty.

GEMARA: The Mishna speaks of idols, and mentions Molech. Said R. Abiu: Our Mishna is in accordance with him who says that Molech is not an idol at all. As we have learned in the following Boraitha: There is no difference whether one has given of his children to other idols or to Molech—he is culpable. R. Eliezer b. R. Simeon, however, maintains: Only if he has done it to Molech he is guilty, but not if to another idol. Said Abayi: R. Elazar b. Simeon and Hanina b. Antiguus have said the same—R. Elazar b. Simeon, in the Boraitha cited; and Hanina, who said in the following Boraitha: Why does the Torah use the term Molech? * To say of every one whom they have accepted as a king over them—be it even a piece of wood—one is guilty if he had transferred one of his children for it. Hence we see that, according to him, one is guilty only concerning Molech, but not concerning another idol. Rabha, however, maintains that Simeon and Hanina differ concerning a temporary Molech, as according to R. Simeon one is not guilty on account of such.

R. Janai said: One is not guilty unless he transfers a child to the servants of the idol, as it reads [Lev. xviii. 21]: " And from thy children thou shalt not give to pass through the fire to Molech." And so also we have learned in the following Boraitha: Lest one say that when he passed his child and has not transferred, he should be guilty, therefore it reads, " Thou shalt not give." If he has transferred and not passed through

---

* The term for king in Hebrew is *melech.*

the fire, he is also not guilty, because it reads, " to pass through the fire." And if one has done both, but not for Molech, one might say he is guilty? Therefore it reads, " to Molech." If one has transferred and passed to Molech, but not through fire, he is also not guilty, because it reads, " through fire." And it is written also [Deut. xviii. 10]: " There shall not be found among thee any one who causeth his son or his daughter to pass through the fire." And we infer one from the other. As there it is mentioned plainly " fire," so here also it is meant fire; and as here is meant Molech, so also there is meant Molech. Said R. Aha b. Rabha: If one has transferred all his children to Molech, he is not guilty, as the verse reads, " and from thy children "—but not all. R. Ashi questioned: How is it if one has passed through the fire a son blind or asleep, or one of his grandchildren? The last question may be answered from the following: It reads [Lev. xx. 3]: " Because of his seed he has given unto Molech." To what purpose was it written? Because in the above-cited verse in Deuteronomy it reads " son " and " daughter," and one might say, but not of grandchildren. Therefore it is written [ibid., ibid. 4]: " When he giveth of his seed," in which grandchildren are included.

Let us see! The Tana begins with verse three [3] and ends with verse four [4]. He did so because of another teaching. One might say that one is guilty only for legitimate children, but not for illegitimate; therefore it reads in verse four, from his " seeds," which includes all.

Said R. Jehudah: One is not guilty unless he let him pass in the usual manner. What was that? Said Abayi: A row of bricks were placed for passing, and on both sides fire was kindled. Rabha, however, maintains that it was by jumping, as children used to jump on Purim. (Rashi explains that they used to have a pit in which fire was kindled, and the people used to jump over it.)

There is a Boraitha in accordance with Rabha: One is not culpable unless he has passed in the usual manner of worship. However, if he passed it by, not jumping, he is not guilty. He is also culpable only when he passed his descendants; but not if his brother, sisters, father, mother, or even himself. R. Eliezer b. R. Simeon, however, makes guilty him who passed himself. There is no difference whether he has passed to Molech or to any other idol. R. Eliezer b. R. Simeon, however, maintains: To Molech, but not to others.

Said Ula: The reason why R. Elazar makes guilty him who passes himself is because it reads: " bkho "—literally, " *in* thee," which means " thyself."   But do not the rabbis also give attention to the word " bkho "?   Is there not a Mishna in Middle Gate (p. 000): And R. Jehudah said: The reason of it is because it is written " bkho "?   There is also another reason—because the verse begins with " although, indeed."

R. Jose b. Hanina said: Three times korath is mentioned concerning idolatry: once for worshipping it as it is done usually; once as not done usually; and once for Molech, although it was not considered an idol.   And to him that holds that Molech was also an idol, why is a separate korath needed for it?   Is it not included in idolatry?   To him who passes his son not in its usual manner (*i.e.*, although he is not put to death by the court, the punishment of korath rests upon him).   And to him who holds that he who worships idols—*e.g.*, he sings before one—is also considered blasphemous,—to what purpose is korath mentioned concerning blasphemy?   To that which we have learned in the following Boraitha: It reads [Num. xv. 31]: " hekorath tekorath "—" hekorath," which means cut off from this world; " tekorath," from the world to come.   So R. Aqiba.   Said R. Ishmael to him: Is it not written in the preceding verse, " Shall be cut off "?   Are there then three worlds?   Therefore the expression [in 30] means from this world, and the term " hekorath " means from the world to come; and the expression " tekorath " is not to be considered, as the Torah speaks with the usual language of human beings.

MISHNA *IX.*: Baal ob (mentioned in the Scripture) is the python that makes the dead speak from his armpit, and Yidoui means one that makes the dead speak from his mouth.   These two are to be stoned; and he who queries from them is warned [Lev. xix. 31].

GEMARA: Why does our Mishna count both Baal ob and Yidoui, and in Tract Keritoth the Tana mentioned only Baal ob and omitted Yidouim, etc.?   (The discussion here is a repetition from Tract Kheritoth, which is the proper place, where it will be translated.)

The rabbis taught: Baal ob is one who ventriloquizes, and a Yidoui is he who puts a certain bone in his mouth, which speaks from itself.

The rabbis taught: There are two kinds of " ob ": one who brings up the dead, and one who questions a dead head.   He who brings up the dead—it appears before him not in the usual manner, but with its feet on top; and on the Sabbath it does not come up at all. But he who does this with the head of one dead answers as usual, and answers also on Sabbath. Also about this, R. Aqiba was questioned by Turnusrupus: Why is this day (of Sabbath) distinguished from all other days? To which Aqiba answered: Why is this man (Turnusrupus) distinguished from all other men? And he answered: Because it is the will of my master (the king). Rejoined R. Aqiba: Sabbath is also distinguished because it is the will of the Lord of the Universe. Said Turnusrupus: You misunderstand me. My question is: Whence do you know that this day is Sabbath? And he answered: From the river of Sabbation (which rests on this day); and it may also be proved from the fact that he who occupies himself with bringing up the dead cannot do his work on Sabbath; and also the grave of your father may prove that the smoke which comes out of it on all week days does not come out of it on all week days does not come out on Sabbath. Exclaimed Turnusrupus : You have disgraced, ashamed, and insulted me.

Is not he who queries an " ob " the same as one who inquires of the dead? Nay! The latter is as we have learned in the following Boraitha: By " inquire of the dead " is meant he who does not take food all day, and while he suffers hunger he goes to a cemetery, and remains there overnight for the purpose that the unclean spirit should rest upon him. And when R. Aqiba used to read this passage, he would weep, saying: Is not an *a fortiori* conclusion to be drawn from this passage? If one who makes himself suffer from hunger, for the purpose that the unclean spirit should rest upon him, usually succeeds, and the spirit in question rests upon him, so much the more, if one makes himself suffer hunger for the purpose that the pure spirit should rest upon him, should he succeed in reaching his desire; but what can we do if our sins cause that our desire shall not be reached, as it reads [Is. lix. 2] : " But your iniquities have ever made a separation between you and your God "? Said Rabha: If the upright would take care to be clean from any sin whatsoever, they would be able to create a world (and he infers it from the verse just cited). Rabha created a man and sent him up to R. Zera. The latter spoke to him, and he did not answer. Exclaimed R. Zera: I see that thou wast created by one of our colleagues. It is beter that thou shouldst be returned to the earth from which thou wast taken. R. Hanina and R. Oshia were acustomed to sit every eve of Sabbath studying the book of creation, and create a calf like that of the third offspring of a living cow, and they used to consume it on Sabbath.

The rabbis taught: An observer of times is, according to R. Simeon, he who passes the outcome of a certain male over his eye (for the purpose of witchcraft); according to the sages, it is he who dazzles the eyes. R. Aqiba, however, said: The one who reckons times and hours, saying: This day is good to go on the road, such a day is good to buy things, on the eves of the Sabbatic years the wheat is fine, such and such a time is good for picking peas as they will not become verminous.

The rabbis taught: An enchanter is he who says: " My bread has fallen from my mouth to-day, and it is a bad sign "; or, " My cane has fallen from my hands "; or, " My son called me up from my back "; or, " A robin is calling me "; or, " A ram has crossed my way "; or, " A snake is on my right, a fox is on my left, and all this is a bad sign." Or, if one says to a collector: Do not begin with me, as this will be a bad sign for me. And the same is it if he says: " To-day is the first day of the month," or, " It is the Sabbath eve, and if I should pay at this time I will have a bad week " or " a bad month." And the same is the case with them who enchant with cats, birds, and fish (i.e., I will not begin this thing because a cat has crossed my way, etc.). So is the teaching of the rabbis.

MISHNA X.: He who violates the Sabbath with such a labor as is liable to korath if done intentionally, and to a sin offering if unintentionally.

GEMARA: From this we see that there are violations of Sabbath to which neither korath nor a sin-offering apply. What are they?   The limit of the cities (Te'humi), in accordance with R. Aqiba; and kindling, according to R. Jose.

MISHNA XI.: He who curses his father or mother is not punished with a capital punishment, unless he curse them by the proper Name of God.   If he has done so with a pseudonym, according to R. Mair he is guilty, and according to the sages he is not.

GEMARA: Who are the sages?   R. Mnahem b. Jose of the following Boraitha, who said thus: It reads [Lev. xxiv. 16]: " When he prounceth the holy name," etc.   Why is here repeated " the holy name "?   It should read: " If he blaspheme," etc. To teach that in the case of cursing father and mother one is not guilty unless he do so with the Holy Name.

The rabbis taught: It reads [ibid., xx. 9]: "Every one," instead of "one." This came to include a daughter, or an hermaphrodite, or an andogyn. "That curseth his father and his mother." But whence do we know that the same is the case when he curses his father only, or his mother only? Therefore it reads farther on, "his father and his mother has he cursed." Hence the word "cursed" corresponds with the word "mother"; and in the beginning of the verse the word "cursed" corresponds with "father," which is to be explained as that he is equaly guilty if he has cursed his father or his mother. So is the decree of R. Jashia. R. Jonathan, however, said: The beginning of the verse can be explained that it means both together, and also one *or* the other; and in such a case the applicability is to each of them, unless the verse itself explains that both together are meant. "Shall be put to death"—by stoning! But perhaps with some other kind of death mentioned in the Scripture? It reads here, "His blood shall be upon him," and elsewhere it is written, "Their blood shall be upon them." As there it means stoning, the same is it here. But here we have heard of the punishment. Where is the warning? [Ex. xxii. 27]: "The judges thou shalt not revile, and a ruler among thy people thou shalt not curse." "If one's father were one of the two, he is included; but if he was neither a judge nor a Nasi, whence do we know that the same is the case? This can be inferred from the construction of the leading rule in both cases (*i.e.*, one who is to be respected must not be cursed, although the nature of respecting them is not equal), as concerning a judge we are commanded to follow his decision, which is not the case with a Nasi; and concerning the latter we are commanded not to rebel against him, which is not the case with a judge. However, in one case they are equal, in that they are of "thy people," and thou must not curse them. The same is the case with the father, who is also of "thy people" and must be respected by thee. Hence you are warned not to curse him. And lest one say that, after all, we can infer nothing from the case in which they are equal, as their dignity is the reason of their equality, which is not the case with a common father, concerning this it reads [Lev. xix. 14]: "Thou shalt not curse the deaf"—from which we see that the verse speaks of the unfortunates of "thy people." And lest one say that this is also

different, as the misfortune is the reason, the above case of
judge and Nasi proves that this is not so.   And again, their
dignity is the reason?   The case of the deaf proves that it is
not so.   Hence, although the reason of the one is not similar
to that of the other, in one thing, however, they are equal, in
that they are of " thy people " and must not be cursed.   The
same is the case with his father.   And still, lest one say that,
after all, the three above mentioned are distinguished, which
is not the case with the father, it may be said that if the reason
is because of distinction, it would not be necessary for the
Scripture to write all the three, as a judge and a death or a
Nasi and a death would suffice.   Why, then, all the three?   As
it is not needed for itself, apply it to a common father.   And
all this is correct to him who explains the word " Elohim " in
the above-cited verse [Ex. xxii.] with " judges "; but to him
who explains the word " Elohim " as meaning God, what can
be said?   For there is a Boraitha: Elohim in this verse is common, and means " judges."   So R. Ishmael.   R. Aqiba, however, maintains that Elohim is " holy."   And there is another
Boraitha: R. Eliezer b. Jacob said that this verse is a warning
against blasphemy.   He who holds that the word Elohim here
is common, must say that the holiness is inferred from this passage (by drawing an *a fortiori* conclusion—if one is warned
not to curse a human judge, so much the more is he warned
not to curse the Holiness), as we do not find any other warning besides; and he who holds that the word Elohim is " holy,"
the case of a commoner may also be inferred—from the double
Lamed in the word " tekhalel " (curse), which could be expressed " tekhal " with one Lamed.

MISHNA XI.: He who sins with a betrothed damsel is
not guilty to be stoned unless she was a maiden betrothed
and still in her father's house.   Should it happen that two
had sinned with her, the first is to be stoned and the second
choked.

GEMARA: The rabbis taught: It reads [Deut. xxii. 23]:
" if a damsel "—not a *vigaros;* " a maiden "—not one who had
already known man; " betrothed "—not married.   And [ibid.,
ibid. 21] it reads, " in her father's house," excluding if the
father had already transferred her to the mesengers of her
husband.

Said R. Jehudah in the name of Rabh: This is in accordance
with R. Mair.   The sages, however, say: A betrothed damsel,

even if she is still a minor. Said R. Aha of Diphthi to Rabhina:
Whence do you know that the Mishna is in accordance with
R. Mair and excludes a minor—perhaps it is in accordance with
the rabbis excluding a *vigaros* only? And he answered: If so,
the Mishna should state that he is not guilty but as concerning
pression means to exclude a minor also; and about this no more
discussion.

R. Jacob b. Adda questioned Rabh: In accordance with R.
Mair, if it happened one had sinned with a betrothed minor,
does he exclude him from any punishment, or from stoning
only? And he answered: Common sense dictates from stoning only. But is it not written [ibid., ibid. 22]: "Shall both of
them die," which is explained elsewhere, that it means, provided both were alike concerning age? And Rabh kept silent.
Said Samuel: I do not understand why Rabh was silent, and
did not refer him to ibid., ibid. 26, which reads: "He shall die
alone"?

In this point Tanaim differ. "Both shall die" means, provided both were alike concerning age. So R. Jashia. R.
Jonathan, however, said: From the verse [25] is inferred that
he alone must be put to death. But what does R. Jashia infer
from the verse, "He alone," etc.? That which we have learned
from the following Boraitha: If ten men knew her while she
was still a virgin, all of them are to be stoned. Rabbi, however, maintains that only the first one is to be stoned, and all
the others choked, as thus it reads: "And the man that lay
with her shall die alone." What does it mean? Said R. Huna
b. R. Jehoshua: Rabbi holds with R. Ishmael that a betrothed
damsel is to be burned, but not one married. And the verse
which reads about one betrothed is to be explained thus: Only
the beginner is to be burned, but all others are to be choked.
Said R. Bibi b. Abayi: Our master, R. Joseph, does not say
so. But that Rabbi holds with R. Mair, who said that if the
daughter of a priest was married to one who was prohibited
from marrying her, and she has sinned, her death is choking.
And Rabbi meant to say thus: If the beginning of her profana-
tion was sin, then she is to be burned; but if she was already
profaned by an illegal marriage, she is to be choked. And his
expression, "And so also it reads: 'He shall die alone,'" is not
to be taken particularly, but as a remark.

MISHNA *XII.*: A seducer means one who is himself a
commoner and seduces a commoner—*e. g.*, he says: There is an

idol in such and such a place which so and so eats, so and so drinks, and so and so does good, and so does harm.

Concerning all who are liable to capital punishment biblically, it is not allowed to hide witnesses except in this case: If, *e.g.*, he said the above to two persons, they are his witnesses —they bring him up to the court, and they themselves stone him. If, however, he said it only to one, he may say: I have some colleagues who will also follow your adivce, if you will say the same to them. But if he is shrewd, and does not want to talk in the presence of two persons, they may hide witnesses behind a fence, and he may say to him: Repeat to me what you said at first. And if he repeats, he may say to him: How can we leave our Heavenly Father and go to worship idols of stone and wood? If he retracts—well and good. If, however, he answers: This will be good for us and also is our duty, the witnesses who are hidden behind the fence may bring him to court and stone him.

A seducer is considered he who says: I will worship; I will go and worship; Let us go and worship; I will sacrifice to such and such an idol; or, Let us go and sacrifice; I will smoke incense before it; I will go and smoke; Let us go and smoke; I will pour wine before it; I will go and pour; Let us go and pour; I will bow myself; I will go and bow; Let us go and bow.

GEMARA: The Mishna states: A seducer means a commoner. But how would it be if he should say: I am a prophet, and tell you to do so in the name of the Lord? Choking would apply. And also " he seduces a commoner " (individual). But how if he should seduce many? Then also choking would apply and not stoning. We see, then, that our Mishna is in accordance with R. Simeon of the following Boraitha: To a prophet who had misled, stoning applies. R. Simeon, however, said: Choking. To the misleader of a misled town, stoning applies; according to R. Simeon, choking. How, then, will be understood the succeeding Mishna, which states: A misleader is named he who says, " Let us go and worship idols "? To which R. Jehudah in the name of Rabh said: It speaks of the misleader of a misled town, who is to be stoned, which is in accordance with the rabbis. Hence our Mishna is in accordance with R. Simeon, and the succeeding Mishna in accordance with the rabbis. Said Rabhina: Both are in accordance with the rabbis; and by the expression, " he seduced a commoner," he does not mean to exclude a majority. But it was said in the Mishna, " not only "—*i.e.*, not only is he to be stoned who seduces a majority, but even a single commoner.   And R. Papa said: Even the beginning of the Mishna, " the seducer is a commoner," does not mean to exclude a prophet, as it was supposed, but it means to say: He is a commoner idiot, to whom hiding witnesses is allowed, which is not the case with all other criminals.   And how used they to do with such a person? They used to light a candle in the inner chamber, engaging him with talk, and the witnesses were placed in the outer chamber so that they should see him and hear his voice, while he could not see them; and there the person whom he attempted to seduce tried to make him repeat, as stated above in the Mishna.

MISHNA *XII.*: By a misleader is meant one who says: Let us go and worship idols.   A conjurer is liable to be stoned only when he did an act, but not if he dazzled the eyes.   R. Aqiba said in the name of R. Jehoshua: As, for instance, if there are two who gather cucumbers from a field by enchantment—one of them is liable to a capital punishment and one of them is entirely free.   If one has really gathered all of them to one place by witchcraft, he is to be stoned; and the other, who did so only by dazzling the eyes, but in reality the cucumbers remained in their place, is entirely free.

GEMARA: R. Jehudah in the name of Rabh said: The Mishna speaks of the misleader of a misled town.   "*A conjurer*," etc.   The rabbis taught: It reads: " A witch."   There was no difference whether male or female—why, then, the term " witch "?   Because in most cases women used to be engaged in witchcraft.   What kind of death applies to them?   R. Jose the Galilean said: It reads [Ex. xxii. 17]: " Thou shalt not suffer a witch to live "; and it reads [Deut. xx. 16]: " Shalt thou not let live a single soul."   As there it is meant by the sword, the same is the case here.   R. Aqiba, however, said: It is to be inferred from [Ex. xix. 13]: " It shall not live."   As there stoning is meant, the same is the case here.   Said R. Jose: My analogy is from " techaiah "—" let not live " (a female), while your analogy is from " yechaiah "—" shall not live " (a male).   And he answered: My analogy is to infer Israel from Israel, to whom many kinds of deaths are prescribed, while according to your analogy, Israel from the descendants of Noah should be inferred, and there is only one death prescribed for descendants of Noah.   Ben Azai, however, said: Ex. xxii. 17 is to be inferred from the next verse [18]: "Whosoever lieth with a beast," etc.   As to this stoning applies, the same is the case here.   Said R. Jehudah to him: Because this verse is near to the other, therefore the witch should be stoned?   According to my opinion there is another reason.   Ob and Yidoui ought to be included in the case of conjurers—why, then, does the Scripture separate them? Only for the purpose of comparing other conjurers to them. As to them stoning applies, so does it to all conjurers.

According to R. Jehudah: Let Ob and Yidoui be considered as two verses which command one and the same.   And there is a rule that from such nothing is to be inferred.   Said R. Zecharias: Infer from this that R. Jehudah does not hold this theory and maintains that from such it may be inferred.   It reads [Deut. iv. 35]: "There is none else besides him."   Said R. Hanina: Even witchcraft has no effect against a heavenly decree.   There was a woman who tried to take earth from beneath the foot of R. Hanina.   And he said to her: If you think you will succeed in affecting me with your witchcraft, go on and do so, as I am not afraid.   It reads: "There is none else besides Him."   Is that so?   Did not R. Johanan say: It may happen that witchcraft may affect even against heavenly decrees?   With R. Hanina it was different, as his strength was great, being righteous all his life.   Aibu b. Nagri in the name of R. Hyya b. Abba said: In Ex. vii. 11 it reads, "blahatehem," and in ibid. viii. 3 it is written, "blatehem."   The latter means by the act of demons, and the former by the act of sorcery. And so also is it expressed in Gen. iii. 24, "lahat," or the sword which revolveth (revolveth by itself, which looked like witchcraft).   Said Abayi: A conjurer who is particular to use a utensil, it is by a demon, and he who is not particular, it is by witchcraft.

He said again: The Halakhas of witchcraft are similar to the Halakhas of Sabbath.   There are some to which stoning applies; there are some which are not allowed to start with, but if, nevertheless, one has done them, he is free; and some are allowed even to start with.   To him who did an act by witchcraft, stoning applies.   To dazzle the eyes is not allowed to start with, but if one did, he is free.   And it is allowed to start with, as said above.   R. Hanina and R. Oshia were accustomed to create a calf, etc.

Said R. Ashi: I have seen the father of a certain man Karna

scatter strips of silk from his nose. It reads [Ex. viii. 15]: "Then said the magicians of Pharaoh, This is the finger of God." Said R. Elazar: Infer from this that a demon is not able to produce a creation the size of which is less than a barley. Said R. Papa: They are not able to create even the size of a camel; but if they needed it, they got it from far places, which they could not do with smaller creations.

Said Rabh to R. Hyya: I have seen a rider of a camel who took his sword, cut off the head of the camel, and thereafter rung a bell, and the camel stood up. Said R. Hyya to him: Did you see after it stood up, that the place was dirty from blood and dust? There was nothing. Hence it was only a dazzling of the eyes.

It happened that Zera was in Alexandria of Egypt, and bought an ass. Afterward, when he came (to a river) to let the ass drink, it disappeared (the charm was broken), and there stood a landing board. And he was told: If you were not Zera, your money would not be returned, as there is no one who buys something here and does not try it on water. Janai happened to stop at a certain inn and asked for water. And he was supplied with *sthitha* (water mixed with flour), and he noticed that the woman who brought it mumbled. He poured out a little and a serpent came out of it. And then he said to her: I drank from your water, now you may also drink from mine. She did so and became an ass. He then rode upon her to the market. And her associate, who recognized the witchcraft absolved her, and then every one saw that he was riding on a woman.

It reads [ibid., ibid. 2]: "And the frogs came up." Said R. Elazar: It was only one frog which multiplied over all Egypt with its offspring. In this point Tanaim differ. R. Aqiba said the same as Elazar. Said Elazar b. Azariah to him: Aqiba, what have you to do with Haggadah? Leave it, and show forth thy study in the difficulties of Negaim and Ohaloth. It was only one frog to whose croaking all other frogs were gathered.

"*R. Aqiba said,*" etc. Did R. Aqiba indeed learn this from R. Jehoshua? Is there not a Boraitha: When R. Eliezer became sick, R. Aqiba and his colleagues came to make him a sick-call. He was under a canopy, and they were placed in his palace. That day was an eve of Sabbath, and Hurcanos, his son, entered to undress his phylacteries.* His father re-

---

* See our "Phylacterien Ritus," p. 49, footnotes.

buked him, and he went out as if he had been under the ban, and said to his colleagues: It seems to me that the mind of my father is not clear. And R. Eliezer, who heard this, said to them: And I think that the minds of both his mother and himself are unsound, as they occupy themselves with undressing phylacteries on account of which the Sabbath would not be violated, even if they were to remain upon him the whole Sabbath, while so long as they have not as yet prepared other things for Sabbath, which would be a violation subject to a capital punishment if done on Sabbath.

When the above-mentioned sages saw that his mind was clear, they approached him a distance of four ells, and became seated. He then questioned them: To what purpose is your call? To which they answered: We came to learn Torah from you. And to his question: Why have you not come until now? They answered: We had no time. He then exclaimed: I wonder if these people will die a natural death! Said Aqiba to him: And what will be my lot? And he said: Yours will be still harder than theirs. He then took his two arms, put them on his heart, and said: Woe to ye! my two arms, which are as two parchments of the Holy Scrolls, of which nothing can be read when they are rolled together (he meant that when he should die, all his wisdom would go with him, as there were none to whom to teach it). I have studied much and taught much. I have studied much, and have not diminished from the wisdom of my masters even to the extent of what a dog laps from the sea. I taught much, and my disciples have not diminished from my wisdom—even as the painting pencil which is inserted in a tube. And not this only, but I have learned about three hundred Halakhas as to planting cucumbers, and there was no man who could question me something concerning them except Aqiba b. Joseph. As it once happened, I was on the road with him, and he said to me: Rabbi, teach me something about planting cucumbers. And I said something, and the whole field was filled with cucumbers. And he said to me: Rabbi, with this you taught me the planting of them; now teach me the removing of them. And I said something and all were gathered to one place. Hence we see that he had learned this of R. Eliezer, and not of R. Jehoshua? He learned it from R. Eliezer, but did not understand thoroughly. But thereafter, however, he learned this from R. Jehoshua thoroughly, and it remained in his mind. But how could he do so? Have we not learned in a Mishna that he who does an act with witch-craft deserves a capital punishment? To learn it is different. As the Master said: It reads [Deut. xviii. 9]: " Thou shalt not learn to do "—which means: Thou must not learn to do, but thou mayst learn it to understand it for the purpose of deciding cases.

CHAPTER VIII.

MISHNA *I.*: A stubborn and rebellious son—at what age
may he be considered such? From the time he brings forth
two hairs till they encompass the face: it does not mean the
chin, but the bottom (pubes); but the sages used to speak with
delicacy.

It reads [Deut. xxi. 18]: "If a man have a stubborn and
rebellious son," etc. A son, and not a daughter; a son, but
not a mature man. However, a minor is free from such a
charge, as the commandment's obligation does not as yet rest
upon him.

GEMARA: Whence do we know that a minor is free?
Whence do we know! Does not the Mishna give the reason,
"because the commandment's obligation does not as yet rest
upon him." And secondly, where do we find that the Scripture has made a minor liable, so that in this case it is necessary to free such? We mean to say thus: Is, then, the punishment of a stubborn son because of his sins? He is punished
because of his future (as will be explained farther on). Then
it would be supposed that the same is the case even when he is
still a minor. And again, the Mishna itself states, "a son, but
not a mature man." And if it did not explain thereafter that
a minor is free, we might say that a minor is also included.
Said R. Jehudah in the name of Rabh: It reads: "If a man has
a son," which means a son who has grown up almost to maturity.

"*Till they surround,*" etc. R. Hisda said: A minor who has

born a son—the latter does not become a rebellious son: which means, when a man 'has a son, but not a son who has a son. But was not what R. Jehudah said in the name of Rabh inferred from the same verse? It should read, " If there shall be a son to a man."

And from what is written, " when a man has a son," we infer also what R. Hisda said. However, he differs with Rabha, who said elsewhere that a minor cannot beget children. As it reads [Num. v. 8] : " But if a man have no kinsman." And to the question: Is it possible that a man in Israel should have no kinsman? it was said that the verse speaks about the robbery of a proselyte (who has no kinsman in Israel). But why does the Scripture mention a man? It should read, " if he has no kinsman," to teach that if the proselyte was already a man you have to inquire; for perhaps he has begotten children, and thus has kinsmen. But if he was a minor, you have not to inquire, as a minor cannot beget children. Abayi objected to him from [Lev. xix. 20] : " And if a man lie," etc.— as to which a Boraitha states, " A man ! " But whence do we know that the same is the case with a minor after the age of nine years and one day, who is already fit to have connection with a woman? Therefore it is written, " *and* if a man," to add the minor just mentioned. (Hence we see that such is already fit to beget children.) Rejoined Rabha: He is fit to have connection, but not to beget children, which is equalized to grain which has not as yet grown up to a third of its usual growth; and if such were sown, it would not reproduce. Is this so? Did not the disciples of R. Ishmael teach: It is written, " a son "; but not when he is a father. Now let us see how was the case. Shall we assume that his wife was pregnant just after he grew two 'hairs, and that he begot the child before the above-mentioned encompassing was completed. Has she, then, so much time? Did not R. Khruspdai say that the prescribed time for a rebellious son is only three months? You must then say she was pregnant before he grew two hairs, and begot a child before the encompassing was complete. Hence we see that a minor begets children? Nay! she was pregnant after he grew two hairs, and begot after the encompassing. And the difficulty about what was said by Khruspdai was explained by R. Dimi after his return from Palestine thus: In 'thei West it was said, " a son," but not one who is fit to be called a father, as he has already a pregnant wife.

The text says: Khruspdai in the name of R. Sabatta said: The time for a rebellious son is only three months. We, however, have learned in a Mishna that the prescribed time is from when he grows two hairs until the encompassing is complete. However, if the completion was before three months, the time has already elapsed; and the same is the case when the encompassing was not completed after the three months had elapsed.

R. Jacob of the city of N'har Pauqud was sitting before Rabhina, and said in the name of R. Huna b. Jehoshua: From Khruspdai's theory we may infer that a woman who bears in the seventh month cannot be recognized as pregnant after the first third of her pregnancy. For if it were so, why was it said in the West that he is fit to become a father after three months —would not two and a third suffice, as then the pregnancy is already recognizable? Answered Rabhina: This cannot be taken as evident, as the majority do not bear children in the seventh month, but in the ninth. All this was declared to R. Huna b. Jehoshua, and the latter exclaimed: Do we, then, consider a majority in criminal cases? The Torah says: "The congregation shall judge, the congregation shall save"; and you say that we shall go after a majority. His answer was brought back to Rabhina, to which the latter replied: Is it indeed so—that we do not consider a majority in criminal cases? Have we not learned in a Mishna that if one witness says it was in the second of the month and the other says that it was on the third, their testimony is valid, since to one the intercalation of the month was known, but not to the other. Now, if a majority which does not know of the intercalation should not be considered, why should their testimony be valid? Say they are aware of it, but they contradict each other! Hence we must say that the majority is considered.

R. Ahiah b. Rabba b. Nahmani in the name of R. Hisda, according to others the latter in the name of Zeeli, said: All agree that a minor of nine years and one day is fit to have connection with a woman, and in a case of adultery it is considered; and they agree also that at less than eight years of age one is not fit, and it is not considered. And the point of their difference is from the age of eight up.

The school of Shammai holds: We may infer from the first generation. And the school of Hillel holds: We may not.

And whence do we know that the first generation produced children at the age of eight? From [Gen. xi. 27]: "Now these are the generations of Therach: Therach begat Abram, Nachor, and Charan." Abram was one year older than Nachor, and Nachor was one year older than Charan. And it reads [ibid., ibid. 29]: "And Abram and Nachor took themselves wives: the name of Abram's wife was Sarai; and the name of Nachor's wife was Milcah, the daughter of Charan, the father of Milcah, and the father of Yiscah." And R. Itz'hak said: There is a tradition that Yiscah is identical with Sarai. Now, how much was Abram older than Sarai? Ten years. And how much was he older than her father? Two years. Hence, when Charan bore Sarai he was eight years. But perhaps Abram was the younger, and the enumeration in Scripture is not particular, being according to their wisdom. And that the Scripture used to enumerate according to wisdom, and not age, may be seen from [ibid. vi. 10]: "And Noah begat three sons—Shem, Ham, and Japheth." And from the latter passage it is inferred that Shem was the youngest, and nevertheless he is named first, because of his wisdom. Said R. Kahana: I told this to R. Zebith of Nahardea, and he answered: Ye learned this from the cited passage. We, however, infer this from [ibid. x. 21]: "But unto Shem also, the father of all the children of Elier, the brother of Japheth the elder." Hence we see that Japheth was the oldest of all the brothers.

Now the question, "Whence do we know that the first generations produced children at eight years?" still remains unanswered. This is to be inferred from the following. It reads [Ex. xxxv. 30]: "And Moses said unto the children of Israel, See, the Lord hath called by name Bezaleel the son of Uri, the son of Chur, of the tribe of Judah"; and in I. Chron. ii. 19, 20, it reads: "And when Azubah (the wife of Caleb) died, Caleb took unto himself Ephrath, who bore unto him Chur. And Chur·begat Uri, and Uri begat Bezaleel." And when Bezaleel was engaged in building the Tabernacle, he was at least thirteen years old. As it reads [Ex. xxxvi. 4]: "Every man from his own work which they were doing"; and one is not called a man before the age of thirteen. And there is a Boraitha: The first year Moses prepared all that was necessary for the Tabernacle, and in the second year he erected it and sent the spies. And it reads [Joshua, xiv. 7]: "Forty years old was I when Moses the servant of the Lord sent me"; and [ibid., ibid. 10]: "Behold, I am this day eighty and five years old." Now, take off fourteen, the age of Bezaleel from the forty of Joshua when he was sent as a spy, and there remain twenty-six; take off two years for the three pregnancies with Uri, Chur, and Bezaleel, and there remain twenty-four. Hence each of them produced at the age of eight.

"*A son, and not a daughter,*" etc. There is a Boraitha: R. Simeon said: According to common sense, a daughter should be more open to the charges of stubbornness and rebelliousness, as it is to be supposed that her future will be to stand in the way and entice men to sin. But so is the decree of the Scripture—"a son, and not a daughter."

MISHNA *II.*: When does such become guilty? When he consumes ατρι τημόριον of meat and drinks half a lug of Italian wine. R. Jose, however, maintains: Meat not less than a manna, and wine not less than a whole lug. If, however, he ate at a banquet of a meritorious society, or at the intercalation of a month, or at second tithe in Jerusalem; or he ate carcasses, illegal meat, or reptiles, and second tithe and consecrated things which were not redeemed, or mixed grain of first tithe from which the heave-offering was not separated. There is a rule: If he ate a thing which is meritorious, or, on the contrary, a thing which is a transgression—if he consumes any kind of food but not meat, any kind of beverages but not wine —he cannot be condemned as a stubborn and rebellious son, unless he eats meat and drinks wine. As it reads [Deut. xxi. 20]: "He is a glutton and a drunkard." And although there is no direct support in the Scripture that gluttony means meat, and drunkenness, means wine, a hint of this is to be found in [Prov. xxiii. 20]: "Be not among those that drink wine, among those that overindulge in eating meat." *

GEMARA: R. Zerah said: The term "tertimory" mentioned in the Mishna—I don't know how much it weighs. But from the fact of R. Jose having doubled the measure of wine from half a lug to a lug, I understand that he means also to double the weight of meat. Hence a "tertimory" must be half a manna.

R. Hanan b. Muldha in the name of R. Huna said: He is not guilty unless he consumes the meat and the wine raw. Is that so? Did not both Rabha and R. Joseph say that he who consumes meat and wine raw is not to be condemned as a stub-

---

* The term in Hebrew is "zaulel v' saube," which Leeser translates "a glutton," etc. In Proverbs, however, he translates the same term with "overindulging," which also means gluttony.

born and rebellious son? Said Rabhina: By raw wine is meant refined and not refined, and by meat is meant cooked and uncooked, as usually consumed by thieves.

Both Rabha and R. Joseph said: If he consumed salted meat and drank wine from the press, he cannot be condemned as a stubborn and rebellious son. What is to be considered salted meat? When it has lain in salt for three days. And what is called wine from the press? When it is still fermenting.

R. Itz'hak said: It reads [Prov. xxiii. 31]: " Do not look on the wine when it looketh red "—meaning that you shall not look for wine which makes red the faces of the wicked in this world, and makes them pale in the world to come. Rabha said: You shall not look for wine which causes bloodshed.*

When R. Dimi came from Palestine, he said: About the verse [ibid., ibid. 29, 30]: " Who hath woe? who hath sorrow? who hath quarrels? who hath complaints? who hath wounds without cause? who hath redness of eyes? They that tarry late over the wine; they that come to seek for mixed drink." It was said in the West that he who tries to explain them from their beginning to their end is correct, and he who tries to explain them from their end to their beginning is also correct.†

Eubar the Galilean lectured: Thirteen vavs are enumerated in the Scripture concerning wine, as in Genesis ix., from 20 to 25, there are thirteen vavs: " And Noah, who was a husbandman, began his work, and he planted a vineyard. And he drank of the wine, and became drunken; and he uncovered himself within his tent. And Ham, the father of Canaan, saw the nakedness of his father, and told it to his two brothers without. And Shem and Japheth took a garment, and laid it upon the shoulders of both of them, and went backwards, and covered the nakedness of their father; and their faces were turned backwards, and they saw not their father's nakedness. And

---

* The term in Hebrew for " becoming red " is " yithadom," and for " blood " the term is " dom " ; and Rabha divides " yithadom " into two—yitha, dom—literally, " will bring blood."

† Rashi explains the passage thus : From the beginning to the end means, " To whom is woe ? " etc. To them that tarry late over the wine. And from the end to the beginning means, " For whom is it right to tarry late over wine ? " For those who are crying woe—e.g., mourners, and those who have quarrels, and wounds without cause, and those who have redness of eyes because they are stout or are idle— these may drown their troubles in the wine.

Noah awoke from his wine, and discovered what his younger son had done unto him." *

R. Hisda in the name of Uqba, according to others Mar Uqba in the name of R. Sakkai, said: The Holy One, blessed be He, said to Noah: " Noah, why didst thou not learn from Adam the First that all the troubles he had were caused by wine "? And this is in accordance with R. Mair who maintains that the tree of whose fruit Adam the First partook was a vine. As we have learned in the following Boraitha: R. Mair said that the tree of whose fruit Adam the First partook was a vine, as there is no other thing which causes so much lamentation as wine does. And R. Jehudah said: It was wheat, as a child is not able to call mother or father before it has experienced the taste of wheat. R. Nehemiah said: It was a fig-tree, as their remedy came from the same thing by which they had transgressed. For it reads [Gen. iii. 7] : " And they sewed fig leaves together."

It reads [Prov. xxxi. 1] : " The words of king Lemuel, the prophecy with which his mother instructed him." Said R. Johanan in the name of R. Simeon b. Jochai: Infer from this that his mother tied him to a pillar, saying: " What (hast thou done), O my son? and what, O son of my body? and what, O son of my vows? " " O my son "—all are aware that thy father has feared Heaven, and now that people see thee going in a wrong way, they will say: " It was caused by his mother." " The son of my body " means: All the wives of thy father never saw the king again after their pregnancy, which was not the case with me, as I have troubled myself to see him again after pregnancy, for the purpose that my child should be of good health. " The son of my vows "—all the wives of thy father used to vow to the sanctuary for the purpose that their child should be fit for the throne, and I have vowed that my son should be full of wisdom, and fit for prophecy. " Not for ꝛ kings, O Lemuel, not for kings (is it fitting) to drink wine, nor for princes (rausnim) strong drink! " She said to him: " What hast thou to do with kings who drink wine, become intoxicated, and say: " For what purpose do we need God " (" Lomo-el "—literally, " why God ")? " And to rausnim strong drink." Is it right that he to whom all the mysteries of the world are revealed should drink wine to intoxication

---

* There are sixteen " ands " in these passages, three of which, being for connection only, are excluded..

—according to others: He to whose door all the princes of the world are hastening, shall he drink wine to intoxication? Said R. Itz'hak: And whence do we know that Solomon repented and confessed to his mother? From [ibid. xxx. 2]: "Surely I am more brutish than any man, and have not the understanding of a common man." "Than any man" means Noah. As it reads [Gen. ix. 20]: "And Noah, who was a husbandman, began his work, and he planted a vineyard." "Of a common man" means Adam the First (the term for this in Hebrew being "adam").

"Of a meritorious society," etc. Said R. Abuhu: He is not guilty unless he consumed the above-mentioned meat and wine with a society of reckless persons (as then there is no hope that he will depart from his way after he is bound to such a company). But does not our Mishna state "a meritorious society"—he does not become a stubborn and rebellious son? From which it is to be understood that if it was not a meritorious one, he is culpable even if not all of the society were reckless men? The Mishna comes to teach us that if it happened that to the meritorious banquet were invited men all reckless, he is nevertheless not culpable, as he was engaged in a meritorious banquet and eating and drinking to excess will not become his habit.

"At the intercalation of the month," etc. Was there then used meat and wine at the meal of intercalation? Does not a Boraitha state only bread and peas? The Mishna comes to teach us that although they were used only to bread and peas, and one in spite of this took for this meal meat and wine, he is not culpable, as the meal was of a meritorious nature and it will not become a habit.

The rabbis taught: To the intercalation meal no less than ten persons were invited, and nothing else was used but bread and peas; and it was prepared only on the thirtieth day, and not in the daytime but at evening. But is there not a Boraitha, "not at evening but in the day"? As R. Hyya b. Abbah said to his sons: Try to go to this meal when it is yet day, before sunset; and also to leave before sunrise, that people shall know that you were engaged in a meal of intercalation.

"Second tithe," etc. Because he consumed it in the usual way, it will not become a habit.

"Carcasses," etc. Said Rabha: If he has consumed meat of fowls, he is not to be charged as a stubborn son. But does

not our Mishna state " carcasses, illegal meat," etc., from which
it is to be understood that if it was legal he is to be charged?
Our Mishna means that even if he has eaten this to complete
the prescribed quantity—*e.g.*, he has eateen a " tertimory " less
an eighth, and this eighth he ate from illegal meat—he is also
not culpable, for the reason stated farther on.

"*A thing which is meritorious,*" etc.—means a meal of condolence.

"*A transgression*"—means when he ate on a fast day of the
congregation.   And what is the reason?   It reads [Deut. xxi.
20]: " He will not hearken to our voice."   " Our voice "—but
not of him who does not hearken to the voice of the Omnipotent.

"*But not meat,*" etc.—means to add even pressed figs of the
city of Kaëla, which cause intoxication.

"*But not wine*"—means even honey and milk, as we have
learned in the following Boraitha: If one consumed pressed
figs of Kaëla and drank honey and milk and entered the sanctuary, he is culpable as to [Lev. x. 9] " wine and strong drink,"
etc.

"*He eats meat and drinks wine,*" etc.   The rabbis taught:
If he consumes any kind of food, but not meat, any kind of
beverages but not wine, he cannot be condemned as a stubborn and rebellious son unless he eats meat and drinks wine.
bles, it will not become a habit.   In the second case, although
there is no direct support in the Scripture that gluttony means
meat and wine, a hint to this is to be found in—" Be not among
those that drink wine, among those that overindulge in eating meat."   And it is also written [ibid., ibid. 21]: " For the
drunkard and the glutton will come to poverty; and drowsiness clotheth a man in rags."   Said R. Zerah: He who sleeps
in a house of learning, his wisdom is rent to pieces.   As it
reads: " And drowsiness clotheth a man in rags."

MISHNA *III.*: If he has stolen from his father and consumed on *his* premises, or he has stolen from strangers and
has consumed on the premises of still other strangers, or he has
stolen from strangers and consumed on the premises of his
father, he is not charged as a stubborn and rebellious son unless
he stole from his father and consumed on the premises of
strangers.   R. Jose b. Jehudah maintains: Unless he stole from
his *mother* and father.

GEMARA: In the first case, when he stole from his father

and consumed on the premises of the father, because he trembles, it will not become a habit.   In the second case, although he does not tremble after stealing, as it cannot be frequently done, it will not become a habit.   From strangers, and consumed on the premises of his father, there are both, because this can be done only occasionally and when consuming he trembles for his father.   Unless he stole from his father and consumed on the premises of strangers—which includes both, because it can be done frequently and without any trembling.

"*From his mother*," etc.   Where did his mother get this, so that it should belong to her only?   Is there not a rule that all a woman buys belongs to her husband?   Said R. Jose b. Hanina: He took it from the meal which was prepared for his his father and mother.   But did not R. Hana b. Mouldha in the name of R. Huna say that he is not culpable unless he buys meat and wine cheap and consumes them?   Say that he has stolen the money which was prepared to buy a meal for his father and mother; and if you wish, it might be said that some one else gave it to his mother, with the condition that her husband should have no share in it.

MISHNA *IV.*: If the father is willing to transfer the case of the son in question to the court and the mother is not willing, or *vice versa*, he cannot be accused as a stubborn and rebellious son, unless both are willing to do so.   Furthermore, R. Jehudah says: If his mother was not fit to be the wife of his father, their son cannot be charged as a stubborn and rebellious son.

GEMARA : What does the Mishna mean by the words " was not fit"?   Shall we assume that his father married a woman who was under the liability of the korat, or capital punishment by the court?   Why?   After all, the father is *his* father and the mother is *his* mother.   Hence it must mean that she was like to his father.   And so also we have learned plainly in the following Boraitha: R. Jehudah said : If his mother was not alike to his father in her voice, in her appearance and her height, he cannot be charged as the son in question.   And what is the reason? Because it reads : " He does not hearken to her voice." As we see that their voices must be alike, the same is the case with the appearance and height.   According to whom is the following Boraitha?   The case of a stubborn and rebellious son never existed and will never occur, and it was written only for the purpose of studying and the reward for it.   It is in accordance with R. Jehudah (who requires such things as can never occur).   And if you wish, it is in accordance with R. Simeon, who said in the following Boraitha thus : Does the law indeed dictate that because this boy consumed a " tertimory " of meat and drank half a lug of Italian wine his father and mother shall deliver him to be stoned ? Hence such a thing neither occurred nor ever will be, and it is written only for studying. R. Jonathan, however, said :: I myself have seen such, and have sat on his grave.

According to whom is the Boraitha that a case of a misled town never occurred and will never be—and was written only for studying? In accordance with R. Eliezer, who said in the following Boraitha thus : A misled town in which there is to be found even one mezuza (a piece of parchment on which a portion of the Holy Writ is written to be placed on the doorpost) cannot be condemned as misled town, because it reads [Deut. xiii. 17]: " And all its spoils shalt thou gather into the midst of the market-place thereof, and thou shalt burn them with fire." And as there is a mezuza this cannot be done, as it reads [ibid. xii. 4] : " Ye shall not do so unto the Lord your God." R. Jonathan, however, said : I have seen such and I myself have sat on its heap.

According to whom is the following Boraitha?: A house of leprosy never occurred and will never be, and it is written only for studying, etc. In accordance with R. Elazar b. Simeon, who says in the following Mishna : A house of leprosy cannot be condemned unless the leprosy was of the size of two beans upon two stones at the two walls in the corner—the length of two beans and the width of one.

There is a Boraitha : R. Eliezer b. Zadok said : There was a place within the limit of the city of Azah which was named the "ruin of leprosy." And R. Simeon, head of the village Akhu, said : It happened once that I went to Galilee and saw a place which they used to mark, saying, It was because stones of leprosy were placed there.

MISHNA *V.*: If one hand of his father or mother is missing, or they limp, or are dumb, blind, or mute, he cannot be condemned as a stubborn son. As it reads [Deut. xxi. 19]: " Then shall his father and his mother lay hold on him "—which cannot be done with one hand. " And bring him out." This cannot be when they limp. " And they shall say "—not when they are mutes. " This our son "—not when they are blind. " He will not hearken "—not when they are dumb.

They must first warn him in the presence of two witnesses and then bring him to the court of three judges, who punish him with stripes. And only then when he offends again must he be tried before twenty-three judges, but must not be stoned un-less the first three judges are among the twenty-three. As it reads : " This our son "—which means, this is our son who was beaten according to *your* decision.

GEMARA : Infer from our Mishna that wherever the Scrip-ture commands something, it must be taken literally? (See above, Chapter VI., p. 000.) With this passage it is different, as it is entirely superfluous. (It should read : " Ye shall deliver him at the gate of that city, to be stoned.") But where is it written that he must first be beaten? Said R. Abuhu : From an analogy of the expressions [Deut. xxi. 18] : " And they chastise him," which same is to be found in ibid xxii. 18. And also from the expression " son," which same is to be found in ibid. xxv. 2, which speaks of stripes. " *This our son.*" But is not this verse needed for this not when they are blind? It should read : " He our son." Why "this"? To infer both statements.

MISHNA *VI.* : If he runs away before the decision of con-demnation is rendered and the encompassing (mentioned in the first Mishna) occurred afterwards, he is free. But if he runs away after the decision was rendered, the encompassing which occurs afterwards does not free him.

GEMARA : R. Hanina said : A descendant of Noah who blasphemed, and thereafter he embraced Judaism, is free from capital punishment, because the law concerning him was changed (for when he was yet a heathen one witness and one judge sufficed, while as an Israelite two witnesses and three judges are needed). And also capital punishment was changed—as to a heathen the sword applies, and to an Israelite stoning ; and as he cannot be punished with stoning (for at the commission of the crime he was yet a heathen), he is entirely free.

Shall we assume that our Mishna, which states that if he runs away before the decision is rendered and the encompassing in question occurred afterwards, he is free, is also because, there being a change, the punishment is also changed? Nay, here it is different; because, if he were to commit the crime at the time after the encompassing, capital punishment would not apply at all. Should we say that the second case stated : If he runs away after the decision was rendered, the encompassing in question does not free him—forms an objection to R. Hanina? Do you wish that after the decision was rendered the change should affect the decision? After the decision is rendered he is considered as dead, which changes cannot affect.

Come and hear another objection: A descendant of Noah who killed his neighbor or committed a crime with his neighbor's wife, and afterwards he embraced Judaism, he is free from capital punishment. But if he did the same with an Israelite while he is yet a heathen, he is guilty even if, after the crime, he becomes a Jew. And why? Say, because it was a change, the capital punishment should also be changed? It requires a change in both—in the trial and in the kind of punishment. Here, however, the change is only in the trial (as said above), but not in the punishment, as either to a heathen or an Israelite the sword applies.

MISHNA *VII.*: A stubborn and rebellious son is tried because of his future. The Scripture prefers that he should die innocent, and not be put to death because of his sins. For the death of the wicked is both a benefit to them and a benefit to the world, while to the upright it is a misfortune for them and for the world. Drinking and sleeping are a benefit to the wicked and to the world, while they are so doing (do they not do harm to the world), and the reverse is it with the upright (because when they are drinking or sleeping they cannot do any good). Separation of the wicked is also a benefit for themselves and for the world; the reverse, however, is the case with the upright. The assembling of the wicked is a misfortune for them as well as for the world, while as to the upright it is a benefit for themselves and for the world. The idleness of the wicked is a misfortune for them and for the world (because in the time of their idleness they will conspire to do harm, but the repose of the upright is a benefit for them as well as for the world).

GEMARA: There is a Boraitha: R. Jose the Galilean said: Is it possible that because this boy ate a "tertimory" of meat and drank half a lug of Italian wine he shall be stoned? But the Torah foreshadows the final thought of the son in question, as in the future he will squander his father's property, and pursuing his habit, which he will find difficult, he will proceed to rob people in the street. Therefore the Torah said: "He shall rather die while he is still innocent than be put to death because of his sins, as the death of the wicked is a benefit," etc., as stated above in the Mishna.

MISHNA *VIII.*: In the case of "breaking in" [Ex. xii. 1],

for which there is no liability if one is killed by a detector, one is also punished because of his future crimes (*i.e.*, because of his intention to kill his opponent, although no crime involving capital punishment was as yet committed). And therefore, if he broke a barrel while breaking in, if according to the laws he must not be killed when caught (*e.g.*, a father who breaks into the premises of his son, who could not have intended to kill his son if he made opposition, and therefore if his son kills him he is liable to capital punishment, he must pay for damaging the barrel. But with respect to other persons who, if killed by the detector, would not be punished, he is free.

GEMARA : Said Rabha : The reason why the Scripture freed the detector if he killed the burglar, is because it is certain that a man cannot control himself when he sees his property taken. And as the burglar must have had the intention to kill anyone, in such a case, who should oppose him, the Scripture dictates that if one comes to kill you, hasten to kill him first.

Rabh said : A burglar who broke in and succeeded in taking some utensils and escaped, he is free from paying for the utensils. Why so ? Because he acquired title to them by his blood. Said Rabha : It seems to me that Rabh's decision was in case he broke the utensils; and as they are no longer in existence, he is free from paying their value. But if he took them and they still exist, he must return them. [Says the Gemara : By God ! Rabh's decision was even if they were still in existence, and his reason is that if they were taken by a burglar of that class, the opponent being guilty of shedding his blood, for which the Mishna makes him liable, would he not be responsible if the utensils were broken or taken away by force by someone else ? He would be, because they were already under his control. The same is the case with an ordinary burglar, as by his blood he has acquired title to them, and therefore he is not obliged to return them.] However [continued Rabha], it is not so, as the Scripture considers the things stolen by the burglar to be under his control only concerning a contingency—*i.e.*, if they were taken away from him. But the Scripture never meant him to acquire title to them when they were still in his possession, for he is considered as a borrower.

It happened that rams were stolen from Rabha by burglary, and thereafter they were returned to him ; but he was not willing to accept them because the above decision came from the mouth of Rabh.

The rabbis taught : It reads [Ex. xxii. 2] : " If the sun be risen upon him, there shall be blood shed for him." What is meant by the sun being risen upon him? Does the sun rise upon him only? It means therefore if it is as clear to you as the sun that it is impossible to be at peace with him, then you may kill him, but not otherwise. There is another Boraitha: If it is as clear to you as the sun that it is possible for you to be at peace with him, then you should not kill him; but if not, you may. Hence the Boraithas contradict each other? It presents no difficulty: one speaks in case a father breaks into his son's house, whose usual intention is not to kill his son, and the other case speaks of the reverse—namely, when the son breaks into the house of his father.

Rabh said: Anyone whatsoever who should break into my house, I would kill him, except R. Hanina b. Shila. If it should happen that he should break in, I would not kill him, as I am sure that he would have mercy upon me as a father for his son.

The rabbis taught: The expression " blood shed " mentioned in ibid., ibid. 1 and 2 means that it makes no difference whether such a case happened on week days or on a Sabbath. Let us see! The teaching that a burglar may be killed even on Sabbath is correct, lest one say as there is a rule that the execution by the court does not violate the Sabbath the same applies here. But why the teaching that the burglar must not be killed, the same being the case if the burglary occurred on Sabbath? Even on week days he is not to be killed?

Said R. Shesheth : The teaching was needed in case it happened that while breaking in on Sabbath a heap of earth covered him. If he is of that class who are to be killed, then the heap must not be removed on Sabbath; if of the other class, it must be done to save the man, if still alive.

The rabbis taught: It reads " to be smitten so"—by any man whatsoever ; " he die "—through any kind of death possible. This teaching was necessary. Lest one say, only if he were killed by the owner, who could not control himself; but if he were killed by some other detector, he is liable, it comes to teach us that the burglar is considered a life-seeker, who may be killed by anyone.

The rabbis taught: The text speaks only of breaking in— whence can it be proven that the thief found on one's roof, in one's yard, or in any building whatsoever may be killed? Therefore it reads, " If a thief be found," which means in any place whatsoever. But if so, why is the term " breaking in " mentioned?

To say that his breaking in serves the place of warning (for he knew what he might expect).

Said R. Huna: Even a minor who seeks one's life may be killed for self-protection. He holds that one who seeks one's life does not need any warning, be he of age or a minor.

R. Hisda objected to him from a Mishna (Ohaloth, VII., 7): If the head of a child were already without the womb, it must not be killed to save the life of its mother in case of danger, as one's life must not be given for that of another. And why not consider the child as the seeker of the life of its mother, so that it shall be killed? There it is different, as the child cannot intend to seek the life of its mother, and the danger in question is decreed by Heaven.

MISHNA *IX.*: The following may be killed for self-protection: He who pursues one to kill him, and he who pursues a betrothed damsel, or pursues a male person to lie with him; but he who pursues an animal for this purpose, or he who intends to commit idolatry or to violate the Sabbath, must not be killed before the crime is committed.

GEMARA: The rabbis taught: Whence do we know that one may kill for self-protection? From [Lev. xix. 16]: "Thou shall not stand idly by the blood of thy neighbor." But how can you so infer from this passage? Is it not needed to that of the following Boraitha: Whence do we know that if one sees his neighbor drowning in a river, or a wild beast or robbers seize him, he is obliged to save him? From the verse just cited? Yea, so it is. And that one may be killed in self-protection, is to be inferred by an *a fortiori* conclusion which is to be drawn from "a betrothed damsel." If in this case, in which one only intended assault, the Torah says he may be killed in self-protection, how much the more a seeker of life. But do we then punish from an *a fortiori* conclusion? The school of Rabbi taught that this is not only an *a fortiori* conclusion, but also an analogy. As it reads [Deut. xxii. 26]: "As a man riseth against his neighbor and striketh him dead, even so is this matter." And what have we to learn from the case of a murder? This passage is intended to throw light (on the case of a violated betrothed) and is at the same time receiving light.* He compares a murder to a betrothed damsel. As in case of a damsel one may be killed in self-protection, the same is it in the case of a murder.

* A proverbial phrase: "This one comes as a teacher and turns out a learner" (Jastrow).

And whence do we know that so is the case concerning a betrothed damsel? From what was taught in the school of R.
Ismael. It reads [ibid. xxi. 27]: "There would have been none
to aid her"—which means, if there were one he must help her
under all circumstances, even to killing her pursuer.

The rabbis taught in addition to what is stated in the Mishna
concerning self-protection : However, in the pursuing by a high-
priest of a widow, or by a common priest of a divorced woman,
or of one with whom the ceremony of Halitah was performed, or
even in the pursuing of a betrothed damsel who had already had
connection with some one, killing in self-protection is not allowed.
And R. Jehudah said : Also, if the damsel herself said to the
pursuers of her assaulter : Let him go—although it is to be
supposed that she said so, only because of fear lest the pursuers
should kill her—he must not be killed before the crime was committed. Whence is all this deduced? From [ibid., ibid. 26]:
" But unto the damsel shalt thou not do anything: there is in
the damsel no sin worthy of death." It is written " naar "
(youth), and it reads " naaro "—from which we infer, both him
who is pursuing a male for the purpose of sin and a betrothed
damsel. And from the term " sin " we infer crimes of a kind to
which the punishment of korath applies; and from " worthy of
death," we infer those who are to be executed by the court.

The Boraitha states: R. Jehudah said : Also if the damsel
herself said, etc. What is the point of their difference? Said
Rabha: They differ in case the damsel cares for her honor, but
without sacrificing her life for it. According to the rabbis the
Scripture cares for the violation of her honor, and as she also
cares for it, though without life-sacrifice, she must be saved even
by killing her pursuers. And according to R. Jehudah, the
Scripture commands to kill him, only in case the damsel herself
is willing to sacrifice her life for her honor, but not otherwise.

Said R. Papa to Abayi: Let us see! In case a high-priest is
pursuing a widow, is not this also a violation of her honor?
Why, then, is he not to be killed? Is not the Scripture particular about the honor of a woman? And Abayi answered: For
the honor of a damsel, who is ruined forever, the Scripture is
particular to save her even to the killing of the pursuer, which is
not the case with a widow.

It says farther on, " sin "—meaning those who are liable to be
punished with death. There is a contradiction from the following: Among the assailants of damsels who must pay a fine

besides the bodily punishment, is counted also one who assaults his sister (the punishment for which is korath). Now, if he is to be killed while pursuing, he must be counted in the class subject to capital punishment. . And there is a rule that he who commits a crime subject to capital punishment is absolved from paying a fine. Said Abayi: The Boraitha which states that he must pay a fine treats of a case in which she could be saved by injuring one of the members of her pursuer's body, and it is in accordance with R. Jonathan b. Shaul who said in the following Boraitha thus: A seeker of life whom the pursued killed, although he was able to protect himself by injuring a member of the pursuer's body—it is to be tried as a case of capital punishment. And what is the reason of Jonathan? It reads [Ex. xxi. 22, 23]: " If men strive . . . and if any mischief follow, then shalt thou give life for life." And R. Elazar said: The cited verses treat about him who intended to kill his opponent. And nevertheless it reads: " And yet no further mischief follow, he shall be surely punished." Now, if you say that the law dictates that the pursuer must not be killed in case his crime could be prevented by injuring one of the members of his body, it is correct that he is to be fined. But should you say that even in the latter case there is no liability if the pursuer was killed—his offence being in the class subject to capital punishment—why, then, is he to be fined? And should you say that he is fined because his intention was to kill another, and the fine belongs to another person, we understand from Rabha's decision * (First Gate, pp. 269 and 270) that it is not so.

" *He who pursues an animal,*" etc. There is a Boraitha: R. Simeon b. Jochai said: The one who intends to worship idols may be killed (if there is an impossibility of preventing his crime otherwise). And this is to be drawn by an *a 'fortiori* conclusion thus: When the dishonoring of a commoner is to be saved even by killing the pursuer, so much the more because of a heavenly dishonor. But is one to be punished because of an *a 'fortiori* conclusion? R. Simeon holds that so it is. There is another Boraitha: R. Eliezar b. Simeon said: The same is the case with one who intends to violate the Sabbath. He holds with his father, that one may be punished from a decision drawn from an

---

* See p. 269, third line from the bottom, which begins : " This decision of Rabha," to Mishna 7, which is here repeated literally, with the difference that there it is Rabba and here it is Rabha. Concerning the difference in the names, see Thosphat Khethuboth, 30*b*, paragraph beginning with the name " R. Ashi."

a 'fortiori conclusion. And he infers the violation of Sabbath from the case of idolatry by the analogy of the expression "violation,' which is termed in Hebrew "chillul," and is to be found in both cases. Said R. Johanan in the name of R. Simeon b. Jehozadok, in the Ethic of Beth Nithza: "In the city of Suda it was voted and resolved that if one were compelled, under threat of being killed, to commit any one of all the crimes which are mentioned in the Torah, he might commit it and not be killed, except idolatry, adultery, and bloodshed." But is not the case the same with idolatry as the following Boraitha states: R. Ismael said: Whence do we know that, if one were told under threat of being killed, to worship an idol, he should rather worship than be killed? From [Lev. xviii. 5]: "He shall live in them"; *i.e.*, but not die in them. But lest one say that the same is the case when he is told to do so publicly, therefore it reads [ibid. xxii. 32]: "And ye shall not profane my holy name; so that I may be sanctified." Hence we see that privately he may rather worship than die? They (R. Johanan and R. Simeon b. Jehozadok) hold with R. Eliezer who said in the following Boraitha thus: It reads [Deut. vi. 5]: "And thou shalt love the Lord thy God with all thy heart, and with all thy soul, and with all thy might." Why, then, with all thy soul and with all thy might—is not one of them sufficient? Because people are of different natures. There are among them some who prize their body more than their money—for them it is written, "with all thy soul." And there are some others who prize their money more than their body, and for them it is written, "with all thy might? And from this we infer that even if one were told to commit idolatry privately, he must not do so, even under threat of being killed. This is concerning idolatry. But whence do we know that the same is the case with adultery and bloodshed. From the following Boraitha: Rabbi said: It reads [ibid. xxii. 26]: "For as when a man riseth against his neighbor" (See above, p. ooo). He compares a murder to the case of a betrothed damsel. As concerning a betrothed damsel one may be killed to save her, the same is it in the case of a murder. And as concerning a murder one is obliged to sacrifice his own life rather than kill another by command, the same is the case with a betrothed damsel—she is held to be killed rather than be ravished. And whence do we know that in a murder case one is obliged to sacrifice his own life, etc. This is common sense. Thus it happened to one who came before Rabha. (See Pcsachim, p. 37, line 11.)

When R. Dimi came from Palestine, he said in the name of
R. Johanan: All this was said when there was no civil decree by
the government to violate religious duties; but if there was, one
must sacrifice himself even for a most lenient commandment.
And when Rabbin came, he said in the name of the same authority: Even when an evil decree did not exist, he might do so
privately; but publicly, one must sacrifice his life, even for a most
lenient commandment. What is meant by a most lenient commandment? Said Rabba b. R. Itz'hak in the name of Rabh: (In
days of religious persecution you must resist, even to changing
the shoe-strap. And what is to be considered publicly? Said
R. Jacob in the name of R. Johanan: If this is to be done in the
presence of no less than ten Israelites. R. Jeremiah questioned:
How is it if there were nine Israelites and one heathen? Come
and hear what R. Janai the brother of R. Hyya b. Aba taught:
It reads [Lev. xxii. 32]: "In the midst of the children of Israel,"
and [Num. xvi. 21]: "From the midst of this congregation";
and from the analogy of the expression "midst," we infer that,
as in the case of Korach there were no less than ten, and all
Israelites, the same is the case with the sanctification in question.
But was not Esther compelled to sin with Ahassuerus, in the
presence of more than ten Israelites? Said Rabha: In case they
do it for their own benefit it is different; as, if this were not the
case, how could we lend copper vessels to the Persians for the
purpose that they should fill them in their houses of worship with
live coals at the time of their holidays? But as this is for their
own benefit, it is not considered a transgression; and Rabha is in
accordance with his theory elsewhere, that if a heathen commands
an Israelite to cut hay on Sabbath for his cattle, with threat of
killing him, he shall rather cut the hay than be killed. But if he
tells him, "Cut it and put it in the river," from which we see that
he wants only to overcome his religious scruples, it is better for
him to resist and be killed than to comply with his command.

R. Ami was questioned: Is a descendant of Noah commanded
to sanctify the Holy Name, or not? And Abayi answered:
Come and hear! "There were seven commandments which were
given to the descendants of Noah," etc. Now, if they were commanded to sanctify the Holy Name, there would be eight. Said
Rabha to him: From this we can infer nothing, as by the seven
commandments is meant all that pertains to them (and sanctify-
ing the Holy Name pertains to the negative commandment of
idolatry). However, how should this question be decided? Said

Adda b. Ahaba: It was said in the college: It reads [II. Kings v. 18 and 19]: "For this thing may the Lord pardon thy servant, that when my lord goeth into the house of Rimmon to prostrate himself there, and he leaneth on my hand, and I prostrate myself also in the house of Rimmon, . . . and he said unto him, Go in peace." Now, if a descendant of Noah were commanded concerning sanctification, Elisha would not say to him, "Go in peace," but would keep silent. This also is not a support, as Nahman's request was considered privately as no Israelites were present. Said R. Jehudah in the name of Rabh: It happened to one that he saw a woman and became sick through his infatuation, and he consulted physicians, who saw that there was no remedy for him unless he had connection with her, and the sages decided that he should rather die than have connection. The physicians, however, said: "Let her stand before him naked; perhaps this may do something in his behalf. But even this the sages did not allow. Let her talk to him behind a fence. Even this the sages forbade. R. Jacob b. Idi and Samuel b. Na'hmani differ. According to one she was a married woman, and according to the other she was single. Single! Why such strictness? Said R. Papa: Because of the dishonor of her family, as a daughter of an Israelite must not be sold for prostitution. And R. Ahbah b. R. Ika said: To prevent such becoming a habit among the daughters of Israel. But why did he not marry her? Said R. Itz'hak: This would not satisfy him. As it reads [Prov. ix. 17]: "Stolen waters are sweet, and bread of secrecy is pleasant."

CHAPTER IX.

MISHNA *I.*: To the following the punishment of burning applies: To one who has intercourse with a woman and her daughter, and to a daughter of a priest who has sinned. Under the general rule of a woman and her daughter comes his own daughter, the granddaughters of his daughter and son, the daughter of his wife, her granddaughters of her daughter and her son, his mother-in-law, and the mother of his mother and father-in-law.

GEMARA: The Mishna does not state a woman whose daughter he has married, but "a woman and her daughter," which seems to be that the intercourse with both of them was a sin, and this can only be with his mother-in-law and her mother. And from the expression, "Under the general rule of a woman and her daughter," it is to be assumed that both are mentioned in the Scripture, which is not so, as the mother of his mother-in-law is only inferred from an analogy. Read: If one has had intercourse with a woman whose daughter he has married. Whence is this deduced? From what the rabbis taught: It reads [Lev. xxi. 4]: "And if a man take a woman and her mother." This is concerning a legal wife and her mother. But whence do we know that the same is the case with the illegal daughter of a ravisher (referring to Deut. xxii. 28), and her granddaughters from her daughter and her son? From the analogy of the expression "incest" (zimha), which is to be found here in the verse cited and also in Lev. xviii. 17. And as there it speaks of an ordinary woman, and it is plainly mentioned the granddaughters of her son and daughter, the same is the case here (that all of them must be punished by burning).

And whence do we know that the males who have committed the crimes in question are also to be punished by burning, the same as the females? Again from the same analogy of the expression zimha. As there the verse speaks of the male perpetrator of the crime, so also in the case here we are not to make any difference in the punishment between males and females. And whence do we know that the latter generations—*i.e.*, the daughters and the granddaughters—are to be equalized to the earlier generations —*i.e.*, the mothers of one's father and mother-in-law? Again from the analogy of the same expression. As there the Scripture does not make any difference between the expression in verse 15, which speaks of a father with his daughter-in-law, and that of the seventeenth, which speaks of the latter generations, and at the end of which it reads: for *they* are near kins-"women," which refers to all of them, so here the punishment of the earlier generations is to be equalized to that of the latter.*

The father of R. Abbin taught: Because there is no definite commandment in the Scripture concerning the daughter of a ravisher, it was necessary for the scripture to state [Lev. xxi. 9]. "And if the daughter of *any* priest"—"esh cohn," instead of " cohen." From which we infer that, were she a legal or an illegal daughter, if he sins with her, she must be burned.

But if so, let the punishment of burning apply only to the daughter of the abuser, but not to the abuser himself, as so is the case with the daughter of a priest in which the punishment applies only to her, but not to her abuser. Said Abayi: Concerning the daughter of a priest it reads: " Her father does she profane." Exclude this case, in which the father is profaning her. Rabha, however, said: For this no verse is necessary, as it is common sense. In the case of a priest's daughter, if you have excluded her abuser from burning, he is nevertheless left under the category of choking, which applies to any one having intercourse with a married woman. But here, if you exclude the abuser from the punishment which applies to her, under what category can you put him? Should you put him under the category of those who have had intercourse with single women, who are free from any

---

* It is impossible to give a literal translation of this Boraitha with even an abstract of the explanation as discussed by the Amoraim at length in the text. It is so complicated that the Amoraim themselves could not explain it without correcting the Boraitha or without giving to it an entirely strange interpretation. As was said by Rabha : " In any event, the analogy of expressions cannot be used without objections and difficulties." We therefore give a free rendering of the Boraitha, omitting the discussion.

punishment, is it possible that she should be burned for this crime, and he who is the abuser of her mother and the seducer of herself should be free? Now we have had the punishment for such, but where is the warning? It is correct for both Abayi and Rabha as they infer the warning from the same which states the punishment. But according to the father of R. Abbin, whence is deduced? Said R. Ailea, from [Lev. xix. 29]: "Do not profane thy daughter, to cause her to be a prostitute." R. Jacob, the brother of R. Abha b. Jacob, opposed: Is not the verse just cited necessary to that of the following Boraitha: "Thou shalt not profane thy daughter," etc? Lest one say that it speaks of a priest who marries his daughter to a Levite or an Israelite, therefore it reads "to cause her to be a prostitute." Hence it speaks only of him who gives his daughter other than in marriage. From the "ll" in the word "techallel" (profane), instead of "tochal," which would have the same meaning, the warning in question may also be inferred. And both Abayi and Rabha, who have inferred the warning in this case from the same verse mentioning the punishment—what do they infer from the verse just cited? Said R. Mani: Him who marries his daughter to an old man, as the following Boraitha states: "You shall not profane your daughter," etc. According to R. Eliezer: He who marries his daughter to an old man is meant; and according to R. Aqiba, he who leaves his daughter unmarried until she becomes "vigaros."

R. Kahana in the name of R. Aqiba said: There is none poor in Israel, but a shrewd-wicked and he who has left his daughter unmarried until "vigaros." How is this to be understood? Is not one to be called a shrewd-wicked if he left his daughter unmarried for his own benefit, that she should do the housework until "vigaros"? Said Abayi: He means thus: There is none poorer than he who is compelled because of his poverty to leave his daughter unmarried until "vigaros," as then he is equal to a shrewd-wicked.

R. Kahana in the name of R. Aqiba said again: Be careful in your counsellor in order that you shall not listen to him who counsels you for his own benefit.

R. Jehudah said in the name of Rabh: He who marries his daughter to an old man and he who marries his minor son to a woman of age; to both the verses [Deut. xxix. 18, 19]: "In order that the indulgence of the passions may appease the thirst (for them): The Lord will not pardon him," apply.

The rabbis taught: Concerning the verse Lev. xx. 14, in which the words "him and them" are mentioned, R. Ismael and R. Aqiba differ. According to the former it means "him and one of them," and according to the latter, "him and both of them." What is the point of their differences (even R. Ismael agrees that both of them are to be punished)? Said Abayi: They differ only as to the texts from which the law is derived. According to R. Ismael, who maintains "him and one of them," it is because in Greek εν means one, and the expression in the passage is " es'-en." Hence, biblically his mother-in-law is to be burned, while her mother is inferred only rabbinically by an analogy of expression. And according to R. Aqiba both of them are meant in this verse. Hence both, biblically, are to be burned. Rabha, however, maintains that the point of their difference is an intercourse with one's mother-in-law after the death of his wife. According to R. Ismael, even then she must be burned, as in the verse cited it reads "and them," which makes no difference whether his wife is still alive or dead. And according to R. Aqiba, after the death of his wife, it is only a prohibition, but not a crime to which burning applies.

MISHNA II.: To the following, punishment with the sword applies: To a murderer and the men of a misled town. A murderer who strikes his neighbor with a stone or with an iron so that he dies; if one pressed down a person while he is in water or in fire, preventing him from coming out, until he dies—he is guilty. If, however, he pushes him into water or into fire and he was able to come out, but nevertheless dies without being prevented by him who pushed him, he is not guilty of a capital crime. If he sets a dog or a serpent upon him, he is not guilty of a capital crime. If, however, he applies the snake to his body with his hand, and it bites him to death, R. Jehudah makes him guilty of a capital crime, and the sages free him.

GEMARA: Samuel said: Why is there not mentioned in the Scripture the word "yod" concerning iron in Num. xxxv. 16, as is done concerning stones and wood in ibid., ibid. 17, 18? Because even a fragment of iron brings death. So also we have learned in a Boraitha: Rabbi said: It is known to Him who created the whole world by one word, that a fragment of iron may bring death, and therefore He has not prescribed any size concerning iron. (Says the Gemara:) This is only when he pierced him with it; but if (he struck him with iron), it must be of a size to cause death.

" *If he presses down*," etc. The first part teaches a preponderance, and so does the second. The preponderance of the first part is that, although he did not push him, but only prevented him from coming out, he is nevertheless guilty of a capital crime. And the preponderance of the second part is that, although he pushed him in, yet, so long as the victim could come out and was not prevented, he is not guilty of a capital crime. But whence do we know that one is guilty for pressing down? Said Samuel: From [ibid., ibid. 21]: "Or if in *enmity* he have smitten him with his hand," which means to include him who pressed him down.

There was one who urged cattle of his neighbor into the sun until they died. And Rabbini made him liable, but R. A'hal b. Rabh freed him. The former made him liable because of an *a ʾfortiori* conclusion drawn from a murderer. As concerning a murderer the Scripture makes a difference between intentionally and unintentionally, between accident and premeditation, and nevertheless makes guilty the presser; and as concerning damages, where there is no difference between intentionally and unintentionally, between accident and premeditation, so much the more should a pusher be liable. And as to the reason of R. A'hal, who freed him, said R. Mesharshia: The reason of my grandfather, who freed him, is the above-cited verse: " He that smote him shall surely be put to death, for he is a murderer," meaning only in case of murder is one guilty of pressing, but not in a case of damages.

Rabha said: If one bound a person, and he died thereafter of hunger, he is not guilty of a capital crime. If, however, he bound him and put him in a sunny place, and he dies because of the sun, or he puts him in a cold place and he dies of cold, he is guilty. But if he put him in a sunny or a cold place, where there was not as yet either sun or cold, and thereafter, when it came, it caused his death, he is not guilty of a capital crime.

The same said again: If one bound a person and left him before a lion, he is not guilty of a capital crime. (Rashi explains that he could not save himself from the lion even if he were unbound. Rashi's reasons are not quite clear to us.) But if he bound him in a place where mosquitoes are abundant, he is guilty. R. Ashi, however, maintains that even in the latter case he is not guilty, as the mosquitoes which were on his body at the time he tied him, went away, and others came. Hence he did not cause his death directly.

It was taught: If one places a vat over a person and he dies from heat, or he removes the ceiling to let the cold come in, and he dies from cold—Rabha and R. Zerah—one of them makes him guilty and the other frees him. Says the Gemara : It seems that Rabha is the one who frees him, as it is in accordance with his theory. Said above : If one bound a person and he dies of hunger, he is free. On the contrary, it seems R. Zerah is the one that makes him free, as it is in accordance with his theory elsewhere : He who puts a person in a house closed from all sides so that the air cannot go out, and lights a candle, which causes his death, is guilty. Hence we see that the reason of making him liable is the lighting of the candle, and if this were not done he would be free? Nay ! It may be said that the heat which caused his death began with the lighting of the candle. The same is the case with the vat—the heat began just when he turned it over him.

Rabha said again : If one pushed a person into an excavation in which a ladder stood for coming out, and someone came and removed the ladder, or even if he himself removed it after he pushed him in, he is not guilty of a capital crime, as at the time he pushed him in he was able to come out.

The same said again : If one shot an arrow at a person who wore an armor and someone removed the armor, or even if he himself removed it after he shot, he is not guilty of a capital crime, as at the time he shot the arrow it could not injure him.

And he said again : If one shot an arrow at a person who was supplied with spices which could cure the wounds from the arrow, and someone came and scattered them, or even if he himself scattered them before the arrow reached him, he is not guilty, because the victim, at the time he shot, could be healed by the spices. Said R. Ashi : According to this theory he would not be guilty if there should be spices in the market which could cure the wounds? Said R. Ahbah, the son of Rabha, to R. Ashi : How is the law if it happened that spices were brought to him after he was shot, and he did not make use of them? And he answered : In such a case the court would not overlook this, and would accept the defence to his advantage.

Rabha said again : If one throws a stone at a wall, with the intention of killing a person with it, the stone, however, killing the man only by the rebounding, he is guilty of a capital crime. In explanation of this, it was taught, e.g., ball-players—if one threw a ball with the intention of killing someone, he is to be put to death, and if it was unintentionally, he is to be exiled. Is this not self-evident? The teaching that one is to be put to death, if done intentionally, was necessary. Lest one say that such a warning was of a doubtful nature, as who could predict that the ball would kill him by rebounding so that he should be forewarned of it, he comes to teach us that he is nevertheless guilty.

R. Tachlifa of the West taught in the presence of R. Abuhu concerning those who play ball: If the ball killed one by rebounding within a distance of four ells from the wall, he is free from exile, but if it exceeded four ells, he is guilty.

Said Rabhina to R. Ashi: Let us see, how was the case! If the player was pleased with the rebounding of the ball, then let him be guilty if the man was killed even within a nearer distance (as the law of killing a man unintentionally prescribes). And if he was not pleased with the rebounding, let him be free even at a greater distance. And he answered: The greater the distance a ball rebounds, the more is the pleasure of the ball-player.

It was taught: R. Papa said: If one bound a person and turned a stream of water upon him, it is considered as if the man were killed directly by his arrow, and he is guilty of a capital crime. However, this is only when he was killed by the first stream which poured upon him; but if he dies from the continued flow, it is not considered direct killing, but only a cause of death.

The same said again: If one throws a stone on high and it swerves and kills a man, he is guilty. Said Mar. b. R. Ashi to him: Let us see what is the reason of your theory! Because the stone went by his force? But if so, the force must only be considered when it went on high; and when his force ends it should fall down vertically. But according to your theory it swerves, hence it is not by his force. It must be said, however, if this cannot be called his exact force, it may nevertheless be considered a part of his force.

The rabbis taught : If one was assaulted by ten different persons, no matter whether at once or at different times, and was killed, none of them has to suffer capital punishment, as according to the Scripture it must be known who was the cause of the death. R. Jehudah b. Bathyra, however, holds: In case the assault was made by one after the other, the last one is guilty, for he hastened his death.* Said R. Johanan: Both parties took their theories from one and the same passage [Lev. xxiv. 17]: " And he that taketh the life of all the soul of man." † The rabbis hold that all the "soul" means one is not guilty unless he

---

* Against our method, here are repeated a few lines from First Gate, pp. 55 and 56 ; but we could not do otherwise, because of the explanation in the text.

† Leeser's translation does not correspond.

takes the whole soul. And R. Jehudah holds that it means all that was as yet left of the soul.

Said Rabha: All agree that if one kills a person whose wind-pipe and larynx (gullet) are cut, or whose skull is fractured, he is free (for it is considered as if he had attacked a dead man). And they agree also that, if one killed a person who was struggling with death through sickness caused by Heaven, he is guilty of a capital crime. And the point of their difference in the above Boraitha is, if one killed a man who was struggling with death through sick-ness caused by man. According to the rabbis, it is similar to him whose windpipe, etc., are cut. But according to R. Jehudah b. Bathyra, it is similar to him who was struggling with death through sickness caused by Heaven.

A disciple taught in the presence of R. Shesheth: The above-cited verse, which commences with "and a man," means if one struck a person with an article which can cause death, but the man was not entirely without life, and another came and put an end to him entirely, the latter is responsible, as the ordinary opinion is in accordance with R. Jehudah b. Bathyra.

Rabha said: If one kills a person whose windpipe and larynx are cut he is free; but if the latter killed a person, if this was in the presence of the court, he is guilty. As it reads [Deut. xiii. 6]: "And thou shalt put the evil away from the midst of thee." But if not in the presence of the court, but in the presence of other witnesses, he is free, as their testimony cannot be taken into consideration, because they cannot be made collusive (as their in-tention was to kill a man already dead). And there is a rule that such a testimony as was given by those cannot be made collusive is not considered as testimony at all.

And he said again : Although the witnesses who had testified against the man whose windpipe, etc., were cut were thereafter found collusive, they are not to be put to death ; if the windpipe, etc., of the witnesses themselves were cut at the time they testi-fied, and thereafter they were found collusive, they are to be put to death, because of the above-cited verse. R. Ashi, however, maintains that they are not, because the witnesses who made them collusive could not be punished if their testimony were found false, as their intention was to kill men who are considered al-ready dead.

And Rabha said again : An ox of such a kind, if he killed a per-son, is guilty. But if the ox was a healthy one and his owner was of that kind, he is free; because it reads [Ex. xxi. 29]: "The ox

should be put to death and the owner also." And as in this case
the owner is considered already dead, and the expression "he
shall also be put to death," does not apply to him, we therefore do
not apply to the ox the beginning of the verse. R. Ashi, however, maintains that even if the ox was of that kind, he is also
free for if its owner would be such it would be free ; therefore it
is to be free when it itself is of this kind.

"*If he set a dog or a serpent,*" etc. Said R. Abbah b. Jacob:
If you wish to know the reason of their difference, it may be said
thus: According to R. Jehudah, the venom of the serpent is
always between its teeth (*i. e.*, with the bite of the serpent the
venom is injected into the body, which causes death directly) and,
therefore, if he applied the serpent to the body he is to be decapitated, and the serpent is free. And according to the sages, the
poisoning comes after the bite, from the venom of the serpent
Hence the biting did not cause death directly, and therefore the
serpent must be stoned and he who applied it is free from capital
punishment.

MISHNA *III.* : If one strikes a person with a stone or with
his fists, and he was diagnosed (by the physicians of the court) to
die, and thereafter he improved, and was diagnosed to live, and
then again becomes worse and dies, he is guilty of a capital crime.
R. Nehemiah, however, maintains that he is free, because it is
reasonable to say that he did not die directly from the blow, but
from some other cause.

GEMARA : The rabbis taught: The lecture of Nehemiah
concerning this matter was thus : It reads [Ex. xxi. 19]: "If he
rise again and walk abroad upon his crutch, then shall he that
smote him be acquitted." Can it be supposed that one should
be put to death because he struck a person who later walks in the
market, if there were not a passage which commands the contrary? We must then say that the passage means that if when
he was struck he was diagnosed to die, and thereafter he improved, walked in the street, and was diagnosed to live, and then
became worse and died, he is nevertheless free. What do the
opponents of R. Nehemiah infer from the words " be acquitted "?
That the person who struck must be kept in arrest until the outcome shall be known. R. Nehemiah, however, maintained that
no verse is necessary for this, as this is to be inferred from the
woodgatherer, who was arrested immediately after committing
the crime. Why did not the rabbis also infer from the woodgatherer? (Moses was aware that) he was surely guilty of a capital

crime, but did not know whas kind of death applied to him. But concerning the murderer in question, it is not known whether he came under the category of capital punishment at all ? R. Nehemiah, however, infer this from the blasphemer, of whom Moses did not know whether he came under the category of capital punishment at all, and nevertheless he was imprisoned. The rabbis, however, do not infer this from the blasphemer, as according to their opinions it was only a decision for that time, as we have learned in the following Boraitha: Moses our master was aware that the woodgatherer was guilty of capital crime. As it reads (Ex. xxxi. 14]: "Everyone that defileth it shall be put to death." But he did not know what kind of death; as it reads: [Num. xv. 34]: Because it had not been declared what should be done to him." Concerning the blasphemer, however, it is not so written, but : "To the decision of the Lord," hence Moses was not aware whether he came under the category of death at all.

The rabbis taught: If one struck a person and he was diagnosed to die, but he nevertheless remained alive, they may free him. And if he was diagnosed to die and he improved, the sick man must be examined again, and appraisement made concerning the money which is to be collected from his smiter; and if thereafter he becomes worse and dies, he must be charged according to the second examination. So is the decree of Nehemiah. The sages, however, maintain that there is no other examination after the first. There is another Boraitha: If he was diagnosed to die, but he did not, he must be examined again. But if the first opinion was that he would live no second examination as to dying may take place (for if it happened that he dies, it is probably not from the previous blow). If, however, he was diagnosed to die, and he becomes better, the sick man must undergo an appraisement concerning money. And if thereafter he becomes worse and dies, his murderer must pay for damages and the suffering of the deceased, to the heirs from the time he was struck till his death. And this anonymous Boraitha is in accordance with R. Nehemiah, who frees such from capital punishment.

MISHNA *IV.* : To the following, capital punishment does not apply : To one who intended to kill an animal and killed a man, an idolator and killed an Israelite, a miscarried child and killed a mature one. The same is the case with one who intended to strike another on the loins with an article which was not sufficient to cause death, but the blow was made on his heart, for which it was sufficient, and he dies; or if he intended to strike him on the heart with an article which was sufficient to cause death if striking same, but he struck the loins and the man dies, although it was not sufficient to cause death if struck on the heart or even if he intended to strike an adult with an article which was not sufficient for such, but it happened that he struck a minor and he dies, as for a minor it was sufficient; or, on the contrary, if he intended to strike a minor with an article which was sufficient for such, but not for an adult, and it happened that he struck with it an adult and he nevertheless dies. To the following, however, capital punishment does apply: To one who intended to strike a person on the loins with an article which was sufficient for this purpose, and he strikes him to death on his heart, or if he intended to strike an adult with an article which was sufficient to cause his death, but it happens that he strikes to death a minor with it. R. Simeon, however, maintains: Capital punishment does not apply even to him who intended to kill a certain person, and it happened that he killed another.

GEMARA: To which part of the Mishna belongs R. Simeon's theory? If to the latter part only it should read: And R. Simeon frees him (*i.e.*, him who intended to kill an adult and killed a minor). We must then say that it belongs to the first part, which states: an animal—an idolater—an Israelite—a miscarried child, etc., to which capital punishment does not apply, from which it is to be understood that if there were two resembling persons, and he intended to kill one and killed the other, capital punishment does apply. And to this R. Simeon came to say that even in such a case capital punishment does not apply. Now, let us see! If, *e.g.*, there were Reuben and Simeon, and the murderer said, " I intend to kill Reuben and not Simeon," and finally Simeon was killed, and not Reuben—this is the case in which the first Tana and R. Simeon differ. But how is it if the murderer said, "I intend to kill one of them"; or the murderer mistook Simeon for Reuben? Does R. Simeon differ even in this? Come and hear the following Boraitha: R. Simeon said: Capital punishment does not apply, unless one said, "I intended to kill so and so," and he did so. And what is his reason? [Deut. xix. 11]: "But if any man be an enemy to his neighbor and lie in wait for him," which means only when he killed the intended person. Said the disciples of Janai: And what do the rabbis say to this verse? It excludes him who throws a stone into an excavation in which men are standing, without the intention of killing any particular one. Now, let us see! According to the rabbis, who apply capital punishment to him who killed one person, although he intended to kill another, the verses Ex. xxi. 22 and 23, "If men strive . . . then shalt thou give life for life," are in accordance with the explanation of R. Elazar, stated above, that the verses speak about him who intends to kill. But how should this passage be explained in accordance to Simeon's theory? In accordance with Rabbi of the following Boraitha: "Thou shalt give life for life" means money (*i.e.*, the value of the woman should be paid to her heirs). You say "money," but perhaps it means literally "life"? The expression here "thou shalt give," is to be explained similarly to ibid., ibid. 22 : "He shall give according to the decision," etc. As there it means money, the same is the case here.

Rabha said: The following statements, taught in the school of Hiskia, correspond neither with Rabbi nor with the rabbis mentioned above. Namely: It reads [Lev. xxiv. 21]: "And he that killeth a beast shall make restitution for it, and he that killeth a man shall be put to death." As in the case of a beast there is no difference whether it was intentionally or unintentionally, by an error or by premeditation, while he was ascending or descending, he is always liable and must pay. The same is it in the latter case of a human being: there is no difference whether it was intentionally, etc.,—he is absolved from any money payment.

Now let us see what is meant by the expression "unintentionally" concerning a human being. Shall we assume, *i.e.*, that it was done without any intention? Then it was an error, which has been already mentioned. Why, then, the repetition? You must then say that it means, if he intended to kill one and killed another person, and nevertheless it states that he is absolved from any payment. Now, if he should hold with the rabbis that such is guilty of a capital crime, then such a statement is not necessary, as there is a rule that no payment is required in a case of capital punishment. We must therefore say that it does not agree with them; nor can we say, on the other hand, that it agrees with Rabbi, as the latter requires payment, while Heskia does not.

MISHNA *V.* : A murderer mixed up among others—all of them are free. R. Jehudah maintains : All of them must be taken to χυφος (a life-long prison, to be done with as explained farther on). If it happen that the persons sentenced to deaths of different kinds, and are so mixed that it is not known who comes under this kind of death and who under another, all of them must be executed with the more lenient death, *e.g.*, if those who are to be stoned are mixed up among those who are to be burned, according to the sages all of them must be executed by burning, as stoning is more rigorous; and according to R. Simeon all of them are to be executed by stoning, as burning is more rigorous. Said R. Simeon to the sages: Were burning not more rigorous, it would not apply to a daughter of a priest who had sinned. Answered the sages: Were stoning not more rigorous, it would not apply to a ʿblasphemer and an idolater. If they who are to be slain by the sword are mixed among those who are to be choked, according to R. Simeon they must be decapitated, and according to the sages, they must be choked.

GEMARA: What does the Mishna mean by the words, "among others"? Does it mean others who are innocent? Is it not self-evident that they are all free? And secondly, could R. Jehudah say that such are to be imprisoned? Said R. Abuhu in the name of Samuel: It speaks of a murderer who was not as yet sentenced, and was mixed among those who were already sentenced; and as the verdict of death must be rendered only in the presence of the criminal, therefore all of them are free from execution according to the rabbis. R. Jehudah, however, maintains that such cannot be entirely free, since they are murderers, and therefore, they must be taken to the kyphos.

Resh Lakish said: The Mishna does not mean human beings at all, but oxen—*i.e.*, whether an ox which was not as yet sentenced to death was mixed among others which were already sentenced is the point of their difference. According to the rabbis the ox must be judged the same as its owner. As its owner cannot be sentenced to death if not present, the same is the case with the ox; and as he is now mixed among others, all of them are free. And R. Jehudah maintains that all of them must be taken to the kyphos.

Said Rabha: How can such an explanation be given to the Mishna? Does not a Boraitha add to this: Said R. Jose: Even if among the others was Abbah Halafta (who was known as a great man). How, then, can the Mishna be interpreted that it means other murderers or oxen? Therefore explains he: It means if, *e.g.*, two were standing shoulder to shoulder and an arrow came out from one of them and killed a person, both of them are free. And to this R. Jose said: Even if Abbah Halafta was among the two, and it is certain that Abbah Halafta would not commit such a crime. Nevertheless, the other is free. And the saying of R. Jehudah belongs to another case, as the Mishna is not completed, and should read thus: And if an ox which was sentenced to death was mixed among other innocent oxen, they must all be stoned. R. Jehudah, however, maintains that all of them must be taken to the kyphos, and it is in accordance with the following Boraitha: If a cow has killed a human being, and thereafter gave birth, before she was sentenced to death, the offspring is valid; but if it happened after she was sentenced, the offspring is invalid. And if such were mixed among others, and even if some of the others among which it is mixed were mixed with still others, all of them must be taken to the kyphos. R. Elazar b. Simeon, however, maintains: All of them are to be brought to the court and stoned.

"*All who were sentenced to death,*" etc. Infer from this that if one is forewarned of a rigorous crime, it suffices for a lenient one. (This question was not yet solved.) Said R. Jeremiah: The Mishna speaks of a case where the criminal was warned in general; and it is in accordance to the Tana of the following Boraitha: All the crimes to which capital punishment applies, the perpetrators of them are not put to death unless there were witnesses who warned them, and unless they warned them that they were liable to die by the decision of the court. And according to R. Jehudah, only when they notified them by which kind of death they would be executed.

The first Tana, who does not require that they should be notified by which death, infers it from the case of the woodgatherer; and according to R. Jehudah, nothing is to be inferred from the case of the woodgatherer, as it was only a decision of that time.

"*Among those who are to be burned,*" etc. R. Ezekiel taught to Rami his son: If those who are to be burned were mixed among those who are to be stoned, according to R. Simeon, they are to be executed by stoning, as burning is more rigorous. Said R. Jehudah (his older son) to him: Father, do not teach so, for, according to your teaching (as " those who are to be burned were mixed among those who are to be stoned ") it seems that the majority of them come under the category of stoning : Hence the reason why they are to be stoned is not because it is more lenient, but because so was it to be done with the majority. And to the question of his father : How, then, shall I teach ? The answer was : As our Mishna states : If those who are to be stoned were mixed among those who are to be burned, R. Simeon said, etc. But if so, how is the latter part, " And the sages said that they are to be executed by burning, because burning is more rigorous," to be understood? Also here the reason may be that the majority who are to be executed come under the category of burning? Nay! The expression of the rabbis, "stoning is more rigorous," was not as a reason, but as an answer to R. Simeon. And it is to be explained thus: If they were mixed among those who are to be burned, it must be done with them in accordance with their majority. And your supposition to care about the minority, because we have to select for them a lenient death, does not hold good, as in reality stoning is more rigorous. Said Samuel to R. Jehudah: Genius! do not express yourself in such terms to your father, as there is a Boraitha: If a son saw his father transgressing what is written in the Scripture, he must not say to him, "Father, you have transgressed the law," but, " Father, so and so is written in the Scripture."

But is it not finally one and the same? It means he shall say: " Father, there is a verse in the Scripture which reads so and so," and in such a tone that it shall not seem a rebuke, but an intimation.

MISHNA VI.: If one committed a crime which deserves two kinds of death (e.g., one who has intercourse with his mother-in-law who is married, commits two crimes—with a married woman, to which choking applies, and with his mother-in-law, to which burning applies), he must be tried for the more rigorous one. R. Jose, however, maintains: According to that act, he began first. (Illustrations in the Gemara.)

GEMARA: Is this not self-evident? Should one who has committed another crime which brings an easier punishment be benefited by it? Said Rahba: It speaks of where he was tried for a case which deserved a lenient death, and was sentenced, and then committed a crime to which a more rigorous death applies. Lest one say that this man is to be considered as already killed and not to be tried again, it comes to teach us that he must be tried and punished with the more rigorous death.

The brother of R. Jose b. Hanna questioned Rabba b. Nathan: Whence is this law deduced? (And the answer was:) from Ezek. xviii. 10-13; " . . . Upon the mountains he eateth . . . and his eyes he lifteth up to the idols of the house of Israel . . . and the wife of his neighbor he defileth . . . " To bloodshed the sword applies, to adultery with a married woman choking applies, and to idolatry stoning applies, and it ends with "his blood shall be upon him," which means stoning. Hence he is to be executed with the more rigorous one. R. Na'hman b. Itz'hak opposed: Perhaps all the crimes mentioned in this passage come under the category of stoning, namely, a "dissolute son," means a stubborn and rebellious son, to whom .stoning applies; "he defileth the wife of his neighbor" means a betrothed damsel, to whom also the same applies; "to the idols he lifteth up," which is idolatry, to which stoning applies? If it were so, then what came Ezekiel to teach? And lest one say that he was only repeating what is in the Scripture, then he ought to have done as did Moses our master, who said [Deut. xvii. 18]: He shall write the *repetition* of the law." *

R. Abbah b. Hanina lectured about the passage [ibid. 6]: "Upon the mountains he eateth not," which ends with [ibid. 9]: "He is righteous, he shall surely live." Is it possible that, because he has not committed such crimes, he should be called righteous? Therefore these verses must not be taken literally, but "upon the mountains he eateth not" means that he does not live upon the reward of the meritorious acts done by his parents; "his eyes he lifteth not up to the idols" means that he never walked overbearingly; "and the wife of his neighbor he defileth not," means that he never tried to compete in the special trade of his neighbor; "unto a woman on her separation he cometh not near" means that he never tried to derive any benefit from the treasure of charity—and to this it reads: "He is righteous, he shall surely live."

Rabban Gamaliel, when he came to this passage, used to weep, saying: It seems as if he who has done all of them is righteous, but not he who has done only one. Said R. Aqiba to him: According to your theory, the verse [Lev. xviii. 24]: "Do not defile yourself with all of these things," also means with all of them, but one of them is allowed? Hence it means to say with "any" of them. The same is to be said here: If one does one of the things mentioned above, he is righteous.

"*A crime which deserves two kinds*," etc. There is a Boraitha: How is R. Jose's decision in our Mishna to be illustrated?—*e.g.*, if the crime which he committed with this woman was that she became first his mother-in-law and then married. Hence the prohibition of having intercourse with her applied, even before she

---

* Leeser's translation, " a copy of the law," is entirely wrong.

married again. Then he must be tried under the crime " with a mother-in-law." But if she became his mother-in-law after her marriage, then he must be tried under the crime " with a married woman," as the prohibition against intercourse with her existed already before she became his mother-in-law.

Said R. Adda b. Ababah to Rabha: In the first case, in which she married after she became his mother-in-law, why should he not also be tried for the crime with a married woman? Did not R. Abuhu say that R. Jose agrees in case a prohibition were added. (*E.g.*, when she was his mother-in-law but unmarried, she was prohibited to him only, but allowed to the whole world, and when married she became prohibited to the whole world. Hence one prohibition was added. And in such a case R. Jose agrees that the second crime must also be taken into consideration.) And Rabha answered: Adda, my son, do you want us to execute him twice? (R. Jose considers the added prohibition to be only concerning sin-offerings, when incurred through error.)

MISHNA *VII.*: He who receives stripes, and relaxes into the same crime, and is punished again and does not repent, the court takes him to the kyphos, and feeds him with barley until his abdomen bursts.

GEMARA: Because he received stripes twice, should the court imprison him in the kyphos forever? Said Jeremiah in the name of Resh Lakish: The Mishna speaks of crimes to which korath applies, and he was forewarned of stripes, and was punished twice for the same crime. And as this man deserves death by Heaven, but his time has not yet come, and we see that he devotes his life to sin, the court imprisons him to hasten his death. Said R. Jacob to R. Jeremiah b. Tahlifa: Come and I will explain to you the real meaning of Resh Lakish: The Mishna means that he has committed the same crime thrice, for two of which he has received stripes. And as the court does not see any remedy for him, it puts him in the kyphos after the third time. If, however, he has committed different crimes to which korath applies, he is not taken to the kyphos, as he is not considered as devoting his life to this crime, but as one careless concerning prohibitions.

" *He who receives stripes twice,*" etc. Twice, although he was not punished a third time! Shall we assume that our Mishna is not in accordance with R. Simeon b. Gamaliel, who says that until one has repeated the same crime thrice it is not considered a hazakah* (habit). Said Rabhina: It may be even in accordance with R. Simeon, as the crime was committed thrice, and he considers it a habit, although he was not beaten thrice.

An objection was raised from the following: He who has committed a crime twice to which the punishment of stripes applies receives the stripes twice ; repeating same a third time, the court puts him in the kyphos. Abba Shaul, however, maintains that even to the third time he receives stripes, and only after he has committed the crime a fourth time does the court imprison him. Is it not to be assumed that the Tanaim of this Boraitha differ in the same point as R. Simeon b. Gamaliel and Rabbi differ—namely, whether it should be considered a hazakah after two times, which is the opinion of Rabbi, or after three times, according to R. Simeon? Nay ; all agree with R. Simeon. And the point of their difference is that, according to the first Tana, the crimes which were committed thrice counted, and according to Abba Shaul, the stripes, and not the crimes, are to be counted.

Where is to be found an allusion in the Scripture to the kyphos in question? Said Resh Lakish [Ps. xxxiv. 22]: " The evil will slay the wicked." And the same said again : It reads [Eccl. ix. 12] : " For man also knoweth not his time, like the fishes that are caught in an evil net," from which the same is to be inferred.

MISHNA *VIII.* : He who kills a person, not in the presence of witnesses, is taken to the kyphos and is fed on scant bread and water.

GEMARA : But whence do we know if it was not in the presence of witnesses? Said Rabh : If there was only one witness, or even if there were two who saw this from separate places. And Samuel said : If he committed the crime without forewarning. And R. Hisda in the name of Abimi said : Even when the witnesses contradicted themselves in unimportant matters—as, *e.g.*, a Mishna stated above : Ben Sakkai examined them concerning the size of figs, etc., and they were not contradicted in the examination.

"And is fed with scant bread and water." And above it was said that he was fed with barley? Said R. Shesheth : In both cases it is meant that he was first fed with scant bread and water till his abdomen shrank, and afterwards with barley, from which it swelled till it burst.

MISHNA *IX.* : If one steals a kisvah, or one curses his

---

neighbor, invoking God as "a carver," or one has intercourse with a female heathen, zealous people (like Pinehas) have a right to strike him when caught in the act. If a priest performed the serv-ice in the Temple while he was unclean, his fellow-priests would not bring him to the court, but the youths would take him out of the sanctuary and split his head. If a common Israelite served in the Temple, according to R. Aqiba, he was choked by the court, and according to the sages he would come to his death by Heaven.

GEMARA: What is meant by "*kisvah*"? Said R. Jehudah: It means service vessels [*cf.* Num. iv. 7]. And where is there to be found an allusion to this in Scripture? [Ibid., ibid, 20]: "That they may not go in to see when the holy things are covered, and die."

"*Who curses*," etc. R. Joseph taught: May the carver strike his carving. And another explanation by Rabah b. Mari is: May the carver strike him himself, and his creator and his creation.

"*One who has intercourse*," etc. R. Kahana questioned Rabh: What is this punishment if there were no zealous men? Rabh forgot his traditional answer to this, and it happened that it was read before R. Kahan in a dream, etc. [Mal. ii. 11]: "Judah hath dealt treacherously, and an abomination hath been com-mitted in Israel and in Jerusalem; for Judah hath profaned the sanctuary of the Lord which he loveth, and hath married the daughter of a strange god." And he came to Rabh and told him that so was it read to him, and therefrom Rabh recollected that this passage was an answer to his question, as it reads immediately after it: "The Lord will cut off, unto the man that does this, son and grandson, out of the tents of Jacob, and him that bringeth near an offering unto the Lord of hosts"—which means, if he was a scholar, that he should not have a son among the scholars or a grandson among the disciples; and if he was priest, that he should not have a son who should bring an offering, etc. Hyya b. Abuhu said: He who has had intercourse with the daughter of an idolater is considered as if he mingles himself with the idols. As it reads: "He hath married the daughter of a strange god." Has, then, an idol a daughter? Hence it means as is just mentioned above.

When R. Dimi, or Rabbin, came from Palestine, he said that the court of the Maccabees decreed: He,who does so transgresses concerning the following four things: Neda (menstruation), Shif'ha (female-slave), Goiye (strangers in faith), and prostitution.

Said R. Hisda: If one comes to the court with the question, "May one take revenge on the criminal mentioned above?" his question must not be answered. And so also said Rabba b. Hana in the name of R. Johanan, and not only this, but if it should happen that Zimri were killed by Phinehas after he separated himself from Cozbi, Phinehas would be put to death for this crime. Furthermore, if Zimri, seeing that Phinehas seeks his life, were to kill him in self-protection, he would not be punished, as Phinehas would be considered a seeker of life.

It reads [Num. xxv. 5]: "Moses said to the judges of Israel," etc. The tribe of Simeon went to Zimri ben Saul and said: They (the judges) are judging cases of capital punishment, and you keep silent! What did he do? He gathered twenty-four thousand of his tribe and went to Cozbi, pleading with her to listen to him. And to her answer, "I am a princess, the daughter of a king, and my father commanded me not to listen to any one but the greatest of Israel," he said: I myself am a prince of a tribe in Israel, and I am greater than Moses, as I am from the second tribe, while he is from the third. He took her by the locks of her hair, and brought her to Moses, saying: Son of Amram, is this damsel allowed to me, or prohibited? And should you say that she is prohibited, I would ask you, Who allowed to you the daughter of Jethro? Moses, however, had forgotten the traditional Halakha, and he and all who accompanied him wept. As it reads [ibid., ibid. 6]: "And these were weeping by the door of the tabernacle of the congregation."

And farther on it reads: "And Phinehas saw." What did he see? Said Rabh: He saw Zimri's act, from which he recollected the traditional Halakha. And he said to Moses: Granduncle, didst thou not teach me, on thy descending from Mount Sinai, that zealous men might take revenge on him who has had intercourse with the daughter of an idolater? To which Moses answered: Let him who reads the letter be the carrier—*i.e.*, let him who gives the advice be its executor.

Samuel, however, said: Phinehas saw [Prov. xxi. 30]: "There is no wisdom, nor understanding, nor counsel against the Lord—*i.e.*, in a case where there is a violation of the Holy Name the honor of the master must not be considered (and therefore Phinehas did it without the consent of his master Moses).

R. Itz'hak, in the name of R. Elazar said: He saw the angel who destroyed the people. It reads: "Arose and took a javelin in his hand." From this it may be inferred that one must not enter with arms into the house of learning. He took out the javelin from its sheath, sharpened it, and replaced it in the sheath so that it should not be visible; and went to the headquarters of Simeon's tribe, saying: Whence do we know that the tribe of Levi is greater than Simeon's? And the people who were there thought: Phinehas himself is coming to do the same as Zimri has done. Hence the scholars decided that this is allowed.

Said R. Johanan: Six miracles occurred to Phinehas when he came to smite Zimri. One—Zimri has not separated himself, etc (The continuation of the Haggadah will be translated farther on.)

"*If a priest performed the service . . . while he is defiled,*" etc. R. Ahbah b. Huna questioned R. Shesheth: Is a priest who does service, being defiled, deserving of death by Heaven, or not? And he answered: This we have learned in our Mishna: "A priest who does service in the Temple, being de- filed, his fellow-priests would not bring him to court, but the youths would take him out and split his head." Now, if it should be supposed that he was guilty of death by Heaven, why did not they leave him to the heavenly punishment? Rejoined he: Do you mean to say that he was not guilty at all? Is there such a thing—that Heaven frees him and we should put him to death? Yea! Does not the court put one who is twice beaten with stripes in the kyphos and cause him to die? (What com- parison is this?) Did not R. Jeremiah say that it speaks of crimes of a kind to which korath applies? Hence such an offender deserves death. But is the case not the same with him who steals a kisvah, and with the two other cases mentioned in our Mishna? To all of them it is taught that there are allusions in the Scripture implying that they deserve death, viz., concerning a kisvah [Num. iv. 20]: "That they may not go in to see when the holy things are covered, and *die*," concerning one cursing his neighbor, etc., it was explained by R. Joseph that it looks like blasphemy, and concerning an intercourse with a daughter of an adulterer, Rabh recollected his tradition, as said above.

An objection was raised from a Boraitha which states: And the following are liable to death by Heaven: An unclean priest who served in the Temple, etc. Hence we see that his punish- ment is death, R. Shesheth being objected to, and the objection remains.

The same Boraitha continues thus: The following deserve death by Heaven: One who eats grain in which the heave-offering is mixed, an unclean priest who eats a heave-offering while defiled, and a commoner who partakes of the heave-offering, a commoner who performs service in the Temple, a priest, while defiled, serving in the Temple, a priest who has had a legal bath after defilement and performs the service in the Temple before sunset, the same is if he performs the service without the prescribed dress, or he who performs service before the prescribed offering after defilement is brought, and also he who serves without the prescribed washing of his hands and feet, or he serves while drunk, or without having cut his hair at the prescribed time. However, one uncircumcised, a mourner while the corpse is not yet buried, and he who worships while sitting, do not come under the category of death by Heaven, but are only forewarned. A priest who has a blemish and he who derives benefit from the sanctuary intentionally—according to Rabbi he comes under the category of death by Heaven, and according to the sages he comes under the category of the forewarned.

Concerning heave-offering mentioned in the Boraitha, said Rabh: A commoner who partakes of heave-offering is to be punished with stripes. Said R. Kabana and R. Assi to him: Let the master say he deserves death by Heaven. And he answered: It reads [Lev. xxii. 9, 10]: "They die therefore . . . I am the Lord who sanctify them. And no stranger shall eat of a holy thing." Hence between "they will die" and "no stranger shall eat" intervenes "I am the Lord," etc., to teach that the punishment of death does not apply to a stranger. But does not the above Boraitha state that such comes under the category of punishment by Heaven? Do you want to contradict Rabh from a Boraitha? Rabh is a Tana, and has the right to differ.*

"*If a common Israelite served in the Temple*," etc. There is a Boraitha: R. Ismael said: It reads [Num. xviii. 7] : "And the stranger that cometh nigh shall be put to death"; and [ibid. xvii. 28] "Everyone that cometh near at all unto the tabernacle of the Lord shall die." As the verse just cited speaks of death by Heaven, the same is the case with the former.

R. Aqiba, however, said : Here the Scripture says : "And die therefore "; and [Deut. xiii. 6] : "And that prophet, or that dreamer of dreams, shall be put to death." And as there it means by stoning, the same is the case here. And R. Johanan

---

* All that is mentioned in the Boraitha cited is inferred from different passages in the Scripture by analogy of expression, followed by a discussion at length about them, which does not belong here and is therefore omitted.

b. Nuri said : As a false prophet is punished with choking, the same is the case here. What is the point of their difference? R. Aqiba holds that the expression "put to death" must be analogized with "put to death," and not "put to death" with "shall die." And R. Ismael holds that we should equalize a commoner with a commoner, and not a commoner with a prophet. According to R. Aqiba, however, a prophet who has misled is worse than a commoner.

And the point of difference between R. Aqiba and R. Johanan b. Nuri is the same wherein R. Simeon and the rabbis differ in the following Boraitha : To a prophet who has misled, stoning applies; according to R. Simeon, however, choking applies. But does not a Mishna above state (p. 239): R. Aqiba said : Choking applies. There are two Tanaim who differ concerning R. Aqiba's statement. Our Mishna mentioned R. Simeon, who said so, in accordance with R. Aqiba's theory; but the Boraitha is in accordance with the rabbis, who are of the opinion, with R. Aqiba, that choking applies.

CHAPTER X.

MISHNA *I.* : To the following, choking applies : To him who strikes his father or mother, to him who steals a living soul of Israel, to a judge rebelling against the Great Sanhedrin, to a false prophet, to him who prophesies in the name of an idol, to the paramour of a married woman, and to the collusive witnesses of the married daughter of a priest who has sinned, and to her abuser.

GEMARA : Whence do we know that choking applies to the smiter of his father or mother? From [Ex. xxi. 15] : " Put to death " ; and wherever the Scripture mentions death without specifying what kind, choking is meant. But perhaps the verse cited means " when he kills him or her " ? How can it be supposed if one who kills a stranger is executed by the sword, that he who kills his father should be executed by choking, which is more lenient? However, this is correct according to him who holds that choking is lenient; but according to him who holds that the sword is lenient, what can be said? Therefore, from [ibid., ibid. 12] : " He that smiteth a man so that he die," and from [Num. xxxv. 21] : " Smitten with his hand that he die," we infer that when it is not mentioned " that he die," it means smitten only. And it was necessary for the Scripture to write both of the following passages, namely [Ex. xxi. 12] : " He that smiteth a man so that he die," and [Num. xxxv. 30]: " Whoever it be that killeth a person (soul)," for if the first only were written, one might say that one is liable only when he kills an adult, but not a minor; and if the second only were written, one might say that one is liable even if he killed a miscarried child or one who was born in the eighth month, and therefore both are necessary.

But from the above theory it is to be understood that if one smote his father he is guilty of a capital crime even if he did not wound him. Why, then, does the succeeding Mishna state that he is *not* guilty unless he wounds him? This is inferred from [Lev. xxiv. 21]: "And he that smiteth a beast shall make restitution for it, and he that smiteth a man shall be put to death."* As concerning a beast the striker is not liable unless he makes a wound, as in ibid. 18 it reads "nefesh" (soul, blood of it), the same is the case if he smote a person—he is not guilty unless he made a wound. R. Jeremiah opposed: According to this theory, if one has made lean an animal by using it to carry stones, should he not be responsible? Therefore we must say, as verse 30 is not necessary for this case, because of verse 18, apply it to human life. If so, why the analogy? In accordance with what was taught by the school of Hiskia (above, p. 233). But this is only correct for him who agrees with the school of Hiskia. But for him who does not agree with this theory, to what purpose is the analogy? To teach that, as there is no liability if one wounds an animal for the purpose of curing it, the same is the case with a human being. A similar question was propounded by the schoolmen: May one bleed his father to cure him? R. Mathna said: From "Thou shalt love thy neighbor as thyself" it may be inferred that he may. And R. Dimi b. Henna said: It is inferred from the analogy just mentioned. As there is no liability for wounding an animal to cure, the same is the case with a human being. Rabh did not allow his son to take out a string from his finger, lest he might wound him unintentionally, which is prohibited for one to do to his father; and Mar b. Rabhina did not allow his son to open for him a wound, for the same reason.

R. Shesheth was questioned: May a son be a messenger from the court to punish his father with stripes, or to put him under the ban?† Said Rabba b. R. Huna: And so also was it taught by the school of R. Ismael: Concerning all the crimes mentioned in the Torah, the court must not appoint the son of the criminal to strike, to curse his father, etc., except in the case of a seducer, about whom it reads [Deut. xiii. 9]: "Nor shall thy eye look with pity on him," etc.

MISHNA *II.*: A son is not guilty of a capital crime unless he wounds his father by striking him. Cursing is in one respect

---

* Lesser's translation does not correspond.

† A discussion at length about this matter is omitted from the text, as most of the objections and answers are already translated, or will be translated in their proper places. Here, however, it is of no importance at all, as the question is solved by Rabha without any objection or opposition.

more rigorous than striking, as for the latter one is guilty when done to his living father only, and for the former he is guilty even if he did it after his father's death.

GEMARA: The rabbis taught: It reads [Lev. xx. 9]: "His father and mother has he cursed," which means even after his death. And this is repeated only for this purpose, lest one say that one is guilty for striking his father and for cursing him. Hence, as the former applies to a living father only, the same is the case with the latter. But this is correct only for R. Jonathan, as according to him the verse just cited is superfluous; but for R. Jashiah, who uses this verse for inferring father *or* mother (above p. 192), whence does he deduce the above statement? From [Ex. xxi. 17]: "And he that curseth his father," etc. But let the Mishna state that in another respect striking is more rigorous than cursing, as concerning the former one is guilty if he did so to his father even if he were of another faith, which is not the case with cursing (according to the opinion of some Tanaim). The Tana of our Mishna holds that cursing is compared to striking even in the latter case; *i.e.*, one is also guilty if he curses his father who is of another faith.

Shall we assume that the Tanaim of our Mishna differ in the same way as the Tanaim of the following Boraithas, one of which states: If one's father was a Samaritan, he is forewarned against striking him, but not against cursing; and the other states: He is forewarned neither against striking nor against cursing? The schoolmen who learned these Boraithas thought: Both Boraithas agree that at the beginning the Samaritans were true proselytes (this refers to II. Kings, vii. 23–34), but at that time they were decadent. Hence the point of their difference is that, according to one Boraitha, striking is equal to cursing, and according to the other it is not? Nay! All agree that they are not equal, consequently the point of their difference is, whether the ancient Samaritans were true proselytes, or only embraced Judaism from fear of the lions. Hence they were not considered Israelites at all, but heathens.

MISHNA III.: If one steals a person, he is not guilty of a capital crime, unless he brings him upon his own premises. R. Jehudah, however, said: One is not guilty for only bringing him upon his premises, but after he used him for work. As it reads [Deut. xxiv. 7]: "And he treateth him as a slave."

If one steals his own son and sells him, R. Ismael, the son of R. Johanan b. Beroka, makes him guilty; the sages, however, free him. If one steals a person who is half free and half slave, *i.e.*, a slave of two owners, one of whom has freed him, R. Jehudah makes him guilty, and the sages free him.

GEMARA: And the first Tana of our Mishna does not require any work (notwithstanding that so it is written in the Scripture)? Said R. Ahbah b. Rabha: They differ if he worked with him to the value of less than a perutha. (According to the first Tana he is guilty, and according to R. Ismael he is not.)

R. Jeremiah questioned: How is the law if one steals a person while asleep and sells him in this condition, or if he stole a pregnant woman for the purpose of selling her embryo, is it considered treating as a slave, or, because he has not done it in the usual manner, is it not so considered? Usual manner! Let him say that there was not any kind of slavery at all? He speaks of when he used the sleeping one as a support and the pregnant woman as a protection against the wind (and as she is more stout because of the embryo, the protection is stronger). And to this was the question: "Is it considered slavery, or, because it was in an unusual manner, is it not? This question is now decided.

The rabbis taught: It reads [Deut. xxiv. 7]: "If a man be found stealing any one of his brethren of the children of Israel." From this we know only concerning a male, but whence do we know concerning the stealing of a female? It reads [Ex. xxi. 16]: "And he that stealeth a man—whatsoever. However, from both verses we know about a man who stole either a male or a female. But whence do we know that the same is the case when a woman steals a male or female? As to this, it reads in the verse above cited: "Then shall that thief die," meaning what person soever.

There is another Boraitha: The verse just cited means that there is no difference whether he stole a male or a female, a proselyte, or a bondsman who was freed, or a minor. However, if he stole him and did not sell him, or even if he sold him, but he is still on his own premises, he is not condemned to capital punishment. If he sold him to the father or brother of the stolen one, or to some one else of his relatives, capital punishment does apply. However, for stealing slaves it does not. This Boraitha was repeated by one of the disciples before R. Shesheth, and he rejoined: I teach: R. Simeon said: It reads: "From his brethren," which means that he is not guilty unless he took him out from the control of his brother. And you teach: He is guilty of a capital crime if he sold him to his father or brother.

Go and teach that he is free. (Says the Gemara:) And what is the difficulty? Why not say that the Boraitha is in accordance with the rabbis? This cannot be supposed, as there is a rule that all the anonymous Mishnayoth are in accordance with R. Mair, anonymous Tosephtas in accordance with R. Nehemiah, anonymous Siphra in accordance with R. Jehudah, and anonymous Siphri in accordance with R. Simeon. And all of them are after R. Aqiba's instructions. And the Boraitha above cited is to be found in Siphri.

"*If one stole his own son*," etc. What is the reason of the rabbis, who free him? Said Abayi: It reads [Deut. xxiv. 7]: "If a man be found 'stealing,'" which means to exclude him who is often with him. Said R. Papa to Abayi: According to your theory [ibid. xxii. 22]: "If a man be found lying with a woman," etc., is also to be explained to exclude him who is often with her; *e.g.*, in the house of so and so, which is crowded, and men and women are often together—should one not be liable for adultery? And he answered: I call your attention to [Ex. xxi. 16]: "And he will be found in his hand" (which is not the case with a father, whose son is usually in his hand). Said Rabha: According to this theory, teachers of schoolchildren and masters with their disciples are considered often together, and if it happened that one of the masters stole one of the children, he is free from capital punishment.

"*Half a slave*," etc. There is a Mishna (First Gate, p. 193): R. Jehudah says that there is no disgrace for slaves. And ibid. 195 (*q.v.*), the reason of R. Jehudah is given from [Deut. xxv. 11]. However, what would be his reason here? Thus: "From his brethren" means to exclude slaves; "children of Israel" means to exclude a half slave; "of the children of Israel" means again an exclusion, and means to exclude the same. And there is a rule that an exclusion after an exclusion comes to add. Hence a person who is half slave and half free is added to those for whom guilt is incurred. The rabbis do not hold his theory that "of his brethren" means to exclude slaves, as a slave is also considered a brother who is obliged to perform all the commandments which are obligatory on a woman. Hence, according to them, "children of Israel" means to exclude a slave, and "of the children of Israel" means to exclude half a slave and half a free man. But whence do we know about the forewarning of stealing a person of Israel? According to R. Jashiah: From [Ex. xx. 13]: "Thou shalt not steal." And according to R.

Johanan: From [Lev. xxv. 42]: "They shall not be sold as bondmen are sold." And they do not differ, as one master counts the negative commandment of stealing, and the other the negative commandment of selling.

The rabbis taught: "Thou shalt not steal," in the third commandment, means human beings. But perhaps it means simply money? It may be said: Go and learn it from the thirteen methods by which the Torah is to be explained, one of which is that a word or (passage) is to be explained from its connection or from what follows,* and as the connection of this passage speaks of human beings, you must explain also that "stealing" applies to human beings. There is another Boraitha: It reads [Lev. xix. 11]: "Ye shalt not steal," meaning money. You say money, but perhaps it means human beings? Go and learn it from the thirteen methods, etc., one of which is that a word or (passage) is to be explained from what follows. And as the continuation of this passage is concerning money [ibid. 13], so also stealing is to be explained as meaning money.

It was taught: If there were two parties of witnesses, and one party testified that one stole a human being and the other testified that he sold him, and thereafter one of the parties, or both, were found collusive, they are not to be put to death, according to Hiskia. According to R. Johanan, however, they are. Hiskia's reason is that he holds in accordance with R. Aqiba, who used to say (Last Gate, p. 135): A case, but not half a case. And R. Johanan is in accordance with the rabbis, who said: Even for half a case. R. Papa, however, said, concerning the witnesses of selling: All agree that they are to be put to death. But the point of their difference is concerning the witnesses of the stealing. According to Hiskia they are not to be put to death, because stealing and selling are two separate crimes. R. Johanan, however, is of the opinion that the stealing is the beginning of the selling. The latter, however, agrees that the first witnesses concerning a stubborn and rebellious son are not to be put to death if found collusive, as they could say: Our intention was only that he should be punished with stripes, as it is said above that the son in question is not put to death unless he first received stripes.

Said Abayi: There are three cases concerning a stubborn and

---

* "We refer the reader for the real meaning of this method to Mielziner's "Introduction to the Talmud" (par. No. 50 of page 174).

rebellious son. In two of them all agree, and in one of them they differ. Namely, concerning the first witnesses in this case, all agree that they are not to be put to death if collusive, as they could say: Our intention was only that he should receive stripes. And their claim must be taken into consideration. And also all agree concerning the second witnesses of same, that they are to be put to death, as the first witnesses are considered as concerning stripes only. Hence the second witnesses only would be the cause of death to the criminal son, if they were not collusive; and they have done the whole case even according to R. Aqiba, who requires the whole, and not half a case.

And the third case in which they differ is, if there were two parties of witnesses, one of which testifies: " In our presence he stole," and the other testified: " In our presence he consumed." And as the law regarding the criminal son dictates that he is not to be put to death unless he stole from his father and consumed on the premises of strangers, both things depend on each other. Hence according to R. Aqiba each of the parties has done only half a case. And if one or both were found collusive, they cannot be put to death for half a case; and according to the rabbis they can, as they make one guilty for half a case.

MISHNA *IV.*: A judge rebelling against the Great Sanhedrin (to whom, as stated in the first Mishna of this chapter, choking applies) is commanded in the Scripture as in Deut. xvii. 8-13. There were in Jerusalem (at the time of the Temple) three courts: one was situated at the gate of the Temple Mount (this was the east gate, inside of the surrounding wall, preceding the women's court); and another was situated after the women's court, but preceding the court of the common Israelites; and the third one was situated in the Temple treasury for congregational sacrifices. And in case a judge in the country had a dispute about the law with his colleagues, as to which the Scripture commands to bring their case before the court in Jerusulem, they came to the first court, situated at the above-mentioned gate. And the judge in question related his case before the court : I have lectured thus and thus, and my colleagues have lectured otherwise—thus and thus. I have taught in accordance with my lecture so and so, and my colleagues so and so. And if this court were able to decide it traditionally, they rendered their decision; and if not, they came before the other court, explaining the same again. If this court were able to decide it traditionally, they rendered their decision; and if not, all of them came to the Great Sanhedrin, which was in the Temple treasury, from which the law proceeds to all Israel, wherever found. As it reads [ibid., ibid. 10] : " From that place which the Lord will choose, and thou shalt observe to do according to all that may instruct thee." Then if the judge returns to his own city and continues his lectures as before, he is not culpable. If, however, he gives his decision for practice, he is subject to capital punishment. As it reads [ibid., ibid. 12] : "And the man that will act presumptuously," etc., which means that he is not culpable unless he decides for practice.

A disciple who is not a judge, who decides for practice against the decision of the Great Sanhedrin, is not culpable. Hence the rigorousness which lies upon him, not to give his decision in any law (until he shall be forty years of age), becomes lenient concerning the punishment.

GEMARA: The rabbis taught: It reads [ibid., ibid. 8]: " khi j'pola," literally, " if it will wonder." Hence the passage speaks of the wonder (prime) judge of the courts. " *Mimcho*"— " from thee," means a counsellor. As it reads [Nahum, i. 11] : " There is gone forth (mimcho) out of thee he that devised evil against the Lord, the counsellor of infamous things." " Dabhor" —" a matter," means a Halakha ; L'michphat means a decision of money matters. " Between blood and blood " means blood of menstruation and the blood of purification after birth (referring to Lev. xii. 4) or blood of infliction. " Between plea and plea " means criminal and civil cases and cases of stripes; " Between lepers and lepers"—bodily leprosy, leprosy of houses, of dress, etc.; " matters "—excommunications, appraisement of things belonging to the sanctuary ; " controversy"—a thing which came from a controversy between a husband and wife (ref. to Num. v. 11-25); breaking the neck of the heifer (Deut. xxi.)—the purification of men who were afflicted with leprosy ; " within thy gates "—about gathering grain of the poor, forgetters of sheaves and peah (corner tithe) ; " shalt thou arise "—from thy court. " Get thee up "— infer from this that the Temple was the highest building in all Jerusalem, and the land of Israel was situated higher than all other countries. " Unto the place "—infer from this that the place is the cause of the situation of the high court.

The rabbis taught : A rebelling judge is not guilty unless he gave his decision in a matter to which, if done intentionally, korath applies ; and if unintentionally, a sin-offering. So is the decree of R. Mair R. Jehudah said : As to a matter of which the source is to be found in the Scripture, and the interpretation is by the scribes.   R. Simeon, however, maintains: Even as to one observation of the many observations of the scribes.

Said R. Huna b. Hinna to Rabha: Can you explain to me this Boraitha which has enumerated all the cases inferred from Deut. xvii. 8, in accordance with R. Mair's decree?   And Rabha said to R. Papa: Go and explain it to him.   And he explained thus: The Boraitha which states a counsellor, means him who is able to establish leap years and to appoint the days of the month.   And a difference of opinions may cause the eating of leavened bread on Passover; namely, according to some a leap year may be established during the whole month of Adar, and according to others only until Purim.   Hence if the law is in accordance with one of them, and it was done to the contrary, people would eat leaven on Passover.   The Halakha which is mentioned in the same Boraitha means the difference of opinion between R. Johanan and Resh Lakish concerning the tenth day of menstruation—whether it is still to be counted menstruation blood or of infliction (explained in Tract Nidda, 72b).   Criminal cases means the case concerning the daughter of a coercer mentioned above.   Concerning blood of menstruation, Akabia b. Mahalalel and the rabbis differ (Nidda, 19a).   Concerning blood of purification, Rabh and Levi differ (ibid. 35b).   Concerning blood of infliction, R. Eliezer and R. Jehoshua differ (ibid. 36b).   Concerning civil cases, Samuel and R. Abuhu differ (above, p. 7).   Concerning criminal cases, Rabbi and the rabbis differ (above, p. 3); stripes, R. Ismael and the rabbis differ (in the first Mishna of this tract); leprosies, R. Jehoshua and the rabbis differ (Nidda, 19b); leprosy of houses, R. Elazar b. Simeon and the rabbis differ (above, p. 4); leprosy of dresses, Jonathan b. Abtulmes and the rabbis (Nidda, 19a); appraisement of men, R. Mair and the rabbis (Arachin, 5a); excommunications, Jehudah b. Bathyra and the rabbis (ibid. 28b); sanctification, Eliezer b. Jacob and the rabbis (above, p. 32); controversies concerning a woman who is suspected by her husband, R. Eliezer and R. Jehoshua (Sota, 2a); breaking the neck of the heifer, R. Eliezer and R. Aqiba (ibid. 45b); purification of leprosy, R. Simeon and the rabbis (above, p. 137); gathering, the schools of Shamai and Hillel (Tract Negaim, XIV. 9); forgotten sheaves (the same, ibid., ibid.); peah, R. Ismael and the rabbis (Themura, 6a).   (And of all of them, the sources are in the Scripture and the explanation is by the scribes.)

" *There were three courts*," etc.   Said R. Kahana: If he says, " I have it from a tradition," and they (the Great Sanhedrin) also say the same, he is not put to death. And the same is the case if he says : So is it according to my opinion ; and they also say : According to our opinion. And so much the more if he says : I have it from a tradition ; and they say : So is it according to our opinion. And only when they say : We have it from a tradition ; and he says : According to my opinion it is the contrary—then (if he gives his decision for practice) he is put to death. And an evidence in support of this is that Akabia b. Mehalalel, who decided against the Great Sanhedrin, was not killed. R. Elazar, however, maintains that even if he says, " I have it from a tradition," and they say, " So it is according to our opinion," he is put to death, for the reason that quarrels should not increase in Israel. And your evidence from Akabia b. Mehalalel does not hold good, as he was not killed because his decision was not for practice. An objection was raised from our Mishna: I have lectured, etc. Does not the latter expression mean that he taught so from a tradition? Nay! " I taught so because of my opinion, and they taught so from a tradition."

Come and hear another objection: R. Jashiah said: The following three things I was told by Zeerah, one of the citizens of Jerusalem : A husband who has sacrificed his claim against his wife, it is considered (and his wife is not to be brought to the court) ; and the same is the case if the parents of a stubborn and rebellious son have sacrificed their claim ; and the same is it also if the high court were willing to sacrifice their honor in the case of a rebelling judge. And when I came to my brethren in the South, they yielded to me concerning the first two, but not con-cerning the third—for the reason that quarrels should not be increased in Israel. Hence the reason as to a rebelling judge is not to increase quarrel, and there is no difference whether he says, " I have it from a tradition " or " from my own opinion." This objection remains.

There is a Boraitha : R. Jose said : Formerly there was no quarrel in Israel, but a court of seventy-one was situated in the Temple treasury, and two courts of twenty-three sat at the gate of the Temple Mount and at the gate of the common Israelites ; and the same courts of twenty-three were established in every city of Israel ; and if there was a matter of difference concerning which it was necessary to inquire, they used to bring it before the court of their own city. And if they were able to decide from a tradition, they did so ; and if not, they brought it to the court of a near-by city ; and if also they could not decide it, they brought it before the court which was at the gate of the Temple Mount, and thereafter to that of the common Israelite, and he related to them : So have I lectured, etc., and so have I taught, etc. And if they had any tradition concerning this, they explained it ; and if not, all of them came before the court of the Temple treasury, in which the judges sat from the morning daily offering until that of the evening on week days. And on Sabbaths and on holidays they used to take their place in the chamber of the surrounding wall, and the question was laid before them. If they could decide it, they did so ; and if not, they stood up to vote, and their decision was according to the majority. However, since the disciples of Shamai and Hillel who had not accomplished their study increased in number, quarrels were increased in Israel, and it seemed as if the law came from two different lawgivers.

From the court of the Great Sanhedrin they used to write and send to all the cities of Israel : Whosoever is wise, modest, and is liked in the eyes of his people may be a judge in his own city. And thereafter, if he deserved it, he was advanced to the court at the gate of the Temple Mount ; and farther on, until he reached to be a member in the court of the Temple treasury.

A message was sent from Palestine : Who is the man who has surely a share in the world to come ? He who is modest, bends his head when he goes in, and the same when he goes out ; is always studying the Torah, and does not become proud thereof. And the rabbis gave their attention to R. Ula b. Abba (who possessed all these qualifications).

"*Returned to his own city,*" etc. The rabbis taught : He is not guilty unless he himself practised according to his decision ; or, he decided so for others, and they practised. It is correct when he so decided for others, etc., as if he did so before he was not subject to a capital punishment. But if he himself has done according to his decision, he is guilty even before he goes to the higher courts? Previously, if he gave a good reason for his decision, it would be accepted ; but after he came from the court, no longer is any reason accepted.

MISHNA *V.* : The punishment of him who transgresses the decision of the scribes is more rigorous than for that which is plainly written in the Scriptures, *e.g.*, if one says, " I do not see any commandment in the Torah about tephyllin (phylacteries)," with the intention of transgressing that which is written concerning them (*i.e.*, giving another interpretation to Deut. vi. 8, etc.), he is free. However, if he (the rebelling judge) should

decide that the phylacteries must contain five Totaphoth (portions), instead of the four enacted by the scribes, he is guilty.

GEMARA: Said R. Elazar in the name of R. Oshia: One is
not considered a rebelling judge unless he decides upon a thing
the sources of which are in the Scripture and the explanation is
by the scribes, and there is something to add. However, if it is
added, it harms the whole matter; and we cannot find such a
thing in the whole Scripture but phylacteries, according to E.
Jehudah (who maintains the four portions in question are to be
attached one to the other *).

MISHNA V.: (The judge in question) was not put to death
by the court of his own city, and also not by the court of the
great Sanhedrin which was established temporarily in the city of
Jamnia, but was brought to the supreme council in Jerusalem,
kept in prison until the feast days, and executed on one of the
feast days. As it reads [Deut. xvii. 13]: "And all the people
shall hear and be afraid." So R. Aqiba. R. Jehudah, however, maintains that he must not be tortured by postponing the
execution, but must be put to death immediately after being sentenced; and messengers were sent out to all the inhabitants of
Israel that the judge so and so was sentenced and executed by
the court for such and such a crime.

GEMARA: The rabbis taught concerning what was said by
R. Aqiba mentioned in our Mishna: R. Jehudah rejoined:
Does the Scripture read: "The people shall see and be afraid?"
It reads: "They shall *hear* and be afraid." Why, then, should

---

* For the explanation of this passage we published a book, "Ursprung und
Entwickelung des Phylacterien Ritus bei den Juden" (Pressburg, 1883), in which
it is explained thoroughly. It is remarkable that the chief commentator of the
Talmud (Rashi) does not give any sensible explanation hereon, other than that he
dislikes the interpretation mentioned in our text in parentheses, and he would say that
the expression, "according to R. Jehudah," means what was said by him elsewhere
—that one is not guilty unless the matter discussed contains a study which
relies upon the teaching of the sages how to practise. Thosphat remarks that
R. Oshia, the author of this saying, ignores all that was inferred from Deut. xvii. 8,
said above, without any other explanation. All the other commentators, however,
keep silent.

Our book, mentioned above, is written in the language of the Talmud, and the
very essence of this strange passage is that this Mishna was written after the Jewish
Christians began to add to the four portions of the Scripture (viz.: Ex. xiii. 1-10;
ibid., ibid. 11-17; Deut. vi. 4-9; and ibid. xi. 13-21) the first portion of John in the
New Testament. For the sources from which we establish that so was the custom
of the Jewish Christians in the first centuries, A.C., we refer to the above-mentioned
book, and also to our little book, "The History of Amulets, Charms, and Talismans,"
published in English (New York, 1893).

this man be tortured? Therefore I say that he is executed immediately, and messengers are sent out to notify the people.

The rabbis taught: The following four crimes must be heralded—of a seducer, a stubborn and rebellious son, a rebelling judge, and collusive witnesses. Concerning the first three it reads: "All the people of Israel (shall hear and be afraid)." And concerning collusive witnesses it reads [Deut. xix. 20]: "And those who *remain* shall hear"—because not all of Israel are qualified to be witnesses.

MISHNA *VI.*: A false prophet who is to be sentenced by the court is only he who prophesies what he (*personally*) has not heard and what he was not told at all. However, he who does not proclaim what he was told to do, or did not listen to another prophet, or he who acted against what he himself was instructed by Heaven, his death depends upon Heaven. As it reads [ibid. xviii. 19]: "I will require it from him."

He who prophesied in the name of an idol, saying, "So and so was said by such and such an idol," although it corresponds exactly with the Hebrew law, he is punished by choking. The same was the case with him who had intercourse with a married woman, as soon as she comes under the control of her husband, even before she has had intercourse with him. The same punishment applies to the collusive witnesses of the married daughter of a priest, and also to her abuser, there is a difference between this case and all other cases of collusive witnesses, who are to be punished with the same death which would apply to the accused if it were true; and also between the adulterer in this case and other adulterers to whom the death of those abused applies.

GEMARA: The rabbis taught: Concerning prophecy, there are three who are to be sentenced by the court; viz., he who prophesies what he has not heard, he who prophesies what was not said to him, and he who prophesies in the name of an idol. And there are three whose death is by Heaven; viz., he who does not proclaim his prophecy, he who acts against what he was told by another prophet, and he who acts against his own prophecy.

Whence is this deduced? Said R. Jehudah in the name of Rabh: It reads [Deut. xviii. 20]: "But the prophet who may presume to speak a word in my name" means him who has prophesied what he has not heard; "which I have not commanded *him*"—although it was commanded to his colleague. "Or who may speak in the name of other gods" means in the name of any

idol. "That prophet shall die" means by choking, as choking
applies to all the deaths which are mentioned in the Scriptures
without specifying which. And the other three above mentioned
are inferred from the preceding verse [19]: "A man who will not
hearken," etc.—which is to be understood both of him who does
not make the people hear it and him who himself does not listen
to it—which ends: "I will require it of him." (Now the illustrations.) He who prophesies what he has not heard—e.g., Zedekiah ben Kenaanah, of whom it is written [II. Chron. xviii. 10]:
"Made himself horns of iron," etc. But why was he guilty?
Did not the spirit of Naboth make him err? As it reads [ibid.,
ibid. 19 to 21]: "And the Lord said, Who will persuade Achab,
the king of Israel, that he may go up and fall at Ramoth-gilead?
And one spake saying after this manner, and another saying
after that manner. Then came forth a spirit, and placed himself
before the Lord, and said, I will persuade him. And the Lord
said unto him, Wherewith? And he said, I will go forth and I
will become a lying spirit in the mouth of all his prophets.
And he said, Thou shalt persuade him, and also prevail; go
forth and do so." And to the question: What spirit? R. Johanan said: The spirit of Naboth Haisraeli. And what is meant
by "go forth"? R. Jehudah said: Go outside of the fence of
my glory (as a liar must not remain in it, hence it was not Zedekiah's fault, as he was deceived by the spirit)? He ought to have
given his attention to what was said by R. Itz'hak: The sense of
a divine oracle is given by Heaven to many prophets equally;
the language, however, by the prophets cannot be identical even
in two of them, as each prophet expresses it in his own language
—e.g. [Jer. xlix. 16]: "Thy hastiness hath deceived thee—the
presumption of thy heart"; and [Ob. i. 3]: "The presumption of
thy heart hath beguiled thee." Here, however, it reads [II.
Chron. xviii. 11]: "And all the prophets so prophesied, saying,
Go up against Ramoth-gilead," etc. Hence, as all prophesied in
identical language, he ought to have known that it was not a true
prophecy. But perhaps Zedekiah did not know what was said
by R. Itz'hak? There was Jehoshaphat, who told him that. As
it reads [ibid., ibid. 6]: "Is there not a prophet of the Eternal
besides?" And to the question of Achab: Are not all these, who
prophesy in the name of the Lord, sufficient? Jehoshaphat
answered: I have a tradition from my grandfather's house that
the sense of a divine oracle is given by Heaven, etc. And here
I hear the same version from all of them. He who prophesies

what was not said to him—*e.g.*, Chananyah ben Azzur, who said
[Jer. xxviii. 2]: "Thus hath said the Lord . . . I have broken the
yoke." And this was only by an *a 'fortiori* conclusion, drawn
from what was said by Jeremiah [ibid. 49]: "Thus hath said the
Lord . . . behold, I will break the bow of Elam." And his *a
'fortiori* conclusion was thus: Elam, who came only to assist the
king of Babylon, should be broken; the king of Babylon, who
himself came to destroy the kingdom of Judah, so much the
more should be broken. [Said R. Papa to Abayi: But this illus-
tration does not correspond, as such a prophecy was not given
to any one? And he answered: For if such an *a 'fortiori* conclusion were to be drawn, it is equal to its having been said to
some one else; however, it was not said to him directly.] He
who prophesied in the name of an idol—*e.g.*, the prophets of
Baal. He who does not proclaim the prophecy—*e.g.*, Jonah b.
Amitthai. He who does not listen to what he was told by
another prophet—*e.g.*, the colleague of Michah; as its reads
[I. Kings, xx. 35, 36]: "And a certain man of the sons of the
prophets said unto his companion, by the word of the Lord,
Smite me, I pray thee. But the man refused to smite. Then said
he unto him, Forasmuch as thou hast not obeyed the voice of
the Lord . . . " And a prophet who acted against that wherein
he himself was instructed by Heaven—*e.g.*, Edah the prophet, of
whom it is written [ibid. xiii. 9]: "For so was it charged me by
the word of the Lord"; and [ibid., ibid. 18]: "And he said unto
him, I also am a prophet like thee." And farther on it is written
[19]: "So he returned with him," ending [34]: "And when he
was gone, a lion met him on the way and slew him." [A disciple
taught in the presence of R. Hisda: He who does not proclaim
the prophecy he was told has to receive stripes. And R. Hisda
said to him: Should one who ate dates from a sieve receive
stripes? Who warned him? And Abayi said: His colleagues,
the prophets. And whence did they know this? Said Abayi:
From [Amos, iii. 7): "For the Lord Eternal will do nothing,
unless he have revealed his secret unto his servants the prophets."
But perhaps the decree was changed by Heaven? If it were so,
all the prophets would be notified. But was not such the case
with Jonah, who was not notified that the decree was changed?
There was the prophecy: Nineveh will be overthrown, which had
two meanings, to be destroyed, and also to be turned over from evil
to righteousness, and he did not understand the real meaning.
" *Who* does not listen to another prophet." But whence is one

aware that he is a true prophet, that he should be punished?
In case he gives him a sign. But was not Michah, who was
punished for not listening to the prophet (as said above), although
he did not give any sign? With him who has long been recognized as a true prophet it is different. For if the case were
not so, how could Isaac have trusted his father that his prophecy
was a true one, since such a commandment was never before
heard, and also no sign was given by Abraham. And also, how
could they rely upon Elijah, who commanded them to sacrifice
outside of Jerusalem, which was prohibited by the Scripture?
Hence, because they were recognized prophets, one must listen
to them in any event.*

The rabbis taught, concerning what was taught by rabbis
(above, p. 151) as to a prophet who had misled, to whom stoning
applies according to the rabbis, and choking according to R.
Simeon: Said R. Hisda: The point of their difference is in case
one removed the whole portion of the Scripture concerning idolatry, saying: I was so commanded by Heaven. Or even if he
said: To perform some of its worship and to abolish the rest.
But if he removed a portion which speaks concerning other commandments, all agree that choking applies. And if he told to
perform some of them and abolish the others, he is free according
to all. R. Hamnuna, however, said: The point of their difference
is if he removed a portion of any commandment, be it concerning idolatry or some other; and also in performing some worship
of idolatry and abolishing the rest. As it reads: "From the
way"—which means even a part of it. But if he prophesied as
to performing some of the commandments and abolishing the
others, all agree that he is free.

The rabbis taught: If one commands by prophecy to remove
a commandment from the Scripture, he is guilty; but if to abolish
some of it, and perform the remainder, R. Simeon frees him.
However, concerning idolatry, even if he commands "To-day
worship," and on the morrow to abolish it, all agree that he is
guilty. Hence it contradicts the explanations of both R. Hisda
and R. Hamnuna? Abayi, who holds with R. Hisda, explained
the Boraitha just cited: According to his theory—viz., if one
commands by prophecy to remove a commandment from the
Scripture—all agree that he is to be choked. "As to performing
some," etc., R. Simeon makes him free, and the same do the

---

* Here are also some Haggadas, which we transfer to the Haggadic chapter.

rabbis. But concerning idolatry, even if he said: "To-day wor-ship," and on the morrow to abolish, he is subject to a capital punishment—according to the rabbis by stoning, and according to R. Simeon by choking. Rabha, however, who holds with R. Hamnuna, explains according to his theory thus: He who com-mands by prophecy to remove, etc., either concerning idolatry or some other commandment, is subject to a capital punishment —each of the masters according to his opinion. "As to perform-ing some," etc., R. Simeon makes him free, and so also do the rabbis. Concerning idolatry, however, even if he says: "To-day," etc., he is guilty accordingly—each of the masters according to his opinion.

R. Abuhu in the name of R. Johanan said: In every case men-tioned in the Torah, if a true prophet commands you to trans-gress, you may listen, except as to idolatry, when you must not listen, even if he were to stop the sun for you, as was done by Joshua.

R. Jose the Galilean said: "There is a Boraitha: The Torah foreshadowed the final mind of idolatry and therefore gave force to it, for the purpose that one should not listen to him who commands to commit it, even if he were to stop the sun for him in the middle of the sky. Said R. Aqiba: God forbid that the sun should be stopped for them who are acting against His will. But it means even, e.g., Hananiah b. Azzur, who was a true prophet when he began to prophesy, and became a false one only afterwards.

"*Collusive witnesses of the married daughter of a priest*," etc. Whence is this deduced? Said Abhah b. R. Ika: From the following Boraitha: R. Jose said: Why is it written: "Then shall ye do unto him . . . unto his brother." (Would it not be sufficient if it should read: "As he purposed to do"?) Because all who are to be put to death biblically, their collusive witnesses and their abusers are punished with the same, except in the case of the married daughter of a priest, where she is to be burned, but not her abuser, who is to be choked. However, concerning her collusive witnesses, it would not be known whether they were to be equalized to him or to her? Therefore the expression, "unto his brother," which means, not unto his sister.

END OF TRACT SANHEDRIN, PART I. (HALAKHA),
AND OF VOL. VII. (XV.).

VOLUME VIII. (XVI.)—TRACT SANHEDRIN.

PART II.—(HAGGADA.)

CHAPTER XI.

MISHNA *I.* : All Israel has a share in the world to come. As it reads [Is. lx. 21] : " And thy people—they will all be righteous, for ever shall they possess the land, the sprout of my planting, the work of my hands, that I may glorify myself." The following have no share in the world to come : He who says that there is no allusion in the Torah concerning resurrection, and he who says that the Torah was not given by Heaven, and a follower of Epicurus R. Aqiba added, him who reads books of the Hizunim and him who mumbles over a wound, reciting the verse [Ex. xv. 26] : " I will put none of those diseases upon thee, which I have brought upon the Egyptians ; for I the Lord am thy physician." Abba Shaul said : Also he who speaks out the Holy Name with its vocals.* Three kings and four commoners have no share in the world to come. The three kings are Jeroboam, Achab, and Menasseh. R. Jehudah, however, said : Menasseh has a share in the world to come. As it reads [II. Chron. xxxiii. 13] : " And he prayed unto him and he permitted himself to be entreated by him, and heard his supplication and brought him back to Jerusalem unto his kingdom." And he was answered : He was returned to his kingdom, but not to the world to come. The four commoners are Bileam, Doeg, Achitopel, and Gechazi.

GEMARA : Is he who does not believe that the resurrection is hinted at in the Torah such a criminal that he loses his share in the world to come? It was taught : He denies resurrection, therefore he will not have a share in it, as punishment corresponds to the deed ; for all retributions of the Holy One, blessed

---

* The explanation of this term, with a difference, is found in the Gemara farther on. It is prohibited to mention the name of Jehovah as it is written, and we read it with the expression "Adonay." See a footnote in Chapter VII. We have to add thereto, that none of the Jews—not even the reformers of that time—dared to mention this Holy Name as it is written, and wherever it was mentioned they read it "Adonay."

be He, are in correspondence with man's doing. And R. Samuel b. Na'hmani in the name of R. Jonathan said : Whence do we know that so it is? From [II. Kings, vii. 1, 2] : " Then said Elisha, Hear ye the word of the Lord : Thus hath said the Lord, About this time to-morrow a seah of fine flour shall be sold for a shekel, and two seahs of barley for a shekel, in the gate of Samaria. Then answered the lord of the king, on whose hand he used to lean, the man of God, and said, Behold will the Lord make windows in the heavens, that this thing shall be? And he said, Behold, thou shall see it with thy eyes, but thereof shalt thou not eat." And this chapter ends [ibid. 20] : " And it happened unto him so ; for the people trod him down in the gate and he died." But perhaps this was because Elisha cautioned him ? As R. Jehudah in the name of Rabh said : If a sage cautions some one, even if the one cautioned had not deserved such, it falls upon him nevertheless? If it were so, it should read : And the people trod on him and he died." Why in the *gate*? Thus because of his protest which he made at the gate.

Where is resurrection hinted at in the Torah ? [It reads, Num. xviii. 28] : " And ye shall give thereof the heave-offering of the Lord to Aaron the priest." Should, then, Aaron remain alive forever? He did not even enter into the land of Israel. How, then, could Israel give him heave-offering? Infer from this that he would experience resurrection and Israel would give him heave-offering. Hence here is a hint of resurrection. The school of R. Ismael, however, taught : (Nothing is to be inferred from this,) as the words " to Aaron " mean priests who are similar to him— viz., scholar as he was. And from this it is inferred that no gift whatsoever should be given to a priest who is ignorant. Samuel b. Na'hmani in the name of R. Jonathan said : Whence do we know that one must not give heave-offering to a priest who is an ignoramus? From [II. Chron. xxxi. 4] : " To give the portion of the priests and the Levites, in order that they might hold firmly to the law of the Lord." Hence the priest who knows to hold firmly the law has a portion, but not he who is ignorant of the law. R. Johanan said that he who does so causes death to the ignorant priest. As it reads [Lev. xxii. 9] : " That they may not bear sin through it, and die therefor, if they profane it." The disciples of R. Eliezer b. Jacob taught that [ibid., ibid. 16] also applies to him who gives heave-offering to an ignoramus.

There is a Boraitha : R. Sinai said : The hint of resurrection in the Torah is to be found in [Ex. vi. 4] : " And as I did also establish my covenant with them, to give unto them the land of Canaan." It does not read "to you" (as it should, the patriarchs of that time being already dead), but "to them"—hence this is a hint that they would be restored. The Minim questioned Rabban Gamaliel : Whence do you deduce that the Holy One, blessed be He, would restore the dead? And he answered : From the Pentateuch, Prophets, and Hagiographa. However, they did not accept it. From the Pentateuch—[Deut. xxxi. 16]: "Thou shalt sleep with thy parents 've-qom,'"—"*and arise.*" * And they answered : Perhaps this word ve-qom is connected with its succeeding words.

From the Prophets—[Is. xxvi. 19] : "Thy dead shall live, my dead bodies shall arise. Awake and sing, ye that dwell in the dust ; for a dew on herbs is thy dew, and the earth shall cast out the departed." And they answered : Perhaps the verse cited means those dead who were restored by Ezekiel [chap. xxxvi.]. In the Hagiographa—[Solomon's Song, vii. 10] : "And thy palate like the best wine, that glided down for my friend gently, exciting the lips of those that are asleep." And they answered : This cannot be taken as an evidence, for it is not certain that "are asleep" means the dead. [(Says the Gemara :) R. Johanan, in the name of R. Simeon b. Jehozodok, used to cite this verse with his statement that if a Halakha is mentioned in the name of a dead sage the lips of the latter move (mumble) in his grave.] Thereafter, when Gamaliel mentioned to the Minim [Deut. xi.

---

* The translation of this verse by the translator of the Bible according to the sense does not correspond. The reason, however, of the Talmud's opinion is because it should read, "Sleep with thy father, and the people will go astray." Hence the word "arise" is superfluous. Furthermore, as it reads, "*and* arise," it is therefore enumerated among the five verses of which the explanation was doubtful to the most famous Tanaim of the Talmud. These verses are : Gen. iv. 7 : The word "sheath," which has two meanings, "atone" and "carry" (the sin)—whether it belongs to its preceding words and the former is the meaning, or to its succeeding words and the latter is the meaning ; Ex. xxv. 34 : the word "almond-shaped"—whether it belongs to the candlestick or to its succeeding words ; ibid. xvii. 9 : whether the word "to-morrow," mentioned in this verse, belongs to preceding or succeeding words ; Gen. xlix. 7 : whether the word "cursed" ends verse 6 (at that time the verses were not as yet marked) or it is the beginning of verse 7 (explained elsewhere) ; and the verse in question cited, whether the word "ve-qom" belongs to the preceding or succeeding words. This was said by Issi b. Jehudah, the greatest authority among the ancient Tanaim, to whom even the word Rabban was not added, as to Hillel and Shammai. (See Passover, 236, explaining who Issi b. Jehudah was.) And after him no lesser authorities than Rabban Gamaliel and R. Jehoshua b. Chananjah interpreted this verse on the assumption that the word "ve-qom" belongs to its preceding words. Hence, in accordance with our method, we could not omit this strange supposition.

9], " And the Lord hath sworn unto your fathers to give unto them," which does not read "to ye," but "to them "—hence it is a hint of resurrection from the Torah—it was accepted. According to others he mentioned before them [Deut. iv. 4]: " But ye that did cleave unto the Lord your God are alive every one of you this day " which means, as this day every one of you is alive, so will it be in the world to come. The officers of Rome questioned R. Jehoshua b. Hananiah: Whence do you know that the Holy One, blessed be He, will restore the dead and that there is also revealed before Him all that will be in the future? And he answered : Both things are inferred from Deut. xxxi. 16, cited above. And to their answer : Perhaps the word " ve-qom " belongs to its succeeding words, he rejoined : Accept at least the half (the second question)—that there is revealed before Him all that will be in the future. The same was taught also by R. Johanan in the name of R. Simeon b. Jehai, that from this verse both the resurrection and that there is revealed before Him all that will be in the future is inferred.

There is a Boraitha : R. Eliezer b. Jose said: I have shown the falsification in the books of the Minim, who used to say that there is no hint about resurrection in the Pentateuch. And I said to them : You have falsified your Torah, but you have nothing in your hand to say that there is no hint of resurrection. Does it not read [Num. xv. 31]: " That person shall be cut off, his iniquity is upon him "? Upon him—when? Does it not mean after he shall be cut off? Hence it means even in the world to come. (Questioned the Gemara :) Above, this passage is explained by R. Aqiba and R. Ishmael. But neither of them has explained what means " his iniquity shall be upon him "? They may explain it as in the following Boraitha : Lest one say that he will be cut off even after his repentance, therefore " the iniquity is upon him " means only when it is still upon him, but if he repented it is no more upon him.

Queen Cleopatra questioned R. Mair thus : I am aware that the dead will be restored. As it reads [Ps. lxxii. 16]: " And (men) shall blossom out of the city like herbs of the earth." My question, however, is : When they shall be restored, will they be naked or dressed? And he answered : This may be drawn by an *a fortiori* conclusion from wheat. A grain of wheat which is buried naked comes out dressed in so many garments : the upright, who are buried in their dress, so much the more shall they come out dressed in many garments.

Cæsar questioned Rabbon Gamaliel : You say that the dead will be restored. Does not the corpse become dust? How, then, can dust be restored? And the daughter of Cæsar said to R. Gamaliel : Leave the question to me and I myself shall answer it. And she said (to her father) : If there were two potters in our city, of whom one should make a pot from water and the other from clay, to which of them would you give preference? And he said : Certainly to him who creates from water; for if he is able to create from water, he is undoubtedly able to create from clay. (And she said: This is an answer to your question.)

The school of R. Ismael taught : One may learn it from glass-wares, which are made by human beings, and if they break there is a remedy for them, as they can be renewed : human beings, who are created by the spirit of the Lord, so much the more shall they be renewed (restored).

There was a Min who said to R. Ami : You say that the dead will be restored. Does not the corpse become dust? How, then, can dust be restored? And he told him : I will give you a parable showing to what this thing is similar. A human king said to his servants : Go and build me a palace in such a place, where there is no earth and no water. And they did so : and after it collapsed he commanded the same to build it for him in a place where there was earth and water. And they answered : We cannot do so. And he became angry, saying : When you could build it in such a place where there was no earth and no water, ought you not to be able to build it where they are? And if you don't believe it, go into a valley and see a mouse, which is half flesh and half earth (it being believed that there is a species of mice developed from earth), and to-morrow it multiplies and becomes all flesh. And should you say that it takes much time till it becomes so, go up into the mountain, and see that to-day you cannot find even one helzun,* and on the morrow, after rain, you will find the mountains full of them.

There was another Min who said to Gebiah b. Psisa : Woe to you, wicked, who say that the dead are restored. The living die—should the dead come to life? And he answered : Woe to you, wicked, who say that the dead will not come to life. That which has not existed at all comes to life—shall those who had

---

* It is explained elsewhere that the color of its body is like to that of the sea, the body itself like that of a fish, and that it comes out once in seventy years, and also that with its blood the Tkheles were dyed. See also the description of it in S'hönhack's Dictionary.

life once not come to life again? Said the Min to him : You call
me wicked. If I arise, I will kick thee and level thy hump from
off thee (drive out thy conceit). And he rejoined : If you do so,
you will be a specialist physician, and you will receive a great
reward.

The rabbis taught : On the twenty-fourth of Nissan the contractors of duty were taken off from Judah and Jerusalem. This
was when the Africans summoned Israel before Alexander of
Macedonia, claiming that the land of Canaan belonged to them.
As it reads [Num. xxxiv. 2] : "The land of Canaan according to
its boundaries "—and that they were the descendants of Canaan.
Said Gbiah b. Psisa to the sages : Permit me, and I will appear
before Alexander as advocate of the defendant Israel, and if they
defeat me, say to them, "You have defeated an ignoramus among
us "; and if I defeat them, say to them, "The law of Moses has
defeated you." He got this permission, and did so. Then he
said to them : What is your evidence? And their answer was :
From your Torah. Then said he : I in defence will also bring
my evidence from the same. It reads [Gen. ix. 25] : "And he
said, Cursed be Canaan ; a servant of servants shall he be unto
his brethren." Now, to whom belongs the estate of a slave, if
not to his master. And not this only, but I summon you before
the king for the many years you have not done any service for
us. And Alexander commanded them to give answer, for which
they requested from him three days' time. And he gave it to
them. And as they could not find any right answer at the appointed time they fled, leaving their fields, which were sown, and
their vineyards, which were planted. And this year was a Sabbatical one.

It happened again that the Egyptians summoned Israel before
Alexander of Macedonia, demanding from them the gold and
silver which they had borrowed from them at the time of their
exodus. As it reads [Ex. xii. 36] : "And the Lord hath given
the people favor in the eyes of the Egyptians, so that they gave
unto them what they required ; and they emptied out Egypt."
And Gbiab b. Psisa requested from the sages permission to be
the advocate of the defendant Israel, with the same reason mentioned above. He got this permission, and did so. Then he
said to them : What is your evidence? And their answer was :
From your Torah. Then said he : I in defence will also bring
my evidence from the same, which reads [ibid., ibid. 40] : "Now
the time of the residence of the children of Israel, which they dwelt

in Egypt, was four hundred and thirty years." Hence I demand of you the wages for the labor of six hundred thousand men whom your parents compelled to work for them all the time they were in Egypt. And Alexander decided that the Egyptians should give a proper answer—for which they requested three days' time, which was allowed to them. But they could not find a satisfactory answer, and they fled, leaving their sown fields and their planted vineyards. And also this year was a Sabbatical one.

· And it happened again that the descendants of Ishmael and the descendants of Keturah summoned Israel before Alexander, claiming to have a share in the land of Canaan, as they also were descendants of Abraham. And again Gbiah b. Psisa requested for permission to be Israel's advocate, which he received. And the same question of evidence was put to them, and their answer was: From your Torah [Gen. xxv. 12 and 19], which shows that Ishmael as well as Isaac were Abraham's children. And he then also brought his evidence from the same [ibid., ibid. 5 and 6]: " And Abraham gave all that he had unto Isaac. But unto the sons of the concubines that Abraham had, Abraham gave gifts; and he sent them away from Isaac his son." Now, on a father who made a *legatum* (bequest) to his children, and separated them while he was still alive, can they have any claim thereafter!

Antoninus said to Rabbi: The body and the soul of a human may free themselves on the day of judgment by Heaven. How so? The body may say: The soul has sinned; for since she has departed I lie in the grave like a stone. And the soul may say: The body has sinned; for since I am separated from it, I fly in the air like a bird. And he answered: I will give you a parable to which this is similar: A human king, who had an excellent garden which contained very fine figs, appointed two watchmen for it—one of whom was blind, and the other had no feet. He who was without feet said to the one who was blind: I see in the garden fine figs. Take me on your shoulders, and I shall get them, and we shall consume them. He did so, and while on his shoulders he took them off, and both consumed them. And when the owner of the garden came and did not find the figs, and questioned them what became of them, the blind one answered: Have I, then, eyes to see them, that you should suspect my taking them? And the lame one answered: Have I, then, feet to go there? The owner then put the lame one on the shoulders of the one who was blind, and punished them together. So also the Holy One, blessed be He—He puts the soul in the body and punishes them together. As it reads [Ps. l. 4] : " He will call to the heavens above, and to the earth beneath, to judge his people." " To the heavens above" means the soul, and " to the earth beneath " means the body.

Antoninus again questioned Rabbi : Why does the sun rise in the east and set in the west ? And he answered: If it were contrariwise, you would also question the same. Rejoined Antoninus : I mean to say, why does he set in the west (let him go around without setting, until he reach the place where he arose)? And he answered : For the purpose of greeting with peace his Creator (as the Shekhina is in the west). Rejoined again Antoninus : Let him then travel to half of the sky, greet the Creator, and set? This would harm the laborer, and those who are on the road.

The same questioned again the same : At what time does the soul come into the body—at the moment of conception, or at the time the embryo is already formed? And the answer was : When it is already formed. Said Antoninus to him : Is it possible that a piece of flesh shall keep three days or more without being salted, and it shall not become stinking? And therefore it must be said : At conception. Said Rabbi : This teaching I accepted from Antoninus, and a support to him is to be found in [Job, x. 12] : " And thy providence watched over my spirit."*

Antoninus questioned Rabbi again : At what time does the evil spirit reach man? At the time the embryo is formed, when it comes out from the womb? And he was answered: At the time it is formed. Rejoined Antoninus : If so, the embryo would kick the entrails of the mother and go out ; therefore it must be from the time it comes out. And Rabbi said : This teaching I received from Antoninus, and he is supported by Gen. iv. 7 : " Sin lieth at the door."

Resh Lakish proposes the following contradiction : It reads [Is. xxxv. 6] : " Then shall the lame leap as a hart, and the tongue of the dumb shall sing " ; and [Jer. xxxi. 7 †] : "Among them the blind and the lame, the pregnant woman and she that

---

* Conception in Hebrew is termed " pqiddha," and the term in the verse cited is " up-qudos'ha." Hence the analogy.

† In Leeser's translation of the Bible, which we follow in our edition, there is an error, as the first verse of Jer. xxxi. is misplaced and ought to be the twenty-fifth of xxx., with which it ends, and chap. xxx. begins with : " Thus hath said the Lord." Hence the verse cited is 7, and not 8, as in Leeser.

travaileth with child together." (Hence the passages contradict each other.) It must therefore be said: They will be restored with the blemishes they had in their life, and thereafter they will be cured.

Ula advanced another contradiction: It reads [Is. xxv. 8]: " He will destroy death to eternity; and the Lord Eternal will wipe away the tear from off all faces, and the shame of his people will he remove from off all the earth; for the Lord hath spoken it "; and [ibid. lxv. 20]: " There shall no more come thence an infant . . . for as a lad shall one die a hundred years old "? This presents no difficulty. The former speaks of Israel's self, and the latter of those concerning whom it reads [ibid. lxi. 5]: " And strangers shall stand and feed your flocks, and the son of the alien shall be your ploughmen and your vintners."

R. Hisda also advanced a contradiction: It reads [ibid. xxiv. 23]: " And the moon shall be put to the blush and the sun be made ashamed; for the Lord of hosts will reign on mount Zion "; and [ibid. xxx. 26]: " And the light of the moon shall be as the light of the sun, and the light of the sun shall be sevenfold, as the light of the seven days "? This presents no difficulty. The latter speaks of the time when the Messiah shall appear, and the former, of the world to come. And to Samuel, who maintains that there will be no difference between this time and the time of Messiah, except that Israel will no longer be under the dominion of foreigners, the explanation of these contradictory verses may be thus—that the latter speaks of the camp of the upright and the former of the camp of the Glory of the Shekinah.

Rabha propounded another contradiction: It reads [Deut. xxxii. 39]: " I make one die and I make one alive "; and further on it reads: " I wound and I heal "? It means that the Holy One, blessed be He, says: All that I made to die shall I bring to life again, and thereafter shall I cure what was wounded.

The rabbis taught: Lest one say that the verse just cited means, I make one die and another one shall I bring to life. therefore it reads, " I wound and I cure." As wounding and curing apply to one person only, the same is the case with death and life—they apply to one person. This is an answer to those who say that there is no hint in the Torah about resurrection.

There is a Boraitha: R. Mair said: It reads [Ex. xv. 1]: "Then Moses and the children of Israel will sing this song." It does not read " sang," but will sing (yoshir). This is a hint of resurrection in the Torah. Similar to this is [Joshua, viii. 30]: "Then Joshua will build an altar." It does not read "did build," but "will build." This is also a hint of resurrection. (Says the Gemara): However, this cannot be taken as a support, as the same expression is to be found in I. Kings xi. 7, and nevertheless it does not mean in the future, but in the past.

R. Jeoshuah b. Levi said: It reads [Ps. lxxxiv. 5]: "Happy are they who dwell in thy house: they will be continually praising thee." It does not read "praised thee" in the past, but in the future. Hence it is a hint of resurrection.

The same said again: He who sings to his Creator in this world will be rewarded by singing the same in the world to come, as the verse just cited reads.

Hyya b. Abah in the name of R. Johanan said: It reads [Is. lii. 8]: "The voice of thy watchmen—they raise their voice, together shall they sing; for eye to eye shall they see, when the Lord returneth unto Zion." It does not read "sung," in the past, but in the future. Hence it is a hint of resurrection.

The same said again in the name of the same authority: In the future all the prophets together will sing a song of praise with one voice, as the verse just cited reads.

R. Jehudah said in the name of Rabh: He who hesitates in declaring a Halakha to a disciple is considered as if he would rob him of the inheritance of his parents. For it reads [Deut. xxxiii. 4]: "The law which Moses commanded us is the inheritance of the congregation of Israel." Hence the law is considered as an inheritance to all Israel since the creation of the world.

R. Hana b. Bizna in the name of R. Simeon the Pious said: He who hesitates in declaring a Halakha to a disciple, even the embryos in the entrails of their mothers denounce him As it reads [Prov. xi. 26]: "Him that withholdeth corn, the people* will denounce." And what is the reward for declaring such? Said Rabha in the name of R. Shesheth: He will be rewarded with the blessing with which Joseph was blessed, as the end of the verse cited reads: "But blessing will be heaped upon the head of the one that selleth it," which means Joseph; as it reads [Gen. xlii. 6]: "And Joseph, he was the governor over the land, he it was that sold corn to all the people."

---

* The Hebrew term for "people" is "Leum," and for "corn" "bor," and he infers from the analogy of expression that the latter means the Torah and the former means embryos.

R. Shesheth said again : He who teaches the Torah in this world will be rewarded by teaching it in the world to come.   As it reads [Prov. xi. 25] : " He that refresheth (others) will do same in the future." *   Rabha said : Resurrection is hinted at in the Torah in [Deut. xxxiii. 6] : " May Reüben live, and not die "— which means that he may live in this world, and not die in the world to come.   Rabhina, however, maintains that it is hinted at in [Dan. xii. 2] : " And many of those that sleep in the dust of the earth shall awake, some to everlasting life, and some to disgrace and everlasting abhorrence."   And R. Ashi said : From [ibid., ibid. 13] : " But thou, go (thy way) toward the end ; and thou shalt rest, and arise for thy lot at the end of the days."

R. Elazar said : A leader of a congregation, who leads them humbly, will be rewarded by leading the same in the world to come.   As it reads [Is. xlix. 10] : " For he that hath mercy on them will lead them, and by springs of water will he guide them."

The same said again : Great is wisdom, as it was placed between two divine names [I Sam. ii. 3] : " For a God of knowledge is the Lord."

And he said again : Great is the Temple, as the word " mik- dash " (Temple) [Ex. xv. 17] is also placed between two divine names.

R. Adda b. Karthinaah opposed : According to this theory " revenge " is also great, as it is also placed [Ps. xciv. 1] between two divine names.   And he was answered : And it is in accord- ance with Ula.   (This will be translated in Berachoth, as the proper place.)   R. Elazar said again : Every man who possesses wisdom may consider himself as if the Temple were built in his days, as both " wisdom " and " temple " are placed between two divine names.   And he said again : A man who possesses true wisdom will finally become rich.   As it reads [Prov. xxiv. 4] : " And thorough knowledge are chambers filled with all manner of precious and pleasant wealth."   And he said again : He who does not possess any knowledge does not deserve that one should have mercy with him."   As it reads [Is. xxvii. 11] : " For it is not a people of understanding : therefore he that made it will not have mercy on it, and he that formed it will show it no favor." And he said again : He who feeds one who does not possess any

---

* Leeser's translation does not correspond.   It seems also that in the Bible which was before the sages of the Talmud " yorah " had an *h* at the end, as so it is cited, while in our Bibles it ends with an " *a*," and has another meaning.

knowledge, chastisement will be the reward for it. As it reads
[Ob. i. 7]: "They that eat thy bread have struck thee secretly a
wound. There is no understanding in him." And he said again:
Such a man as has no knowledge will finally be exiled. As it
reads [Is. v. 13]: "Therefore are my people led into exile, for
want of knowledge." * R. Jehudah said: Exile atones for three
things. As it reads [Jer. xxi. 9]: "He that remaineth in this city
shall die by the sword, or by the famine, or by the pestilence; but
he that goeth out and runneth away to the Chaldeans that be-
siege you, shall remain alive, and his life shall be unto him as a
booty."

R. Johanan, however, said: Exiles atones for everything. As
it reads [ibid. xxii. 30]: "Thus hath said the Lord, Write ye
down this man as childless, as a man that shall not prosper in his
days; for no man of his seed shall succeed to sit upon the throne
of David, and to rule any more in Judah." And in I Chron. iii.
17, it reads: "And the sons of Yechonyah: Assir, Shealthiel his
son." And there is a tradition that Assir, Shealthiel is one person, and was Nehemiah b. Chachalyah. And why was he called
Assir? Because he was conceived in prison. (The term in
Hebrew for prisoner is Azzir.)

R. Elazar said: A house in which the words of the Torah are
not heard in the nights will finally be burned. As it reads [Job,
xx. 26]: "Entire darkness is laid by for his treasures: a fire not
urged by blowing will consume him; it will destroy any one left
in his tent." The Hebrew term for left is "sharid." As it reads
[Joel, iii. 5]: "Among the remnant (shridim)." And he said
again: He who does not benefit scholars by his estate will never
see a sign of blessing: As it reads [Job, xx. 21]: "Nothing was
spared from his craving to eat; therefore shall his wealth not
prosper." (There also the Hebrew term is "sharid," which,
according to him, means a scholar, as analogized above.) And
from the same passage the same inferred that he who does not
leave any bread after his meal will not see any blessing. But did
not the same say elsewhere that he who left pieces of bread after
his meal is considered as if he were to worship idols? This presents no difficulty. In the latter saying he means, after finishing
the meal he puts a whole loaf on the table, which is prohibited.
As it reads [Is. lxv. 11]: "That set out a table for the god of
Fortune and that fill for Destiny the drink-offering." On the

former saying he speaks of leaving some crumbs of bread for the poor. The same said again : He who changes his word is considered as if he were to worship idols. As Gen. xxvii. 12 reads : " Seem to him as a deceiver "; and as in Jer. x. 15 : They are vanity, the work of deception." And he said again : A man shall always be modest, but nevertheless shall be strong in his mind, so that he shall not be overruled by any one. (As then he may be sure that he will exist.) Said R. Zera : A hint of this is to be found in the following Mishna (Negaim vii. 3): If there seems to be leprosy in a house which is dark, windows must not be opened for investigation. (Hence if one is strong in his mind, and at the same time modest, his defects cannot be investigated.)

R. Tabi in the name of R. Joshiah said : It reads [Prov. xxx. 16]: " The nether world, and a barren womb; the earth which is not satisfied with water ; and the fire which never saith, Enough." What correspondence is there between the nether world and the womb? This is only to say that as the nature of the womb is, if something be brought in, to give it out, the same is the case with the nether world—it gives out what is brought in. And it is to be inferred by an *a fortiori* conclusion thus : A womb into which corpses are privately brought gives them out with much noise, the nether world, into which corpses are brought with much noise, so much the more shall they come out with great noise. And this may be an answer to those who say that resurrection is not hinted at in the Torah.

The disciples of Elijah taught : The upright who will be restored in the future by the Holy One, blessed be He, will never return to dust. As it reads [Is. iv. 3]: " And it shall come to pass that whoever is left in Zion, and he that remaineth in Jerusalem, shall be called holy, everyone that is written down into life in Jerusalem." And as the Holy One is forever, so also those who are mentioned in this verse will be forever. And lest one say, " What will they do at the time the Holy One, blessed be He, shall renew his world," as it reads [ibid. ii. 17]: " And exalted shall be the Lord *alone* on that day." The upright in question will be supplied with wings similar to the wings of the eagles, and they will fly over the world. As it reads [Ps. xlvi. 3]: " Therefore will we not fear when the earth is transformed, and when mountains are moved into the heart of seas." And lest one may say that they will be inflicted—to this it is written [Is. xl. 31]: " Yet they that wait upon the Lord shall acquire new strength ; they shall mount up with wings as eagles; they shall

run and not be weary; they shall walk and not become faint."
But why not infer from the dead who were restored by Ezekiel,
and who died again? He (Elijah) holds with him who says that
in reality Ezekiel did not restore any dead at all, and the whole
prophecy was only a parable for the Jewish nation that it would
be restored again. And this is related in the following Boraitha:
The dead whom Ezekiel restored arose on their feet, sang a song,
and died again. And what kind of a song was it? The Lord makes
one die justly, and mercifully restores him. So R. Eliezer. R.
Joshua said: The song was from I Sam. ii. 6: "The Lord killeth,
and maketh alive; he bringeth down to the grave, and bringeth
up." R. Jehudah, however, said: Really, it was only a parable.
Said R. Nehemiah to him: If really, then it is not a parable; and if
a parable, it is not really. Say, then, in reality it was a parable.
R. Eliezer b. R. Jose the Galilean, however, said: The dead who
were restored by Ezekiel went to the land of Israel, married, and
brought forth sons and daughters. And R. Jehudah b. Bathyra
arose on his feet, saying: I myself am a descendant of them, and
these are the phylacteries which I inherited from my grandfather,
who told me that they were used by the restored. But who were
the restored dead in question? Said Rabh: They were the sons
of Ephraim who erred concerning the promised time of redemption from Egypt. As it reads [I Chron. vii. 20–23]: "And the
sons of Ephraim: Shuthelach, and Bered his son, and Thachath
his son, and Eladah his son, and Thachath his son, and Zabad his
son, and Shuthelach his son, and Eser and Elad whom the men of
God that were born in that land slew . . . And Ephraim
their father mourned many days, and his brethren came to comfort him." Samuel, however, said: They were the men who dis-
believed in resurrection. As it reads [Ezek. xxxvii. 11]: "Then
said he unto me, Son of man, these bones are the whole house of
Israel; behold, they say, Dried are our bones, and lost is our
hope; we are quite cut off." R. Jeremiah b. Abah said: They
were the bodies of men in whom there was no sap of any meritorious act. As it reads [ibid., ibid. 4]: "O ye dry bones, hear
ye the word of the Lord." And R. Itz'hak of Nabhar said: They
were the men who did what was mentioned in [ibid. viii. 10]: "So
I went in and saw; and behold there was every form of creeping
things, and cattle, abominations, and all the idols of the house of
Israel, engraven upon the wall all round about." And it reads
[ibid. xxxvii. 2]: "And he caused me to pass by them all round
about," etc. And R. Johanan said: They were the dead of the

valley of Dura, whom Nebuchadnezzar killed. This is what he said elsewhere, that from the river Achar to the city of Rabath in the valley of Dura there were young men of Israel who were exiled by Nebuchadnezzar the wicked, who were so beautiful that there were none similar to them under the sun; and the women of Chaldea became sick when they looked upon them. The king then commanded to slay them all and to tread down their faces.

The rabbis taught: At the time Nebuchadnezzar threw Chananya, Mishael and Azaryah into the caldron the Holy One, blessed be He, told Ezekiel to go and restore the dead of the valley of Dura, and the vessels which were made from the bones of those who were slain by Nebuchadnezzar kicked him in the face. And to his question, "What is the matter?" he was told that the colleagues of those whom he had thrown into the caldron were engaged in restoring the dead of the valley of Dura. He then said [Dan. iii. 33]: "His signs—how great are they! and his wonders—how mighty are they! his kingdom is an everlasting kingdom, and his rule is over every generation." Said R. Itz'hak: May hot melted gold be put in the mouth of that wicked, for if an angel had not come and shut his mouth, he would have brought to shame all the songs and praises which were said by David in the Psalms.

The rabbis taught: Six miracles occurred on that day: (a) The caldron floated upwards; (b) it broke; (c) its foundation was crumbled by the heat; (d) the golden image fell upon his face; (e) men from four kingdoms were burned; and (f) Ezekiel restored the dead in the valley of Dura. All of them are known traditionally. However, concerning the men from the four kingdoms, there is to be found in the Scripture [Dan. iii. 2]: "And King Nebuchadnezzar sent to assemble (his) lieutenants, the superintendents and the governors, the judges, the treasurers, the counsellors, those learned in the law, and all rulers of the provinces; and [ibid., ibid. 12]: "There are certain Jewish men," etc., and further on (27) it reads: "And the lieutenants, superintendents and governors, and the king's counsellors, being assembled together, saw these men," etc. (Hence four of those mentioned in verse 2 are missed.)

The disciples of R. Eliezer b. Jacob taught: Even at the time of danger one shall not change the dress belonging to his dignity. As it reads: [ibid., ibid. 21]: "Then were these men bound in their mantles," etc. Said R. Johanan: Upright men are greater than angels, as it reads [ibid., ibid. 25]: "He answered and said, So, I see four men unbound, walking in the midst of the fire, and there is no injury on them ; and the appearance of the fourth is like a son of the gods." (Hence the angels are mentioned last.)

R. Tanhin b. Hanilai said : When Chananyah, Mishael, and Azaryah came out of the caldron, the nations came and kicked Israel in their faces, saying : Ye have such a God, and ye bowed yourself to the image! They (Israel) immediately confessed, saying [ibid. ix. 7] : " Thine, O Lord, is the righteousness, but unto us belongeth the shame of face, as it is this day."

R. Samuel b. Nah'maine, in the name of R. Jonathan, said : It reads [Solomon's Song, vii. 9] : " I thought, I wish to climb up the palm-tree, I wish to take hold of its boughs." I thought, I will take hold of the whole tree, but now I claim only one branch (of the palm Israel)—that of Hanania, etc. R. Johanan said : It reads [Zech. i. 8] : " I saw this night, and behold there was, a man (ish) riding upon a red horse," etc. " This night "—the Lord intended to plunge the whole world into night. " Behold there was a man "—the Holy One, who is named [Ex. xv. 3] " ish, lord of war." " Upon a red horse "—he intended to plunge the world into blood, but after looking upon Chananyah, Mishael and Azaryah he gave up his intention. As it reads further on, " And he was standing among the myrtle-trees (hadisin)." And by myrtle-trees are meant the upright. As it reads [Esther, ii. 7] : " And he brought up Hadassah." And " deep valley " means Babylon. As Is. xliv. 27 reads: " That saith to the deep, Be dry, and thy rivers will I dry up." " Behind them were red "—immediately the red which were filled with anger became pale, and the red became white. Said R. Papa: Infer from this that if one sees a white horse in his dream, it is a good sign. But what became of Chananyah, Mishael, and Azaryah after they came out of the caldron (as there is no further mention of them)? According to Rabh, they died from an evil eye ; and according to Samuel, they died in order not to bring further shame on Israel. R. Johanan, however, said that they returned to Palestine, married, and begot children. As it reads [Zech. iii. 8] : " Do but hear, O Joshua the high-priest, thou and thy fellows that sit before thee, for men of wonder are they." And who were the men to whom wonder was done, if not Chananyah, etc.? But where was Daniel at the time that they were thrown into the caldron? Said Rabh: He went to dig a river in the city of Tiberius. And Samuel said: He was sent by Nebuchadnezzar to bring a certain kind of grass from Palestine, to build it in Babylon. And R. Johanan says: He was sent to bring swans from Alexander of Egypt. But was it not said above by Tudus the physician that no swan left Alexandria without removal of the womb (for the purpose that they should not multiply in other countries)? He brought little ones, and the Egyptians were not aware that he took time for the purpose that they should multiply in Babylon.

The rabbis taught : According to the advice of the following three, Daniel went away before the affair of Chananyah, etc., happened: The Holy One, blessed be He, Daniel himself, and Nebuchadnezzar. The Holy One, for the reason that people should not say they were saved because of Daniel's good deeds. Daniel said : I shall go away that it shall not be done with me as in Deut. iii. 25 : " The graven images of their gods shall ye burn with fire." And Nebuchadnezzar said: Let Daniel go, in order that people shall not say I have burnt my god in fire. And whence do we know that Nebuchadnezzar worshipped him? From [Dan. ii. 46] : " Then did king Nebuchadnezzar fall upon his face, and he bowed down to Daniel."

It reads [Jer. xxix. 21-23] : " Thus hath said the Lord of hosts, the God of Israel, concerning Achab the son of Kolayah, and of Zedekiah the son of Maasseyah, who prophesy unto you in my name falsehood . . . And a curse shall be derived from them for all the exiled of Judah who are in Babylon, saying: May the Lord make thee like Zedekiah and like Achab, whom the king of Babylon roasted in the fire." It does not read whom he " burned," but whom he " roasted." And R. Johanan in the name of R. Simeon b. Johai said : Infer from this that they were roasted as people roast grain. It reads farther on [ibid., ibid 23] : " Because they have done scandalous deeds in Israel, and have committed adultery with the wives of their neighbors." What had they done? They went to the daughter of Nebuchadnezzar. Achab said: The Lord has commanded me to tell thee that thou shalt listen to Zedekiah. And the latter said the same—that she should listen to Achab. And she went and told this to her father. To which he answered: It is known to me that their God abhors incest. When they shall come to you again, send them to me. She did so. And to the question of Nebuchadnezzar: Who told you to do so? they said: The Lord. " But Chananyah and his colleagues told me that such a thing is prohibited." And they answered : We are also prophets as they are, and this command was given to us, of which they were not aware. Then said the king : I would try you as I did Chananyah and his colleagues. And to their claim, " They were three, and we are only two," he gave them the choice of any one they liked, who should be thrown with them into the caldron. And they selected Jehoshua the high-priest, thinking that his merit was so great that it would save them also. Jehoshua was then brought, and all three were thrown into the caldron. They were burned, but Jehoshua was saved; only his garments were singed. And this is what it reads [Zech. iii. 1-3]: "And he showed me Jehoshua the high-priest standing before the angel of the Lord. And the Lord said unto the accuser, The Lord rebuke thee, O accuser," etc. Satan said to him: I know that you are an upright man, but why did the fire affect your garments, which was not the case with Chananyah, Mishael and Azaryah? And he answered: They were three, and I one. And to the question: Was not Abraham the patriarch also only one when he was thrown into the caldron? he answered, With Abraham there were no wicked ones whom permission was given to the fire to affect, but with me were two wicked, and permission was given to the fire. And this is what people say: Two dried pieces of charred wood burn the third which is wet.

But why was he punished? Said R. Papa: Because his sons married such as were not fit to be the wives of priests, and he did not object; and this is meant by "filthy garments," mentioned in the verse cited.

R. Tanhun said: Bar Kappara lectured in Ciporias thus: It reads [Ruth. iii. 17]: "These six barleys gave he unto me." How is to be understood six barleys? It cannot be meant literally, for would a man like Boas give six grains of barley as a gift? And it also cannot be said "measures of barley," as it is not customary for a woman to carry six measures. Therefore the six barleys were a hint that in the future six sons would come out from her, each of whom would be blessed with six blessings: viz., David, Messiah, Daniel, Chananyah, Mishael, and Azaryah. David—as it reads [I Sam. xvi. 18]: "Then answered one of the servants, and said, Behold, I have seen a son of Jesse the Bethlechemite, who is skilful as a player and a mighty valiant man, and a man of war, and intelligent in speech and a person of good form, and the Lord is with him." Messiah—as it reads [Is. xi. 2] "And there shall rest upon him the spirit of the Lord, the spirit of wisdom and understanding, the spirit of counsel and might, the spirit of knowledge and of the fear of the Lord." Daniel, Chananyah, Mishael, and Azaryah—as it reads [Dan. i. 4]: "Lads in whom there should be no kind of blemish, but who should be handsome in appearance, and intelligent in all wisdom and acquainted with knowledge, and understanding science, and such as should have the ability to serve in the king's palace, and that these should be taught the learning and the language of the Chaldeans." (Hence all of them were blessed with six things.)

[Concerning the verse cited about David, said R. Jehudah in the name of Rabh: The whole verse is a slander, said by Doeg the Edomite. "Who is skilful as a player"—who knows how to propound questions; "mighty valiant man"—who knows how to answer questions; "a man of war"—who understands argument in the disputations of the Torah; "intelligent in speech"*—he understands from one thing another one; "a person of good form"—who is able to give good reasons for Halakhas; "the Lord is with him"—the Halakha always prevails with him. To all the things mentioned above Saul said: "My son Jonathan possesses all the same qualities. But when he heard that the Halakha prevailed with him, a qualification which he himself did not possess (for concerning Saul it reads [I Sam. xv. 47]: "And whithersoever he turned himself, he caused terror," and about David it is written: "In whatsoever he turned to be he was successful" †), he was dejected, and began to be jealous. But whence do we know that it was Doeg who said so? From [ibid. xvi. 18]: "One of the servants"—the most distinguished of them; and [ibid. xxvi. 8]: "And his name was Doeg the Edomite, the chief of the herdsmen that belonged to Saul." Concerning the verse cited about Messiah, it reads also farther on "vahari'hu" (animated), from which R. Alexandri infers that he is always overloaded with the divine commandments and chastisements resting upon him as "re'hayim" (a handmill). And Rabha said: The term "vahari'hu" means smelling—i. e., he judges by smelling. As farther on it reads: "And not after the sight of the eyes shall ye judge, and not after the hearing of the ears . . . (but nevertheless) he judges with righteousness the poor and decides with equity for the suffering ones of the earth, and he shall smite the earth with the rod of his mouth, and with the breadth of his lips shall he slay the wicked." Hence, if not by the eye and not by the ear, it must be by smelling; and therefore the sages did not recognize Bar Kochba, who claimed to be the Messiah and ruled

---

* The Hebrew term for this is "nabun dabhar"—literally, "understanding things." Leeser, however, took it as "dibur," meaning "talk."

† This passage is not to be found in the Scripture (see footnote in the original, 93*b*).

two and a half years, because he did not judge by smelling. And now concerning the verse cited about Chananyah, Mishael, etc., that they had no blemish. Said R. Haman b. Hanina: Not even a scratch was to be found on their bodies. "The ability to serve in the king's palace"—that they were able to restrain themselves from laughing, sleeping, and dreaming, and even from departing for one's necessity for fear of the king. It reads farther on [ibid. 6]: "Now there were among these, of the children of Judah," etc. According to R. Elazar, all of them were of the tribe of Judah; and according to Samuel b. Na'hmane, Daniel only was of Judah, but Chananyah, Mishael, and Azaryah were of other tribes.

It reads [Is. lvi. 5]: "I will indeed give unto them . . . an everlasting name." Said R. Tanhun: Bar Kappara lectured in Ciporias that this means the book of Daniel, which is named after him.* Let us see! All which is written in the book of Ezra was said by Nehemiah b. Chackhalyah. Why, then, was it not named after him? (The book of Nehemiah in our Bible was not as yet separated from Ezra in the time of the Talmud.) Said R. Nehemiah b. Abah: Because he was proud of it. As it reads [Neh. v. 19]: "Remember for me, my God for good, all that I have done for this people." But did not David also say similar to this [Ps. lvi. 4]: "Remember me, O Lord, when thou favorest thy people?" This was said only as a prayer.

R. Joseph said: The book was not named after him because he slandered the former governors. As it reads [Neh. v. 15]: "Former governors . . . had made it heavy . . . had taken of them bread and wine, besides forty shekels." And in this slander Daniel, who was greater than he, was also included, as he was of the former governors who made their exodus from Babylon a long time before Nehemiah. And whence do we know that Daniel was greater than he? From [Dan. x. 7]: "And I, Daniel, saw alone this appearance; but the men that were with me did not see the appearance; nevertheless a great terror fell upon them, so that they fled to hide themselves." Who were these men? Said R. Jeremiah, and according to others, R. Hyya b. Abah: Haggai, Zechariah, and Malachi. In one respect he

---

* In the text this is inferred from the term " sarissim," which has two meanings —" servants " and " eunuchs "; and [Is. xxxix. 7] in the prophecy to Hiskia it is said that his descendants will be sarissim in the palace of the Babylonian king. Here (lvi. 4) this prophecy was said to the sarissim who would keep the Sabbath ; and Daniel was a descendant of Hiskia, and among the sarissim who were taken to Nebuchadnezzar's palace.

was better than they, for he saw the appearance, but they did not. And in another respect they were better than he, as they were prophets, while he was not. But why were they shocked when they saw nothing? Though they did not see it, their guardian angels did. Said Rabhina: Infer from this, that if a man is shocked, unaware of the cause, his guardian angel must be aware of it; and his remedy is stepping back four ells, or reading the portion of Shema. And if he stands in a dirty place, where it is not allowed to recite the portion of " Shema Israel," he may say, " The goats of the butcher are stronger than I."

It reads [Is. ix. 6] : " For promoting the increase of the government, and for peace without end," etc. Said R. Tan'hun: Bar khapara lectured in Ciporias about this verse thus: Why is the first word of this verse distinguished? In all other words if a " mem " happens to be among its letters, if at the beginning or in the middle, it is an open one מ. Here, however, the " mem," which is the second letter of this word, is closed ם, which is usually only at the end of a word? It is because the Holy One, blessed be He, was about to make Hiskiah the Messiah, and Sanherib who declared war against him as a substitute for Gog and Magog the future nations who will declare war against the Messiah. Said the divine attribute of justice for Him: Lord of the Universe, David, the king of Israel, who recited before Thee so many songs and praises, Thou madest him not a Messiah; Hiskiah to whom Thou hast done so many miracles, and he recited neither songs nor praises—shouldst Thou make him a Messiah? And therefore the " mem " was closed (as a hint to this). The earth, however, opened her mouth and said : Lord of the Universe, I will recite songs before Thee instead of this upright, and Thou, I pray Thee, make him a Messiah. And she did so immediately, as it reads [ibid. xxiv. 16]: " From the edge of the earth have we heard songs ' Glory be to the righteous.' " And the governor of the world also said before Him : O Lord of the Universe, do, I pray Thee, the desire of this upright. Then a heavenly voice was heard saying: " It is my secret, it is my secret! To which the prophet exclaimed: Woe is me! Tell what time will it be postponed? And the heavenly voice answered: " Till the treacherous will have dealt treacherously." And Rabha, and according to others, R. Itz'hak, explained this: Until disgrace after disgrace will have come upon Israel.

It reads [ibid. xxi. 11]: " The prophecy concerning Dumah. Unto me one calleth out of Le'ir, Watchman, what of the night?

Watchman, what of the night? Said R. Johanan: The angel who rules the souls after their departure from this world, is named Dumah. And the latter said that all spirits gathered themselves to him questioning him: What said the watchman of the world (the Lord) about the exile which is equalized to night? And he answered. So said the watchman : The morning cometh, but previously will be a long, long night. If, however, ye desire to pray that He shall hasten it, try to do so by repenting of your sins, and coming again prepared for redemption.

It was taught in the name of R. Pepiyas: It is a shame for Hiskiah and his associates not to have recited any song until the earth recited hers, as the verse "from the edge of the earth," etc., cited above, reads. Similar to this it reads [Ex. xviii. 10]: "Blessed be the Lord who hath delivered you." And it was taught also in the name of Pepiyas: It was a shame for Moses and the six hundred thousand Israelites with him who didn't say this benediction till Jithro came. It reads [ibid., ibid. 9]: "Vayi'had" (rejoiced) Jithro, the Hebrew term "had" means to sharpen. And according to Rabh, it means that he passed a sharp razor upon the flesh of his body. (He performed the cere-mony of circumcision). And according to Samuel it means that his whole body pained as if stuck with sharp needles. Said R. Papa : This is what people say: One shall not dare to disgrace any heathen before a descendant of a proselyte, even if he is of the tenth generation.

It reads [Isa. x. 15]: "Therefore will the Lord, the Eternal of hosts, send forth among his 'bmashmanov' (fat ones) leanness." What is meant by the term "bmashmanov"? (in Hebrew shamuno means eight). The Lord said: Hiskiah who has eight names shall take revenge on Sanherib who also has eight names. Hiskia's eight names are enumerated in [Isa. ix. 5] : "For a child is born unto us, a son hath been given unto us, and the government is placed on his shoulders and his name is pele, yaez, el gibaur, abbi, ad, sar, shalaum." And concerning Sanherib it reads [II Kings, xv. 9] : "Thiglash pilesser" [ibid., ibid. 19]: "Pul" [II Chron. xxviii. 20]: "Pilnesser" [II Kings, xvii. 3]: "Shalma-nesser" [Isa. xx. 1]: "Sargon" and [Ezra, iv. 70] : "Assnapper, rabha, v'yaqira." The name Hiskia is not counted, for he was named so because God strengthened him. And the name San-herib is also not counted, for he was named so because he said vile words against Heaven.

Said R. Johanan : Why was he named Assnapper, the honored and the great? Because he did not speak evil of the land of Israel, as it reads [II Kings, xviii. 32]: " Until I come and take you away to a land like your own," etc.

Rabh and Samuel. According to one he was a clever king, because if he would have said that he would take them in a better land than theirs they would consider him a liar. And according to the other he was a fool, for what use could it be for them to go in a land which is not better than their own? To where did he exile the ten tribes of Israel? According to Mar Sutra to Africa, and according to R. Hanina to the mountains of Slug. However, the ten tribes of Israel slander the land of Israel, for when they reached the city of Sus they said that it was like their own land. And when they came to the city of Elmin they said that it is like our Elmin (Jerusalem). And when they reached the second Sus they said that it was much better than their own land.

It reads [Isa. x. 16]: " And under his glory shall be kindled." According to R. Johanan it means " under his dress garments," as he used to call garments glory. Hence the body was burned, but not the garments. R. Elazar, however, maintains " under his glory " means under the flesh—*i.e.*, only the soul was burned as by the children of Aaron.

There is a Boraitha in the name of R. Joshua b. Kharha: Pharaoh who personally blasphemed Heaven, was also punished by Heaven. Sanherib, who blasphemed though a messenger, was also punished though a messenger. Concerning Pharaoh, it reads [Ex. v. 2]: " And Pharaoh said, Who is the Everlasting, whose voice I am to obey?" And he was punished by Heaven, as it reads [ibid. xiv. 27]: " And the Lord overthrew the Egyptians in the midst of the sea." And also [Habakkuk, iii. 15]: "(But) thou didst pass along over the sea." Concerning Sanherib it reads [II Kings, xix. 23]: " By thy messengers thou has blasphemed the Lord." He was punished through a messenger, as it reads [ibid., ibid. 35]: " And it came to pass . . . that an angel of the Lord smote in the camp of the Assyrians, one hundred eighty and five thousand.

R. Hanina b. Papa propounded a contradiction from [Isa. xxxvii. 24: " I will enter into the height of its summit." [II Kings, xix. 23]: " I will enter into the lodgings of its summit." Thus thought Sanherib: I will first destroy the lower dwelling and thereafter the higher one. R. Jehoshua b. Levi said: It reads [ibid. xviii. 25]: " Now am I come up without the Lord('s will) against this place to destroy it ?   The Lord hath said to me, Go up against this land, and destroy it." What is it?   He heard the prophet who said [Isa. viii. 6-7] : "Forasmuch as this people despiseth the waters of Shiloach that flow softly, and rejoice in Regin and Remalyabu's son," etc.   Said R. Joseph : Were it not for the translation of this verse into Chaldaic, we would not understand its meaning.   The translation is thus : Because this people despised the kingdom of David, who ruled them gently like the waters of Shiloach which flow gently, and grew fond of Regin and the son of Remalyabu.

R. Johanan said : It reads [Prov. iii. 33] : "The curse of the Lord is in the house of the wicked"—Peckach b. Remalyabu, who used to consume forty saas of pigeon as a dessert. "But the habitation of the righteous will he bless"—Hiskia, king of Judah, whose whole meal consisted of a liter of herbs.

It reads [Isa. viii. 7 and 8] : "The king of Assyria . . . and he shall penetrate into Judah, overflood and flood over, even to the neck shall he reach.   Now as Sanherib acted in accordance with the prophecy, why then was he punished?   The prophet prophesied concerning the ten tribes, and he himself made up his mind to go to Jerusalem.   Then came the prophet and said [ibid., ibid. 23] : "And no fatigue (befalleth) him that oppresseth them." And R. Elazar b. Breakhya explained the passage thus : A people who are occupied with the study of the law will not be delivered over to their oppressor. "In the first time, he made light of the land of Zebulun and of the land of Naphtali, and at the last he will deal hard, with the way by the sea, on the other side of the Jordan, (up to) the Galilee of the nations"—not like the first, who threw off the yoke of the Thorah, but like the latter, who tolerated the heavy yoke of the Thorah, and therefore deserved that a miracle should happen to them as happened to those who passed the Red Sea and to those who stepped over the Jordan. Hence if he will retract to turn away from Jerusalem, well and good, but if not, I will make him a shame among all other nations.

It reads [II Chron. xxxii. 1] : "After these things and veritable events came Sanherib the king of Assyria, and invaded Judah, and encamped against the fortified cities, and thought to break them open for himself." Is such a present given to the men of truth?   And also what is meant by "after"?   Said Rabhina : It means after the Holy One, blessed be He, had sworn, saying, If I would tell Hiskiah that I will bring Sanherib, and deliver him in his hands, he would say I want neither to be scared nor to have him delivered to me. And therefore the Lord swore that he will bring him in, as it reads [Isa. xiv. 24 and 25]: "Sworn hath the Lord of host, saying, Surely as I have purposed, so doth it come to pass ; and as I have resolved, so shall it occur. To break Asshur in my own land, and upon my mountains will I tread him under foot ; then shall his yoke be removed from off them, and his burden shall be removed from off their shoulders."

Said R. Johanan: The Holy One, blessed be He, said: Sanherib with his companions shall come and be made a crib for Hiskiah and his associates.

It also reads [ibid. x. 27]: " And it shall come to pass in that day, that his burden shall be removed from off thy shoulder, and his yoke from off thy neck, and the yoke shall be broken because of the fatness." Said R. Itz'hak of Nafha: The yoke of Sanherib was broken because of the fats of Hiskia which he used to kindle in the prayer house and in house of learning. He placed a sword on the gate of the house of learning as a sign that he who will not occupy himself with the Thorah shall be slain by the sword. And thereafter a search was made from the city of Dan to the city of Beersheba, and there was not found one ignoramus among them. And also from the city of Gebeth to the city of Antiphras, and there was not found one who was not acquainted with the law of purification, even among the women and children. And to that generation it reads [ibid. vii. 21]: " And it shall come to pass on that day, that a man shall nourish (but) one young cow and two sheep." And (23): " And it shall come to pass on that day that every place, where there are (now) a thousand vines worth a thousand silver shekels, shall be—yea, this shall be (given up) to briers and thorns," which means though the vine was so valuable it was left to briers and thorns because all of them occupied themselves with the study of the law.

It reads [ibid. xxxiii. 4]: " And your spoil shall be gathered as the cricket gathereth." The prophet said to Israel: Gather your spoils. And to the question: Shall each one gather for himself or shall it be divided into equal shares? the prophet answered : As the cricket gathereth—as the gathering of the cricket is each one for himself, so also shall be your gathering. And when they objected, saying, Is there not among these the property of the ten tribes which was robbed by the Assyrian? he answered:

19

So long as it was mingled among it, it is not considered the property of the ten tribes.*

R. Huna said: Ten trips had the wicked made on that day, as it reads [ibid. x. 28 to 32]: " He cometh to Ayath, he passeth on to Migron; at Michmash he layeth up his baggage: They go through the pass; they take up their lodgings at Geba; Rama trembleth; Gib'ah of Saul fleeth. Let thy voice resound, O daughter of Gallim! listen Layshah; O poor Anathoth! Madmenah is in motion (the inhabitants of Gebin)," etc. Are there not enumerated more than ten places? Verse 30 the prophet said to the assembly of Israel thus : Those daughter of Gallim means Abraham, Isaac and Jacob, who performed divine commandments as numerous as the waves of the sea. Layshah means be not afraid of Layshah, which means Sanherib, but of Nebuchadnezzar, who is equalized to a lion, as it reads [Jer. iv. 7]: " The lion has come up from his thicket. O poor Anathoth!"—there will come a prophet from Anathoth, Jeremiah, who will prophesy the destruction of Jerusalem.

(Verse 32): "As yet will be remain at Nob." What does this mean? Said R. Huna: There was one day more appointed for the punishment of the iniquity of Nob. And the astrologers told Sanherib that if he could reach Jerusalem on that day he would be victorious. He therefore hastened his march and made a journey of ten days in one. And when he reached Jerusalem a ladder was made for him, upon which he ascended to view the whole city which was visible from that place. And it appeared to him very small, so that he exclaimed : Is this the city of Jerusalem for which I have troubled all my forces? Is she not smaller and weaker than all the great cities and countries which I have besieged with my powerful arm? He nodded his head, and gestured with his hands over the mountain of the Temple in Zion and over the court of the Temple in Jerusalem. And as his army wanted to put their hands on Jerusalem immediately, he told them that they were at present too tired, but on the morrow every-one of them should bring with him a piece of the wall which surrounds it. Concerning that night, however, it reads [II Kings, xix. 35]: " And it came to pass, on that same night, that an angel of

---

* This answer is inferred from the end of the cited passage with a strange interpretation. However, it was impossible for us to translate it, as the Hebrew term "gebin" was translated by Leeser with "locusts," and according to the Talmud it means water-pipes, the source of which is unknown to us. We therefore gave the answer without the reason.

the Lord . . . . smote . . . . of the Assyrians one hundred eighty and five thousand men ; and when the people arose early in the morning, behold they were all dead corpses."

Said R. Papa : This is what people say : If the judgment is postponed over one night, there is hope that it will be abolished entirely.

It reads [II Sam. xxi. 16] : " And Yishbi at Nob, who was of the children of the Raphah, the weight of whose spear was three hundred shekels of copper, he being girded with a new armour, thought to slay David." What is meant by "Yishbi at Nob"? Said R. Jehudah in the name of Rabh : It means that this happened because of that which was done to the city of Nob. The Lord said to David : How much longer will the iniquity of Nob rest upon thee ? Thou caused the destruction of the priest's city of Nob. Thou caused the iniquity of Doeg the Edomite, and through thee Saul and his three sons were killed. Now thou hast the choice of one of the following two. Either thou shalt not leave any issue, or that thou couldst be delivered over to thy enemies. And he answered : Lord of the Universe, it is better for me to be delivered over to the enemy than my descendants shall be destroyed.

It happened then that David went to a village and the Satan appeared to him in the form of a ram. He shot an arrow at it, but it did not reach it. So he ran after it till he passed the border of the Philistines. And when Yishbi of Nob saw him he said : This is he who killed my brother Goliath. He bound him, gagged him and put him under an olive press. However, a miracle occurred in that the earth under him became soft, and he was not killed. To this it is written [Ps. xviii. 37] : " Thou enlargest my steps under me, so that my joints do not slip." That day was an eve of Sabbath. And Abishai b. Zeruyah used to wash his head with four pitchers of water, and spots of blood appeared on the water. According to others, a dove flew to him, flapped her wings as if in trouble. And he said the assembly of Israel is equalized to a dove. Hence it must be that David the king of Israel is in trouble. He went to David's house but did not find him there. And he said, I was taught : One must not ride on a king's horse, must not sit on his chair, etc. But how is it at the time of danger ? He went to the college and questioned concerning it. To which he was answered that at the time of danger one may. Then he rode upon the king's mule and miraculously the earth jumped towards him. And while riding he saw

Arpa, the mother of Yishbi, sitting and spinning. When she saw him she broke the thread of her spindle and threw it at him with the intention of killing him (simulating that it had accidentally slipped). Then she said : Young man, hand me my spindle. And he took the spindle, threw it at her head, and she was killed. When Yishbi of Nob saw Abishai, he said : Now there are two, and they will be able to kill me. He took David and threw him up high, and placed the point of his spear so that David should fall upon it, and be killed. And Abishai mentioned a certain holy name, through which David remained between the sky and the earth. [But why didn't David himself mention such a name? Because a prisoner cannot liberate himself from prison without help.]

Abishai then questioned David what he was doing there. And he narrated before him what the Lord told him and what his answer to it was. Said he to him : Reverse thy prayer. Thy grandson may go and sell wax, but thou thyself must not take any trouble upon thee. Rejoined David : If it must be so, then succor me to pray. For it reads [Sam. xxx. 17] : " But Abishai the son of Zeruyah succoured him." And R. Jehudah, in the name of Rabh, said that he succored him in prayer. Thereafter Abishai mentioned another holy name and took David up on the knees, and both ran away. And Yishbi ran after them. And when they reached the village of Kubi (situated on the boundary of Palestine) they thought: Let us stop here and fight him. However, they went to the village of Tri and said to themselves that two cubs of a lion are able to kill a big lion. When the fight began they said to him : Go back, and you will see that your mother is dead. And when he heard this he became weak, and then they killed him. And this is what is written [ibid. 17]: " Then swore the men of David unto him, saying : Thou shall go out no more with us to battle, that thou mayest not quench the lamp of Israel."

The rabbis taught : To the following three the earth jumped: To Eliezer the servant of Abraham, to Jacob our father, and to Abishai b. Zeruyah: To the latter, as it was said above. To Eliezer the servant of Abraham, as it reads [Gen. xxiv. 42]: " And I came this day unto the well." " This day " means on the same day he went from home. To Jacob our father, as it reads [ibid. xxviii. 10 and 11]: " And Jacob went out from Beer-sheba and went towards Charan. And he " vayiphga " (lighted) upon a certain place and tarried there all night, because the sun was set," etc. When he reached Charan he said: Is it right of me not to have prayer when I passed the place my parents passed? He resolved to return, and soon after his resolution the earth jumped and he met Bethel.

And another explanation is that "vayiphga" means praying, as it reads [Jer. vii. 16]: "But thou—pray not thou in behalf of this people, nor lift up in their behalf entreaty or prayer, nor make an intercession ("al-tiphga") to me, for I will not hear thee." "And tarried there all night," etc. He wanted to return after he prayed, but the Holy One, blessed be He, however, said: This upright came to my inn and he should go away without staying over night. He made, therefore, the sun set immediately. And this is what it reads farther on [ibid. xxxii. 32]: "And the sun rose unto him as he passed by Penuel." Does the sun only rise to him and not to the whole world? Therefore said R. Itz'hak, it means the sun which has set for his sake has risen now for him.

And whence do we know that David's children were destroyed? From II Kings xi. 1: "And when Athalyah the mother of Achazyahn saw that her son was dead, she arose and destroyed all the seed royal. But did not Yoash remain? There in the case of Nob also Ebyathar remained, as it reads [I Sam. xxii. 20]. And R. Jehudah said in the name of Rabh: If from Achimelech's family there would not one have remained there would not have remained from David's family a single soul.

R. Jehudah in the name of Rabh said: Sanherib the wicked, when he came to attack, brought with him forty-five thousand princes with their concubines in golden carriages, and eighty thousand valiant men which were clothed in coats of mail, and sixty thousand girded with swords, who ran before the army. And the remainder were riders. Similar to this army was the one that attacked Abraham. And such will come in the future with Gog and Magog. In a Boraitha it was taught: The length of his camp was four hundred parsus, and the width of the necks of his horses were forty parsus. And the total of camp was two hundred and sixty thousand, less one. Questioned Abayi: What is meant by "less one"? Less one thousand, less one hundred, or less one literally? The question was not decided.

There is a Boraitha: The first part of 'Sanherib's army passed the Jordan by swimming, as it reads [Is. viii. 8]: "He shall penetrate into Judah, overflow," etc.; the middle part standing on their feet, as it reads: "Even to the neck shall he reach." (The water was so diminished by the swimming of the first part, that these had to pass over on foot.) And by the last part (the Jordan was so dry) that the dust whirled up by the tramping of their feet. And they found no water to drink, and they had to bring it from another place; as it reads [ibid. xxviii. 25]: "I have dug and drunk water." But is it not written that the angel smote only one hundred eighty and five thousand, and when they arose early in the morning they were all corpses? Said R. Abuhu: This enumerates only the officers of the army. Said Rabhina: It seems to be so from [II Chr. xxxii. 21]: "And the Lord sent an angel, who cut off every mighty man of valor and leader and captain in the camp of the king of Assyria, and when he returned with shame of face to his own land, he went into the house of his god, and (those) that were come forth from his own bowels felled him there with the sword."

With what did the angel smite them? R. Eliezar said: With his hand. As it reads [Ex. xiv. 31]: "And Israel saw that great hand which the Lord had shown," i.e., that which will take revenge on Sanherib. And R. Jehoshua said: With the finger. As it reads [ibid. viii. 15]: "Then said the magicians unto Pharaoh, this is a finger of God," "this" means the one which will take revenge on Sanherib. And R. Eliezar b. R. Jose the Galilean said: The Holy One, blessed be He, said to Gabriel: Is thy sickle (of death) polished? And he answered: Lord of the Universe, it is ready, polished, since the six days of the creation. As it reads [Is. xxi. 15]: "From the drawn sword, from the bent bow." R. Simeon b. Jochai said: That was the time when the fruit became ripe, and the Holy One said to Gabriel: When thou will go to make the fruit ripe, by the way, thou shalt attend to them. As it reads [ibid. xxviii. 19]: "For morning by morning shall it pass by, by day and by night; and the mere understanding of the report shall cause terror." Said R. Papa: This is what people say: When thou passest by the door of thy enemy, look at it. According to others the angel blew into their nostrils till they died. As it reads [ibid. xl. 24]: "When he breathed upon them, they withered." R. Jeremiah b. Abah said: They died from the striking of his hands. As it reads [Ezek. xxi. 22]: "I will strike my hands together, and I will cause my fury to be assuaged." ·

And Itz'hak of Nafha said: He revealed their ears so that they hear the songs of the angel and become death from it. As it reads [ibid. xxxiii. 3]: "When thou liftedst thyself up nations were scattered." And how many remained of them? According to Rabh, ten, as it reads [ibid. x. 19]: "And the rest of the trees of his forest shall be few in number, so that a boy may write them down." And what can a boy write a י (yad) which counts ten. And Samuel said: Nine, as it reads [ibid. xvii. 6]: "Two or three berries on the top of the uppermost bough, four to five on the outmost branches of a fruitful tree." And R. Jehoshua b. Levi said: Fourteen, as the just cited verse reads two, three . . . four, five. R. Johanan, however, said: Only five, and they were Sanherib and his two sons, Nebuchadnezzar and Nebusaradan, the latter is known by tradition, and concerning Nebuchadnezzar, it reads [Dan. iii. 25]: "And the appearance of the fourth is like a son of the gods," and if he would not have seen him first, how would he know how an angel looks? And concerning Sanherib, it reads [II Kings xix. 37]: "And it came to pass, as he was prostrating himself in the house of Nisroch his god, that Adrammelech and Sharezer his sons smite him."

R. Abuhu said: Were it not for the following verse it would be impossible to believe. It reads [Is. vii. 20]: "On the same day, will the Lord shave with the razor that is hired, from among those on the other side of the river, with the king of Assyria, the head and the hair of the feet, and also the beard shall it entirely remove." The Lord sent an angel, who appeared before Sanherib as an old man, and questioned him: When thou wilst return to the kings of the East and the West, whose sons thou broughtst with thee, and who were killed, what excuse canst thou give to them? And he answered: I myself am trembling about this. Canst thou advise me what to do? And he rejoined: Go and change thyself that thou mayest not be recognized. And to the question how should this be done, he told him, Bring me scissors and I will cut your hair off. And to the question where he shall take the scissors, he showed him a certain house, telling him to go there and that he will find what he needs. He went there, and found angels who had appeared before him as men, engaged in grinding the kernels of dates. And he asked them for a scissors. To which they answered, grind one kernel and thou wilst get it. He did so and got the requested scissors. But when he returned it grew dark, and he was told to bring light. And while carrying the light, the wind blew and caught his beard, and therefore he was compelled to cut off his hair and his beard. And this is what is written, "and also the beard shall it entirely remove." [Said R. Papa, this is what people say: Then

you are engaged in cutting the hair of an Aramaen, cinge his
beard, and you will have to laugh for a long time.] When he
went away he found a board from the ark of Noah. And he
exclaimed, This is the great God, who saved Noah from the flood.
I vow that if I will succeed in the future, I will sacrifice my two
sons to him. This his sons heard, and therefore they killed him,
and this is what is written in the above cited verse [II Kings,
xix. 37].

It reads [Gen. xiv. 15]: " And he divided himself against
them, he and his servants by night (lajlha), and smote them."
Said R. Johanan: The name of the angel who came to assist
Abraham was lajlha (night), as it reads [Job, iii. 3]: "And the
night when it was said, There hath been a male child conceived,"
etc. And R. Itz'hak of Nafha said: The term lajlha concerning Abraham means that the stars of the night assisted him in
his war as they did in the war with Sissera [Judges, v. 20]:
" From heaven they fought—the stars in their courses fought
against Sissera." Said Resh Lakish: The explanation of Nafha
is better than that of the bar Nafha (Johanan, who is always
called bar Nafha).

R. Johanan said: When this upright (Abraham) reached the
city of Dan he became weak, as he saw that in the future his
children will worship idols in Dan, as it reads [I Kings, xii. 29]:
" And the other put he in Dan." And also this wicked (Sanherib)
did not feel strong until he reached Dan, as it reads [Jer. viii. 16]:
"From Dan was heard the snorting of his horses."

R. Zera said: Although R. Joshua b. Levi sent a message, in
which among other things he said be careful with the children of
the gentiles, as it happens very often wisdom emanates from
them, the following may be nevertheless proclaimed. It reads
[ibid., xii. 1 to 3]: "(Too) righteous art thou, O Lord, that I
could plead with thee; yet must I speak of (the principles of)
justice with thee: Wherefore is the way of the wicked happy?
Do all those prosper that deal treacherously? Thou hast
planted them; they have also taken root; they grow; they also
bring forth fruit: thou art near in their mouth, and far from
their mind." And he was answered [ibid., ibid. 5]: " If thou hast
run with the footmen, and they have wearied thee, how then
canst thou contend with the horses? and if in the land of peace,
(wherein) thou trusted, (they wearied thee), how then wilt thou
do in the swelling of the Jordan?" As a parable to this is: One
who proclaims that he is able to run three parsus in front of

horses in the swamps.   And a pedestrian happened to say to him
that he is able to do the same.   And he tried to run in front of
him three miles and became tired.   And then he said, If you become tired by running in front of me, how much the more in front
of horses?   If only from three miles, how much the more from
three parsus?   If you become tired on dry land, how much the
more would you become so in the swamps!   Similar to this was
it said to Jeremiah.   Thou art wondering that I have rewarded
that wicked for the four steps he was running for the sake of my
glory: how much more will you wonder when I will come to pay
the reward of Abraham, Isaac and Jacob, who used to run for
me like horses!   And this is what is written [ibid. xxiii. 9]: "To
the prophets—Broken is my heart within me ; all my bones shake ;
I am like a drunken man, because of the Lord, and because of
his holy words."

But what four steps are meant ?   Those of [Isa. xxxix. 1] : At
that time sent Merodach-baladon, the son of Baladon, the king
of Babylon, letters and presents to Hezekiah, for he had heard
that he had been sick, and was becoming strong again."   And to
this it reads also [II Chron. xxxii. 31] : "And in the same manner
in the business of the ambassadors . . . who sent unto him to inquire concerning the wonder that had happened in the land."
(And what is it?)   What R. Johanan said : That the day on
which Achaz died consisted of only two hours.   And when Heskiah became sick and thereafter recovered, the Holy One, blessed
be He, returned the ten hours to that day, as it reads [Isa. xxxviii.
8] : Behold, I will cause the shadow of the degrees, which is gone
down on the dial of Achaz by the sun, to return backward ten
degrees.   So the sun returned ten degrees, by the degrees which
he was gone down."   Merodach-baladon then questioned why
that day is so long.   And he was told, because Hiskia was sick
and recovered.   He said then : If there is such a man, must he
not be greeted ?   Write him a letter of greeting.   And they
wrote, Peace to the king Hiskiah, peace to the city of Jerusalem,
and peace to the great God.

At that time Nebuchadnezzar was Merodach's scribe.   But
this letter was written in his absence.   When he returned and
heard of this he asked them what they wrote.   And they told
him so and so.   And he exclaimed : Ye named Him the great
God, and greet Him at the end !   It ought to have been written,
Peace to the great God, peace to the city of Jerusalem, and peace
to Hiskiah !   And they told him that the dictator of the letter

should be the messenger. He then ran after the messenger to make him return. But after he ran four steps Gabriel came and stopped him. And R. Johanan said : If Gabriel would not have stopped there would be no remedy for the people of Israel.

What does the term " ben baladon " mean ? It was said that Merodach's father was a king whose appearance was changed to that of a dog. And his son baladon sat on the throne. And when he used to sign his name he did so in conjunction with his father's for the sake of his honor. And to this it reads [Malachi, i. 6] : " A son honoreth his father, and a servant his master." A son honoreth his father, as just mentioned, and a servant his master, as in [Jer., lii. 12 and 13] : " And in the fifth month on the tenth day of the month, which was the nine-teenth year of King Nebuchadnezzar, the king of Babylon, came Nebusaradan, the captain of the guard, (who) served the king of Babylon, unto Jerusalem. And he burnt the house of the Lord," etc. But was Nebuchadnezzar, indeed, at that time in Jerusalem ? Is it not written [II Kings xxv. 20] : " And Nebusaradan, the captain of the guard, took these, and conducted them to the king of Babylon to Riblah." And R. Abuhu said that Riblah is iden-tical with Autukhia ? R. Hisda and R. Itz'hak b. Abudimi : One said that the image of Nebuchadnezzar was engraved on his carriage, and the other that the fear of Nebuchadnezzar rested upon Nebusaradan, so that it always appeared to him that he was standing by him.

Rabha said : Three hundred mules loaded with iron saws which cut iron were given to Nebusaradan by Nebuchadnezzar while going to attack Jerusalem. And all of them were broken at one gate of Jerusalem, as it reads [Ps. lxxiv. 6] : " And now they hew in pieces the carver work thereof altogether with hatchets and hammers." Seeing this he thought to return, but a heavenly voice was heard : " Jumper, the son of a jumper, O Nebusaradan, jump now, and thou wilst succeed, as the time for the destruction of the sanctuary and for the burning of the Temple has arrived." And one saw remained with him, and with it he struck the gate, and it opened, as it reads [ibid., ibid. 5] : " (The enemy) is known as one that lifteth up high axes against the thickets of a forest." Then he slew every one coming under his hand till he reached the Temple and kindled it. However, the Temple wanted to fly away, but it was prevented by Heaven and was trodden down, as it reads [Lamentations, i. 15] : "A wine-press hath the Lord trodden over the virgin, the daughter of

Judah." Nebusaradan became proud of all this, and a heavenly voice was heard saying: "You slew a killed nation, a burnt temple have you burned, grind flour have you grind," as it reads [Isa. xlvii. 2]: "Take the mill and grind meal; uncover thy locks, lift up the train, uncover the thigh, pass over the rivers." It does not read "and grind wheat," but "grind meal."

He then saw the blood of Zecharyah the prophet, which was boiling. He asked: What is it? And he was told that it is blood of sacrifice which was spilled. And he said: I will bring such blood and see if it will be similar. He did so, but it didn't correspond. Said he to them: Reveal to me this secret, for if not I will scratch your flesh with iron combs. They told him then that it was that of a priest and prophet, who had prophesied the destruction of the Temple and was slain. Said he to them: I will reconcile him. He slew the rabbis over his blood, but it didn't become quiet. He brought then the little school children, slew them, and it didn't effect. He slew then the young priest over it, and it didn't cease to boil. He slew then altogether nine hundred and forty thousand, and still the blood did not rest. He approached the blood, saying: Zecharyah, the best of thy people I slew; dost thou want that I shall slay all of them? And the blood immediately rested. He then repented, thinking they had suffered so much only for one person. I who have shed so much blood, how much will I have to suffer? He then ran away, sent his will to his house, and became a proselyte.

The rabbis taught: Naamani's proselytism was only to perform the seven commandments given to the descendants of Noah. Nebusaradan, however, was a true proselyte, from the descendants of Sissera were such who studied the law in Jerusalem, and from the descendants of Sanherib were such who taught the Torah among a majority of Israelites, and they are Shmayah and Abtalia. From the descendants of Haman were such who learned the Torah in the city Bne-Brack. And even the descendants of Nebuchadnezzar, the Holy One, blessed be He, thought to enter them under the wings of the Shekinah. But the angels prayed before Him: Lord of the Universe, he who has destroyed your house, burned your Temple, shouldst thou enter him under the wings of the Skekinah? And this is what reads [Jer. li. 9]: "We would have healed Babylon, but she was not healed." And Ula said this means Nebuchadnezzar. Samuel b. Na'hman, however, said: It means the waters along the (dry, or stony) palms of Babylonia.

Ula said: Amon and Moab were the two bad neighbors of Jerusalem, and when they heard the prophets prophesying the destruction of same, they sent to Nebuchadnezzar, "Come up," and to his answer that he is afraid that they will do to him as they have done with their former enemies, they said to him [Prov. vii. 19]: "For the man is not in his house," and by the man is meant the Lord. He, however, sent to them; he is near to them, and will return. They sent again to him, "He is gone on a journey a great way off." Nebuchadnezzar, however, sent to them: I am aware that among them are upright, who will pray for them to Him and He will return; and they answered: The bag of money hath he taken with him, and by a "bag of money," the upright are meant, as it reads [Hosea, iii. 2]: "So I bought me such a one for fifteen pieces of silver," etc. He sent again: The wicked of them will repent, pray, and will be listened to. And they answered: He has already appointed a time for repenting, as it reads [Prov. vii. 19]: "By the day of kesa only will he return," and the term kesa means "an appointed time," as it reads [Ps. lxxxi. 4]: "Blow on the new moon, the cornet at the time appointed (kesa) on the day of our feast." He, however, sent to them: It is winter, and I cannot come up because of snow and rain. And they sent to him: The mountains will protect thee, as it reads [Is. xvi. 1]: "Send ye the lambs of the ruler of the land from Sela, through the wilderness unto the mount of the daughter of Zion." He (Nebuchadnezzar) sent to them: When I will arrive there I will have no place to reside. And they answered: Their graves are better than your palaces, as it reads [Jer. viii. 1 and 2]: "At that time, saith the Lord, shall they bring out the bones of the kings of Judah, and the bones of the princes, and the bones of the priests, and the bones of the prophets, and the bones of the inhabitants of Jerusalem, out of their graves. And they shall spread them out before the sun, and the moon and all the hosts of heaven, which they have loved, and which they have served, and after which they have walked."

R. Na'hman said to R. Itz'hak: Have you heard when the fallen son will come? And to the question, Who is it? He answered: The Messiah. And the Messiah you call "The fallen son"? And he said: Yea, for it reads [Amos, ix. 11]: "On that day will I raise up the tabernacle of David, which is fallen." And he answered: Thus said R. Johanan: In the generation in which the son of David will come scholarly men will decrease, and by the remainder their eyes will protrude from sighing and sorrow, many chastisements and many evil decrees will be renewed, one will not cease as yet, while another will have come.

The rabbis taught: In this Sabbatic period in which the son of David will appear in the first year there will be fulfilled what is written, in [Amos, iv. 7] : " And I caused it to rain upon one city, and upon another city I caused it not to rain." In the second year, arrows (tokens) of famine will be sent. In the third, a great famine, from which men, women, and children, pious men and men of good deeds will die, and the Torah will be forgotten by their scholars. In the fourth there will be abundance, and not abundance. In the fifth there will be great abundance, and the people will eat, drink, and enjoy themselves, and the Torah will return to her scholars. In the sixth, voices will be heard saying that the Messiah is near. In the seventh, war will be, and at the end of the seventh, ben David will come. Said R. Joseph : Were there not many Sabbatical periods which were like this, but still he did not come? Said Abayi : Were then the above-mentioned voices heard in the sixth? And was there in the seventh war? And secondly, has it then happened in the same order as said above? There is a Boraitha. R. Jehudah said : The generation in which the son of David will come, the houses of assembly will be converted into houses of prostitution. Galilee will be destroyed. The place called Gablan will be astonished. Men of the borders of Palestine will travel from one city to another, but will find no favor. The wisdom of the scribes will be corrupted. Men fearing sin will be hated. The leaders of that generation will have the nature of dogs. And truth will be missing, as it reads [Is. lix. 15] : " And thus is the truth missing." What does this mean? It was said in the college that it passes away like flocks.* " And he that departeth from evil is regarded as foolish." Said the school of Shila : He who turns away from evil is regarded as foolish in the eyes of the people. Said Rabha : Previously I thought there is no truth in the whole world. However, I met thereafter a certain rabbi named Tubuth, according to others R. Tibumi, and if the whole world filled with gold would be given to him, he would not change his word or tell a lie. It happened once that he came to a city named Kushta (truth). And the inhabitants of

---

* The Hebrew term for flocks, " eder," and concerning truth, the expression is, " neaderes."

that city would not change their word, and it never happened
that one should die an untimely death. And he married one of
its inhabitants, and she bore him two children. It happened
once that his wife washed her head and a female neighbor came
to ask for her, and he thought that it was not nice to say that
she is washing her head, and therefore said that she is out.
And the two children died. And when the inhabitants came to
ask him what was the reason that such an unusual thing happened
to him, he told them the truth. And they requested him to
move away from their city in order not to cause untimely death.

R. Nehuraia taught: The generation in which the son of
David will come, young men will make pale the faces of the old,
old men will rise before youth, a daughter will rebel against
her mother, a daughter-in-law against her mother-in-law, the
leaders of the generation will have the nature of dogs, and a son
will not be ashamed when his father reproaches him.

There is a Boraitha: R. Nehemiah said: The generation in
which ben David will come, insolence will increase, an evil man
will be honored, respect will be missed, the vine will give forth its
fruit abundantly; wine, however, will be dear, and all the governments will be turned over to *Minuth* (will embrace the relig-
ion of the Minim), and no preaching will avail. And this is a
suppport to R. Itz'hak, who said that ben David will not come
unless all governments will be turned over to *Minuth*. Where
is to be found a hint to this in the Scripture? [Lev. xiii. 13]:
" It is all turned white, he is clean."

The rabbis taught: It reads [Deut. xxxii. 36 and 37]: " For
the Lord will espouse the cause of his people, and bethink himself concerning his servants: When he seeth that their power is
gone, and the guarded and fortified are no more." Ben David
will not come until the denouncers will increase. According to
others, unless the disciples will decrease; and still according to
others, until the pockets will be empty of aperuthar. And some
others also say unless they will renounce their hope to be redeemed. And this is as R. Zera found the rabbis occupying
themselves with the question of the Messiah. And he told them,
I beg you do not make the thing further than it is, as there is a
Boraitha that the following three come suddenly after renouncing all hope for them, viz., the Messiah, found and a bite of a
serpent. R. Ktina said: For six thousand years the world will
continue, and in the seventh it will be destroyed. As it reads
[Isa. xii. 11]: " And exalted shall be the Lord alone, on that day."

Abayi, however, said two thousand will be destroyed, as it reads [Hosea, vi. 2]: "He will revive us after two days. There is a Boraitha in accordance with R. Ktina: As in the Sabbatic period, the seventh year is a release, so will it be with the whole world that one thousand years after six will be a release, as above cited verse [Isa. xii. 1] and [Ps. xcii. 11]: "A Psalm or song for the Sabbath day," which means the day which will be all Sabbath. And as [ibid. xc. 4]: "For a thousand years are in thy eyes but as the yesterday when it is passed."

The disciples of Elijah taught: The world will continue for six thousand years, the first two thousand of which were a chaos (Tahu), the second two thousand were of wisdom, and the third two thousand are the days of the Messiah, and because of our sins many, many years of these have elapsed, and still he has not come. Elijah said to R. Jehudah, the brother of R. Sala the Pious: The world will continue for no less than eighty-five jubilaic periods, and in the last jubilaic period ben David will come. And to the question: At its beginning or at its end? he answered: I don't know. Has this passed already, or will it come? He also answered, I don't know. R. Ashi, however, said: Elijah told him thus: Until the above mentioned time will pass you shall not have any hope for him. But after that time, you may hope.

R. Hanan b. Tahlipha sent a message to R. Joseph: I met a man who possessed scrolls written in Assyrian characters and in the holy language. And to my question from where he got it, he answered: I hired myself to the Persian army, and among the treasures of Persia I found it. And it was written therein that after two thousand, two hundred and ninety-one years of the creation, the world will remain an orphan, many years will be the war of whales, and many more years will be the war of Gog and Magog, and the remainder will be the days of the Messiah. But the Holy One, blessed be He, will not renew the world before seven thousand have elapsed. And R. Aha b. R. Rabha said: After five thousand years from to-day.

There is a Boraitha: R. Nashan said: The following passages bore a hole to the depth (i.e., as no one can fathom the depth, so no one can come to the exact meaning of these), viz. [Habukkuk, ii. 3]: "For there is yet a vision for the appointed time, and it speaketh of the end, and it will not deceive: Though it tarry, wait for it; because it will surely come, it will not be delayed." It is not as our masters lectured about this from [Dan. vii. 25]:

"And they will be given up into his hand until a time and times and half a time." And not in accordance with R. Simlai, who used lecture about this form [Ps. lxxx. 6] : "Thou feedest them with the bread of tears, and givest them tears to drink in great measure." And also not in accordance with R. Aqiba, who used to lecture about this from [Haggai, ii. 6] : "For thus said the Lord. . . . Yet one thing more (will I do), it is but little, when I will cause to quake the heavens and the earth, and the sea, and the dry land." But the first kingdom was of seventy years, the second of fifty-two, and the kingdom of Bar Kochha, two years and a half.*

What does the verse "Speaketh of the end" mean? Said R. Samuel b. Na'hman, in the name of R. Jonathan : Blown out shall be the souls of those who are sitting and appointing times for the arrival of the Messiah. Because they usually err, and when the appointed time comes and the Messiah does not appear, they say that he will not come any more. But every one has to wait for him, as it reads : "Wait for him, because he will surely come." And lest one say, We are awaiting but He does not wait, therefore it reads [Isa. xxx. 18 :] "And therefore will the Lord wait, to be gracious unto you, and therefore will he exalt himself, to have mercy upon you." But if He and we are awaiting, who prevents Him to come? The divine attribute prevents. But if so, what is the use of our waiting? To receive reward for waiting, as the cited verse ends : "Happy are those that wait for him."

Abayi said : There are no less than thirty-six upright in every generation who receive the appearance of the Shekhina (see Succah, p. 68, and there it reads every day instead of every generation.) Is this so? Did not Rabha say that the row in front of the Holy One, blessed be He, contains eighteen thousand parsus, as it reads [Ezek. xlviii. 35] : "All around it shall be eighteen thousand rods"? This presents no difficulty. Abayi speaks of those who are looking in a "*speculare*," which gives the right light. And Rabha speaks of those who are looking in such, which does not give the right light. But are there, indeed, so many? Did not R. Simeon b. Jochai say : I see the very greatest men in the world are very few, etc. (see ibid., ibid., line 6)? This presents no difficulty. R. Simeon b. Jochai speaks of those who may enter without permission, and Rabha speaks of those who must have

---

* We do not understand the connection of this passage. And also Rashi, after quoting many commentaries, ignores them, and says that all these legends are not from a Mishna, nor from a Boraitha.

permission.   Said Rabh: All the appointed times for the appearance of the Messiah have already ceased.   And it depends only
on repentance and good deeds.   Samuel, however, said: It is sufficient for the mourner to remain with his own sorrow (*i.e.*, the
suffering of Israel for such a long time is sufficient that they
should be redeemed even without repentance.) And on this point
the following Tanaim differ.   R. Eliezar said: If the people of
Israel will repent they will be redeemed, but not otherwise.   Said
Jehoshua to him: According to you, if they will not repent they
will not be redeemed at all?   (Replied R. Eliezar *) : The Holy
One, blessed be He, will appoint, for this purpose, a king whose
decrees concerning Israel will be as severe as Haman's were.   And
this will bring them back to the better side, and they will repent.

There is another Boraitha: R. Eliezar said: If the people of
Israel will repent they will be redeemed, as it reads [Jer. iii. 14]:
"Return, O backsliding children, I will heal your backslidings."
Said R. Jehoshua to him: Is it not written [Isa. lii. 3]: "For thus
hath said the Lord, for naught were you sold, and without silver
shall ye be redeemed," *i.e.*, for naught were you sold to the idolaters, and not because of repentance and good deeds will you be
redeemed.   Rejoined R. Eliezar: But does it not read [Malachi
iii. 7]: "Return unto me, and I will return unto you, said the
Lord"?   Rejoined he: Does it not read [Jer. iii. 14] : "For I am
become your husband, and I will take you one of a city and two
of a family, and bring you to Zion"?   Said R. Eliezar again: It
reads [Isa. xxx. 15]: "In repose and rest shall ye be helped."
And R. Jehoshua answered : I call your attention to [ibid. xlix.
7]: "Thus hath said the Lord, the Redeemer of Israel, his Holy
One, to him who is despised by men, to him who is abhorred by
nations, to the servants of rulers, kings shall see it and rise up,
princes, and they shall prostrate themselves, for the sake of the
Lord who is faithful."   And R. Eliezar rejoined: To this it is
written [Jer. iv. 1] : "If thou wilt return, O Israel, saith the Lord,
unto me, must thou return."   Said R. Jehoshua to him : I call
your attention to [Dan. xii. 7]: "Then heard I the man clothed
in linen, who was above the waters of the stream ; and he lifted
up his right hand and his left hand unto the heavens, and swore
by the Everliving One that after a time, times and a half, and
when there shall be an end to the crushing of the power of the
holy people, all these things shall be ended."   And R. Eliezar

---

* This of the parenthesis is from the Palestinian Talmud.

20

kept silent. Said Rabha : The appointed time for the Messiah cannot be more revealed than in this passage, as it reads [Ez. xxxvi. 8] : " But ye, O mountains of Israel, ye shall send forth your boughs, and your fruits shall ye bear for my people Israel." R. Elazar said also from [Zech. viii. 10] : " For before those days, there was no reward for man, nor any reward for beast ; and for him that went out or came in there was no peace, because of the oppressor." What do the last words in this passage mean ? Said Rabh : Also the scholars, of whom it reads [Ps. cix. 165] : " Abundant peace have they who love thy law," will also have no peace from the oppressor. Samuel, however, said : The cited verse means the Messiah will not come until high prices will be for all articles of life. R. Hanina said : The son of David will not come unless even a piece of fish will be sought for a sick one and it will not be found, as it reads [Ez. xxxii. 14) : " Then will I make clear their waters, and cause their rivers to flow like oil." And it reads also [ibid. xxix. 21] : " On that day will I cause to grow a horn for the house of Israel, and unto thee will I open the mouth in the midst of them.* R. Hana b. Hanina said : Ben David will not appear unless every office of the government, even the least one will be removed from the children of Israel, as it reads [Isa. xviii. 5] : " He will both cut off the tendrils with pruning-knives, and the sprigs will he remove and cut down." And thereafter it reads [ibid. 7] : " At that time shall be brought as a present unto the Lord of hosts a people pulled and torn." And Zera, in the name of R. Hanina, said : Ben David will not come until the haughty men of Israel will cease to be, as it reads [Zeph. iii. 11] : " For then will I remove out of the midst of thee, those that rejoice in thy pride, and thou shall never more be haughty again on my holy mount." And thereafter it reads [12] : " I will leave remaining in the midst of thee an humble and poor people, and they shall trust in the name of the Lord." R. Simlai said, in the name of R. Elazar b. Simeon : Ben David will not come unless there will cease to be judges and officers of Israel, as it reads [Isa. i. 25 and 26] : " And I will turn my hand against thee, and I purge away as with lye thy dross, and remove all thy tin. And I will restore thy judges as at first, and thy counsellors as at the beginning," etc.

Said Ula : Jerusalem will not be redeemed but by charity, as

---

* See Samuel Eidles (Mahrsho) about the strange analogy of these two passages. It is remarkable in that the text quotes the verse xxix. 21 after that of xxxii. 14.

it reads [Isa. i. 27]: " Zion shall be redeemed through justice, and her converts through *zdaha*" (the meaning of which is both righteousness and charity). Said R. Papa : When insolence shall cease to be in Israel, the *magus* of the Persians who causes much trouble will also cease to be, as it reads [ibid., ibid. 25]: " And purge away as with lye thy dross, and remove all thy tin." When judges of Israel will cease to be, the brutal executions of the Per sian court-servants will be abolished, as it reads [Zeph. iii. 15]: " The Lord hath removed mishophtakha (literally " the judges from thee"), he hath cleared away thy enemy." R. Johanan said : When you see that wisdom decreases continually from a generation, you may hope for the Messiah, as it reads [II Sam. xxii. 28]: " And the afflicted people thou wilt save." And he said again : If you see chastisements and evils are increasing in a generation like the waters of the rivers, await the Messiah, as [Isa. lix. 19]: " For there shall come distress like a stream." And the next verse reads: " But unto Zion shall come the redeemer." He said again : Ben David will appear either in a gen-eration in which all will be upright or in one in which all shall be wicked. " All upright," from [ibid. lx. 21]: " And thy people —they all will be righteous, for ever shall they possess the land." And " all wicked," from [ibid. lix. 16]: " And he saw that there was no man, and wondered that there was no intercessor." And [ibid. xlviii. 11]: For my own sake, for my own sake, will I do it."

R. Alexandri said : Jehoshua b. Levi propounded a contradic-tion : It reads [ibid. lx. 22]: " I the Lord will hasten it in its time." " Hasten" and "in its time" contradict each other. And the answer was that if they will be worthy I will hasten it, and if not, they must wait till the right time will come. The same said again that the same authority propounded another contradiction from [Dan. vii. 13]: " Behold with the clouds of. heaven came one like a son of man . . ." [Zech. ix. 9]: " Lowly and riding upon an ass." And the answer was, if they will be worthy he will come with the clouds of heaven, and if not, he will come upon an ass.

The king Sabur said to Samuel : You say that your Messiah will come upon an ass, let me send him the best horse of my sta-ble. And he answered him : Do you then possess a horse of a hundred colors as the ass of the Messiah? (a joke to a joke). R. Jehoshua b. Levi met Elijah standing at the gate of the cave of R. Simeon b. Jochai and asked him if he will have a share in the world to come. And he answered: If it will be the will of this Lord. Said R. Jehoshua: Two persons have I seen and the voice of the third have I heard.* I questioned him further when the Messiah will appear. And he answered: Go and ask him himself. " But where is he to be found?" "At the gate of Rome, among poor people inflicted with wounds." "And how can I recognize him?" All the inflicted poor open the bandages of all their wounds, fix all of them and then dress them. And he opens one bandage, fixes the wound and dresses it, and then goes on to the next one, for the reason that perhaps he will be cold and there will be a delay till all the wounds are dressed. R. Jehoshua went to him, and when he met him he said: Peace be to thee, my master and teacher. And he answered: Peace be with thee, son of Levai. And to Jehoshua's question: When will the master appear? he answered: This day. When Jehoshua met Elijah again, the latter questioned him as to what the Messiah said to him. And he said: Peace be with thee, son of Levai. Said Elijah: He assured you of a share for thyself and for thy father in the world to come. Rejoined Jehoshua: He made a fool of me by saying that he will come this day. And Elijah answered: The expression " this day " means as in [Ps. xcv.]: " Yea this day, if you will hearken to his voice."

The disciples of R. Jose b. Kisma questioned him when the son of David will appear. And he answered: I am afraid you will request from me a sign. And they assured him that they would not. He then said to them: When this gate will fall, be rebuilt and fall again, be rebuilt again and fall again. And before it will be rebuilt for the third time the Messiah will appear. The disciples then said: Our master, give us a sign. " Have you not promised that you will not ask of me for any sign?" They answered: Nevertheless we would like to have it. And he said: If it is as I say, the spring of the cave of Paneas shall be converted into blood. And so it happened. While dying he said to his disciples: Put my coffin very deep into the earth, for there will not be one tree in Babylon to which a horse of the Persians will not be tied. And there will not remain one coffin in the land of Israel from which the horses of the Modoites will not eat straw.

Rabh said: Ben David will not arrive until Rome shall have dominated over Israel nine months (see Yomah, p. 13, where it

---

* The explanation of this may be found in Samuel Eidles (Marsho).

is said, "over the entire world"; see there the sources also). Said Ula: Messiah may appear in the near future; I, however, wish not to see him. And the same said Rabba. R. Joseph, however, said: I pray for his coming in my days, and that I shall have the preference to sit in the shadow of his ass. Said Abayi to Rabba: Why does the master not wish to see the Messiah? Is it because of the lot which will be at that time? Is there not a Boraitha that the disciples of R. Elazer questioned him: What may one do to be saved from the lot of the Messiah? And he answered: He shall occupy himself with the Torah and with bestowing favors to the people, and you, master, are doing both; why then are you afraid? And he answered: Perhaps sin will cause me to suffer by the lot. And this is in accordance with R. Jacob b. Idi, who propounded the following contradiction: It reads [Gen. xxviii. 15]: "And, behold, I am with thee, and will keep thee withersoever thou goest." And [ibid. xxxii. 8]: "Then Jacob was greatly afraid, and he felt distressed." Hence after he was promised by the Lord, he was still afraid? And the answer was that he was afraid perhaps his sins caused what happened, as we have learned in the following Boraitha. It reads [Ex. xv. 16]: "Till thy people pass over"—*i.e.*, their first coming to Palestine; "till this people pass over"—*i.e.*, their second coming to Palestine from Babylon; from which we may infer that the second coming ought to be equal in miracles with the first. And why did not miracles occur at the second coming? Because of their sins. R. Johanan also said: The Messiah may come, but I shall not see him. Said Resh Lakish to him: What is your reason? Is it because of [Amos, v. 19]: "As if a man were to flee from a lion, and a bear should meet him; and he enter into the house, and lean his hand against the wall, and a serpent should bite him." Come, and I will show you a similarity to this in the world at this time—*e.g.*, one is going to his field and a bailiff meets him (trying to contes this title to the field): is this not equal as if a lion should meet him? And when he enters the city a collector from the government meets him: is this not equal as if a bear should meet him? And when he enters his house and finds his sons and daughters starving: is this not equal as if a serpent would bite him? It must then be because of [Jer. xxx. 6]: "Ask ye now, and see whether a male doth give birth to a child? Wherefore do I see (gebher) every man with his hands on his loins as a woman in giving birth? and why are all faces turned pale?"

What is meant by " I see every *gebher*? Said Rabba b. Itz'hak in the name of Rabh: Him (God) from whom all the strength comes. And what is meant by "*all* faces turned pale"? Said R. Johanan: The heavenly household and the household of the earth, as at the time the Holy One, blessed be He, said: Both Israel and the nations are my work, why then should I destroy the one for the other? Said R. Papa: This is what people say: If the ox which is liked by the owner falls while going on his way, and he is compelled to substitute for it a horse which he does not like very much, when the ox, however, becomes better it is difficult for him to remove the horse because of the ox.*

R. Giddel said in the name of Rabh: The years of abundance in the time of the Messiah, will benefit Israel. Said R. Joseph: Is this not self-evident? Who else then should have benefit from them, Hilek and Bilek (as in English Dick and Harry)? This was said by him in order to deny R. Hillel's theory, who said farther on, that Israel has no more to wait for a Messiah, as they have consumed him already at the time of Hezekiah. Said Rabh: The world is created only for such men as David. And Samuel said: For such men as Moses. And R. Johanan said: For such men as the Messiah. But what is his name? The disciples of R. Shilah said: Shilah is his name, as it reads [Gen. xlix. 10]: " Until Shilah will come." The disciples of R. Janai said *Jinun* is his name, as it reads [Ps. lxxii. 17]: " In the presence of the sun, Jinun is his name." And the disciples of R. Hanina said: Hanina is his name, as [Jer. xvi. 13]: " So that I will not grant you Hanina." (Favor.) According to others, Menachem b. Hiskia is his name as in [Sam. i. 16]: " For from me in Menachem (comforter) that should refresh my soul." And the rabbis said: The sufferer of the house of Rabbi is his name, as [Is. liii. 4]: " But only our diseases did he bear himself, and our pains he carried: while we indeed esteemed him stricken, smitten of God and afflicted." Said R. Na'hman: If Messiah is among the living he is a man like myself, of whom it reads [Jer. xxx. 21]: " And their leader shall be of themselves, and their ruler shall proceed from the midst of them." Said Rabh: If he is among the living it is our holy rabbi, and if he was from the death it was Daniel. Said R. Jehudah in the name of Rabh: In the future the Holy One, blessed be He, will create for them

* Rashi explains this thus: When Israel sins, the power is given to the nations. And therefore when Israel repents, and has to be redeemed, it is hard for Heaven to destroy the enemies because of Israel. (See also Marsho.)

another David, as it reads [ibid., ibid. 9] : "And David their king, whom I will raise up unto them." It does not read " I raised," but " I will raise." Said R. Papa to Abayi, Does it not read [Ezek. xxxvii. 25] : " David my servant shall be prince unto them forever " ? As it is now a Cæsar and a half Cæsar.

R. Simlai lectured: It reads [Amos, v. 18] : " Wo unto you that long for the day of the Lord ! for what do you wish the day of the Lord? It is (one of) darkness and not of light." It is similar to a cock and a bat who were waiting for light. The cock said to the bat, I look out for the light, because the light is mine (I see it), but for what purpose do you wait for it ? And this is what a Min said to R. Abushu : When will your Messiah appear ? When your people will be surrounded with darkness. Rejoined the Min : Do you caution me ? And he answered : No, but [Isa. lx. 2] reads : " For behold, the darkness shall cover the earth, and a gross darkness the people ; but over thee will shine forth the Lord, and his glory will be seen over thee."

There is a Boraitha : R. Eliezar said : Forty years will be the days of the Messiah. As it reads [Ps. xcv. 10] : " Forty years long did I feel loathing on this generation." R. Elazar b. Aza-ryah said : Seventy years, as [Isa. xxiii. 15] : " Seventy years like the days of one king." By " one king " the Messiah is meant. Rabbi, however, said : It will continue three generations, as [Ps. lxxii. 5] : " They shall fear thee, as long as the sun shineth, and in the presence of the moon throughout all generations." R. Hillel, however, said : There is no more any Messiah for Israel, as they have consumed him already in the days of Hiskia. Said R. Joseph : May the Lord forgive R. Hillel ! Hiskia was at the time of the first Temple, and Zacharyah prophesied at the time of the second Temple, and said [Zech. ix. 9] : " Be greatly glad, O daughter of Zion ; shout, O daughter of Jerusalem ! Behold, thy king will come unto thee, righteous and victorious is he lowly, and riding upon an ass, and upon a colt the foal of a she-ass.

There is another Boraitha : The days of the Messiah are forty years, as it reads [Deut. viii. 3] : " And he afflicted thee, and suf-fered thee to hunger," and [Ps. xc. 15] : " Cause us to rejoice as many days as those wherein thou hast afflicted us." Hence, as their journey in the desert was forty years, so long will be the days of the Messiah ; so R. Eliezar. R. Dusa, however, said : Four hundred years, as in [Gen. xv. 13] : " And they will afflict them four hundred years." And as the above cited verse reads, " to rejoice as many days as thou afflicted us," hence it is four hundred years. Rabbi said: Three hundred and sixty-five years, according to the days of the year when counted after the sun, as [Isa. xxiii. 4]: "For the days of vengeance was in my heart, and the year of my redeemer was come." What is meant, the day of vengeance is in my heart? Said R. Johanan: I revealed it to my heart, but not to any other member of my body. And R. Simeon b. Lakish said: I revealed it to my heart, but not to the angels. Abimi b. Abuhu taught: Seven thousand years will be the days of Messiah, as it reads [ibid. lxii. 5]: "And as a bridegroom is glad over the bride, so will be glad over thee thy God," which is seven days, and each day of the Lord is a thousand years.

R. Jehudah said in the name of Samuel: The days of the Messiah will be as from the day of creation till now, as it reads [Deut. xi. 21]: "As the days of heaven over the earth." R. Na'hman b. Itz'hak said: As from the day of Noah till now, as [Isa. liv. 9]: "For as the waters of Noah is this unto me; as I have sworn," etc.

R. Hyya b. Aba in the name of R. Johanan said: All the prophets have prophesied only for the days of the Messiah, but concerning the world to come it reads [ibid. lxiv. 3]: "No eye (also) had seen a god beside Thee." And he differs with Samuel, who says that there is no difference between this world and the days of the Messiah only concerning the dominion of foreigners over Israel. R. Hyya said again in the name of R. Johanan: The prophets prophesied only to those who have repented, but concerning the entirely upright, it reads: "No eye has seen," etc. And they differ with R. Abuhu, as he said that at the place where those who have repented will be placed, entirely upright cannot be placed, as it reads [Isa. lvii. 19]: "Peace, peace to him that is afar off, and to him that is near." Hence "afar off" is first, and then is "that is near." And what is meant by "far off"? Who previously was far off and now is near. And what is meant by "near"? He who was first near, and is also now near. R. Johanan, however, explained "far off" means one who was always far off from sin, and "near" means one who was near to sin, but now is far off.

The same said again in the name of the same authority: The prophets prophesied only to him who marries his daughter to a scholar, to him who is in business for a scholar, and to him who benefited the scholars by his estate, but to the scholars themselves "an eye has not seen," etc. What is this? Said R. Jehoshua b. Levi: This is the wine which is preserved in

the grapes since the days of the creation.   And Resh Lakish
said: That is the Eden which no eye has seen.   And lest one
say that Adam the First was there?   Adam dwelt only in
the garden.   And lest one say that both are one and the same.
To this it reads [Gen. ii. 10] : " And a river went out of Eden
to water the garden."

" *And he who says that the Torah is not given by Heaven,*" etc.
The rabbis taught: It reads [Num. xv. 31] : " Because the word
of the Lord hath he despised and his commandment hath he
broken."   It means him who says that the Torah is not given
by Heaven.   According to others it means an Epicurean.
Still another explanation is that " the word of the Lord hath he·
despised," means him who explains the Torah against the true
law.   " His commandment hath he broken "—means circumcision, Hikorath—shall be cut off from this world.   Tikorath
—from the world to come.   Said R. Elazar the Modoi: It is
inferred from this that he who profanes the sanctuary, who despises the festivals, he who breaks the covenant of Abraham
our father, he who explains the Torah in a wrong way, he who
makes pale in public the face of his neighbor, although they
possess wisdom and good deeds, have no share in the world to
come.   There is another Boraitha: " He hath despised the word
of God," means him who says that the Torah was not given
by Heaven, and even if he says that the Torah is given by
Heaven, except such and such, which is not by the Holy One,
but by Moses himself.   And even if he says that the whole
Torah is by Heaven except such and such an explanation, such
an *a fortiori* conclusion, such an analogy of expression, they are
considererd as despising the word of the Lord.

There is another Boraitha.   R. Mair said: The just cited
verse means him who learned the Torah but does not teach
it.   R. Nathan said: It means him who does not care for the
Mishna.   R. Nehoraim said: It means him who is possible to
study the law, but does not.   R. Ismael, however, said: It
means an idolater.   How does he infer this from this passage?
As in the following Boraitha: The disciples of R. Ismael taught:
" He hath despised the word of the Lord," means him who has
despised the words which were said to Moses at Sinai, " I am
the Lord thy God, there shall not be any other god before thee."

R. Jehoshua b. Karcha said: He who learns the Torah and
does not repeat it, is similar to him who sows but does not harvest.

R. Jehoshua said: He who learned the Torah and forgot it, is similar to a woman who bears children and buries them. Said R. Aqiba: One shall systematize his study as a song which is to be sung daily (and this will cause his singing in the world to come). Said R. Itz'hak b. Abudimi: Where is an allusion to be found to this in the Scriptures? [Prov. xvi. 26]: "The desire of the laborer laboreth for him; for his mouth imposeth it on him," which means he is laboring here and the Torah labors for him in another place. R. Elazar said: Every man is created to labor, as it reads [Job, v. 7]: "But man is born unto labor." From this, however, we do not know if it means mental or manual labor. As the end of the above-cited verse [Prov. xvi. 26] ends "for his mouth imposeth it on him," hence mental labor is meant. But still I am not aware if it means wisdom or gossip. But as [Josh. i. 8] reads: "This book of the law shall not depart out of thy mouth," hence it means for the labor of the Torah. And this is what Rabha said: Every body is a δρυφατο. Well is to him who is a "druphanto" for the Torah. Resh Lakish said: He who occasionally studies the Torah lacks sense, as it reads [Prov. xxii. 18]: "For it is a pleasant thing if thou keep them within thy bosom, if they be altogether firmly seated upon thy lips."

The rabbis taught: It reads [Num. xv. 30]: "But the person that doth aught with a high hand," means Menasseh b. Hiskia who was offending the legends of the Torah by saying: Has not Moses written something better than in [Gen. xxxvi. 22]: "And Lotan's sister was Thimna," or that she was a concubine of Eliphaz b. Esau, or that of [ibid. xiii. 14]. "And Reuben went in the days of the wheat harvest and found mandrakes in the field." A heavenly voice was then heard [Ps. l. 20]: "Thou sittest and speakest against thy brother, against thy own mother's son thou utterest slander." And to him also applies [Isa. v. 18]: "Woe unto those that draw iniquity with the cords of falsehood, and as with a wagon-rope, sinfulness." What does a "wagon-rope" mean? (See Succah, p. 80, line 3.) But what means in reality the verse "Lotan's sister was Thimna"? Thimna was a princess, as it reads [Gen. xxxvi. 40]: "Duke Thimna," and a dukedom is a kingdom without a crown; and she desired to become a proselyte, but Abraham, Isaac, and Jacob did not accept her. And she went and became the concubine of Eliphaz b. Esau, saying it is better to be a servant in this nation than to be a princess of another.

And the offspring from her was Amalek, who troubled Israel as a punishment to their parents, who ought not to have driven her out.

"*Reuben went in the days of harvest,*" etc.   Said Rabha b. Itz'hak in the name of Rabh: Infer from this that the upright do not stretch their hands out to robbery.   What are the *dudaim* which Reuben found?   According to Rabh they were *jabruchen*, and according to Samuel mandrake flower.   R. Alexandri said: Those who occupy themselves with the Torah for her own sake cause peace to reign in the heavenly household and in the household here below, as it reads [Isa. xxvii. 15]: "If he but take hold of my strength, make peace with me, make peace with me."   And Rabh said: He is considered as if he had built both palaces of heaven and earth, as it reads [ibid. li. 16]: "And I have placed my words in thy mouth, and with the shadow of my hand have I covered thee: to plant the heavens and to lay the foundations of the earth."   R. Johanan said: He is also considered as a protector of the world, as it reads "with the shadow of my hand have I covered thee."   Levi said: He makes redemption sooner, as this verse ends "to say to Zion, Thou art my people."   Resh Lakish said: He who teaches the Torah to his neighbor's son the verse considers him as if he had created him, as it reads [Gen. xii. 5]: "And the persons they had obtained in Charan."   R. Elazar said: He is considered as if he has created the law, as it reads [Deut. xxix. 8]: "Keep ye therefore the words of the covenant, and do them."   And Rabha said: He is considered as if he created himself from the same verse; do not read authom, but athem (ye yourselves).   R. Abuhu said: He who hastens his neighbor to do a meritorious act, the verse considers him as if he himself has done it, as it reads [Ex. xvii. 5]: "And thy staff wherewith thou smotest the river take in thy hand and go."   Did he, then, smite the river?   Did not Aaron do this?   Hence it was written to teach that the verse considers him as if he himself has done it.

"*Epicurean,*" etc.   Both Rabh and R. Hanina said: He who disgraces a scholar is meant.   And both R. Johanan and R. Jehoshua b. Levi said: He who disgraces his neighbor in the presence of a scholar.   It is correct according to them who said that an Epicurean is he who has done as in the latter case, as then he who disgraces a scholar himself is considered as explaining the Torah a wrong way.   But according to them who

say that he who disgraces a scholar himself is considered only
an Epicurean, who then is considered as explaining the Torah
wrongly? *E.g.*, Menassah b. Hiskia.   There were those who
taught the same concerning the latter part of the Mishna, " who
explains the Torah not according to the true law."   And to this
Rabh and R. Hanina said: He who disgraces a scholar.   And
Johanan and Jehoshua b. Levi said: He who disgraces his
neighbor in the presence of a scholar.   And the question was,
if he who disgraces his colleague in the presence of a scholar
is considered as explaining the Torah wrongly, who then is
considered an Epicurean?   Said R. Joseph: *E.g.*, those who
say, What good do the rabbis do to us?   They read and study
the Torah for their own sake.   Said Abayi to him: Such are also
considered as explaining the Torah wrongly, as it reads [Jer.
xxxiii. 25]: " Thus said the Lord, If my covenant be not day
and night, I would not have appointed the ordinances of heaven
and earth." *   This is inferred also from [Gen. xviii. 26]:
" Then will I spare all the places for their sake."   So R. Na'h-
man b. Itz'hak.   And an epicurean is considered—*e.g.*, if one
sits before his master and recollects a Halakha stated some-
where else and says, so and so we have learned there, but does
not say: And the master said so.   Rabha, however, said: An
epicurean is considered—*e.g.*, the disciples of Benjamin the
physician, who used to say, What good have the rabbis done
for us?   They have never permitted us to eat a crow, and they
have not prohibited us to eat a dove (hence all remains as it is
in the Scriptures).   It happened that a question of legal or
illegal meat was brought before Rabha from the house of Benjamin the physician, and he saw a reason to permit the use of
it, and he said then: See, I have permitted you a crow.   The
same happened again and he saw a reason to prohibit it, and
also said: See, I have prohibited a dove to you.   R. Papa said:
Even he who speaks of the rabbis in the same language as when
he speaks of common people.   However, he himself forgot his
statement in talking about the rabbis, and thereafter when he
recollected it, he fasted.   Levi b. Samuel and R. Huna b. Hyya
used to prepare mantles for the holy scrolls in the college of
R. Jehudah.   When they came to the Book of Esther, they
said: For this certainly no mantle is needed.   Said R. Jehudah
to them: Even such a language is as used by the followers of

---

* Translated according to the Talmud.

Epicurus. R. Na'hman said: He who named his master by his name without adding "my master." As R. Johanan said: Why was Gechazi punished? Because he named his master by his name [II Kings, viii. 5]: "This is our son whom Elisha restored." R. Jeremiah was sitting in the presence of R. Zera ard said: The Holy One, blessed be He, will create a river in the future, which will issue from the holy of holy chamber, and on its edges the best fruit will be grown, as it reads [Ezek. xlvii. 12]: "And by the stream upon its banks, on this side and on that side, shall grow up all kinds of trees for food, the leaves of which shall not fade, and the fruit of which shall not come to an end, every month shall they bring forth new ripe fruit; because its water is that which issueth out of the sanctuary; and their fruit shall serve for food, and their leaves for remedies."

And there was a certain old man who said: Thanks, so also said R. Johanan. Said R. Jeremiah to R. Zera: Is such a language also not used by the epicureans? And he answered: Nay, he is only supporting you, and if you have heard that such a language must not be used, it is what is said in Last Gate (pp. 210 and 211, from "it is written" to "Rabha"). What means "leaves for remedies"? R. Itz'hak b. Abudimi and R. Hisda. One said: To make the dumb speak. And the other: To open the womb when there is a difficulty in bearing the child. And so also was it taught by Hiskia, to open the mouth of the dumb and by Bar khapara, to open the womb. R. Johanan, however, said: It is to be explained literally remedies for everything. R. Samuel b. Na'hmani said: It means a remedy for the appearance of those who have studied with their mouth, as R. Jehudah b. Simon lectured: He who makes his face black by studying the Torah in this world, the Holy One, blessed be He, will make radiant his face in the world to come, as it reads [Sol. Song, v. 15]: "His countenance is as Lebanon, excellent like the cedars." R. Tanhun b. Hanilai said: He who starves because of the words of law in this world, the Holy One, blessed be He, will satiate him in the world to come, as it reads [Ps. xxxvi. 9]: "These will be abundantly satisfied with the fatness of thy house; and of the stream of thy delight wilt thou give them to drink." When Abdimi came from Palestine, he said: The Holy One, blessed be He, will give in the future to every upright his handful of reward, as it reads [ibid. lxviii. 20]: "Blessed be the Lord; day by day he loadeth us (with benefits); our God is our salvation." Said Abayi to him:

How is it possible to say so? Is it not written [Isa. xl. 12]:
" Who hath measured in the hollow of his hand the waters, and
meted out the heavens with the span "? And he answered:
Why are you not used to study Haggadah? It was said in the
West in the name of Rabha b. Mari: The Holy One, blessed be
He, will give in the future to every upright man, three hundred and ten worlds, as it reads [Prov. viii.]: " That I may
cause those that love me ‎ש‎," etc., and these two letters count
310. (And this is called a handful.)

There is a Boraitha: R. Mair said: The measure with which
one measures will be measured out to him—*i.e.*, as man deals,
he will be dealt with, as it reads [Isa. xxvii. 8]: " In measure,
by driving him forth, thou strivest with him." Said R. Jehoshua to him: How is it possible to say so? *E.g.*, if one gives
to a poor man a handful of charity, will then the Holy One,
blessed be He, give the donator His handful? Does it not
read " he meted out the heavens with a span "? Said he to him:
And you do not say so? What measure is greater of good or
of evil? You must say that the former is greater than the
latter, as concerning good it reads [Ps. lxxviii. 23 and 24]:
" Then he ordained the skies from above, and the doors of
heaven he opened; and he let rain down upon them manna to
eat, and the corn of heaven gave he unto them." And concerning evil it reads [Gen. vii. 11]: " The windows of heaven
were opened." (It is said elsewhere that the size of a door is
as the size of four windows.) Now, come and read what is
written about chastisement. [Isa. lxvi. 24]: " And they shall
go forth and look upon carcasses of the men that have transgressed against me; for their worm shall not die, nor shall their
fire be quenched; and they shall be an abhorrence unto all
flesh." And how is this to be understood? We know that in
this world, if a man puts his finger in the fire, immediately he
is burned. You must then say, that as the Holy One, blessed
be He, gives strength to the wicked to receive their punishment. The same is the case with the upright; he gives them
strength to be able to accept their reward.

" *The books of the Hizumni.*" In a Boraitha it was taught:
In the books of the atheists. R. Joseph said: One must not
read even in the book of Ben Sirra. Said Abayi to him: Is it
because it reads: Thou shalt not take off the skin of a fish,
even that of the ear, as the skin will be damaged, but roast it
in fire, and eat with it two loaves of bread? Is not similar to

this also written in the Scripture [Deut. xx. 19] : " Thou shalt not destroy the trees thereof," etc.?   And if because it reads: " A daughter to a father is a false treasure, as because he is afraid of her, he does not sleep in the night.   When she is a minor, perhaps she will be seduced.   When she becomes of age, perhaps she will sin, when she becomes vigaros, perhaps she will not marry.   If she is married, perhaps she will have no children.   And when she becomes old, perhaps she will become a witch? "   Similar to this, the rabbis also said : The world cannot be without males and females, however happy are those who have male children, etc.   And if because there is written " Thou shalt not bring worry in thy heart," as such has killed strong men.   This was also said by Solomon [Prov. xii. 25] : " If there be care in the heart of a man, let him suppress it." (See Yomah, p. 140, for explanation.)   And if because it reads: " Prevent many people to enter thy house,' as not all of them are fit to come into it; this was said also by Rabbi in a Boraitha elsewhere.   Therefore we must say, because it reads there, " He who has a long and thin beard is shrewd."   And he who has a thick one is a fool.   He who blows off the foam, it is sign that he is not thirsty.   And he who says with what he shall eat his bread, take the bread away from him.   And he whose beard is parted in two, the whole world will not overrule him.

Said R. Joseph : However, the good teachings which are in this book may be proclaimed.   It reads there : A good woman is a good gift, she may be given to one who fears God.   A bad woman is leprosy to her husband, and there is no remedy for him till he divorces her, and be cured.   A beautiful woman, happy is her husband, the numbers of his days are doubled. Turn away thy eyes from a beautiful woman, as thou canst be easily caught in her net.   Abstain thyself from drinking beer and wine with her husband, as by the appearance of a beautiful woman many were destroyed.   And numerous are those who were killed by such.

A great number of pedlars were wounded by the husbands who found them trading with their wives.   As a spark kindles a coal, or like a coop full of birds, so are their houses full of deceit.   Many may be who wish you peace, however thy secrets you may reveal only to one from thousand.   Be careful with words even with her that lies on thy bosom.   Don't worry of the morrow, as thou knowest not what the morrow may bring.   For perhaps thou wilt not exist any more to-morrow, and thou hast worried for a world which belongs not to thee. All the days of a poor are bad. Ben Sirra said: Also the nights, as his roof is lower than others, the rain from these falls on his. And his vineyard is usually on the top of the mountain, and the manure which he brings up for it is blown off to the other vineyards which are lower. (Here is repeated from Last Gate, p. 328, paragraph commencing with R. Zera in the name of Rabh said, till Mishna VI. See there also footnote.)

The rabbis taught: If one reads a verse of the Songs of Solomon in a different manner than it is written, and makes a song of it; or any other verse in the drinking-places not in its proper time, causes evil to the world, because the Torah, dressed in a sack, stands before the Holy One, blessed be He, and says: Lord of the Universe, thy children have made of me a fiddle on which frivolous persons play. And He said to her: My daughter, with what else, then, shall they occupy themselves while they are eating and drinking? And she said before Him: Lord of the Universe, if they are masters in the Scriptures, they may occupy themselves with the Pentateuch, Prophets, and Hagiographa; if they understand Mishnayoth, they may study Mishna, Halakha, and Haggadah, and if they are Talmudists they may study Halakhas in time of Passover on Pesach. Of Pentecost at that time. And the Halakhas of Feast of Tabernacle at that time. R. Simeon b. Elazar in the name of R. Simeon b. Hanania testified: If one reads a verse in its proper time, he benefits the world, as it reads [Prov. xv. 23]: "And a word spoken at the proper time, how good is it."

"*He who mumbles over a wound,*" etc. Said R. Johanan: Provided he also spits, as the name of Heaven must not be mentioned by spitting. It was taught: Rabh said: Even a verse which does not contain the name of Heaven—*e.g.*, a plague, if it will be on a man. And R. Hanina said: Even the words: And He has called to Moses.

The rabbis taught: One may ask the fortune tellers who tell fortunes by certain oils or eggs. But it is not advisable to do so, because they often lie. They usually mumble over the oil in a utensil, but not over that which is in the hand, and therefore one may use the oil from the hand, but not that in a utensil. R. Itz'hak b. Samuel b. Marta happened to be in a certain inn. They brought him oil in a utensil, and he anointed himself with it, and blisters came out on his face. When he went to the market a certain woman saw him, and said: I see on your face a sickness caused by witchcraft. And she did something for him and he was cured.

Abba said to Rabba b. Mari: It reads [Ex. xv. 26] : " I will put none of those diseases upon thee . . . as I the Lord will heal thee." Now if he did not put any, why the cure? Said R. Johanan: This verse explains itself. " If thou wilt diligently hearken,"etc., I will not put disease upon thee, but if thou wilt not hearken, I will. However, at any rate, I will heal thee.

Rabba b. b. Hana said: When R. Eliezar became sick his disciples came to make him a sick call, and he said to them, I have high fever, and they began to weep. R. Aqiba, however, smiled. And to the question: Why are you smiling? he returned the question: Why are you weeping? And they answered: Is it possible not to weep when we see the Holy Scrolls are in such a distress? Rejoined he: And therefore I smile, for so long as I have seen our master's wine does not become sour, his flocks undamaged, his oil unspoiled, and his honey unfermented, I was afraid that perhaps he received all his reward in this world, now as I see him in trouble, I rejoice. Said he to him: Aqiba, have I failed to perform or transgressed anything of that what is written in the whole Torah? And he answered: You, master, yourself taught us [Ecc. vii. 20] : " For no man is so righteous upon earth, that he should do always good and never sin."

The rabbis taught: When R. Eliezar became sick four elders entered to make him a sick call—R. Tarphun, R. Jehoshua, R. Elazar b. Asaryah, and R. Aqiba. Exclaimed R. Tarphun: You are better to Israel than drops of rain, as the latter are only in this world, while you are in both, in this and in the world to come. Exclaimed R. Jehoshua: You are better to Israel than the planet of the sun, which is only in this world, while you are in both. And R. Elazar b. Asaryah exclaimed: You are better to Israel than a father and mother, who are only in this world, etc. R. Aqiba, however, exclaimed: Pleased are chastisements. And R. Eliezar answered: Support me, and I will hear the statement of Aqiba, my disciple, who says: " Pleased are chastisements." And he said: Aqiba, whence is this known to you? And he answered: From the following: It reads [II Kings, xxi. 1 and 2] : " Twelve years old was Menasseh when he became king, and fifty and five years did he reign in Jerusalem . . . and he did what is evil in the eyes of the Lord." It reads also [Prov. xxv. 1] : " Also these

21

are the proverbs of Solomon, which the men of Hezekiah, the king of Judah, have collected." Could it be possible that Hiskia taught the law to the whole world, but not to his son Menasseh? It must then be said that of all the troubles which Hiskia has troubled himself to bring him, and from all his toil to correct him nothing was done, and only until chastisement had turned him over to the better side, as it reads [II Chron. xxxiii. 10-14]: "And the Lord spoke to Menasseh, and to his people; but they listened not. Wherefore the Lord brought over them captains of the army belonging to the king of Assyria; and they took Menasseh prisoner with chains, and bound him with fetters, and led him off to Babylon. And when he was in distress he besought the Lord his God, and humbled himself greatly before the God of his fathers. And he prayed unto Him, and He permitted Himself to be entreated by him, and heard his supplication and brought him back to Jerusalem unto his kingdom. Then did Menasseh feel conscious that the Lord is indeed the (true) God." Learn from this that chastisements are pleased.

The rabbis taught: Three men (biblical personages) came with indirectness (instead of praying in a straightforward manner), and they were Cain, Esau, and Menasseh. Cain who says [Gen. iv. 13]: "My sin is greater than I can bear." He said before Him: Lord of the Universe, is then my sin greater than that of the six hundred thousand Israelites who will sin before Thee in the future, and Thou wilt forgive them? Esau said [Ex. xxvii. 38]: "Hast thou then but one blessing, my father?" And Menasseh, who at the beginning called to many gods, and only finally called to the God of his parents.

"*Abba Shaul,*" etc. There is a Boraitha: Provided he does so out of the sanctuary in a profane language.

"*Three kings,*" etc. The rabbis taught: Jeroboam means who made Israel quarrel among themselves. According to others, who has made a controversy between them and their Heavenly Father. Ben Nebat means the son of him who had a vision, but did not see (interpret it properly). As the following Boraitha Nebat is identical with Michah and with Sheba ben Bichri Nebat because of the reason said above. And Michah, because he became poor while occupying himself with building. And his real name was Sheba ben Bichri.

The rabbis taught: There were three who had a vision, but have not seen it properly. Nebat Achitopel and the astrol-

ogers of Pharaoh. Nebat saw that some light will come out from 'him. He thought he 'himself will become a king, and he erred, as this was his son Jeroboam. Achitopel saw also the same. He thought that he 'himself will become a king, but he erred, as it was his daughter, Bath Sheba, from whom Solomon came out. And the astrologers of Pharaoh, who saw that the redeemer of Israel will be beaten through water, and therefore advised Pharaoh to command. [Ex. i. 22] : " Every son that is born ye shall cast into the river." And they erred, as this was [Num. xx. 13] : " These are the waters of Meribah where the children of Israel quarreled." But whence do we know that Jeroboam has no share in the world to come? From [I Kings, xiii. 34] : " Blotted out, and destroyed from the face of the earth. Blotted out from this world and destroyed from the world to come. Said R. Johanan: What has Jeroboam done that he was rewarded to be king? Because he rebuked Solomon. And why was he punished? Because he rebuked him in public, as it reads [ibid. xi. 27] : " And this was the occasion that he lifteth up his hand against the king: Solomon built up the Milo and closed up the breach of the city of David his father." He said to 'him : David, thy father 'hath broken in holes in the surrounding wall of Jerusalem, for the purpose that it shall be easier for Israel to enter the city. And thou hast fenced it for the purpose to make an *angaria* to Pharaoh's daughter. What means " and 'he lifteth up his hands "? Said R. Na'hman: He took off his phylacterious in his presence.*
R. Na'hman said again: The insolence of Jeroboam destroyed 'him from the world, as it reads [ibid. xii. 26-28] : " And Jeroboam said in his heart, Now may the kingdom return to the house of David. If this people go up to prepare sacrifices in the house of the Lord at Jerusalem, then may the heart of this people turn again unto their lord, even unto Rehoboam, the king of Judah, and they might kill me, and return to Rehoboam, the king of Judah." He said: We have a tradition that in the Temple there are no seats except for the kings of the house of David. Now if they see that Rehoboam, the king, is sitting and I am standing, then they will say that he is the king and I am his servant. And if I will sit, Rehoboam's people will say that I am a rebel, and they will kill me, and therefore (28) : " Whereupon the king took counsel, and he made two calves

---

* An explanation to this you will find in our " Amulets," Charms and Talismans, p. 28.

of gold, and saith unto the people, You have been long enough
going up to Jerusalem; behold here are thy gods, O Israel,
which have brought thee up out of the land of Egypt." What
is meant by "the king took counsel"? Said R. Jehudah: He
has conjoined an upright to a wicked, and said to them: Will
you sign your name to all what I will command you? And
they said: Yea. "Even to worship an idol"? The upright
answered: God forbid. But the wicked saith to him: Do you
think a man like Jeroboam will worship idols? He wants only
to try us. And in this thing even Achiyah, the Shilonite, erred
and signed his name. As Jehu, who was one of the greatest of
upright about whom it reads [II Kings, x. 30]: "Forasmuch
as thou hast acted well in doing what is right in my eyes, and
hast done in accordance with all that was in my heart unto the
house of Achab: children of the fourth generation after thee
shall sit upon the throne of Israel." And thereafter it reads
(31): "And Jehu took no heed to walk in the law of the Lord
the God of Israel with all his heart: he departed not from the
sins of Jeroboam, who induced Israel to sin." But what caused
him to sin? Said Abayi: There is a covenant to one's lips. He
said [ibid., ibid. 18]: "Achab hath served Baal a little: Jehu will
serve him much." And Rabha said: He saw the signature of
Achiyah the Shilonite and he erred, as reads [Hosea, v. 2]:
"And for murdering they who had rebelled (against God) con-
cealed themselves in deep places; but I will inflict correction on
them all." Said R. Johanan: The Holy One, blessed be He,
said: They laid deeper plans than that of mine: I said: He
who does not ascend to Jerusalem for the festivals transgresses
a positive commandment only, and they say that he who will
ascend to Jerusalem shall be slain by the sword.

It reads [I Kings, xi. 29]: "And it came to pass at that time
when Jeroboam went out of Jerusalem, that the prophet Achiyah the Shilonite found him on the way; and he had clad himself with a new garment; and these two were alone by themselves in the field." It was taught in the name of R. Jose:
"At that time" means the time which was designated for chastisement. [Jer. ii. 18]: "In the time of their punishment shall
they vanish," was also taught in the name of the same authority,
means at the time designated for chastisement. [Isa. xlix. 8]:
"In the time of favor have I answered thee," according to the
same authority: The time which is designated for doing good
[Ex. xxxii. 8]: "But on the day when I visit I will visit their

sins upon them," according to the same, at the time which is designated for chastisement. And the same is with Gen. xxxviii. 1: "And it came to pass at *that time.*" It reads [I Kings, xii. 1]: "And Rehoboam went to Shechem (. . .) to make 'him king." It was taught in the name of R. Jose. That place was designated for trouble. In Shechem, Dina was assaulted in the same place, Joseph was sold by 'his brothers, and in the same place the kingdom of David was divided. And (ibid. 29) "Jeroboam went out of Jerusalem." Said R. Hanina b. Papa: It means he went out of the destiny of Jerusalem (*i.e.,* was to have no share in the welfare of Jerusalem). "And the prophet Achiyah . . . with a new garment," what does it mean? Said R. Na'hman: As a new garment has no spots so also the wisdom of Jeroboam was clean, without any error. According to others: They renewed things which no ear has ever heard of. And what is meant by "The two were alone in the field"? Said R. Jehudah in the name of Rabh: All other scholars were like the plants of the field in comparison with them. According to others: All the reasons for the commandment of the Torah were revealed to them as a field.

It reads [Michah, l. 14]: "Therefore shalt thou have to give presents to *Moreshe thgath*: the houses of Achzib shall become a deception to the kings of Israel." Said R. Hanina b. Papa: A heavenly voice was heard saying: "To him who has killed Goliath the Philistine and inherited to you. the city of Gath, should ye send away his descendants?" Therefore the house of Achzib shall be a deception to the kings of Israel. It reads [II Kings, xvii. 21]: "And Jeroboam misled Israel from following the Lord, and caused them to commit a great sin." Said R. Hanina: As one throws a stick by means of another stick—*i.e.,* he makes Israel to sin against their will. Said R. Aushia: Until Jeroboam came, Israel had to bear the iniquity of one golden calf, and from that time farther on for two and three. Said R. Itz'hak: Every evil dispensation which came upon Israel contained in it a twenty-fourth part as punishment for the golden calf, as the above cited verse [Ex. xxxii.] states. Said R. Hanina: After twenty-four generations this verse was fulfilled, as it reads [Ezek. ix. i]: "The ' *pkudas* ' of the city came already at an end."*

---

* Leeser translates Ex. xxxii. 8 *pokdi* and *pokadi* with "will visit," and here he translates the same term with "charge" (by the way, both translations are wrong). The Talmud, however, has its way of saying that the *pokdi* of that verse had ceased

It reads [I Kings, xiii. 33]: After this event Jeroboam returned not from his evil way. After what! Said R. Abba:
After the Holy One, blessed be He, held Jeroboam by his garment, saying: Repent, and I and David Ben Yishai and thou
will walk in the Garden of Eden. And to Jeroboam's questions:
Who will have the preference? he said: Ben Yishai. And he
rejoined: If so I don't want it.

R. Abuhu used to lecture about the three kings and became
sick, and he made up his mind not to lecture about them, and
he was cured. However, he lectured about them as before,
and to the question of his disciples: Have you not made up
your mind not to lecture any more about them? he answered:
Did they then repent that I shall do so?

R. Ashi appointed a time for lecturing about the three kings,
and said: On the morrow we will begin our lecture about our
colleague Menasseh. He then appeared to him in a dream, and
said to him: You call me a colleague and a colleague of your
father? Answer me the question: Where must one begin to
cut the bread by the benediction of *thamotzi*? And he said: I
don't know. Rejoined Menasseh: If you are not aware to answer even that what I questioned you how can you call me
a colleague? Rejoined R. Ashi: Teach this to me, and to-
morrow I will proclaim it in your name in the college. And he
said: From that part where it begins to bake when in the oven.
Said R. Ashi again: If you are so wise, why did you worship
idols? And Menasseh answered: If you would have been at
that time you would have lifted up the edges of your dress, that
they shall not impede you to run after me to worship the idols.
On the morrow said R. Ashi to the rabbis: Let us lecture
about the great men. Achab—means " Ach," a thorn to
Heaven, and " ab," a father to idolatry, as it reads [I Kings,
xvi. 31]: " And it came to pass as if it had been too light a
thing for him to walk in the sins of Jeroboam." Said R. Johanan: The lenient things which were done by Achab were
more rigorous than the rigorous things done by Jeroboam.
And why then does the Scripture make Achab dependent on
Jeroboam, because Jeroboam was the beginner and all his followers were dependent upon him.

It reads [Hosea xii. 12]: " Their altars also are as stone

at that time. It is important that it counts from Moses to Ezekiel twenty-four generations.

heaps." Said R. Johanan: There was not one heap in the land of Israel upon which Achab had not placed an idol and bowed himself to it. And whence do we know that he has no share in the world to come? From [I Kings, xxi. 21]: "Behold, I will bring evil upon thee, and I will sweep out after thee and will cut off from Achab every male and the guarded and fortified in Israel." "Guarded" means in this world, and "fortified" in the world to come.

R. Johanan said: For which good deeds was Omri (Achab's father) rewarded that he obtained the kingdom? Because he added one great city to the land of Israel, as it reads [ibid. xvi. 24]: "And he bought the mount Samaria of Shemer for two talents of silver, and built on the mount, and called the name of the city which he had built, after the name of Shemer, the lord of the mount, Samaria."

R. Johanan said again: Why was Achab rewarded by the prolongation of his kingdom for twenty-two years? Because he respected the Torah which is written with the twenty-two letters of the alphabet, as it reads [ibid. xx. 2, 7, and 9]: "And he sent messengers to Achab, the king of Israel, into the city. And he said unto him: Thus hath said Ben-hadad, Thy silver and thy gold are mine; thy wives also and thy children, even the best are mine. And the king of Israel answered and said, According to thy word, my lord, O king, thine am I, and all that I have. And the messenger returned and said: Thus hath said Ben-hadad, to say (to thee) I have indeed sent unto thee, saying, 'Thou shalt give unto me thy silver, and thy gold, and thy wives, and thy children. Nevertheless, about this time to-morrow will I send my servants unto thee, and they will search through thy house, and the houses of thy servants, and it shall be, that whatsoever is pleasant in thy eyes, they shall place it in their hand, and take it away.' Then did the king of Israel call for all the elders of the land, and said, Mark, I pray you, and see that this man seeketh mischief, for he hath sent unto me for my wives, and for my children, and for my silver, and for my gold, and I have not refused them to him. Wherefore he said unto the messengers of Ben-hadad: Say to my lord the king, all that thou didst send for to thy servants at the first will do; but this thing I am not able to do. And the messengers went away, and brought him word again." What is meant by "pleasant in thy eyes" if not the holy-scrolls? But perhaps it means an idol. This cannot be supposed, as it reads farther on

(8): "And all the elders, and all the people said unto him, Thou must not hearken nor consent." But perhaps it means the elders of the same kind as was Achab, as we find such in [II Sam. xvii. 4], that they are also named the elders of Israel. There it does not read " all the people," but here it does; and it is impossible that among them were no righteous, as it reads [I Kings xix. 18]: " And I will leave in Israel seven thousand, all the knees which have not bent unto Baal and every mouth which has not kissed him." Said R. Na'hman: Achab's sins and good deeds were just equal, as it reads [ibid. xxii. 20]: " Who will persuade Achab," hence it is difficult to punish him, as his sins did not overweigh his good deeds. R. Joseph opposed: He of whom it reads [ibid. xxi. 25]: " But indeed there was none like unto Achab," etc., etc. And you say that his sins and good deeds were equal? The reason, however, that it was necessary to persuade him, is because he was liberal with his money and assisted many scholars from his estate, and therefore half his sins were atoned. And there came out a spirit," etc. (see above). It reads [ibid. xvi. 33]: " And Achab made a grove; and Achab did yet more, so as to provoke the Lord the God of Israel to anger, than all the kings of Israel that had been before him." Said R. Johanan: He wrote on the gates of Shemer: Achab denies the God of Israel, and therefore he has no share in Him.

Menasseh means " he has forgotten the Lord." According to others it means that he made Israel to forget their Heavenly Father. And whence do we know that he has no share in the world to come? From [II Kings, xxi. 3]: " And he built up again the high places which Hezekiah hath destroyed and he reared up altars for Baal and made a grove as Achab the king of Israel hath done." As Achab has no share in the world to come the same is the case with Menasseh.

" R. Jehudah said Menasseh has a share," etc. Said R. Johanan: Both infer their theory from one and the same passage [Jer. xv. 4]: " And I will cause them to become a horror unto all the kingdoms of the earth on account of Menasseh the son of Hezekiah." According to one: Because Menasseh has repented and the other kings have not. And according to others: Because he himself had not repented. Said R. Johanan: He who said that Menasseh has no share in the world to come weakens the hands of those who are repenting. As a disciple taught before. R. Johanan: Menasseh repented thirty-

three years, as it reads [II Kings, xxi. 1-3]: "And fifty-five
years did he reign in Jerusalem . . . and he made a grove
as Achab did." How long did Achab rule? Twenty-two years;
take off the twenty-two from the fifty-five years which Menasseh
reigned, there remains thirty-three years.

R. Johanan said in the name of R. Simeon b. Jo'hai: It
reads [II Chron. 13]: "And 'he prayed unto Him, and He
permitted himself *v'ychtar** instead of *voyethar*. Infer from this
that the Lord made for him an opening like a *machteres* (opening) in the Heaven to receive him; because of the opposition
of the divine attribute.

The same said again in the name of the same authority ::
In [Jer. xxvi., xxvii. and xxviii., the first verses]: "In the beginning of the reign of Yehoyakim. . . . The beginning
of the reign of Zedekiah." Were there not rulers before them?
But this signifies that the Lord was about to return the world
to tahu vebahu because of Yehoyakim. But when he looked
upon his generation who were upright, he reconsidered it. And
the reverse was the case with Zedekiah. He wanted to destroy
the world because of his generation, but when he looked upon
him he reconsidered it.

But does it not also read about Zedekiah [II Kings, xxiv.
18]: "And he did what was evil in the eyes of the Lord"?
This was because he had to warn them, but did not do so.

The same said again in the name of the same authority:
It reads [Prov. xxix. 9]: "If a wise man contend with a
foolish man, whether he be angry or whether he laugh, he will
have no rest." The Holy One, blessed be He, said: I became angry with Achaz and delivered him to the king of Damascus. What had he done? He sacrificed and smoked incense to their gods, as [II Chron. xxviii. 2]: "And he sacrificed unto the gods of the people of Damascus, who had smitten
him; and he said, "Because the gods of the kings of Syria do
help them (therefore) will I sacrifice unto them, that they may
help me." But they only became to him a stumbling-block
for him and for all Israel. I smiled on Amazia and had delivered the kings of Edom to 'his hand. And what has he done?
He brought their gods and bowed himself to them, as it reads
[II Chron. xxv. 14]: "After Amasyahu was come home from

---

* Such a word is not found. However, perhaps it was in the Bible of the author
of this saying (see Marsho).

smiting the Edomites he brought the gods of the children of Le'ir, and set them up unto himself as gods, and before them he used to prostrate himself and unto them he used to burn incense." Said R. Papa: This is what people say: You can do nothing with the ignoramus; weep before him, laugh with him, he does not care. Woe is to him who does not understand between good and evil. It reads [Jer. xxxix. 3]: "In the middle gate." Said R. Johanan in the name of R. Simeon b. Jo'hai: This was the place the Sanhedrin decided upon Halakhas. Said R. Papa: This is what people say: Should the hook which was used by the herd, etc. (see Middle Gate, p. 216, line 14 from the bottom). R. Hisda said in the name of R. Jeremiah b. Aba: It reads [Prov. xxiv. 30-31]: "By the field of a slothful man I once passed along, and by the vineyard of a man void of sense: And, lo, it was all grown over with thorns, nettles had covered its surface, and its stone wall was broken down." "By the field of a slothful man," etc., means Achaz, "void of sense" means Menasseh, "with thorns" means Amon, "nettles had covered," etc., means Yehoyakim, "broken down"—Zedekiah, in whose days the temple was destroyed.

The same said again in the name of the same authority: Four sects will not receive the glory of the Shekhina; viz., the scorners, as it reads [Hosea, vii. 5]: "He groweth his land with scorners"; liars, as it reads [Ps. ci. 7]: "He that speaketh falsehood shall not succeed in my eyes"; hypocrites, as [Job, xiii. 16]: "For a hypocrite cannot come before Him," and slanderers, as [Ps. ii. 5]: "For thou art not a God that hath pleasure in wickedness. Evil cannot abide with thee," and thereafter it reads [7 and 10]: "Thou wilt destroy those that speak lies . . . For there is not in their mouth any sincerity."

The rabbis taught: Menasseh used to learn fifty-five arguments (ways of interpretation) concerning the book of Leviticus, as many as the years of his reign. Achab, eighty-five, and Jeroboam, one hundred and three.

There is a Boraitha: R Mair used to say: Absalom has no share in the world to come, as it reads [II Sam. xviii. 15]: "Smote Absalom"—in this world, and "slew him"—in the world to come.

R. Simeon b. Elazar said in the name of R. Mair: Achaz, Achazyah and all the kings of Israel about whom it is written, "and he did evil in the eyes of the Lord," will not be restored at the time of resurrection, but are also not sentenced to Gehinem.

It reads [II Kings, xxi. 16] : " And also innocent blood, did Menasseh shed in very great abundance, till he had filled (therewith) Jerusalem from one end to another; beside his sin wherewith he induced Judah to sin, to do what is evil in the eyes of the Lord." Here in this college it was explained because he had slain Isaiah. In the West it was explained that he made an image the weight of a thousand persons. And those who were engaged in carrying it from one place to another would die because of the great exertions.

According to whom is what Rabba b. b. Hana said? One soul of an upright is equalized to the whole world—*i.e.*, if one kills an upright, he is considered as if he would slay the whole world. It is in accordance with him who says that Menasseh has killed Isaiah.

Achaz placed the images in the attics of the Temple, as it reads [II Kings, xxiii. 12] : " Altars that were on the upper chamber of Achaz." And Menasseh placed them in the Temple, as it reads [ibid. xxi. 7] : " And he placed a hewn image of the Asherah that he had made, in the house of which the Lord had said to David, and to Solomon, his son, In this house, and in Jerusalem, which I have chosen out of all tribes of Israel will I put my name forever." And Amon placed them in the holy of holy chamber, as it reads [Isa. xxviii. 20] : " For the bed shall be," etc. (See Yomah, p. 10, line 14, for the explanation and continuation which are repeated here. By the way, we have to remark that there is a misprint, Jeremiah instead of Isaiah.)

Achaz abolished the worship and sealed the Torah, as it reads [ibid viii. 16] : " Bind up the testimony, seal up the law among my disciples." Menasseh cut the divine names out (of the Scriptures) and destroyed the altar. Amon burned the Torah and caused spider-webs to be on the place where the altar stood, as it reads [II Chron. xxxiii. 23] : " For he, Amon, made his guiltiness great."

Questioned Rabha, Rabha b. Mari: Why did not the Mishna also count Yehoyakim, of whom it reads [ibid. xxxvi. 8] : " And the rest of the acts of Yehoyakim, and his abominable deeds which he did, and which was found upon him," which, according to one of the sages, means that he engraved the name

of the idol upon his body? And he answered: Concerning
kings I have not heard, but I have heard concerning common
men thus: Why did not the Mishna count Michah? Because
his house was open to travellers (who used to eat and drink
there without being charged).

It reads [Zech. x. 11]: "And he will pass through the
sea (with) distress, and he will smite in the sea the waves."
Said R. Johanan: This is the image which Michah 'had made
in Egypt and which passed with him the Red Sea. There is
a Boraitha: R. Nathan said: From the city of Grab to the
city of Shilah (where the tabernacle was temporarily) is a distance of three miles, and the smoke from the altar in Shilah
used to mix itself with the smoke from the altars which were
made for the image of Michah. And the angels wanted to put
Michah aside, but the Holy One, blessed be He, said to them:
Leave him alone because his house is open to travellers. And
for this were punished the men who took revenge in the case
of the concubine of Gibah (Judges, xix. and xx.). And the
Holy One said to them: Ye took revenge for the honor of a
man, but did not act so for my honor—*i.e.*, they did not care to
destroy the image of Michah, etc.

R. Johanan said in the name of R. Jose b Kisma: Great
are λυρμος entertainments, for a little refreshment plays an es-
sential part, for its refusal estranged two tribes from Israel
(Ammon and Moab), as it reads [Deut. xxiii. 5]: "For the
reason that they met you not with bread and with water, on the
way." And R. Johanan himself said: It estranges relatives
and brings near strangers; shuts the eye not to look upon the
wicked, makes the Shekhina rest on the prophets of Baal, and
even an error in this affair is considered as if it would be done
intentionally. (Now the illustrations.) It estranges relatives—
e.g., Ammon and Moab (who were relatives to Israel). It
brings near strangers—*e.g.*, Jithro, as he said elsewhere that
the reward for [Ex. ii. 20]: "Call him that he may eat bread"
was that his descendants were rewarded to sit among the
Sanhedrin in the chambers of the Temple, as it reads [I Chron.
ii. 55]: "And the families of the scribes who dwelt at Jabez;
the Thirathites, the Shimathites and the Suchathites. These
are the Kenites that came from Chammoth, the father of the
house of Rechab, and [Judges, i. 16]: "And the children of
the Kenite, the father-in-law of Moses, went up out of the city
of palm-trees with the children of Judah into the wilderness of

Judah, which is south of Arad, and they went and dwelt with the people." Shuts the eye not to look upon the evil deeds of the wicked, *e.g.*, Michah, as said above. Makes the Shekhina to rest upon the prophets of Baal, as [I Kings, xiii. 20]: " And it came to pass as they were sitting at the table, That the word of the Lord came unto the phophets, who had brought him back." And even an error is considered as if done intentionally, as R. Jehudah in the name of Rabh said: If Jonathan would have supplied David with some loaves of bread the priests of the city of Nob would not have been slain, Doeg, the Edomite would not have been lost, and Saul and his three sons would not have been killed.

Why does not the Mishna count Achaz among those who have no share in the world to come? Said R. Jeremiah b. Aba: Because he was placed between two uprights (Jotham, his father, and Hezekiah, his son).

And R. Joseph said: Because he was ashamed before the prophet Isaiah, as [Isa. vii. 3]: " And the Lord said unto Isaiah, Go forth now to meet Achaz, thou with Shear Yashub, thy son, to the end of the aqueduct of the upper pool, on the highway of the washers' field." Why is mentioned the washers' field "? Because Achaz was ashamed to look at Isaiah, and to put upon his face the αβλυο of the washers when he passed Isaiah in order not to be recognized.

And why was Amon not counted? Because of the honor of his son, Yeshiyahu. If so, let them not count Menasseh, because of the honor of Hezekiah? There is a tradition that a son can save his father, but not a father his son, as it reads [Deut. xxxii. 39]: " And no one can deliver out of my hands," which means Abraham cannot save Ishmael, and Isaac, Esau. Now, when we come to this theory it may be said that Achaz was not counted because of the honor of Hezekiah. However, the above question, why Yehoyakim was not counted is as yet unanswered. It is because of what was said by Hyya b. Abuiha that on the head of Yehoyakim was written " This and something else "—*i.e.*, one revenge more will be taken from it. The grandfather of R. Praida found a skull in the gates of Jerusalem upon which was engraved: " This and something else." He buried it once and twice, but it came out again. He then said that it must be the skull of Yehoyakim, of whom it reads [Jer. xxii. 19]: " With the burial of an ass shall he be buried, dragged about and cast forth beyond the gates of Jerusalem."

He then said: It is the skull of a king, and it must be nicely treated. He wrapped it in a silk garment and put it in a bag. When his wife saw this she thought it was the skull of his first wife, whom he does not want to forget. And she heated the oven and burned it. This was what was engraved upon it: "This and nothing else."

There is a Boraitha: R. Simeon b. Elazar said: Hiskia praised himself [II Kings, xx. 3]: "And have done what is good in thy eyes" caused what is said [ibid., ibid. 8]: "What sign," etc., and this caused that idolaters were invited to his table [ibid., ibid. 13]. And these altogether caused the exile of his descendants [ibid., ibid. 17]. This is a support to Hiskia, who said that he who invites an idolater to his house and serves on him, causes exile to his children, as it reads [ibid., ibid. 18]: "And of thy sons . . . they shall be court servants in the palace," etc.

Lamentation I. begins with *aichoh* (O'how). Said Rabha in the name of R. Johanan: Why was Israel beaten with aichoh? Because they transgressed thirty-six things to which Korath applies, and the word aicho counts 36. And he said again: Why is Lamentations written according to the alphabet? Because they have transgressed what is written in the Torah, which is written with the letters of the alphabet.

"Doth she sit solitary?" said Rabha in the name of R. Johanan: The Holy One, blessed be He, said: I said [Deut. xxxiii. 28]: "And then dwelt Israel in safety, alone, the fountain of Jacob; in a land of corn and wine; also, its heavens shall drop down dew." And now solitary is their sitting. "The city that was full of people." Said Rabha again in the name of the same authority. They used to marry a minor to an adult and *vice versa*, for the purpose that they shall have many children. "Is become like a widow." Said R. Jehudah in the name of Rabh: Like a widow, but not a widow. Like a woman whose husband has departed to the cities of the countries of the sea, who intends to return. "She that was so great among the nations, the princess among the provinces." Said Rabba in the name of R. Johanan: Everywhere they came they became masters of their masters, as the rabbis taught: It happened with two men who were captured in the mountain of Carmel, and their capturer was walking behind them. Said one of the captured to his colleague: The camel which walks in front of us is blind in one eye and carries two bags, one of wine and the other of oil. And the men who lead it, one of them is an Israelite, and the other is a heathen. Said the capturer to them: Hard-necked people, whence do you know this? And they answered: From the grass which is in front of the camel that is consumed only from one side, hence from the side on which he sees he consumes, and on the other side on which he is blind he leaves it. It carries two bags of wine and oil; because drops of wine sink, and drops of oil float. And the leaders, one of them is an Israelite and the other a heathen; because an Israelite when he needs to do his necessity, usually turns aside, and the heathen does it on the way. The capturer then ran after them and found that it was as they said. He then kissed them on their heads, brought them to his house, prepared for them a great meal, danced before them, saying: " Blessed be He who chose the descendants of Abraham and gave them of his wisdom, and everywhere they go they become masters of their masters." He freed them, and they went in peace to their home.

" *Weeping, are they weeping?* " * Why two weepings? Said Rabba in the name of R. Johanan: One for the first Temple, and the other for the second Temple.

" *In the night,*" means because of what happened in a former night [Num. xiv. 1]: " And the people wept that night." And Rabba in the name of R. Johanan said: This day was the ninth of Ab, and the Holy One, blessed be He, said: " Ye have cried on this night in vain, and I shall ordain it that your genera-tions shall lament on this day forever." (See Taanith, p. 88, line 9.) According to others: In the night, because he who weeps in the night, it looks like the stars and planets are weep-ing with him. And so also with human beings. He who hears one weeping in the night, weeps with him, as it happened with Rabban Gamaliel, whose female neighbor wept because her son died, and he wept with her until the eyelids dropped. On the morrow his disciples recognized it, and they made her move away from his neighborhood. " And her tears are on her cheeks." Said Rabba in the name of R. Johanan: As a woman weeps for the husband of her youth, as it reads [Joel, i. 8]: " Lament like a woman girded with sackcloth for the be-trothed of her youth." " Her adversaries are become chiefs." Said Rabba in the name of R. Johanan: Every one who op-

---

* It is impossible to follow Leeser's translation of the Bible in the Chapter of Haggadah, as the Talmud translates literally.

presses Israel becomes a chief, as it reads [Isa. viii. 3]: "For no fatigue befalleth him that oppresseth them." And the same said again in the name of the same authority: That from the same verse is inferred that an oppressor of Israel never becomes tired.

"*Not for you, ye travellers, behold and see,*" etc. Said Rabba in the name of R. Johanan: From this may be inferred that the Scripture is particular that if one tells his troubles to his neighbor, he should add, "May it not happen to you.' "All that pass this way." Said R. Amram in the name of Rabh: They (the nations) have made of me the perpetrator of a crime to whom burning applies, as about Sodom it reads [Gen. xix. 24]: "And the Lord rained upon Sodom." And here it reads [13]: "From on high hath he sent a fire into my bones."

It reads [ibid. iv. 6]: "For greater is the iniquity of the daughter of my people than the sin of Sodom." Said Rabba in the name of R. Johanan: Jerusalem was punished with such that even Sodom was not. As concerning Sodom, it reads [Ezek. xvi. 49]: "Behold, this was the iniquity of thy sister Sodom: Pride, abundance of food . . . but the hand of the poor and needy did she not strengthen." And concerning Jerusalem, it reads [Sam. iv. 10]: "The hands of merciful women choked their own children." [Ibid. i. 15]: "The Lord hath trodden under foot all my mighty men in the midst of me." As one says to his neighbor: This coin is already out of current.

[Ibid. ii. 16]: "All thy enemies open wide their mouth against thee." (The whole portion is in alphabetical order. Here, however, the *peh* is before the *ayin*, and why? Said Rabba in the name of R. Johanan: Because of the spies, who said with their mouths (peh) what they had not seen with their eyes (ayin).

It reads [Ps. xiv. 4]: "Who eat up my people, as they eat bread (while), they do not call on the Lord." Said Rabba in the name of R. Johanan: It is so the custom of Israel's enemies that he who robs Israel and consumes his bread feels a good taste, while he does not feel any taste if he has not done so. "They do not call on the Lord," means the judges. So Rabh. And Samuel said that it means the teachers of children who are doing their work falsely. (However, what was said in the Mishna) of having and not having a share in the world to come? Who were they who have decided so? Said R. Ashi: The men of the great assembly. Said R. Jehudah in the name of Rabh:

They wanted to count one king more, and the appearance of his father's face came and spread itself before them, but they did not care. And then a fire from heaven came and charred the benches on which they were sitting, but they did not care. Then a heavenly voice said to them [Prov. xxii. 29]: "Seest thou a man that is diligent in his work? Before kings may he place himself: let him not place himself before obscure men." He has built his house during thirteen years, and my house during seven years. But not this only, but he built first my house and then his house. Should he have such luck? And still they did not care. Then came another heavenly voice [Job, xxxiv. 33]: "Should He then according to thy view send a recompense, because thou hast rejected him? Because thou must choose and not I?"

However, the interpreters of notes said that all of them have a share in the world to come, as it reads [Ps. lx. 9 and 10]: "Mine is Gilead," which means Achab, who fell at Ramoth Gilead. "Menasseh"—literally, "Ephraim the stronghold of my head," means Jeroboam, who was an outcome of the tribe Ephraim. "Judah are my chiefs," means Achitopel, who was of the tribe of Judah. "Moab my washpot," means Gechazi, who was beaten because of the business of washing. "Upon Edom will I cast my shoe," means Doeg the Edomite. "Philistia, triumph thou but over me." The angels said before the Holy One, blessed be He: Lord of the Universe, if David, who has killed the Philistines, would come before Thee and would complain to that what Doeg and Achitopel shared in the world to come, what wilst Thou say to him? And He answered: It is for me to make them friends.

It reads [Jer. viii. 5]: "A perpetual backsliding." Said Rabh: A victorious answer has the assembly of Israel given to the prophets. The prophet said to Israel: Repent ye of your sins, as you may look upon your parents who have sinned, where are they? And they answered: And your prophets who have not sinned, where are they? As it reads [Zech. i. 5]: "Your fathers, where are they? and the prophets, could they live forever?" He then said to them: But your parents have repented and confessed, as it reads [ibid., ibid. 6]: "But my words and my decrees, which I commanded my servants, the prophets, behold, they did overtake your fathers: and (then) they returned and said, Just as the Lord of hosts had purposed to do unto us, in accordance with our ways, and in accordance with our doings, so hath he dealt with us." Samuel said: The victorious answer was thus: Ten men came to the prophet and sat down. And the prophet said to them: Repent of your sins. And they answered: A slave whom his master has sold, and a woman whom her husband has divorced, has then one something to do with the other? Said the Holy One to the prophet: Go and say to them [Isa 1. 1]: "Where is your mother's bill of divorcement, wherewith I have sent her away? or who of my creditors, is it to whom I have sold you? Behold, for your iniquities were ye sold, and for your transgressions was your mother sent away?" And this is what Resh Lakish said: This is what is written [Jer. xliii. 10]: "Nebuchadnezzar my slave." It was known before Him, who said a word and the world was created, that Israel will claim so in the future, and therefore He said in advance, "Nebuchadnezzar my slave." And to whom, then, belongs the property of a slave, if not to his master?

It reads [Ezek. xx. 32-34]: "And that which cometh up into your mind shall not at all come to pass (namely), that ye say, We will be like the nations, like the families of the other countries to serve wood and stone. As I live, saith the Lord Eternal, surely, with a mighty hand, and with an outstretched arm and with fury poured out, will I rule over you." Said R. Na'hman: With such an anger may the Merciful One be angry with us and redeem us.

[Isa. xxviii. 26]: "For his God had instructed him rightly, taught him (so to do)." Said Rabba b. b. Hanna: The prophet said to Israel: Repent. And they answered: We cannot, as we are under the dominion of the evil spirit. And he said to them: Overrule him. To which they answered: This can be done only by his God.

It reads concerning Bil'am [Num. xxii. 5]: "The son of Beor." And [Num. xxiv. 3]: "Bil'am, his son Beor." Said R. Johanan: His father was a son to him what concerns prophecy. The Mishna says that Bil'am has no share in the world to come, but other nations will have. Our Mishna is in accordance with R. Jehoshua of the following Boraitha: It reads [Ps. ix. 18]: "The wicked shall return into hell, all the nations that are forgetful of God." "The wicked" means the transgressors in Israel. "All the nations," means idolaters. So R. Eliezer. Said R. Jehoshua to him: Does it read, "*And* all the nations"? It reads "All the nations." This passage is to be explained thus: The wicked shall return to hell, means all the nations that are forgetful of God. And even Bil'am gave a sign concerning himself with his saying [Num. xxiii. 10]: "May my soul die the death of the righteous, and may my last end be like his." If I will die a death of the righteous, then will be my end like his, and if not [ibid. xxiv. 14]: "I am going with my people."

It reads [Num. xxii. 7]: "And the elders of Moab and the elders of Midian departed." There is a Boraitha: Midian and Moab were always enemies with each other. This is a parable to two watch-dogs who were jealous of each other. But it happened that a wolf came to fight one of them. Said the other: If I will not help him the wolf will kill him to-day, and to-morrow he will kill me. And they therefore conjoined together and killed the wolf. Said R. Papa: This is what people say: The χρεχος and the cat (who are always enemies with each other) made a wedding meal of the fat of Bichgada.

It reads [ibid., ibid. 8]: "And the princess of Moab abode with Bil'am." And what became of the princess of Midian? As soon as they heard that Bil'am told them to stay there over night, they thought: Does then exist a father who dislikes his son? (The Holy One is the father of Israel, and will certainly not advise him to curse Israel.)

Said R. Na'hman: Impudence affects even Heaven, as [ibid., ibid. 12] reads: "Thou shalt not go with him," and finally [20]: "Go with them." Said R. Shesheth: Impudence is a kingdom without a crown, as [II Sam. iii. 39]: "And I am this day yet weak, and just anointed king; and these men, the sons of Zeruyah, are too strong for me."

R. Johanan said: Bil'am was lame on one foot and blind on one eye, as [Num. xxiv. 3]: "Whose one eye is open."

[Num. xxxiv. 16]: "Knoweth the knowledge of the Most High." Is it possible for him, who does not know the knowledge of his ass, to be aware of the knowledge of the Most High? It means he was aware of that moment when the Holy One, blessed be He, became angry. And this is what the prophet said to Israel [Michah, vi. 5]: "O my people, do but remember what Balak the king of Moab resolved, and what Bil'am the son of Beor answered him, from Shittim unto Gilgal, in order that ye may know the gracious benefits of the Lord." What do the last words mean? The Holy One, blessed be He, said to Israel: Beware of the gracious benefits

I have done to ye, that I have not become angry on that day in the time of Bil'am, for if I would have done so, there would not remain one living soul from ye. And this is what Bil'am said to Balak: What is the use of my anger when God was not angry these days in spite of what he used to do every day, as it reads [Prov. vii. 12]: "God is indignant (with the wicked) every day." How long is the duration of the anger? One second, as it reads [Ps. xxx. 6]: "For his anger is momentary." And if you wish, it is from [Isa. xxvi. 20]: "Go, my people, enter thou into thy chamber, and shut thy door behind thee: hide thyself for a little moment, until the indignation be passed away." And at what time in the day does He become angry? In the first three hours when the comb of a cock becomes white. But is the comb not white at any other time of the day? At any other time there are red points in the white, and at that time it is white without any points.

There was a Min in the neighborhood of R. Jehoshua b. Levi who caused him great trouble. And on a certain day Jehoshua tied a cock on the posts of his beds, thinking that when the comb will become white I will caution him. However, when that time arrived he slumbered. He said then: I understand from this that such a thing must not be done, even to Minnim.

There is a Boraitha in the name of R. Mair: When the sun rises and the kings put their crowns on their head, and bow themselves down to the sun, the Lord immediately becomes angry.

It reads [Num. xxiv. 21]: "And Bil'am rose up in the morning and saddled his ass." There is a Boraitha in the name of R. Simeon b. Elazar: Love abandons the custom of great men, and the same animosity does. Love abandons their custom, as we have seen by Abraham, who himself saddled his ass (because of his love to the Creator), and the same we saw by Bil'am, who himself saddled his ass, because of his animosity to Israel.

R. Jehudah said in the name of Rabh: One shall always occupy himself with the Torah and divine commandments, even not for the sake of heaven, as finally he will come to do so for its sake. This can be inferred from Balak, who offered forty-two sacrifices, and was rewarded by that what Ruth was the outcome from him. As R. Jose b. Huna said: Ruth was the daughter of Eglon, the grandson of Balak, king of Moab.

Rabha said to Rabba b. Mari: It reads [I Kings, i. 47]: " May God make the name of Solomon more famous than thy name, and make his throne greater than thy throne." Is it the usual way of saying to a king thus? And he answered: It is not to be taken literally; they meant to say " similar to thy name," as if you would not say so, how is to be understood [Judges, v. 24]: " Dwelling in the tent may she be blessed "? Who is meant by " dwelling in the tent," if not Sarah, Rebekha, Rachel, and Leah? Does, then, this passage mean that Ja'el shall be more blessed than they? Hence it is not to be taken literally; and it means " similar to them "; and the same is the case here. However, Rabba b. Mari differs with R. José b. Huni, who said that usually one becomes jealous of every one but of his son and disciple. Of his son, as we see from the above-cited verse concerning Solomon. And of his disciple [II Kings, ii. 9]: " And Elisha said, Let there be, I pray thee, a double portion of thy spirit upon me," and if you wish, from [Num. xxvii. 23]: " And he laid his *hands* upon him," though he was commanded [ibid., ibid. 18]: " Thou shalt lay thy *hand* upon him."

It reads [ibid. xxviii. 16]: " And put a word in his mouth." Said R. Johanan: From all the blessings of that wicked you may learn what he intended to say, if he would not have been prevented. He wanted to say: Israel shall not possess any houses of assembly and of learning. And what was he compelled to say [ibid., ibid. 5]: " How beautiful are thy tents, O Jacob." He intended to say that the Shekhina shall not rest upon them, and said, " Thy dwellings, O Israel."

He intended to say that their kingdom shall not be prolonged, and said, " As streams are they spread forth." He intended to say that they shall not possess olives and vineyards, and said, " As gardens by the river's side." They shall have a bad odor, and said, " As aloe-trees which the Lord had planted." They shall not have kings of nice appearance, and said, " And cedar-trees beside the waters." Their kings shall not be descendants of kings, and said, " Water runneth out of His buckets." Their kingdom shall not rule over other nations, and said, " That his seed may be moistened by abundance of waters." Their kingdom shall not be strong enough, and said, " And exalted above Agag shall be his king." And their kingdom shall not be feared, and said, " And raised on high shall be his kingdom." Said R. Abba b. Kahana: All

Bil'am's blessings were overturned to cautions, except concerning houses of assembly and of learning, as [Deut. xxiii. 6]:
"And the Lord thy God changed unto thee the curse into a
blessing, because the Lord thy God loved thee." It reads
"curse," singular, but not "curses," plural.

Samuel b. Na'hman in the name of R. Jonathan said: It
reads [Prov. xxvii. 6]: "Faithful are the wounds of a friend;
but deceptive are the kisses of an enemy." The caution that
Achiyah the Shilonite cautioned Israel is better for them than
the blessings that Bil'am has blessed them. The former cautioned Israel with a reed, as it reads [I Kings, xiv. 15]: "As
the reed is shaken in the water." As this reed stands in water-
places, the branches of it change, but its roots are many, and
even all the winds of the world when blowing upon it are not
able to uproot it, but it bends in every direction of the wind.
However, when the wind ceases it remains straight in its place.
But Bil'am, the wicked, blessed them with a cedar, which does
not stand in water-places, does not change its branches, and its
roots are few, and although no winds can affect it, however, as
soon as a south wind comes it uproots it and turns it over on
its face. Moreover, a pen for writing the Holy Scrolls, Prophets, and Hagiographa was made from a reed.

Farther on it reads [Num. xxiv. 21]: "And he looked on
the Kenites. . . . Strong is thy dwelling-place," etc.
Bil'am said to Jithro: Kenite, wast thou not with us at the
time we consulted to destroy Israel? How, then, does it come
that thou art placed now among the strongest of the world?
And this is what R. Hyya b. Aba in the name of R. Simlai said:
The following three—Bil'am, Job, and Jithro—were the ad-
visers of Pharaoh, concerning his command of throwing in the
river the children of Israel. Bil'am, who gave this advice, was
killed; Job, who kept silent, was punished with chastisement;
and Jithro, who ran away, was rewarded by having his descendants placed among the Sanhedrin, in the chamber of the
Temple, as the above-cited verse [of I Chron. ii. 55, p. 327]
reads.

"And he took up his parable, and said, Alas, who shall live
when God doth appoint this one?" [Num. xxiv. 23]. Said
R. Johanan: Woe will be to that nation which will try to prevent the redemption of Israel, when the Holy One, blessed be
He, will do it to his children. Who can prevent a lion to come
together with his lioness at the time they are both free?

It reads [ibid., ibid. 14]: "And now, behold, I am going unto my people: come, I will advise thee against what this people will do to thy people in the end of days." This people to thy people! It ought to be the reverse: "I will advise thee against what thy people will do to this people." Said R. Abah b. Kahana: It is similar to one who intends to caution himself, and does it by cautioning his neighbor. (Rashi explains this that Bil'am said as it ought to be, but the verse changed its language.) Bil'am said to Balak: The God of this nation hates incest, and they, I am aware, are fond of linen dresses. Put up shops for them, and place therein prostitutes, an old woman outside, and a young one inside, and they shall sell them linen dresses. He put up shops from Har Shelek to the place of Beth Hayishimon, and placed therein prostitutes accordingly. And when Israel were eating, drinking, and rejoicing themselves and taking a walk, the old woman said to him: Do you want to buy a linen dress for a reasonable price? But the young woman from inside offers it to him thrice cheaper, and finally she says to him: You are at home, choose what you like. And there stood a pitcher full of Ammonite wine, which was not as yet prohibited. And she treats him with a goblet of wine. And after he drinks it, it kindles him as a fire, and he makes his proposition to her. She, however, takes out her idol from her bosom, saying: Worship it. And to his answer: I am a Jew, she said: What is it, it is required only of you to uncover yourself before it. While he was not aware that so was the custom of its worship, as it reads [Hosea, ix. 10]: "But they, too, went to Baal Peor, and devoted themselves unto that shameful idol, and became abominations as those they loved."

It reads [Num. xxv. 1]: "And Israel dwelt in Shittim." Said R. Johanan: Everywhere such an expression is to be found it brings infliction. Here the people began to commit incest. [Gen. xxxvii. 1]: "And Jacob dwelt in the land of his fathers sojourning," and (2) "Joseph brought evil reports of them to his father." [Ibid. xlvii. 27]: "And Israel dwelt in the land of Egypt, in the country of Goshen," and [ibid. 29]: "And the days of Israel drew near that he was to die." [I Kings, v. 5]: "And every man dwelt in safety," and [ibid. xi. 14]: "And the Lord stirred up an adversary unto Solomon, Hadad the Edomite."

It reads [Num. xxxi. 8]: "And the kings of Midian they

slew, besides the rest of their men that were slain . . .
and Bil'am, the son of Beor, they slew with the sword." What
hath Bil'am to do there? Said R. Johanan: He went to take
the reward for the twenty-four thousand Israelites who were
killed through his advice. Said Mar Zutra b. Tubia in the
name of Rabh: This is what people say: A camel wanted to get
horns, and therefore the ears he possessed were cut off.

[Josh. xiii. 22]: "And Bil'am, the son of Beor, the soothsayer." The soothsayer! Was he not a prophet? Said R.
Johanan: At the beginning he was a prophet, but thereafter
became a soothsayer.

A Sadducaer said to R. Hanina: Are you aware of Bil'am's
age when he was slain? And he answered: There is nothing
written about it, but from [Ps. lv. 24]: "Let not the men of
blood and deceit live out half their days," I understand that he
must have been thirty-two or thirty-three when he was killed.
And the Sadducaer answered: Thou sayest well, as I saw the
record of Bil'am, and it was written therein thirty-three years
was Bil'am when he was killed by Pinehas, the murderer.

Said Mar b. Rabhina to his son: About all the commoners
who are mentioned in the Mishna, you have not to be anxious
to lecture of them to their disadvantage, except Bil'am, about
whom you may lecture as much as you like.

About Doeg is found in the Scripture this word differently,
in some places with an *aleph* and in others with double *yods*
instead of an *aleph*. Said R. Johanan: At the beginning
Heaven was worrying that perhaps this man will go out in a
wrong way, and after it happened so, it was exclaimed that this
man is lost by his bad habits.

R. Itz'hak said: It reads [Ps. lii. 3]: "What vauntest thou
thyself of wickedness, O mighty man? the kindness of God
endureth all the time." The Holy One, blessed be He, said to
Doeg: Art thou, then, not mighty in the Torah? Why art
thou fond of slandering?

And the same said again: It reads [Ps. l. 16]: "But unto
the wicked God saith, What hast thou to do to relate my statutes?" The Holy One, blessed be He, said to Doeg the
wicked: What hast thou to relate my statutes when thou
reachest the portion of murderers and the portion of slan-
derer (which thou hast done both)? How wouldst thou explain them?

"Why bearest thou my covenant upon thy mouth?"

[ibid.].   Said R Ami: Infer from this that the study of Doeg was only with his mouth, but not with his heart.

R. Itz'hak said: It reads [Job, xx. 15]: "The wealth which he hath swallowed, will he have to vomit up again: God will drive it out of his belly.' David said before the Holy One, blessed be He: Let Doeg die. And he was answered: Thou must wait until he will have forgotten the Torah, which he has swallowed. And he prayed again: Let God drive it out of his belly.

R. Itz'hak said again: It was said before David: Let Doeg have a share in the world to come. And he answered [Ps. lii. 7]: "Therefore God will also destroy thee forever." Let there at least a Halakha be mentioned in his name in the college. And he answered: "Pluck thee out of his tent." Let his descendants be rabbis. "And root thee out of the land of life."

The same said again: It reads [Isa. xxxiii. 18]: "Where is he who wrote down? where is he that weighed? where is he that counted the towers?" (All this passage is concerning Doeg.) Where is he who counted the letters of the Torah? Where is he who weighs the lenient and rigorous things mentioned therein? Where is he who counted three hundred decided Halakhas (about Levitical cleanness) concerning a turret flying in the air? Said R. Ami: Four hundred questions had Doeg and Achitophel asked concerning turrets flying in the air, and not one of them could be decided. Said Rabha: Is it also a great thing to ask questions?

In the years of R. Jehudah all their studies were confined to the Section of Damages, etc. (See Taanith, p. 71, from line 12 to the end of that chapter.) However, here the answer is: The Holy One, blessed be He, wants the heart of one, but not his mouth, as it reads [I Sam. xvi. 7]: "But the Lord looketh on the heart." Said R. Ami: Doeg was not dead before he had forgotten all his studies, as it reads [Prov. v. 23]: "He will indeed die for want of correction; and through the abundance of his folly will he sink into error." Said R. Johanan: Three angels of destruction attended to Doeg: one who had made him forget his study, and one who burned his soul, and the third who scattered his ashes in prayer and learning houses.

The same said again: Doeg and Achitophel did not see each other, as Doeg was in the days of Saul and Achitophel in the days of David.

And he said again: Both Doeg and Achitophel have not lived

half of their days. So also we have learned in the following Boraitha: All the years of Doeg were only thirty-four, and those of Achitophel thirty-three. R. Jehudah said in the name of Rabh: One shall not bring himself into temptation, as David, king of Israel, placed himself in the power of a trial and stumbled. He said before Him: Lord of the Universe, why is it said the God of Abraham, Isaac, and Jacob, and not the God of David? And he was answered: Because they were tried by Me, and thou wast not. And he said before Him: Lord of the Universe, try me, as it reads [Ps. xxvi. 2]: "Try me, O Lord, and prove me." And he was answered: You will be tried, and, furthermore, I will do with thee a thing which I have not done with the patriarchs, as them I have not informed that I will try, and thee I inform that thou wilt be tried with a case of adultery. And this is what it reads [II Sam. xi. 2]: "And it happened at evening tide that David arose," etc. Said R. Jehudah: He did in the daytime what is usually done at night. And he overlooked a Halakha: There is a small member in the body of a man which is always hungry if one is trying to satisfy it, and is always satisfied if one starves it. "And he walked upon the roof of the king's house; and he saw from the roof a woman bathing herself, and the woman was of a very beautiful appearance." Bath Sheba used to wash her head under a bee-hive. The Satan then appeared before David as a bird, and he shot an arrow at it, and the arrow fell on the bee-hive and broke it, so that Bath Sheba was visible to David. And immediately [ibid., ibid. 3 and 4]: "David sent and inquired after the woman; and some one said, Behold, this is the Bath Sheba, the daughter of Eliam, the wife of Uriyah the Hittite. And David sent messengers and took her; and she came in unto him, and he lay with her, and she had just purified herself from her uncleanness: and she returned unto her house." And this is what it reads [Ps. xvii. 3]: "Thou hast proved my heart; thou hast thought of me in the night; thou hast refined me—thou couldst find nothing; my *zamuthi* (purpose) doth not pass beyond (the words of) my mouth," which means it would be better for me that a *zmama* (a bit) should have been put in my mouth than to have prayed: Try me.

Rabha lectured [Ps. li. 6]: "To thee, thee only, have I sinned, and what is evil in thy eyes have I done; in order that thou mightest be righteous when thou speakest, be justified when thou judgest." David said before the Holy One, blessed be He: It is known before Thee, that if I would want to overrule my impulse (concerning Bath Sheba) I would be able to do so. But I didn't, so people shall not say that the slave has conquered his master. He lectured again: It reads [Ps. xi. 1]: "In the Lord have I put my trust; how can ye say to my soul, Flee to your mountain as a bird?" David said before the Holy One, blessed be He: Lord of the Universe, forgive me this sin for the purpose that people shall not say that your mountain was lost through a bird (as said above that the Satan appeared to David as a bird). He lectured again: It is written [ibid. xxxviii. 18]: "For I am prepared for (my) downfall, and my pain is continually before me." From the six days of creation Bath Sheba was destined for David; however, she came to him only by infliction. And so also taught the disciples of R. Ishmael: Bath Sheba, the daughter of Eliam, was destined to David, but he enjoyed her as an unripe fruit (did not wait until she was his legitimate wife). (Here is repeated from Middle Gate, p. 138, from "Rabha lectured" until "Rabha said.")

R. Jehudah said in the name of Rabh: David was about to worship idols, as it reads [II Sam. xv. 32]: "When David was come to the head where he used to bow himself to God." By "head" is meant an idol, as it is to be found in Daniel that the head of the image was of gold. "Behold, Chushai, the Arkite, came to meet him with his coat rent, and earth upon his head." And he said to him: Is it proper that a king like thyself shall be an idolater? And he answered: Is it proper that a king like myself should be slain by his son? It is better for me to worship an idol privately than that the Holy Name should be profaned publicly. Said Chushai to him: Why, then, hast thou married a handsome woman? And to his answer: The Merciful One has allowed to marry such. Rejoined Cushai: Why have you not given your attention to the interpretation founded on the facts of local junction of texts, as after "A woman of handsome form is near" [Deut. xxi. 11], the 18th verse, which speaks of "A stubborn son"?

R. Dusthai, of the city of Biri, lectured: David's following prayer is similar to a peddler who wanted to sell out his stock little by little. He said before the Holy One, blessed be He [Ps. xix. 13-15]: "Lord of the Universe, who can guard against errors?" And he was answered: They will be forgiven to you.

" From secrets (faults) do thou cleanse me," and the same answer was given. " Also from presumptuous sins withhold thy
servants," and he was also answered that it will be forgiven.
" Let them not have dominion over me "—the rabbis shall not
talk about me, and he was also promised that so it will be.
" Then shall I be blameless "—my sins shall not be written.
And he was answered: This is impossible as the *Jod* which I
took away from the name of Sarai complained before me several years, until Joshua came and I added it to his name, as it
reads [Deut. xiii. 16]: " And Moses called Hoshea, the son of
Nun, Joshua." How then can I omit a whole portion of the
Torah? " Clear from any great transgression "—He said before Him: Lord of the Universe, forgive me the whole sin.
And he was answered: It is revealed before Me what Solomon,
thy son, will say by his wisdom in the future [Prov. vi. 27-30]:
" Can a man gather up fire in his lap, and shall his clothes not
be burnt? Can a man walk along hot coals, and shall his feet
not be burnt?" So it is with him that goeth in to his neighbor's
wife: no one that toucheth her shall remain unpunished. He
then exclaimed: If so, I am lost. And he was answered: Accept chastisements upon thyself. And he did so.

Said R. Jehudah in the name of Rabh: Six months was
David afflicted with leprosy; the Shekhina left him, and the
Sanhedrin separated themselves from him. " Inflicted with
leprosy " [Ps. li. 9]: " Cleanse me from sin with hyssop," etc.
" The Shekhina left him " [ibid., ibid. 14]: " Restore unto me
the gladness of thy salvation." " The Sanhedrin separated
themselves " [ibid. cxix. 79]: " Let those that fear thee return
unto me and those that know thy testimonies." And whence
do we know that all this lasted full six months? From [I Kings,
ii. 11]: " And the days that David reigned over Israel were
forty years; in Hebron he reigned seven years, and in Jerusalem
he reigned thirty and three years. And in [II Sam. v. 5]: " In
Hebron he reigned over Judah seven years and six months, and
in Jerusalem he reigned thirty-three years over all Israel and
Judah." Hence we see that the six months more which are
counted in II Samuel are not counted in I Kings, and this was
because the six months in which he was inflicted with leprosy
were not counted. (Here is repeated from Minor Festivals, p. 13,
line 6: Said R. Jehudah in the name of Rabh—to the end of the
par. See there.) Now about Gechazi. It reads [II Kings, viii.
7]: " And Elisha came to Damascus." What did he do there?

Said R. Johanan: He went to make Gechazi repent of his sins. He tried to do so, but he did not want, saying: I have a tradition from thee, that he who sins and causes others to sin, Heaven gives no opportunity to him to repent. But what has he done to cause others to sin? According to some he put a magnet over the casts made by Jeroboam, and they were suspended in the air. And according to others, he engraved a holy name on its mouth, and it heralded: " I am the God," etc. And according to still others, he drove away disciples from Elisha's college, as it reads [ibid. vi. 1]: " Behold now the place where we dwell before thee is too narrow for us." (And this was after the departure of Gechazi, hence it was not narrow when he was there, because he drove away many disciples.)

The rabbis taught: Exclusion shall always be with the left hand, and inclusion with the right hand, *i.e.*, if one is compelled to repudiate some one, he shall do it easy as with his left hand, and at the same time try to admit him again with his right hand. And not as Elisha has done with Gechazi, whom he rejected with both hands, as it reads [II Kings, v. 23, 27]: " And Naaman said, Give thy assent, take two talents. And he urged him. . . . Whence comest thou, Gechazi?" And he said, Thy servant went not hither or thither. And he said unto him, " My mind was not gone when the man turned around from his chariot to meet thee. Is it time to take money, and to take garments, and oliveyards, and vineyards, and sheep, and oxen, and men-servants, and maid-servants? " Hath then Gechazi taken all this? He took only silver and garments. Said R. Itz'hak: At that time Elisha was occupied with the study of the chapter of eight reptiles (the 14th chap. of Tract Sabbath). Naaman, the captain of the king of Syria, was inflicted with leprosy, and his servant girl, who was captured from Israel, told him that if he will go to Elisha he will be cured. And when he came and was told to dip himself in the Jordan, he said: They ridicule me. But the men with him induced him to do so. He followed their advice and he was cured. And he brought all what he had with him to Elisha, but he did not want to accept it from him. Gechazi, however, departed from Elisha, took what he took, and hid it,* and when he came before Elisha again he saw that the leprosy was flying over his head. Then he said

---

* See Samuel Eigdus Marsho, who tries to explain why all this is repeated here after it is narrated in the Bible. However, he did not succeed.

to him: Has then the time come that you should be rewarded for my studying of the chapter of eight reptiles, as you took from him the value of the eight things mentioned in this passage? And therefore he went out of his presence a leper (as white) as snow. It reads [ibid. vii. 3]: "And there were four leprous men at the entrance of the gate." Said R. Johanan: These were Gechazi and his three sons. There is a Boraitha: The animal impulses of man, a child and a woman, should always be repulsed with the left hand, and at the same time embraced with the right hand. The rabbis taught: Thrice Elisha became sick, etc. (See Middle Gate, p. 229, which is repeated here with the change that the paragraph "until the time of Abraham there was no mark of age," in line 15, reads here after the paragraph, "The rabbis taught," in line 21. See there.)

MISHNA II.: The generation of the flood have no share in the world to come, and are also not judged, as it reads [Gen. vi. 3]: "Lau jodun ruchiy bheodom," literally "My spirit shall not judge in man"—no judgment and no spirit. The generation of dispersion (cf. to ibid., chap. 11) have also no share in the world to come, as it reads [ibid. 8]: "And the Lord scattered them abroad"; and it reads also (9): "From there the Lord scattered them"—"scattered them" in this world, and "from there the Lord scattered them"—in the world to come. The men of Sodom have also no share in the world to come, as it reads [ibid., ibid. 13]: "For the men of Sodom were wicked, and sinners before the Lord exceedingly"—"wicked" in this world, and "sinners" in the world to come. However, they are standing for judgment. R. Nehemiah said: Both of the following are not standing for judgment, as it reads [Ps. i. 5]: "Therefore shall the wicked not be able to stand in the judgment"—the generation of the flood. And "sinners in the congregation of the upright"—men of Sodom. But he was told by the sages: The latter do not stand up among the congregation of the upright, but they stand among the congregation of the wicked. The spies have no share in the world to come, as it reads [Num. xiv. 37]: "Died by the plague before the Lord." "Died"—in this world, "plague"—in the world to come. The generation of the desert has no share in the world to come, as it reads [ibid., ibid. 35]: "In this wilderness shall they be spent"—in this world, and "therein shall they die"—in the world to come. So R. Aqiba. R. Eliezer, however, maintains: To them is written [Ps. l. 5] : " Gather together unto me my pious servants, who make a covenant with me by sacrifice." The congregation of Korah will not be restored at the time of resurrection, as it reads [Num. xvi. 33] : " And the earth closed over them "—in this world, and " they disappeared from the midst of the congregation "—in the world to come. So R. Aqiba. R. Eliezer, however, maintains: To them it reads [I Sam. ii. 6] : " The Lord killeth and maketh alive: he bringeth down to the grave, and bringeth up."

GEMARA: The rabbis taught: The generation of the flood has no share in the world to come, as it reads [Gen. vii. 23] : " And it swept off every living substance "—in this world, " and they were swept from the earth "—in the world to come. So R. Aqiba. R. Jehudah b. Bathyra said: They will neither be restored nor judged, as it reads in the cited verse of the Mishna: " No judgment and no spirit." R. Menahem b. Jose said: Even at the time the Holy One, blessed be He, will return the souls to the corpses, the souls of the generation in question will still be judged hard in the Gehenim, as it reads [Isa. xxxiii. 11] : " Ye shall be pregnant with hay, (and) ye shall bring forth stubble: your breath is a fire, which shall devour you."

The rabbis taught: The generation of the flood were exalted only because of the overflowing goodness, the Holy One, blessed be He, overflooded them, as concerning them it reads [Job, xxi. 9-14] : " Their houses are at peace without any dread, and no rod of God (cometh) over them. The bull of each one gendereth and disappointeth not: the cow of each one calveth, and casteth not her young. They send forth their little ones like a flock, and their children skip about (with joy). They sing to the timbrel and harp, and rejoice at the sound of the pipe. They wear out their days in happiness." The verse continues, and " in a moment they go down to the nether world." This was caused by what they said, " Depart from us and the knowledge of thy ways we desire not," etc. They said: We need the Almighty only for the drops of rain with which He supplies us; however, we possess springs and rivers, of which we can make use. Said the Lord: With the same good I have overflooded them they anger me, I will therefore punish them with the same, I will bring a flood of water, etc.

R. Jose said: The generation of the flood were exalted because the sclerotic coat of the eye which resembles water, as it reads [ibid., ibid. 2] : " And they took themselves wives of all whom they chose," and therefore they were punished with water, which resembles the eye, as [ibid. vii. 11] : " On the same day, were all the fountains of the great deep broken up, and the windows of heaven were opened."

R. Johanan said: The generation in question sinned with the word *rabbha*. [ibid. vi. 5] : " God saw that *rabbha* the wickedness of men, and they were punished with the same word [ibid. vii. 11] : " All the fountains of the deep *rabbha*." And he said again: Three of the hot springs of that time remained forever, and they are, of Gedda, of Tiberius and the great springs of Biram.

It reads [ibid. vi. 12] : " For all flesh has corrupted his way upon the earth." Said R. Johanan: Infer from this that cattle, beast and men had intercourse with each other. Said R. Aba b. Kahana: All of them returned to their usual manner of propagation, except the bird Thushl'mi.*

It reads [ibid., ibid. 13] : " The end of all the flesh is come before me." Said. R. Johanan: Come and see how severe is the force of robbery, as the generation of the flood had committed all kinds of crimes and their evil decree was not sealed until they stretched out their hand to robbery, as it reads (13) " for all the earth is filled with violence through them, and I will destroy them with the earth," and also [Ezek. vii. 11] : " The violence is grown up into the staff of wickedness: nothing is left of them, and nothing of their multitude and nothing of theirs; and there shall be no lamenting for them." Said R. Elazar: Infer from this passage that the violence itself has grown up as a cane and placed itself before the Lord, saying: Lord of the Universe; nothing shall be left of them, etc.

The disciples of R. Ismael taught: In that evil decree Noah was included, but found favor in the eyes of the Lord, as it reads [Gen. vi. 7 and 8] : " For it repenteth me that I have made them. But Noah found grace in the eyes of the Lord."

It reads [ibid., ibid. 6] : " And it repenteth the Lord that he had made man on the earth." When R. Dime came from Palestine, he said: (The Lord said) I have not done well that I prepared for them graves in the earth. (As it might be that if I would leave them alive, they would repent.) And this is inferred from the analogy of the expression " and it repented,"

---

* It is a kind of bird unknown to the commentators, as well as to us.

which is to be found here and in [Ex. xxxii. 14]: "And the Lord bethought himself."

It reads [Gen. vi. 9]: "Noah was a just, perfect man in his generation;" according to R. Johanan in his generation, but not in others who were more righteous. And according to Resh Lakish: In his generation, which was wicked, so much the more in other generations. Said R. Hanina: As a parable to that of R. Johanan, may be, *e.g.*, if one places a barrel of wine among barrels of vinegar. In that place, the good smell of wine is marked, which would not be the case if placed among other barrels of wine. And a parable to that of Resh Lakish, said R. Oshia, may be, *e.g.*, a glass of perfume which was placed in a filthy place, and the smelling was marked, so much the more would it be marked if placed among spices.

It reads further on [Gen. vii. 23]: "And it swept off," etc. If man sinned, what were the sins of the animals? It was taught in the name of R. Jehoshua b. Kar'ha: It is similar to one who made a canopy for his son, and prepared all kinds of delicacies for the wedding-meal, but his son dies before the wedding and he destroys all what he prepared, saying: All this was done only because of my son; now, as he is dead, to what purpose do I need the canopy and all what I prepared? So the Holy One, blessed be He, said: To what purpose have I created cattle and beast, only for the sake of man; now, when man has sinned and is to be destroyed, to what purpose do I need all other creatures? [Gen. vi. 22]: "All that were on dry land died," but not the fishes in the sea.

R. Jose of Tcsarius lectured: It reads [Job, xxiv. 18]: "Swift are such men (to flee) on the face of the water; accursed is their field on the land." Infer from this that Noah, the upright, warned them, saying: Repent and pray to God, for if not He will bring the flood upon you and will make your corpses swim upon the water like bags filled with air; and not only this, but ye will be accursed to future generations (*i.e.*, one will curse this enemy that his lot shall be like yours). And they answered: Let him do so, who prevents him? And he answered: There is one pigeon among ye which must be taken away from this evil (*i.e.*, Methushelech, the upright, who must depart, not to see the evil). And they answered: If it is so, then we will continue on our way and will not hide ourselves in the vineyards.

Rabha lectured: It reads [Job, xii. 5]: "To the unfortunate there is given contempt—according to the thoughts of him that is at ease—prepared (also) for those whose foot slippeth." Infer from this that Noah, the upright, warned them in hard words. But they scorned him, saying: Thou old man, why buildest thou the ark? And to his answer: The Lord will bring the flood, they said: A flood of what? If a flood of fire, then we have an animal by the name of Elita which extinguishes fire. And if of water, we have iron plates with which we can pave the ground (to prevent water coming up). And if of the sky, we have a thing named Akeb or Ikosh, which can prevent it. And Noah answered: He will bring you (the flood) from under your heels, as the just cited verse reads, " prepared for those whose foot slippeth."

Said R. Hisda: With their hot blood have they sinned, and they were punished with hot water, and it is inferred from an analogy of the expression [Gen. viii. 3]: " And the water was appeased," and [Esther, vii. 10]: " And the fury of the king was appeased."

It reads [Gen. vii. 10]: " And it came to pass after the seven days that the waters of the flood were upon the earth." Seven days of what? Said Rabh: The seven days' mourning for Methushelech. From this you may learn that the lamentation of uprights delays the chastisement to come. Another explanation: The Lord appointed for them at first a long time for repenting, and thereafter a short time. And still another explanation: The seven days in which was given them a taste of the world to come, for the purpose that they shall know what good they are losing.

[Ibid., ibid. 2]: " Of every clean heart thou shalt take to thee seven pair of each, the male and his female." Have these animals wives? Said Samuel b. Na'hman in the name of R. Jonathan: It means from those with whom a crime was not committed. And whence did he know this? Said R. Hisda: He passed them by the ark, and those who were accepted by the ark he was certain that no crime was committed, and those who were not, he was certain that a crime was committed. R. Abuhu said: It means from those animals which came by themselves.

[Ibid. vi. 14]: " An ark of gopherwood." What is meant by gopher? R. Adda, in the name of the school of Shila, said: It means an oak tree, and according to others, a cedar tree.

[Ibid., ibid. 16]: " A window shalt thou make." Said R.

Johanan: The Holy One, blessed be He, said to Noah: Put there diamonds and pearls, that they shall give you light as the middle of the day.

"With lower second and third stories shalt thou make it." The lower for manure, the second for animals and the third for man.

[Ibid. viii. 7] : " He sent forth a raven." Said Resh Lakish: A victorious answer has the raven given Noah: Thy master hates me and thou doest the same. Thy master hates, as from the clean he took seven and from the unclean only two, and thou hatest me as thou sends a creature of which you have only two, while from others you have seven. If I would be killed by heat or by cold would not the world be lacking my creation?

[Ibid., ibid. 8] : " He then sent forth a dove *from him.*" Said R. Jeremiah: Infer from this that clean fowls may be kept in the residence of uprights.

[Ibid., ibid. 11] : " And the dove came in to him at the time of evening." Said R. Elazar: The dove said before the Holy One, blessed be He: Lord of the Universe, may my food be bitter like an olive, but I shall receive it from thy hand rather than that it should be sweet like honey, and I shall receive from beings of blood and flesh.

" Plucked off *tereph.*" And whence do we know that tereph means food? From [Prov. xxx. 8] : " Let me eat the bread," in which the same term *tereph* is used.

It reads farther on [Gen. viii. 19] : " After their families." Infer from this that each family was placed separate. R. Hana b. Bisna said: Eliezar, the servant of Abraham, questioned Shem the Great: As all the animals were placed separately, where was your family placed? And he answered: We had great trouble in the ark to feed all the animals. The creature whose habit it is to eat in the daytime we had to feed in the day, and those whose habit it is to eat in the night, we have to feed in the night. A chameleon, my father did not know what its food is. It happened one day that he cut a pomegranate and a worm fell out of it, and the above consumed it, and from that time prepared its food from the worms found in rotten apples. The lion was fed by his fever, as Rabh said: No less than six and no more than twelve months one can live in fever without taking any food. The Aurshina my father found that it slept in a corner of the ark; and to his question: Dost thou need any food, it answered: I saw thou art very busy, and I thought I would not trouble thee. And he blessed her that it shall never die, and this is what it reads [Job, xxix. 18]: "As the chaul (aurshina) shall I have many days."

R. Hana b. Levai said: Shem the Great questioned Eliezar, the servant of Abraham: When the kings of the West and East came to fight you, what have you done? And he answered: The Holy One, blessed be He, took Abraham, sat him down to His right, and we, however, took earth, threw it, and they became swords. Straw and they became arrows, as it reads [Ps. cx. 1]: "Sit thou at my right hand, until I place thy enemies a stool for thy feet." And also [Isa. xli. 2]: "Who waketh up from the east the man whom righteousness met in his steps? He giveth up nations before him, and maketh him rule over kings. That his sword may render them as the dust, as driven stubble his bow." (Here is repeated from Taanith, p. 56, the legend of Nahum of Gim-zu.)

"*The generation of dispersion has no share,*" etc. What had they done? The school of R. Shila said: They wanted to build a tower to ascend to the sky and split it with hatchets, so that the contained water shall pour down. This legend was ridiculed in the West. If they intended to ascend to the sky they ought to have built the tower on a mountain, and not in a valley. Therefore, said R. Jeremiah b. Elazar: They were divided into three parties. The first party said: Let us go there to dwell; the second: Let us go there and worship their idols, and the third: Let us go there to fight. The party that said, Let us go there to dwell, were scattered all over the world, and the party that said, Let us go there and fight, became demons, devils, etc. And the party that said, Let us go there and worship their idols, were scattered to Babylon, to which it reads [Gen. xi. 9]: "Therefore is the name Babel, because the Lord did there confound the language."

Said R. Johanan: From the tower, a third of it was burned, the second was swallowed and a third is still in existence.

"*Men of Sodom,*" etc. The rabbis taught: Men of Sodom have no share in the world to come, as the verse cited in the Mishna. And in addition to it, said R. Jehudah: They were wicked with their bodies and sinners with their money. With their bodies, as it reads [ibid. xxxix. 9]: "How then can I do this great evil and sin against God?" and sinners with their money, as it reads [Deut. xv. 9]: "It will be sin in thee." Be-

fore the Lord means blasphemy. "Exceedingly"—all their
sins were intentionally. In a Boraitha it was taught the reverse: wicked with their money, as it reads [ibid., ibid. 9] "And
thy eye be thus evil against thy needy brother," and sinners with
their bodies [Gen. xxxix. 9]: "And sin against God." "Before the Lord" means blasphemy, and "Exceedingly" means
bloodshed, as it reads [II Kings, xxi. 16]: "And also innocent
blood did Menasseh shed exceedingly." The rabbis taught:
The men of Sodom were exalted because of the overflowing
goodness of the Lord. Concerning them it reads [Job, xxviii.
58]: "The earth out of which cometh forth bread, is under its
surface turned up as it were with fire. Her stones are the
place whence the sapphire cometh; and golden dust is also
there. On the path which no bird of prey knoweth, and which
the vulture's eye hath not surveyed," etc. And they said: As
our land supplies us with sufficient bread, why shall we leave
in travellers who come only to lessen our money? Let our
land forget that there is a foot of stranger, as it reads [ibid.,
ibid. 4].*

He said again: It reads [Ps. lxii. 2]: "How long will ye
devise mischief against a man? Will ye all assault him mur-
derously, as though he were a falling wall, a tottering fence?"
Infer from this that they used to place a wealthy man under
a tottering wall and pushed the wall over him, and robbed him
of his money.

He said again: It reads [Job, xxiv. 16]: "They break into
houses in the dark, in the daytime they lock themselves in: they
know not the light." Infer from this that when they saw a
wealthy man they used to deposit with him balsam, which usually the depositories placed in their treasure box, and in the
night they scent the balsam and rob him.†

R. Jose lectured the same in Ciporias. And the night after
that three hundred burglaries were committed through the
smell of balsam, the town-men troubled him, saying: "You
have shown a way to the thief." And he answered them: How
could I know that all of you are thieves?

The following was enacted in Sodom. He who possessed
one ox had to pasture all the cattle of the city one day, but he
who possessed none at all had to pasture them two days. There

---

* The translation does not correspond.

† Here is also referred to some passages from the Scripture, but which have no
direct bearing, and are therefore omitted.

was an orphan, the son of a widow, to whom they gave their oxen to pasture, and he killed them, saying: Who has one ox shall take one skin, and he who has none at all shall take two skins. And to the question: What is this? he said to them: The final trial must be at the beginning of it. You enacted that he who has one ox shall pasture them one day, and he who has none at all shall pasture them two days. The same is the case with the skins.

He who passed the river on a boat had to pay one zuz. And he who passed the river on foot had to pay two. If one had a row of bricks, every one of them came and took one, saying: I am not causing you any damage by taking one. The same they used to do when one scattered garlic or onions to dry. There were four judges in Sodom. Every one of them had a name which meant false, lie, etc. If it happened that one struck a woman and she miscarried, they used to decide that the woman should be given to the striker, and he shall return her when she will be pregnant again. If it happened that one cut off the ear of his neighbor's ass, they used to decide that the ass should be delivered to the striker, till it shall be cured. If one wounds his neighbor, they decided that the striker shall be paid for bleeding him. He who passed the river on a bridge had to pay four zuz. And he who passed it with one foot had to pay eight zuz. It happened once that a washer came there and they required of him four zuz. And to his claim that he had passed the water on foot, they required eight. And because he didn't pay they wounded him, and when he came to the judge, he decided that he shall pay for bleeding and eight zuz for passing the water.

Eliezar, the servant of Abraham, happened to be there, and was wounded, and when he came to the judge to complain he said: "You must pay for bleeding." And he took a stone and wounded the judge, saying: The payment for bleeding which you owe to me pay them, and my money shall remain with me. They made a condition that he who invites one to a wedding shall be stripped of his garments. There was a wedding at the same time Eliezar happened to be in the city, and none of them wanted to sell him any bread for a meal. He then went to the wedding and took a place at the very end of the table. And when he was asked who had invited him, he said to him who was sitting near by, Thou hast invited me. And for fear that they will believe that he has invited him and that he will be stripped of his garment, he hurried to take his mantle and run away. And so he did to the remainder, and they all ran away, and he ate the whole meal. They had a bed for strangers. If he was too long for this bed they made him shorter, and if too short they stretched him. When Eliezar was there they told him to sleep in the bed, to which he answered: Since my mother is dead I vowed not to sleep in a bed. When a poor man happened to be there every one used to give him a dinar, on which his name was engraved, but they did not sell him any bread until he died. And then each one took his dinar back. There was a girl who used to supply a poor man with bread, which she used to hide in a pitcher while going for water. And when this was found out they smeared her body with honey, put her on the roof of the surrounding wall, and bees came and killed her, and this is what it reads [Gen. xviii.. 20]: "Because the sin against Sodom and Gomorrah is great," etc.

"*Spies . . . and the congregation of Korah*," etc. The rabbis taught: The congregation of Korah has no share in the world to come, as it reads: "And the earth covered them"— in this world, and "they disappeared from the midst of the congregation"—in the world to come. So R. Aqiba. R. Jehudah b. Bathyra said: They are as a lost thing for which the loser inquires, as it reads [Ps. cxix. 176]: "I have gone erringly astray, like a lost sheep; seek thy servant, for thy commandments have I not forgotten." It reads [Num. xvi. 1]: "And Korah took (*vayikah*)." Said Resh Lakish: He purchased for himself a very bad undertaking. "Korah" means, he has made Israel bald-headed. "Ben Yizhar," he who made the world hot as in the middle of the day. "Ben Kehath," he who made blunt the teeth of his parents. "Ben Levi," he who became a companion to the Gehenna. But why is not also written "ben Jacob"? Said R. Samuel b. Itz'hak: Jacob prayed [Gen. xlix. 6]: "Unto their secret shall my soul not come," means the spies. "Unto their assembly my glory shall not be united," means the congregation of Korah. Rabh said: "The wife of On ben Peleth" saved him from being among the congregation of Korah. She said to him: What is the difference to you? If Moses will be master, you are only a disciple, and the same will be for you if Korah will be the master. And to his answer: What shall I do, I was with them in consultation, and swore to take part with them? she said: I know that the whole congregation is holy, as it reads [Num. xvi. 3]:

" For the whole of the congregation are all of them holy; " remain in your house and I will save you.   She made him drink
wine to intoxication, and she made him sleepy in the house,
and she herself sat outside at the entrance of the house, uncovered her head and dishevelled her hair.   And every one
coming to his house, to call upon On, when he saw the uncovered head of the woman, he returned.   She, however, continued to sit there, till the congregation was swallowed.   On
the other hand, the wife of Korah said to him: See what Moses
did.   He proclaimed himself as a king, his brother he made
high-priest, the sons of his brother for adjuncts of the high-
priests.   Heave-offering he commanded to give to the priests,
and even from tithes, which are for the Levites, he commands to
give again one-tenth to the priest.   And not only this, he made
of you fools by commanding all the Levites to shave off all their
hair.   And to his answer: He himself also did so, she said: As all
the glory belongs to him, he does not care, etc. And this is what
it reads [Prov. xiv. 1]: " The wise among women buildeth her
house "—the wife of On ben Peleth.   But the foolish pulleth it
down with her own hands—the wife of Korah.

It reads farther on [Num. xvi. 2]: " So that they rose up
before Moses, with certain men of the children of Israel, in
number two hundred and fifty "—the distinguished of the congregation.   " Called to the assembly "—who were able through
their wisdom to intercalate months and establish leap years.
" Men of renown " —whose name was renowned through all
the world.   " And Moses heard it, and fell upon his face."
What had he heard?   Said Samuel b. Na'hman in the name of
R. Jonathan: That they suspect him of adultery, as it reads
[Ps. cvi. 16]: " Moreover, they envied Moses."

" And Moses went to Dathan and Abiram." Said Resh
Lakish: Infer from this that one must do all that he can not
to strengthen a quarrel (as he himself who was a king went to
Dathan and Abiram [Num. xvi. 25]).   As Rabh said: He who
strengthens a quarrel transgresses a negative commandment.
[Ibid. xvii. 5]: " That he become not as Korah and as his company."   R. Ashi said: Such is worthy to be punished with
leprosy, as here it reads " by the hand of Moses," and [Ex. iv.
6]: " And he put his hand into his bosom, and when he took it
out, behold, his hand was leprous, white as snow."

R. Jose said: He who fights against the kingdom of David
deserves to be bitten by a snake, as [I Kings, i. 9]: " By the

stone Zoheleth," and [Deut. xxxii. 24]: "With the poison of
Zochle aphar (serpents)."

R. Hisda said: He who quarrels with his master is considered as if he would quarrel with the Shekhina, as it reads [Num.
xxvi. 9]: "At the time they quarrelled against the Lord." R.
Hama b. Hanina said: He who has a controversy with his master is considered as if he would do so against the Shekhina, as
it reads [ibid. xx. 13]: "These are the waters of Meribah,
where the children of Israel quarrelled with the Lord." And
R. Hanina b. Papa said: He who murmurs against his master
is considered as if he would do so against the Shekhina, as it
reads [Ex. xvi. 8]: "Not against us are your murmurings, but
against the Lord." And R. Abuhu said: Even one whose
thoughts are against his master is considered as if his thoughts
would be against the Shekhina, as it reads [Num. xxi. 5]:
"And the people spoke against God and against Moses."

It reads [Eccl. v. 12]: "Riches reserved for their owner
to his own hurt." Said Resh Lakish: This means the riches
of Korah. It reads [Deut. xi. 6]: "And all . . . on their
feet." * Said R. Elazar: It means the money which makes
one stand on his feet. And R. Levi said: The keys of Korah's
treasure were of such a weight that three hundred white mules
had to carry them. R. Hama b. Hanina said: Three treasures
were hidden by Joseph in Egypt, one was found by Korah, and
the second by Antoninus ben Arsirus, and the third is still hidden for the upright in the future. R. Johanan said: Korah
was not from those who were swallowed and not from those
who were burned. Not those from who were swallowed, as
[Num. xvi. 32]: "And all the men that appertained unto
Korah," but not Korah himself. And not from the burned.
[Ibid. xxvi. 10]: "The fire devoured the two hundred and fifty
men, but not Korah." In a Boraitha, however, it is stated that
Korah was both burned and swallowed. "Swallowed," as in
the just-cited verse, "And swallowed them up together with
Korah," and "burned," as [ibid. xvi. 35]: "And there came
out a fire . . . and consumed two hundred and fifty," and
Korah was among them.

Rabha said: It reads [Habakkuk, iii. 11]: "At the light of
thy arrows they walked along." Infer from this that the sun
and the moon ascended to Zebul (one of the seven heavens

---

* Leeser's translation does not correspond.

mentioned elsewhere), and said: Lord of the Universe, if thou
wilst take revenge for Ben Amram we will go out to our work,
and if not, we will not. And they were standing until he shot
arrows at them, saying, When my own glory is affected (by
that people are worshipping ye) ye did not protest; and for the
honor of a being of blood and flesh ye do.

Rabha lectured [Num. xvi. 30]: " But if the Lord do create
a new thing, and the earth open her mouth." Moses said before the Holy One, blessed be He: If such is already created,
well and good, but if not, the Lord shall create. Shall create!
Does it not read [Eccl. i. 9]: " And there is nothing new under
the sun "? to bring the opening of the Gehenna near to them.

It reads [Num. xxvi. 11]: " But the sons of Korah did not
die." In the name of Rabbi it was taught: A place was prepared for them in Gehenna, in which they sat and sung a song.
(Here is repeated Rabba b. b. Hana's legend from Last Gate,
p. 206, concerning the children of Korah.)

" The generation of the desert has no share," etc. The rabbis
taught (in addition to the verse cited in the Mishna) [Ps. xcv.
11]: " So that I swore in my wrath, that they should not enter
into my rest." So R. Aqiba. R. Eliezar, however, said they
have a share, as it reads, " Gather unto me my pious servants."
And the verse " I swore in my wrath " is therefore to be explained: I retract from it because it was sworn while I was in
anger. R. Jehoshua b. Karha said: The verse cited by R.
Eliezar was said only for the future generations. " Gather
together unto me my pious servants," means the righteous
which are to be found in every generation. " Who make a
covenant," means Hanania, Meshael and Asaryah, who delivered themselves to the caldron. " By sacrifice," means R.
Aqiba and his colleagues, who had delivered themselves to be
slain because of the words of the Torah. R. Simeon b. Menasia said: They will have a share in the world to come, as it
reads [Isa. xxxv. 10]: " And come to Zion with song!" Said
Rabba b. b. Hana in the name of R. Johanan: R. Aqiba's saying is against his piety, as it reads [Jer. ii. 2]: " I remember
unto thee the kindness of thy youth, the love of thy espousals,
thy going after me in the wilderness, through a land that is not
sown." Hence we see that from their reward even their descendants will be benefited, so much more they themselves.

MISHNA III.: The ten tribes who were exiled will not be
returned, as it reads [Deut. xxix. 27]: " And he cast them into

another land, as this day." As that day will not return, so will they not return. So R. Aqiba. R. Eliezar said: As this day means as usually a day becomes clouded and thereafter lights up again, so the ten tribes, who are now in darkness, the future will lighten upon them.

GEMARA: The rabbis taught: The ten tribes have no share in the world to come, as it reads: " And the Lord plucked them out of their land of anger, and in wrath and in great indignation," means in this world, "and he cast them into another land," means in the world to come. So R. Aqiba. R. Simeon b. Jehudah, the head of the village of Aku, said in the name of R. Simeon: If their acts will be as on that day, they will not return, but if they will repent, they will. Rabbi, however, said: They will have a share in the world to come, and they will return, as it reads [Isa. xxvii. 13]: " And then shall come those who are lost in the land of Asshur," etc. Said Rabba b. b. Hana in the name of R. Johanan: R. Aqiba's saying is against his piety, as [Jer. iii. 12]: reads: " Go and proclaim these words towards the north, and say, Return, thou backsliding Israel, saith the Lord; I will not cause my anger to fall upon you, for I am full of kindness, saith the Lord, I will not bear grudge forever." What is the kindness? As in the following Boraitha: The minors of the wicked of Israel will not have a share in the world to come, as it reads [Malachi, iii. 19]: " For behold, the day is coming which shall burn as an oven; and all the presumptuous, yea, and all who practice wickedness shall be stubble; and the day that is coming shall set them on fire, saith the Lord of hosts, who will not leave them root or bough." " Root," in this world, and " bough," in the world to come. So Rabban Gamaliel.

R. Aqiba, however, said: They will have a share in the world to come, as it reads [Ps. cvi. 1]: "The Lord preserveth *pethayim* (fool)." And in the countries of the sea (Arabia), a child is called pathia. And also [Dan. iv. 11 and 12]: " Hew down the tree and lop off its branches, strip off its leaves and scatter its fruit; let the beasts flee away from under it, and the fowls from among its branches. Nevertheless leave the body of its root in the earth." But what is meant in the former verse, and " he shall not leave them a root or bough "? It means that he shall not leave one commandment or a part of it which they will observe unrewarded, however they will be rewarded for it in this world, but will have no share in the world to come. Another explanation, " root " means the soil, and " bough " the body. However, the minors, children of idolaters, all agree that they will not have a share in the world to come.

It was taught: From what age has a minor a share in the world to come? R. Hyya and R. Simeon b. Rabbi differ. According to one, immediately after birth, and according to the other, from the time he commences to speak. The former infers it from [Ps. xxii. 32]: " Will tell his righteousness to a people just born," and the latter infers it from the previous, " Sera (children) shall serve him; there shall be related of the Lord unto future generations."

It was taught: Rabhina said: From the time he is formed; and R. Na'hman b. Itz'hak said: From the time he was circumcised, as it reads [Ps. lxxxviii. 16]: " I am inflicted and perishing from my youth up." There is a Boraitha in the name of R. Mair: From the time he can answer " Amen," as it reads [Isa. xxvi. 2] : " Open ye the gates, that there may enter in the righteous nation which guardeth the truth (amunim). Do not read amunim, but amen. What is meant by " amen "? It is an abbreviation of El melech neman (literally, God, King of Truth.

It reads [Isa. v. 14]: " Therefore hath the deep enlarged her desire, and opened her mouth without measure (chok)." Said Resh Lakish: It means him who failed to perform even one (chok) law of the Torah. Said R. Johanan to him: Your saying is not satisfactory to their creator. Say the reverse, even he who has studied but one law does not belong to the Gehenna.

[Zech. xiii. 8] : "And it shall come to pass that in all the land, saith the Lord, two parts (of those) therein shall perish, but the third part shall be left therein." Said Resh Lakish: It means a third of Shem's descendants. And R. Johanan said to him: Your saying is not satisfactory for their Lord. And even if you should say: A third of Noah's children will remain and two-thirds will be destroyed, it would also not satisfy Him, but it means one-third of the wicked will remain.*

[Jer. iii. 14]: " I will take you one of a city and two of a family, and bring you to Zion." Said Resh Lakish: It means

* Rashi tries to explain this at length, basing it on a Midrash of which we are not aware. And as it is very complicated, he also tries to give his own explanation, but it seems to us still more complicated, and therefore we have translated almost literally.

literally. And R. Johanan said again to him: Their Lord is not pleased with such an interpretation, but it means one righteous in a city saves the whole city, and two from a family save the whole family. And the very same said Rabh to R. Kahana when he was sitting before him interpreting the just-cited verses literally.

Rabh saw R. Kahana washing his head and improving his complexion, and thereafter came to study in Rabh's college. And he read to him [Job, xxviii. 13]: "And she is not to be found in the land of the living." And to the questions of R. Kahana: Do you caution me? he replied: I only tell you the interpretation of this passage. The Torah cannot be found with him who adorns himself before studying.

There is a Boraitha: R. Simai said: It reads [Ex. vi. 7]: "I will take you to me as a people," and (ibid. 8): "I will bring you in unto the land." The Scripture compares their exodus from Egypt to the coming in their land. As in entering the land only two from six hundred thousand who made their exodus from Egypt, viz., Joshua and Kaleb, had entered, but all others from the age of twenty to sixty died in the desert, so also from those who made their exodus from Egypt were only two from every six hundred thousand, notwithstanding that they numbered six hundred thousand.

Said Rabha: And so it will be in the time of the Messiah, as it reads [Hosea, ii. 17]: "She shall be inflicted there, as in the days of her youth and as on the day of her coming up out of the land of Egypt."

There is a Boraitha: R. Elazar b. Jose said: It happened once that I was in Alexandria of Egypt, and I found a certain old Gentile who said to me: Come, and I will show you what my great-grandfathers have done to yours. A part of them they threw in the sea, a part they slew with the sword and a part they have crushed in the buildings. Says the Gemara: And for this evil Moses, our master, was punished, as it reads [Ex. v. 23]: "He hath done more evil to this people." To which the Holy One, blessed be He, answered: Woe for those who are lost, as such are not to be found now. Several times I have revealed myself to Abraham, Isaac, and Jacob by the name Almighty God, and they have never thought against my retribution, and did not question me for my proper name. I said to Abraham [Gen. xiii. 17]: "Arise, walk through the land in the length of it and in the breadth of it, for unto thee will I give it." And thereafter when he was searching for a grave for his wife Sarah, he could not get it until he bought one for four hundred silver shekels, and, nevertheless, his thoughts were not against my retribution. I said to Isaac [ibid. xxvi. 3]: "Sojourn in this land, and I will be with thee and bless thee," and thereafter when his bondmen wanted to drink water they could not get it without quarrel, as [ibid., ibid. 20]: "And the herdsmen of Gerar did strive with Isaac's herdsmen, saying, The water is ours," and he also had no thought against my retribution. I said to Jacob [ibid. xxviii. 13]: "The land whereon thou liest, to thee will I give it," and thereafter when he wanted to spread a tent for himself, he could not get it until he paid a hundred kessitah, and his thoughts were not against my retribution and he did not ask for my proper name. Thou, however, first hast asked for my proper name, and now thou sayest to me [Ex. v. 23]: "Thou hast in nowise saved thy people." And therefore [ibid. vi. 1]: "*Now* shalt thou see what I will do to Pharaoh," but thou wilst not live to see the war with the thirty-one kings in the time of Joshua.

It reads [ibid. xxxiv. 8]: "And Moses made haste, and bowed his head." What had he seen that he bowed himself? R. Hanina b. Gamla said: He saw the words "long-suffering." And the rabbis say: He saw the word "truth." There is a Boraitha in accordance with him, who said he had seen long-suffering, viz., When Moses ascended to heaven, he found the Holy One, blessed be He, writing the words "long-suffering." And he said before Him: Lord of the Universe, does this mean long-suffering for the righteous ones? And he was answered: Even for the wicked. And to Moses' exclamation: May the wicked be lost! he answered: In the future thou wilst see that my previous words will be necessary for thee. Thereafter when Israel sinned, the Lord said to Moses: Didst thou not say long-suffering for the righteous? And Moses said before Him: Lord of the Universe, but hast Thou not said to me "also to the wicked"? And to this it is written [Num. xiv. 17]: "And now, I beseech thee, let the greatness of the power of the Lord be made manifest as *Thou* hast spoken."

R. Hagga, ascending the steps of the school of Rabba b. Shila, heard a child saying [Ps. xciii. 5]: "Thy testimonies are exceedingly steadfast. In thy house abideth holiness, O Lord, to the utmost length of days." And immediately he began [ibid. xc. 1]: "A prayer of Moses." And he then said: I infer from this that Moses has seen the words "long-suffering."

R. Elazar, in the name of R. Hanina, said, etc. (Here is repeated from Tract Megilla, p. 38, line 23 to p. 39, line 3: However, here is some change at the end of the paragraph which is unimportant.)

* It reads [Isa. viii. 12]: "Call ye not a conspiracy all that this people may call a conspiracy." What conspiracy does it mean? The conspiracy of Shebna, as his college had thirteen great men, and Hiskia's college had only eleven. When Sanherib came to attack Jerusalem, Shebna wrote a note that he and his society are willing to make peace, however Hiskia and his society are not. And this note he put in an arrow and shot it into the camp of Sanherib, as it reads [Ps. xi. 2]: "For lo, the wicked bend their bow, they arrange their arrow upon the string." And Hiskia was afraid, that perhaps the inclination of Heaven will be towards the majority, whose desire was to deliver themselves to the enemy. The prophet then came to him, saying: "Call ye not a conspiracy," etc., i.e., this conspiracy is wicked, and a conspiracy of the wicked is not counted. The same Shebna wanted also to hew out a cave for a grave for himself among the kings of David's house, and this is what the prophet said to him [ibid., ibid. 16 and 17]: "What hast thou here? and whom hast thou here, that thou hast hewn out for thyself here a sepulchre? . . . Behold, the Lord will thrust thee about with a mighty throw. Oh, *man!*" Said Rabh: From this is to be inferred that travelling is harder for a man than for a woman, as, from the expression of the last word of this verse, R. Jose b. Hanina infers that Shebna was punished with leprosy, as the same expression is to be found concerning leprosy [Lev. xiii. 45].

"He will roll thee up as a bundle, and (toss thee) like a ball into a country of ample space." There is a Boraitha: His (Shebna's) desire was to disgrace the house of his master, and therefore his own honor was turned over to disgrace, for when he came out to Sanherib with his society, Gabriel shut the door in the face of his society. And when Sanherib questioned him: Where is thy society? he answered: They have retracted. Exclaimed Sanherib: I see thou hast ridiculed us. And they bored holes in his heels, tied them to the tails of their horses, and dragged his body over thorns.

---

* Transferred from 26a. See also footnote, p. 75.

In the interpretation of [Ps. xi. 3]: " For (if) the foundations be torn down, what would the upright do? " R. Jehudah
and R. Eina differ. According to one it means, if his kin and his
association would be destroyed, how would the promise of the
Lord be? And according to the other, should the Temple be
destroyed by Sanherib, in accordance with the advice of Shebna, what would become of the wonderful miracles of the Lord?
And according to Ula, this passage is to be explained negatively.
If the thoughts of that wicked (Shebna) would not have been
destroyed, what would have become of the upright, Hiskia?
It is correct, the explanation of Ula, and of him who explains
the word " foundation " to mean the Temple, as according to
the former, it means the previous verse (2) which was the basis
of his thoughts. And also concerning the Temple we found in
Mishna, which states that a stone was placed in the Temple
from the time of the first prophets, with the name *shethiha*
(foundation). But he who explains the passage to mean Hiskia
and his society, where is to be found that by the word foundation the upright are meant? [I Sam. ii. 8]: " For the Lord's
are the pillars of the earth, on which he hath set the world.'
" Pillars " are the upright, " on which he hath set "—the foundation.

*The rabbis taught: Man was created on the eve of Sab-
bath. And why? The Minnim shall not say that he was a
partner to the Lord, in the creation of the world. Another explanation is, if a man becomes haughty it may be said to him:
At the time of creation even a fly was created before thou
wert. Still another explanation is that his first act should be
meritorious, in keeping the Sabbath, and also he shall partake
of the Sabbath meal immediately. This is similar to a human
king who built a palace, accomplished it, prepared a banquet
and thereafter invited guests, as it reads [Prov. ix. 1-4]:
" Wisdom hath built her house; she hath hewn out her seven
pillars. She hath killed her cattle; she hath mingled her wine;
she hath also set in order her table. She hath sent forth her
maidens; she invited (her guests) upon the top of the highest
places of the town." " Wisdom hath built her house "—it is
one of the divine affairs of the Holy One, blessed be He, who
has created the whole world with wisdom. " Seven pillars "—
the seven days of the creation. " Killed her cattle," etc.—

---

* Transferred from 38a. See footnote at the end of Chap. IV.

means the seas, the rivers, and all what was necessary for the world. " She sent forth her maidens "—Adam and Eve upon the top of the highest places.

Rabba b. b. Hana propounded a contradiction from ibid. 3, which reads, " on the top of the height," to ibid. (14), on the chair in the 'high places. And he himself answered: First they were placed on the top, and thereafter on a chair. " Void of sense," the Holy One, blessed be He, said: Who made a fool of Adam the first? The woman who told him, etc., as it reads [ibid. vi. 32] : " Whoso committed adultery with a woman lacketh sense." There is a Boraitha: R. Mair used to say: From the whole world was gathered the earth, from which Adam the first was created, as it reads [Ps. cxxxix. 16]: " My undeveloped substance did thy eyes see." R. Oshia said in the name of Rabh: The body of Adam the first was taken from Babylon, his head from Palestine, and all other members, hands, feet, etc., from all other countries, and the earth for his rump, said R. A'ha, was taken from Akra of Agma. R. Johanan b. Hanina said: A day consisted of twelve hours, the first hour the earth for his creation was gathered, the second hour it became an unformed body, and in the third his limbs were shaped; in the fourth the soul entered the body, in the fifth he arose on his feet, in the sixth he named all his beasts and animals, in the seventh Eve was brought to him, in the eighth they went to bed, two persons, and four persons came out of it; in the ninth he was commanded not to eat of the tree, in the tenth he sinned, in the eleventh he was tried, and in the twelfth he was driven out of the Garden of Eden, as it reads [Ps. xlix. 13] : " And Adam though in his splendor endureth not."

R. Jehudah said in the name of Rabh: At the time the Holy One, blessed be He, was about to create a man, He created a *coetus* of angels, and said to them: Would ye advise me to create a man? And they asked Him: What will be his deeds? And He related before them such and such. They explained before Him: Lord of the Universe, what is the mortal, that Thou rememberest him, and the son of men, that Thou thinkest of him? [Ps. vii. 5]. He then put His little finger among them and they were all burnt. And the same was with the second coetus. The third one, however, said before Him: O Creator of the world! the first angels who protested, did they effect? The whole world is Thine, and all what it is pleased before Thee Thou mayest do. Thereafter at the time of the gen-

24

eration of the flood and the generation of dispersion whose deeds were criminal, the same angels said before Him: Creator of the Universe, were not the first angels right with their protest? And He answered: "And even unto old age I am the same, and even unto the time of hoary hairs will I hear" [Isa. xlvi. 4].

R. Jehudah said again in the name of the same authority: Adam the first was from one end of the world to the other, as it reads [Deut. iv. 32]: "Since the day that God created Adam upon the earth, and from the one end of the heavens unto the other end." After he had sinned, the Holy One, blessed be He, laid His hand upon him and reduced him [Ps. cxxxix. 5]. "Behind and before 'hast Thou hedged me in, and Thou placest upon me Thy hand." R. Elazar said: Adam the first was tall from the earth to the sky, as the above cited verse: "The day Adam was created upon the earth and to one end of the heaven." And when he sinned He laid His hand upon him, and diminished him, as the cited verse [Ps. cxxxix.] reads.

R. Jehudah said again in the name of Rabh: Adam the first spoke with the Aramaic language, as [ibid., ibid. 17]: "And how precious are unto me thy thoughts," and the terms in the original Psalm are Aramaic. And this is what Resh Lakish said: It reads [Gen. v. 1]: "This is the book of the generation of Adam." Infer from this that the Holy One, blessed be He, showed to Adam every generation with its scholars, every generation with its lecturers. And when Adam saw the generation of R. Aqiba, he was pleased with his wisdom, but was dejected seeing his death, and said: "How precious are unto me thy thoughts."

The same said again in the name of the same authority: The Minnim* of this generation say that Adam the first was also of their sect. And they infer it from [Gen. iii. 9]: "And the Lord God called unto Adam and said unto him: Where art thou?" i.e., to what is thy heart inclined?

Said R. Johanan: Every place where the Minnim gave their wrong interpretation, the answer of annulling it is to be found in the same place—e.g., they claim from [Gen. i. 26]: "Let us make man." Hence it is in plural. However, in [ibid. 27] it reads: "And God created man in his image" (singular). [Ibid. xi. 7]: "Let us go down" (plural); however,

---

* In accordance with the commentary of Hananel.

[ibid., ibid. 5]: "And the Lord came down" (singular). [Ibid. xxxv. 7]: "And there God appeared" (the term in Hebrew is plural); however [ibid., ibid. 3]: "Unto the Lord who answered me" (singular). [Deut. iv. 7]: "For what great nation is there that hath *gods* so nigh unto it?" However, it reads farther on, "as is the Lord our God every time we call upon *him*." [II Lam. vii. 23]: "Which God went?" (the term in Hebrew is plural). However [Dan. vii. 9]: "I was looking down until chairs were set down, and the Ancient of days seated himself" (singular). But why are all the above-mentioned written in plural? This is in accordance with R. Johanan, who said elsewhere that the Holy One, blessed be He, does not do anything until he consults the heavenly household, as it reads [ibid. iv. 14]: "Through the resolve of the angels is this decree, and by the order of the holy ones is this decision." However, this answer is for all the plurals mentioned, except the last one, "the chairs." Why are they in plural? One for Him and one for David. So R. Aqiba in a Boraitha. Said R. Elazar b. Azaryah to him: Aqiba, how do you dare to make the Shekhina common? It means one chair for judgment and one for mercy. Did Aqiba accept this, or not? Come and hear the following Boraitha: One for judgment and one for mercy. So R. Aqiba. Said R. Elazar b. Azaryah to him: Aqiba, what hast thou to do with Haggada? Give thy attention to Negain and Ohaloth. It means one for a chair to sit upon and one for a footstool.

Said R. Na'hman. He who knows to give a right answer to the Minnim like R. Aidith may discuss with them, but he who is not able to do so, it is better for him that he discuss not with them at all. There was a Min who said to R. Aidith: It reads [Ex. xxiv. 1]: "Come up unto the Lord." It ought to be, "Come up to me." (And when God said to him: Come up to the Lord, there must be one lord more?) And he answered: That is the angel Mattatron (name of the chief of the angels) about whom ibid. xxiii. 20 speaks, as he bears the name of his master [ibid., ibid. 21]: "Because my name is in him." If so, rejoined the Min, let us worship him. It reads, ibid., ibid., ibid., *al tamer be*, and this term means also "exchange." Hence it means thou shalt not exchange him for Me.

Said the Min again: But does it not read "he will not pardon your transgression"? And Aidith answered: Believe me, that even as a guide we refused to accept him, as it reads [ibid. xxxiii. 15]: " If thy presence go not (with us), carry us not up from here."

A Min asked Ismael b. R. Jose: It reads [Gen. xix. 24]: " And the Lord rained upon Sodom and Gomorrah brimstone and fire. From the Lord," etc. From the Lord! It ought to be from Him (hence there was one more lord). And a certain washer said to Rabban Gamaliel, Let me answer him. It reads [Gen. iv. 23]: " And Lemech said unto his wives, Adah and Zellah, Hear my voice, ye wives of Lemech," etc. Wives of Lemech! " My wives," it ought to be? You must then say that so is it customary in the language of the verse, the same is the case here. And to question of R. Ismael to the washer: Whence do we know this? he answered: From the lectures of R. Mair. As R. Johanan used to say, R. Mair's lectures consisted always of a third Halakha, a third Haggadah, and the last third parables. And he said also: From R. Mair's three hundred fox fables we have only three: (a) [Ezek. xviii. 2]: " The fathers have eaten sour grapes, and the teeth of the children have become blunt;" (b) [Lev. xix. 36]: " Just balances, just weights," and (c) [Prov. xi. 8]: " The righteous is delivered out of distress, and the wicked cometh in his stead." *

There was an atheist who said to Rabban Gamaliel: Your God is a thief, as it reads [Gen. ii. 21]: " Lord God caused a deep sleep . . . and he slept; and he took one of his ribs." Said R. Gamaliel's daughter to him: Let me answer him. And she said to him: Would you assist me to take revenge on a thief

---

* In the text nothing is mentioned of what the fables were. Rashi, however, explains it thus : The fox said to the wolf : If you would go in a Jewish yard on the eve of Sabbath to assist them in the preparation of meals for Sabbath, they would invite you for their best meal on Sabbath day. And when the wolf was severely beaten while doing so, he wanted to kill the fox. He, however, told him, this was because your father in assisting them to prepare their meal, consumed the best of it and ran away. And to his question: Should I be beaten because of my father? he answered: Yea, the fathers have eaten sour grapes, etc. However, if you will follow me I will show you a place where you can eat to satiation, and he led him to a well in which two pails were pulled up and down by means of a rope attached to a beam. And the fox entered in one pail, which dropped down to the bottom. And to the question of the wolf : For what purpose did you enter the pail? he answered : I see here meat and cheese which will be sufficient for both of us. And he showed him the reflection of the moon on the water, which he mistook for a round cheese. And asking the fox how he can get it, he was told to enter the other pail, which was on top. And as he was heavier than the fox, the pail with the wolf dropped down and that of the fox came on the top. And to the cry of the wolf : How can I come out? he answered : The righteous is delivered out of distress, etc.

who robbed me this night, by stealing a silver pitcher, however he left a golden one instead? And he said to her: I would like that such thief would come to me every day. Then she said: Was it not better for Adam that one bone was taken from him, and in its stead was given a woman to him, who shall serve him? Rejoined the atheist: I mean why stealing; could He not take it from Adam when he was awake? She then took a piece of meat, put it in glowing ashes, and when roasted took it out and gave it to him to eat. To which he said: It is repulsive to me. Rejoined she: Eve would also have been repulsive to Adam if he could have seen how she was formed.

The same atheist said to Rabban Gamaliel: I am aware of what your God is doing now. R. Gamaliel sighed deeply. And to the question: Why are you singing? he said: I lost every information of my son who is now in the sea countries. Can you perhaps assist me by informing me where he is? And he rejoined: Where shall I know this from? Rejoined Rabban Gamaliel: You don't know what is in this world, and you claim to know what is in heaven?

At another time the same said to Rabban Gamaliel: It reads [Ps. cxlvii. 4]: " Who counted the number of the stars," etc. What prerogative is this? I also can do this. R. Gamaliel took some grain, put it in a sieve, and while straining told him to count the grain. And he rejoined: Let the sieve stand and I will count it. Rejoined R. Gamaliel: The stars are also always moving. According to others R. Gamaliel answered him: Can you tell me how many teeth are in your mouth? And he put his hand in his mouth and began to count them. Rejoined R. Gamaliel: You are not aware of the number of teeth in your mouth, and you claim to know how many stars there are in heaven?

A Min said to R. Gamaliel: He who created the mountains has not created the wind, as it reads [Amos, iv. 13]: " He that formed the mountains and created the wind." And he answered: If so, then concerning a man, of whom it reads [Gen. i. 27]: " And God created," and [ibid. ii. 7]: " And the Lord God formed," should also mean that he who has formed has not created, and *vica versa*. There is in the body of man one span square, in which two holes are to be found—one in the nose and one in the ear. It must be also that he who created one of them did not create the other, as it reads [Ps. xciv. 9]: " He that hath planted the ear, shall he not hear? Or he that hath formed the eye, shall he not see?" And the Min said: Yea, I am of this opinion. Rejoined Gamaliel: How is it, then, when death comes? Are both creators reconciled, to kill their creation together?

A magician said to Rabban Gamaliel: The lower half of your body is created by *ahermes* (God), but the upper half by Hermes (Mercury). And he answered: If it is so, why does then ahernes leave the dirty water coming from the upper half to pass the lower half?

The Cæsar said to R. Tanhum: Let us unite and be a people of one and the same creed. And he answered: Very well; but we who are circumcised cannot be like your people. However, ye are able to be like us if ye will circumcise yourself. And the Cæsar answered: Your answer is right. However, it is a rule that he who conquers the king must be thrown in the *vivarius* to be devoured by the beasts. He was thrown in the vivarius and was not touched. And there was a Min who said to the king: They did not devour him, because they were not hungry. And they then threw him in the vivarius and he was devoured.

Another atheist said to R. Gamaliel: You say that upon every ten Israelites the Shekhina rests. How many Shekhina have you then? Gamaliel then called the servant of the atheist, struck him with a whip, saying: Why didst thou leave the sun enter the house of your master? His master, however, answered: Every one is pleased with the sun. Rejoined Gamaliel: The sun, which is only one of the hundredth millions servants of the Lord, is pleasant to every one, so much the more the Shekhina of the Holy One, blessed be He, Himself.

A Min said to R. Abuhu: Your God is a jester. He commands Ezekiel to lie on his left side and then on his right side [Ezek. iv. 4-6]: "At the same time a disciple came and questioned him: What is the reason of the Sabbatic year?" And Abuhu answered: I will now say something which will be an answer to both of you. The Holy One, blessed be He, said to Israel: Work up the earth for six years and release the seventh for the purpose that you shall be aware that the earth is mine. However, they did not do so, but sinned, and were exiled. It is custom of a human king if a country has rebelled against him to kill all of them if he is a tyrant, and to kill half of them if he is merciful. But if he is full of mercy he chastises

the leaders only; so was it with Ezekiel, the Holy One, blessed
be He, chastised him for the sin of Israel.

There was a Min who said to R. Abuhu: Your God is a
priest, as it reads [Ex. xxv. 2]: " Bring *Me* a *therumah.*" Now
when He buried Moses where did He dip Himself? (Took the
legal bath prescribed for him who touches a corpse.) You
cannot say that He did so in the water, as it reads [Isa. xl. 12]:
" Who hath measured in the hollow of his hand the waters."
And he answered (a joke to a joke): He dipped Himself in
fire, as it reads [ibid. lxvi. 15]: " For behold, the Lord will
come in fire." And to the question of the Min: Is it legal to
dip in fire? he answered: On the contrary, the principal dipping
is in fire, as it reads [Num. xxxi. 23]: " And whatsoever doth
not come into the fire shall ye cause to go through water."

There was a Min who said to R. Abina: It reads [II Sam.
vii. 23]: " And who is like thy people, like Israel, the only
nation on the earth? " What is your proudness about? Are
you not mingled among other nations, of whom it reads [Isa.
xl. 17]: " All the nations are as naught before him "? And he
answered: A prophet of nations themselves has testified concerning us [Num. xxiii. 9]: " And among the nations it shall
not be reckoned."

R. Elazar propounded a contradiction from [Sam. iii. 25]:
" The Lord is good unto those that hope in him " to [Ps. cxlv.
9]: " The Lord is good to all "? This question may be answered with the following parable to one who possesses a fruit
garden. When he waters it, he waters all of them. And when
he hoes to cover up the roots, he does so only to the best of
them, *i.e.,* when He feeds, He feeds the whole world with dis-
criminating, but to save from trouble He helps only those who
hope in Him.

It reads [I Kings, xxii. 36]: " And there went a *rinah* (song)
throughout the camp." Said R. Aha b. Hanina: This is what
is written [Prov. xi. 10]: " And when the wicked perish there
is rinah," means when Achab, the son of Omri, perished, there
was rinah. Is this so? Is it then pleasant for the Holy One,
blessed be He, the ruin of the wicked? Is it not written [II
Chron. xx. 21]: " As they went out before the armed array and
said: Give thanks unto the Lord; for unto everlasting endureth
His kindness "? And R. Johanan said: Why is it not written
here: " He is good," as [Ps. cxviii. 1]: Because the Holy One,
blessed be He, is not rejoicing over the ruin of the wicked, as

R. Samuel b. Na'hman said in the name of R. Jonathan: It reads [Ex. xiv. 20]: "And the one came not near unto the other all the night." At that time the angels wanted to sing their song before the Holy One, blessed be He, but He said to them: "My creatures are sinking in the sea, and ye want to sing." *

It reads [I Kings, xviii. 3]: "And Rehab called Obadiah, who was the superintendent of the house;— now Obadiah feared the Lord greatly." To what purpose does the passage relate that Obadiah feared the Lord? Said R. Itz'hak: Achab said to him, concerning Jacob, it reads [Gen. xxx. 27]: "The Lord hath blessed me for thy sake." And concerning Joseph it reads [ibid. xxxix. 5]: "The Lord blessed the Egyptian's house for the sake of Joseph." I, however, keep thee and my house is not blessed. Perhaps thou art not fearing God? To this a heavenly voice was heard, saying: Obadiah fears the Lord greatly, but the house of Achab is not fit for blessings. Said R. Abah: It is more conspicuous what is said of Obadiah than of Abraham, as about Abraham it reads, " he feared God," and about Obadiah it adds " greatly." Said R. Itz'hak: For what deeds was Obadiah rewarded with prophecy? Because he hid one hundred prophets in a cave, as it reads [I Kings, viii. 4]: " And it happened when Isabel cut off the prophets of the Lord that Obadiah took a hundred prophets, and hid them fifty in one cave, and provided them with bread and water." Why fifty? Said R. Elazar: He learned this from Jacob, who divided his camp into two parts, for the reason that if it should happen that one would be lost the other would be saved. And R. Abuhu said: Because the cave could not hold more than fifty.

It reads [Ob. i. 1]: " The vision of the Lord . . . concerning Edom." And why? The Holy One, blessed be He, said: Obadiah, who lived among two wicked (Achab and his wife) and did not learn from them, shall prophesy to Esau who lived among two upright (Isaac and Rebecca) and did not learn from them. And Ephraim of Kashaha, a disciple of R. Mair, said in the name of his master: Obadiah was an Edomite-proselyte. And this is what people say that the handle of the hatchet to cut the forest is taken from the wood of the same forest. And this also applies to David, who was a descendant of Moab (according to R. Johanan, in the name of Simeon b. Jo'hai), who smote them [II Sam. viii. 2].

It reads [II Kings, iii. 27]: " Then took he his eldest son

---

* The answer is united.

that should have reigned in his stead, and offered him for a burnt-offering upon the wall. And there was great indignation against Israel." Rabh and Samuel. According to one, he sacrificed him to Heaven, and according to the other, to an idol. But if to an idol, why was there great indignation against Israel? It is in accordance with R. Jehoshua b. Levi, who propounded a contradiction from [Ez. v. 7]: "According to the ordinances of the nations have ye *not* acted," to [ibid. xi. 12]: " But according to the ordinances of the nations ye *have* acted." And he himself answered: Ye have not acted according to their good deeds, but ye have acted according to their crimes.

It reads [I Kings, i. 4]: " The maiden was *ad meod* exceedingly." Said R. Hanina b. Papa: She did reach even half the beauty of Sarah, of whom it reads [Gen. xii. 14]: " Behold the woman that she was *very* fair (*meod*).

*It reads [Gen. xxii. 1]: " And it came to pass after these things, that God did tempt Abraham." After what? Said R. Johanan in the name of R. Jose b. Senira: After the words of the Satan to those of [ibid. xxi. 8]: " And the child grew, and was weaned," etc. The Satan said before the Holy One, blessed be He, thus: Lord of the Universe, Thou hast favored this old man with an offspring at his hundredth birthday, and from all the great meals which he prepared for the people he did not sacrifice for Thee even one dove or pigeon. And he was answered: Does he not prepare all this only for the sake of his son? If I would tell him to sacrifice his son to me, he will do it immediately. Hence God tempted Abraham.

And He said: " Take *na* thy son," etc. Said. R. Simeon b. Aba: The expression " *na* " means request. This is similar to the fable of a human king who had to fight many wars, and who had one hero who was victorious in all of them. Finally a war was declared to the same king by a king with a very strong army, and he said to his hero: I pray thee be victorious also in this war; people shall not say that the former wars were not worthy of consideration. So the Holy One, blessed be He, said to Abraham: I proved thee with many temptations, and thou withstood all of them. I request thee withstand also this temptation, in order people shall not say that the former were not worthy of consideration. " Thy son." But Abraham said: I have two sons. " Thy only one." But Abraham said: Both

---

* Transferred from 89*b*, footnote, p. 260.

of them are the only ones to their mothers, "whom thou lovest," but I love both of them, even Isaac. And why so many words? For the purpose that he shall not become insane from such a sudden command.

The Satan preceded him on the way, saying [Job, iv. 2-6]: "If we essay to address a few words to thee, wilt thou be wearied? . . . Behold, thou hast (ere this) corrected many, and weak hands thou was wont to strengthen. Him that stumbled thy words used to uphold, and to sinking knees thou gavest vigor. Yet now, when it cometh to thee, thou art wearied; it toucheth even thee, and thou art terrified." And Abraham answered him [Ps. xxvi. 11]: "But as for me, I will walk in my integrity." And the Satan said again: "Is not then thy fear of God a stupidity?"* And Abraham answered: Remember . . . whoever perished being innocent. When the Satan saw that Abraham did not listen to him, he said to him [ibid. 12]: "But to me a word came by stealth." I have heard from behind the paraganda (the heavenly curtains) that the ram will be for a burnt-offering, but not Isaac. Rejoined Abraham: This is the punishment of liars, that even when they tell the truth, nobody believes them.

R. Levi, however, said: The above cited verse "after these things" means after the exchange of words between Ismael and Isaac. Ismael said to Isaac: I am greater than thee in performing the commandments of the Lord, as I was circumcised when I was thirteen years of age, and thou when thou wert only eight days. To which Isaac answered: Thou art proud against me because of only one member of thy body; if the Holy One, blessed be He, should command me to sacrifice my whole body to Him I would do it immediately, hence, "and God has tempted Abraham."

MISHNA IV.: The men of a misled town have no share in the world to come, as it reads [Deut. xiii. 14]: "There have gone forth men, Belial, from the midst of thee, and have misled the inhabitants of their city." However, they are not killed, unless the misleaders are from the same city and from the same tribe And also not unless the majority are misled. And the misleaders also must be men; if, however, they were misled by women or minors, or a majority of the city were misled, or the misleaders were outsiders, they are to be considered as

---

* According to the interpretation of the Talmud.

individuals, and each of them must have two witnesses and be forewarned.

There is more rigorousness with individuals than with the majority in that respect, that individuals are to be stoned, therefore their property is saved for their heirs. And the majority are to be decapitated, therefore their property is also lost, as it reads [ibid., ibid. 16]: "Then shalt thou smite the inhabitants of that city with the edge of the sword." A caravan with asses or camels, who are travelling from one place to another, who took their rest in a city which was guilty of idolatry, and the caravan while being there was persuaded and worshipped idols, and counting them to those people of the city who were misled, it will be a majority they save the money of the innocent inhabitants of the city, for the guilty ones are still considered individuals, as the caravan is not counted to complete a majority, as it reads, "Devoting it utterly, and all that is therein, and the cattle thereof, to the edge of the sword" (but not of strangers passing by). From this it was also said that the properties which are found in the city belonging to the innocent individuals are also lost in case the majority were misled, but their properties which are placed outside of the city are saved, while by the property of guilty there is no difference wheresoever it is found it must be destroyed, as it reads [17]: "And all its spoils shalt thou gather into the midst of its main street," etc.

If it happened that the city had no main street, such must be established. If there was one outside of the city, it must be taken in, as it reads, "Thou shalt burn with fire the city, and all its spoil entirely." "Its spoil," but not the spoil belonging to Heaven. From this it was said that if there were some goods belonging to the sanctuary, they are to be redeemed. If there was heave-offering, it must remain till it becomes rotten. Second tithe and books of the Holy Writ must be hidden. "Entirely unto the Lord thy God." Said R. Simeon: The Holy One, blessed be He, said: If ye will take judgment on a misled town, I will consider it as if ye would bring to me a burnt-offering. "A ruinous heap forever" means that from that place gardens and vineyards should not be made. So R. Jose the Galilean. R. Aqiba, however, maintains: It reads: "It shall not be built again," means it shall not be built as it was, but gardens and vineyards may be made from it. "There shall not cleave to thy hand aught of the devoted things," for

as long as the wicked exist the heavenly anger lasts. And
when the wicked perish the heavenly anger ceases.

GEMARA: The rabbis taught: There have gone forth
men, but not their messengers. " Men " (plural) no less than
two. And according to others " men " and not " women," -
" men " and not " minors," " sons of Belial," sons who took
off the yoke of Heaven from their necks. " From the midst of
thee," but not if they were from the boundary. " The inhabitants of their city," but not of another one. " Saying "—infer
from this that (if not a majority) witnesses and warning are
needed for every one of them. It was taught: When the land
was divided among Israel, it was allowed to divide one city for
two tribes, according to R. Johanan. Resh Lakish, however,
said: It was not. And R. Johanan objected to Resh Lakish
from our Mishna: However, they are not guilty unless the
misleaders are from the same city and from the same tribe. It
is not to be assumed that even if the misleaders were from the
same city they are guilty when they were men of their own tribe;
hence we see that one city can be divided for two tribes? Nay,
it may be said that his share in this city fell to him from an inheritance, or some one had made him a present of it. He objected to him again from [Joshua xxi. 16]: " Nine cities from
those two tribes." Does it not mean four and a half for one
tribe and four and a half for the other? Hence, one city was
divided for two tribes. Nay, it means four from one and
five from the other. But if so, let the Scripture say from
which tribe five and from which tribe four. This difficulty
remains.

The schoolmen propounded a question: How is it if they
were misled by themselves without any seducer? Shall we
say it reads " and they misled," but not if they were misled by
themselves, or there is no difference? Come and hear. Our
Mishna states: " If they were misled by women and minors,"
etc., they are to be judged as individuals. And why? If misled by themselves is the same as by leaders, let the misleading
by women and minors be considered as if they were misled by
themselves? Nay, these cannot be equalized, for when they
were misled by themselves they acted according to their own
deliberations, but if they were misled by women and minors,
they acted according to the seducer's mind, which was not
worthy of consideration.

" *Unless the majority was misled.*" How is it to be done?

According to R. Jehudah, when they saw two, three, or more guilty of idolatry, they were tried, sentenced, and kept in prison. And so the others, until they formed a majority of the city, and then they are decapitated and their property destroyed. Said Ula to him: By such an act the prisoners are tortured. And therefore said he in such a case those who are sentenced are also stoned, but their property is not to be destroyed until they number a greater part of the city. And only then if more cases happen they are slain, and the property of all who were executed till now is destroyed.

It was taught: R. Johanan was of the same opinion as Ula. Resh Lakish, however, said that if such a case happened courts who investigate all cases must be increased, and all of them turn it over to the supreme council, who sentences them, and they are then slain.

" *Then shalt thou smite the inhabitants of the city*," etc. The rabbis taught: A caravan with asses or camels, etc. (Here is repeated from Last Gate, p. 19, second line to the seventeenth. See there.)

" *Devoting it utterly*," etc. The rabbis taught: Devoting it and that is therein excludes the property of the innocent which is found out of town, and includes the property of them which is inside of the city.

" *All the spoils*," etc. Includes the property of the guilty, which is outside of the town. Said R. Simeon: Why does the Torah say that the property of the innocent, which is inside of the city, is to be destroyed? Because the reason of their residence in this city was their property, and therefore it must be destroyed. The master said: To include the property of the guilty which is outside. Said R. Hisda: Provided they are near by, so that they can be gathered in on the same day. And he said again: The deposits of a misled town are to be saved. Let us see how was the case. If it was deposited by another city in this city, it is self-evident that they are to be saved, as such deposits do not belong to this city at all. And if the men of this city had deposited in another city, why are they to be saved if they are placed near by, so that they can be gathered together on the same day? And if he speaks of those which are far away and cannot be gathered, why then the repetition, he said it already once? It means deposits of another city which are found in this city, but the depositors took the responsibility for them. And lest one say that in such a case it is considered as if it would be their own property, he comes to teach us that it is not so.

R. Hisda said again: If there was an animal, a half of which belongs to one city and the other half to one of another city, it is invalid. However, if there was dough, half of which belongs to one of another city, it is valid; because it can be divided it is considered as already divided, which is not the case with a living animal. He (R. Hisda), however, was doubtful if the slaughtering of a cattle from a misled town effects to put it out of the category of a carcass. Shall we assume that " with the edge of a sword " there is no difference; if it was killed or legally slaughtered it is considered as any carcass, or the legal slaughtering effects that it is not so considered, and if one touches it he does not become unclean, while he does by touching other carcasses? This question was not decided.

" *In its main street,*" etc. The rabbis taught: If there was no main street, it does not become a misled town. So R. Ismael. R. Aqiba, however, said that if there was none, one must be established. And what is the point of difference? One holds that the Scriptures mean a main street which existed already when it became misled, and the other holds that there is no difference if one existed before or was established after.

" *Belonging to the sanctuary,*" etc. The rabbis taught: If there were cattle sanctified to the altar, they must be put to death. Sanctified things for improving the Temple must be redeemed. Heave-offering must be left till it becomes rotten. Second tithe and books of the Holy Writ must be hidden. R. Simeon said: " The cattle thereof," but not cattle of a first-born, and the tenth of cattle (cf. to Lev. xxvii. 30 and 32). " And all that is therein " excludes sanctified money, and money with which tithe is to be redeemed. But why should cattle sanctified to the altar be put to death? Said R. Johanan: Because it reads [Prov. xxi. 27]: " The sacrifice of the wicked is an abomination." And Resh Lakish said: It speaks of when the owners where they were found responsible for it, and it is then considered as if they would be the property of the owners according to R. Simeon.

The text reads: R. Simeon said: " The cattle thereof," etc. Let us see how was the case. If they were without any blemish it is self-evident, as it belongs to the sanctuary, and if they had a blemish, why then should they be different? Said Rabhina:

It speaks of when they were blemished; but "cattle thereof" means those which are consumed in the usual manner of cattle, but not those which were the property of Heaven, and only because of their blemish become the property of men and may be consumed; hence they cannot be considered as property belonging to the city. And he differs with Samuel, who said: An animal which is to be sacrificed when it is without blemish, and redeemed when with a blemish, is excluded from "the cattle thereof." And if it is to be sacrificed while without a blemish, and is not to be redeemed when with a blemish—*e.g.*, a first-born and the tenth of a cattle, it is included in "the cattle thereof."

"*Heave-offering . . . till it become rotten*," etc. Said R. Hisda: Provided the heave-offering was in the hand of the priest already, but if it was still in the hand of an Israelite, it may be given to a priest of another city.

"*The books of Holy Writ,*" etc. Our Mishna is not in accordance with R. Elazar of the Boraitha mentioned above (p. 211), that even if there was one mezuza it cannot be called a misled town. (See there.)

"*Garden and vineyards,*" etc. Shall we assume that the point of their difference is what was said by R. Abin in the name of R. Ilaa: Everywhere you find a general expression in a positive commandment, and the explicit specification to it in a negative commandment, it must not be judged, as in other cases, that there is nothing in the general expression but what is specified in the explicit specification. The one who does not allow to make gardens of it does not hold this theory. And he who allows it holds this theory? Nay, all hold the theory of R. Abin. And the difference of their opinion is the expression "again." According to one "again" means again as it was built, and according to the other "again" means it shall not build for whatsoever. The rabbis taught: If there were uprooted trees, they are invalid, and if they are still attached they are valid. From another city, however, they are invalid even if they were attached. What does "another city" mean? Said R. Hisda: It means Jericho, as it reads [Josh. vi. 26]: "And Joshua adjured (the people) at that time, saying, Cursed be the man before the Lord that will rise up and build this city of Jericho: with his first-born shall he lay its foundation, and with his youngest shall he set up its gates."

There is a Boraitha: Any other city must not be built

under the name of Jericho, and also Jericho shall not be re-built under another name, as it reads [I Kings, xvi. 34]: "In his days did Chiel the Bethelite build Jericho; with Abiram, his first-born, laid he the foundation thereof, and with Segub, his youngest son, set he up the gates thereof." There is a Bo-raitha: From Abiram, his first-born, this wicked has to learn. What does it mean? Thus: To what purpose is it written that Abiram was his first-born and Segub his youngest son? To learn that he buried all his children, beginning from Abiram, the oldest, to Segub, his youngest son. And this wicked should have learned not to continue the building after bury-ing Abiram. Achab was his friend, and both he and Elijah came to condole Chiel. Said the latter to Elijah: Perhaps Joshua's caution was to those who will rebuild Jericho even under an-other name, or any other city under the name of Jericho? And Elijah answered: Yea. Said Achab: How can it be supposed that Chiel's troubles were because of Joshua's caution, when even the caution of Moses his master does not effect, as it reads [Deut. xi. 16]: "Take heed to yourselves," etc., ". . . and serve other gods . . . that there be no rain," etc. And I am worshipping idols on every flower bed, and nevertheless rain did not cease to fall. Is it possible that the caution of Moses should not stand good while that of Joshua should? To this it is written [I Kings, xvii. 1]: "Then said Elijah the Tish-bite, who was one of the inhabitants of Gilad, unto Achab, As the Lord God of Israel liveth, before whom I have stood, there shall not be in these years dew or rain, except according to my words." He prayed and the key of rain was transferred to him. It reads farther on (3) and (6): "Go away from here . . . and the ravens brought him bread and flesh in the morning." Where did they take it? Said R. Jehudah in the name of Rabh: From the kitchen of Achab. "And it came to pass . . . that the brook dried up," etc. When he saw that the whole world is in trouble he went to Zarephath according to the Heavenly command, and it happened (17) "that the son . . . fell sick," etc. And Elijah prayed again that the key of resurrection shall be given to him. And he was answered: Thou knowest that there are three keys in heaven which are not entrusted to a messenger—the key of birth, of rain, and of resurrection. Now when the key of resurrection shall also be given to thee, thou wilst have two keys and heaven only one. Bring, therefore, the key of rain, and then thou wilt receive the key of resurrection.   And this is what it reads [ibid. xviii. 1]: "Go, show thyself to Achab, and *I* will give rain."   A certain Galilean lectured in the presence of R. Hisda: The parable of Elijah, to what is it similar?   To one who shut his door and lost the key from it.   (So Elijah has shut the door of rain and had to depend upon Heaven.)

R. Jose lectured in Ciporias: Father Elijah is sensitive (hot-tempered), dealing with Achab too severely.   Elijah, however, who used to visit R. Jose every day, disappeared for three days. And thereafter when he appeared and was questioned by R. Jose: Why have I not seen the master three days? he answered: Because you called me sensitive.   Rejoined R. Jose: Is this not true?   Hast not thou, master, become angry because of my expression?

"*As long as the wicked exist*," etc.   Whom does it mean? Said R. Joseph: The thieves (who steal from the things which are legally to be devoted).   The rabbis taught: With the appearance of a wicked anger comes to the world, as it reads [Prov. xviii. 3]: "When the wicked cometh, then cometh also contempt, and with dishonorable acts disgrace."   And when the wicked perish good comes to the world, as it reads [Prov. xi. 10]: "And when the wicked perish there is joyful shouting."   When an upright departs from this world evil comes to the world, as it reads [Isa. lvii. 1]: "The righteous perisheth, and no man layeth it to heart: and pious men are taken away without one considering that before the evil the righteous is taken away."   And when an upright comes to the world goodness comes with him, as it reads [Gen. v. 29]: "This one shall comfort us concerning our work and the toil of our hands."

END OF TRACT SANHEDRIN, PART II. (HAGGADA),

AND OF VOLUME XVI.